Political Survival and Sovereignty in International Relations

Why do political actors willingly give up sovereignty to another state, or choose to resist, sometimes to the point of violence? Jesse Dillon Savage demonstrates the role that domestic politics plays in the formation of international hierarchies, and shows that when there are high levels of rent-seeking and political competition within the subordinate state, elites within this state become more prepared to accept hierarchy. In such an environment, members of society at large are also more likely to support the surrender of sovereignty. Empirically rich, the book adopts a comparative historical approach with an emphasis on Russian attempts to establish hierarchy in post-Soviet space, particularly in Georgia and Ukraine. This emphasis on post-Soviet hierarchy is complemented by a cross-national statistical study of hierarchy in the post-World War II era, and three historical case studies examining European informal empire in the nineteenth and early twentieth centuries.

Jesse Dillon Savage is Assistant Professor of Global Politics in the Department of Political Science at Trinity College Dublin.

Political Survival and Sovereignty in International Relations

Jesse Dillon Savage
Trinity College, Dublin

CAMBRIDGE
UNIVERSITY PRESS

University Printing House, Cambridge CB2 8BS, United Kingdom

One Liberty Plaza, 20th Floor, New York, NY 10006, USA

477 Williamstown Road, Port Melbourne, VIC 3207, Australia

314–321, 3rd Floor, Plot 3, Splendor Forum, Jasola District Centre, New Delhi – 110025, India

79 Anson Road, #06-04/06, Singapore 079906

Cambridge University Press is part of the University of Cambridge.

It furthers the University's mission by disseminating knowledge in the pursuit of education, learning, and research at the highest international levels of excellence.

www.cambridge.org
Information on this title: www.cambridge.org/9781108494502
DOI: 10.1017/9781108658461

© Jesse Dillon Savage 2020

This publication is in copyright. Subject to statutory exception and to the provisions of relevant collective licensing agreements, no reproduction of any part may take place without the written permission of Cambridge University Press.

First published 2020

A catalogue record for this publication is available from the British Library.

Library of Congress Cataloging-in-Publication Data
Names: Savage, Jesse Dillon, author.
Title: Political survival and sovereignty in international relations / Jesse Dillon Savage.
Description: Cambridge ; New York, NY : Cambridge University Press, 2020. | Includes bibliographical references and index.
Identifiers: LCCN 2019042232 (print) | LCCN 2019042233 (ebook) | ISBN 9781108494502 (hardback) | ISBN 9781108658461 (ebook)
Subjects: LCSH: International relations. | Sovereignty. | Great powers.
Classification: LCC JZ1310 .S28 2020 (print) | LCC JZ1310 (ebook) | DDC 327.1–dc23
LC record available at https://lccn.loc.gov/2019042232
LC ebook record available at https://lccn.loc.gov/2019042233

ISBN 978-1-108-49450-2 Hardback

Cambridge University Press has no responsibility for the persistence or accuracy of URLs for external or third-party internet websites referred to in this publication and does not guarantee that any content on such websites is, or will remain, accurate or appropriate.

For Elaine Corbett

Contents

List of Figures	page viii
List of Tables	x
Acknowledgments	xi
Introduction: Hierarchy and International Politics	1
1 Political Survival and the Surrender of Sovereignty	21
2 Submission, Resistance, and War: National Politics and Russian Hierarchy in Georgia and Ukraine since Independence	49
3 Subnational Politics and Sovereignty in Post-Soviet Georgia	97
4 Mass Politics and the Surrender of Sovereignty	125
5 European Informal Empire in China, the Ottoman Empire, and Egypt: Hierarchy and Informal Empire in Historical Context	150
6 Cross-National Variation in Sovereignty and Hierarchy	181
7 Hierarchy, Political Order, and Great Power Politics	217
Appendix A	227
Appendix B	237
Bibliography	243
Index	266

Figures

1.1 Causal process and predicted outcomes with perfect information *page* 39
4.1 Change in predicted probabilities on Russian influence as (a) belief in the rule of law and (b) accountability vary from strongly disagree to strongly agree 132
4.2 Change in predicted probabilities for relationship with Russia as Attitudes to Corruption changes from few involved to everyone involved 135
4.3 Changes in predicted probabilities for (a) Trust Local, (b) Trust Executive, (c) Trust Neither, and (d) Trust Both as Rule of Law changes from strongly disagree to strongly agree 141
4.4 Changes in predicted probabilities for (a) Trust Parliament, (b) Trust President, (c) Trust Neither, and (d) Trust Both as Attitudes to Corruption changes from few involved to everyone involved 143
6.1 Marginal effect of competition when modified by corruption 191
6.2 Marginal effect of corruption when modified by competition 192
6.3 Mean level of hierarchy and standard errors conditional on regime type 200
6.4 Mean level of hierarchy across time conditional on regime type 200
6.5 Relationship between hierarchy and independent variables 202
6.6 Marginal effects of competition (CGV) on (a) external control over international autonomy and (b) domestic autonomy as corruption varies 210
6.7 Marginal effects of competition (Polcomp) on (a) external control over international autonomy and (b) domestic autonomy as corruption varies 210
6.8 Marginal effects of corruption modified by competition (CGV) on (a) external control over international autonomy and (b) domestic autonomy as competition varies 211

6.9 Marginal effects of corruption modified by competition
(Polcomp) on (a) external control over international
autonomy and (b) domestic autonomy
as competition varies   212
6.10 Level of hierarchy over Dominican Republic using
V-Dem's measure of autonomy   213

Tables

1.1 Preference ranking of the dominant unit conditional on costs of formal expansion *page* 28
1.2 Preference ranking of subordinate groups conditional on domestic institutions 38
3.1 Comparison of Adjara, Abkhazia, Javakheti, and Kvemo Kartli, 1991–2012 101
4.1 Predicted effects as perceptions of rule of law change for Georgia 139
4.2 Predicted effects as perceptions of corruption change for Ukraine 142
6.1 Relationship results for Models 1–4 193
6.2 Predicted relationship between regime type and hierarchy 199

Acknowledgments

The project began in 2007, and since then, the meandering path that it took to completion and the wide range of empirical evidence and subjects mean that I have racked up many debts along the way.

From the very beginning of the project, Hendrik Spruyt has shown extraordinary generosity in giving both his time and his advice. His willingness to read multiple drafts at both the project's genesis and its completion was far beyond what I could have expected. His comments and help over the years have been crucial to the development of this book and, more importantly, to my development as a political scientist and scholar. I am also very grateful to James Mahoney, who was essential in the development of this project. After every meeting with him, I walked away assured that the project was possible to complete and with numerous ways to improve the work. Jon Caverley's forthright willingness to express when the work was not up to the appropriate standard was always followed by constructive comments and advice about how to improve things. He gave more time than he should have going over my work chapter by chapter on several occasions. His advice and criticism always kept me honest and forced me to clarify my thinking and arguments; for this, I am very grateful.

Jason Seawright has always been very generous with his time, providing advice about methodological and theoretical issues. He has played a large role in my development as a scholar, helping me refine my views about political and social science more generally. Anne Sartori also provided me consistently excellent feedback and sharpened my thinking. Risa Brooks and Ian Hurd read early versions of this project and were instrumental in getting it off the ground. Georgi Derluguian brought a unique perspective to the project. I learned a lot from sitting in his office and discussing post-Soviet politics. Intellectually, his ability to draw connections from macro- to very micro-processes was a pivotal inspiration. He also helped me greatly with my fieldwork, providing contacts and advice about doing research in the region. Will Reno provided great guidance during the early years of this project. Stephen Nelson also provided helpful advice. I amassed many debts to my fellow Northwestern University graduate students at the time: Andrew Kelly, Larkin Terrie, Marissa Brookes, Chris Day, Jen Cyr, Ross Carroll, Rick Hay, Marina Zaloznaya, Mauro Gili, Olivier Henripin, and Natalia Forrat. More generally, those involved with interdisciplinary groups like the Comparative Historical Social Science group, the Formal and Quantitative International Relations group, and the Quantitative methods group provided a welcoming forum for parts of this work.

I owe a huge debt to the Harriman Institute at Columbia University. I was very fortunate to spend nine months there as a postdoctoral fellow. The time and the stimulating intellectual life there provided me with an enviable opportunity to improve the manuscript and sharpen my ideas. I'm very grateful to Kimberly Marten, Alex Cooley, Lincoln Mitchell, Fredrik Sjoberg, and Timothy Frye, among many others who provided support, advice, and feedback during my time at Columbia.

While putting the finishing touches on the book, I have been very lucky to have supportive colleagues in the Department of Political Science at Trinity College Dublin. I have benefited greatly from the support, feedback, and advice of Constantine Bousallis and Will Phelan. Thomas Chadefaux was especially helpful with his feedback.

I also need to thank several people who helped with my fieldwork or on other occasions. In Georgia, I thank Kornely Kakachia, Kety Rostiashvili, Anna Dolidze, and Geta; in Ukraine, I thank Pavlo Kutuev and Serhiy Kudelia. Greg Walters also provided me with contacts in both countries and general advice and conversation about the region. All these people helped me navigate my way through my times in these countries. This fieldwork was partly funded by the Buffet Centre for International and Comparative Studies and the Dispute Resolution Research Centre at Northwestern University and through a Joan Rydon Scholarship from the University of Sydney. In addition, I have at various stages received feedback or advice on the project from Charles Butcher, Victoria Tin-Bor Hui, Dan Nexon, and Andrew Walter, among others.

I am very grateful for the help and advice of the people at Cambridge University Press. John Haslam and Tobias Ginsberg have been a pleasure to work with. In addition, the anonymous reviewers provided invaluable feedback that has strengthened the arguments, the empirics, and the readability of the book. I am very grateful for their careful reading and insightful comments.

While I have been extremely fortunate to have found so many people prepared to help me during the research and writing of this book, my family have been central to this and provided amazing support and encouragement. However, the most crucial person to thank is Elaine

Corbett. She provided me with much love, support, and advice during the years that I worked on this project. The book would be a much poorer product without her reading of drafts and advice on improving the manuscript. Her suggestions have greatly improved the clarity of the arguments and the presentation of the results, while her love, encouragement, and support were essential to keeping me going. I've been incredibly fortunate to have her with me along the way.

Introduction
Hierarchy and International Politics

In late 1991, the Georgian government was involved in multiple domestic conflicts. One outcome of these conflicts was the ouster of Georgia's first president Zviad Gamsakhurdia. In the region of Mingrelia, supporters of the former president then staged an uprising. In the regions of Abkhazia and South Ossetia, ethnic minorities with Russian support defeated Georgian forces, preserving or reestablishing their dominance. Eduard Shevardnadze, recently installed in power by a coalition of warlords and militia leaders, was faced with a choice. In return for agreeing to Russian demands to allow Russian military forces to be stationed in Georgia, joining the Commonwealth of Independent States, and greater Russian influence and control over Georgia's government and sovereignty, Russia would aid him in defeating his Zviadist rivals and increase his chances of political survival. "Prostrate" before Russia, the bargain was struck. Russian military power helped defeat the Zviadist rebels, while continuing to prop up ethnic separatists in Abkhazia and South Ossetia, and Shevardnadze continued to rule.

The choices made during this period – by Shevardnadze, the leaders of the breakaway republics in Georgia, and elite actors among other ethnic minorities – have shaped Georgia's state-building project, domestic politics, and foreign policy during the decades since independence. The decision made by some actors to support Russian involvement in Georgia and their willingness to cede autonomy has provided both opportunities for some and imposed constraints on others.

The most obvious effect of Russia's policy toward Georgia has been the continued survival of Abkhazia and South Ossetia as de facto states. The de facto independence of large parts of Georgian territory has seriously curtailed Georgian state-building efforts. During the 1990s, Russian involvement in the country affected the Georgian state's attempts to assert authority even in regions where violence did not break out with minority groups. In Javakheti, with its large Armenian population and Russian military installation, the central government long felt constrained from asserting its authority fully. Decisions to support or oppose Russia made by sets of elites and the populace in the late 1980s and early 1990s, as Georgia pursued independence, continue to have ramifications for Georgia today.

These events and subsequent dynamics in Georgia demonstrate two important lessons for understanding authority, control, and sovereignty in international politics. First, political survival can be a powerful impetus for actors to give up sovereignty. This is particularly true in environments such as Georgia where access to political power was essential for economic well-being as well. Second, international hierarchies are not only the product of formal governments bargaining away sovereign rights. Russia in part constructed its influence and control over Georgia by contracting with subnational groups, while simultaneously striking bargains with the central government. Combined, these two lessons demonstrate that domestic political interactions are an essential part of any explanation of hierarchy.

Great powers' attempts to exert control over smaller or weaker states have often been met with violent resistance. For example, the European great powers sent thousands of soldiers to China to defeat the Boxer Rebellion, while the Urabi uprising in Egypt led to an eventual invasion and establishment of a formal empire by Britain. In more contemporary cases, Georgian and Ukrainian opposition to Russian power have triggered violent confrontations between these countries and Russia, in 2008 and 2014, respectively. Perhaps equally consequential in determining the structure of global order, though generally receiving less attention, are instances when great power expansion and attempts to establish authority succeed with local support. This book explains when actors within a weaker state will support giving up sovereignty to a more powerful state and when they will resist. In other words, how do great powers establish authority and control in international politics?

The ability of great powers to find support and establish relationships with actors in less powerful states or polities is crucial for achieving their political goals. The United States invaded Afghanistan with the support of the Northern Alliance, a coalition of warlords opposed to the Taliban; Russia now governs Chechnya with the aid of local actor Ramzan Kadyrov and in the past and present has wielded influence over Georgia using local proxies.[1] However, how great powers establish these patron–client relationships and why they persist, despite potential for defection from both sides, is unclear. Specifically, the conditions that cause local actors to welcome such relationships, surrendering a substantial share of

---

[1] Kimberly Marten, *Warlords: Strong-Arm Brokers in Weak States* (Cornell University Press, 2012).

Introduction

their autonomy, are poorly understood. Knowing that local actors are motivated by concerns for political survival and the desire to pursue or retain rent-seeking opportunities will improve our understanding of the constraints and opportunities available to powerful states seeking to expand and exert influence within the international system.

This book helps to explain how certain kinds of political order in the international system emerge or break down. In particular, it contributes to our understanding of hierarchy in international relations and global politics. Hierarchy is a form of authority relationship between states in which a dominant power controls aspects of a subordinate state's sovereignty. Historians and scholars of international relations are increasingly using the concepts of empire and hierarchy to describe the behavior of powerful states in contemporary as well as historical settings. Political units as diverse as the European Union and the United States have been described as empires.[2] Relationships from those between the United States and Latin America to New Zealand's with certain South Pacific islands have been classified as hierarchies.[3] Hierarchy clearly plays a critical role in how we understand international relations.

Under certain conditions, the interaction between the international system and domestic politics creates incentives for actors to surrender their sovereignty, leading to the establishment of hierarchy. Actors in weaker states respond to both the incentives of their domestic political situations and the credibility of the threat from the dominant state when deciding to surrender sovereignty. Somewhat counterintuitively, I find that where subordinate actors extract the most economic benefit from political power through rent-seeking, they are most willing to surrender sovereign rights and political power to external actors.

The bulk of the evidence is drawn from Russia's relationship with the Soviet successor states. By focusing on Russia, I am able to illuminate some of the dynamics that have resulted in conflict between Russia and former Soviet Republics Ukraine and Georgia. To provide evidence of the argument's generalizability, additional support is mustered using two

---

[2] Niall Ferguson, *Empire: The Rise and Demise of the British World Order and the Lessons for Global Power* (Basic Books, 2004); Herfried Münkler, *Empires: The Logic of World Domination from Ancient Rome to the United States* (Polity Press, 2007); Y. H. Ferguson, "Approaches to Defining 'Empire' and Characterizing United States Influence in the Contemporary World," *International Studies Perspectives* 9, no. 3 (2008).

[3] Ahsan I. Butt, "Anarchy and Hierarchy in International Relations: Examining South America's War-Prone Decade, 1932–41," *International Organization* 67, no. 3 (2013); David A. Lake, "Legitimating Power: The Domestic Politics of US International Hierarchy," *International Security* 38, no. 2 (2013); Jason C. Sharman, "International Hierarchies and Contemporary Imperial Governance: A Tale of Three Kingdoms," *European Journal of International Relations* 19, no. 2 (2013).

4   Introduction

different sources. First, a set of qualitative cases studies explores European attempts to limit the sovereignty of China, the Ottoman Empire, and Egypt in the nineteenth and early twentieth centuries. China and the Ottoman Empire are cases where local support allowed a stable informal empire to be sustained, while in Egypt informal empire faced resistance, broke down, and was replaced with British colonialism. This set of cases demonstrates that the relationships hold even in very different international environments to that of the post-Soviet space. Second, a cross-national statistical analysis examines hierarchy worldwide since 1945, demonstrating these dynamics on a global scale.

Hierarchy and the International System

Hierarchy can be and is defined in a variety of ways in international relations.[4] Hierarchy can be understood in a narrow sense as legitimate authority and the sharing of sovereign rights between states or more broadly as stratification in the international system, whether this be in terms of material power or social status. This work focuses on the narrow definition of hierarchy and the establishment of authority relationships between states where some states have the right to command and others an obligation to obey.[5] These authority relations subordinate the sovereignty of one state to another, constituting hierarchy.[6] "When political authority is exercised, the dominant state commands a subordinate state to alter its behavior, where command implies that the former has the right to order the latter to take certain actions."[7] When one state takes control over another's sovereignty, an authority relationship is established. Hierarchy, in other words, can be understood as defining a situation in

---

[4] Janice Bially Mattern and Ayşe Zarakol, "Hierarchies in World Politics," *International Organization* 70, no. 3 (2016); Ayşe Zarakol, *Hierarchies in World Politics*, vol. 144 (Cambridge University Press, 2017); Paul K. MacDonald, "Embedded Authority: A Relational Network Approach to Hierarchy in World Politics," *Review of International Studies* 44, no. 1 (2017); Meghan McConaughey, Paul Musgrave, and Daniel H. Nexon, "Beyond Anarchy: Logics of Political Organization, Hierarchy, and International Structure," *International Theory* 10, no. 2 (2018).

[5] Some accounts offer a more generic definition of hierarchy based on status and power differentials; see Gerry Simpson, *Great Powers and Outlaw States: Unequal Sovereigns in the International Order* (Cambridge University Press, 2004); David C. Kang, "Hierarchy and Legitimacy in International Systems: The Tribute System in Early Modern East Asia," *Security Studies* 19, no. 4 (2010). In contrast, in this work, I focus on dyadic authority relationships.

[6] David Lake, "Beyond Anarchy: The Importance of Security Institutions," *International Security* 26, no. 1 (2001).

[7] David A. Lake, "Escape from the State of Nature: Authority and Hierarchy in World Politics," *International Security* 32, no. 1 (2007).

which the sovereignty of one state is reduced by another in an institutionalized form.

At one extreme end of the anarchy-hierarchy continuum exist hierarchical arrangements such as formal empire or military occupations that can remove all or most of the sovereignty belonging to the subordinate state or polity.[8] At the other end of this continuum is anarchy; each state has complete control over every issue area or sovereign right within its domain of authority.[9] In between are a variety of different forms of hierarchy that reduce the sovereignty of the subordinate state across a range of issues or just one, leaving the subordinate state with varying degrees of authority over these issue areas.[10] The level of hierarchy increases as the subordinate state loses more sovereign rights or loses greater degrees of control over a particular issue area.[11]

Hierarchy can often shape the relationships between great powers. By establishing authority relationships, great powers introduce a form of governance into the international system.[12] Because such authority allows great powers to achieve many of their aims, they often engage in competition to assert control. For example, both Russia and the United States have competed for control and influence in Central Asia, on occasions seeking to outdo their rival to guarantee their position. Such contestation can exacerbate tensions between states.[13]

In addition, hierarchy, or at least its breakdown, can lead great powers to resort to coercion, violence, and war with smaller states.[14] Where states

---

[8] David M. Edelstein, "Occupational Hazards: Why Military Occupations Succeed or Fail," *International Security* 29, no. 1 (2004); Daniel H. Nexon and Thomas Wright, "What's at Stake in the American Empire Debate," *American Political Science Review* 101, no. 2 (2007).

[9] That it has the right to decide over every issue area does not mean the state possesses the capacity to carry out its wishes. Stephen D. Krasner, *Sovereignty: Organized Hypocrisy* (Princeton University Press, 1999).

[10] David A. Lake, "Anarchy, Hierarchy, and the Variety of International Relations," *International Organization* 50 (1996); John M. Hobson and Jason C. Sharman, "The Enduring Place of Hierarchy in World Politics: Tracing the Social Logics of Hierarchy and Political Change," *European Journal of International Relations* 11, no. 1 (2005).

[11] Arguably, the situation of anarchy is an ideal type that rarely, if ever, exists in the international system.

[12] Alexander Cooley and Hendrik Spruyt, *Contracting States: Sovereign Transfers in International Relations* (Princeton University Press, 2009); David A. Lake, "Rightful Rules: Authority, Order, and the Foundations of Global Governance," *International Studies Quarterly* 54, no. 3 (2010).

[13] See, e.g., the destabilizing effects of competition between the United States and Russia for influence in Central Asia. Alexander Cooley, *Great Games, Local Rules: The New Power Contest in Central Asia* (Oxford University Press, 2012); Rajan Menon, "The New Great Game in Central Asia," *Survival* 45, no. 2 (2003).

[14] Jesse Dillon Savage, "The Stability and Breakdown of Empire: European Informal Empire in China, the Ottoman Empire and Egypt," *European Journal of International Relations* 17, no. 2 (2011); Alexander Lanoszka, "Beyond Consent and Coercion: Using

can rely on legitimacy and authority, they are able to rule through peaceful means. In contrast, where their rule is rejected, great powers are often forced to resort to coercion to achieve their ends. In extreme cases this can result in armed conflict and military interventions. For example, the replacement of a local client in Ukraine resulted in Russia intervening militarily in Crimea in 2014 to maintain some control over important assets and authority in the region.

Hierarchy also affects political relationships between smaller states. In return for smaller states supporting their authority, great powers often provide public goods such as peace and order.[15] The United States has been central to ensuring that the western hemisphere has remained virtually free of interstate conflict during the last 150 years. The one exception to this was in the 1930s when the United States, dealing with consequences of the depression and opting for isolationist international policies, withdrew from its hierarchical role in Latin America, resulting in increased levels of conflict in the region.[16]

Hierarchy, then, is known to have many important ramifications for the conduct of international politics. In this book, I focus my attention on hierarchy where the sovereign rights of one state are ceded to another; I examine when informal empire and moderate levels of hierarchy can be stabilized and persist and when the dominant state must opt for an alternative arrangement such as formal empire, a more extreme form of hierarchy, or accept anarchy. The reason for focusing on informal forms of hierarchy, or hierarchy that leaves in place a subordinate actor, is that such forms of hierarchy are the most viable in the current international system where strong norms and sanctions exist that limit the feasibility of territorial annexation, formal empire, and colonialism.

In practice, informal hierarchies can take many forms. Informal empire, where an authority relationship is established between two states but the subordinate state retains de jure sovereignty, is one common historical example.[17] Under informal empire, imperial intermediaries possess greater autonomy than in formal colonial settings and the authority relationships between the core and periphery only concern a limited set of issues.[18] Informal empire removes agency to a lesser extent than formal empire and does so without assuming direct territorial control. However,

---

Republican Political Theory to Understand International Hierarchies," *International Theory* 5, no. 3 (2013).

[15] Butt, "Anarchy and Hierarchy in International Relations." [16] Butt.

[17] Alexander Wendt and Daniel Friedheim, "Hierarchy under Anarchy: Informal Empire and the East Germany State," in *State Sovereignty as Social Construct*, ed. Thomas Biersteker and Cynthia Weber (Cambridge University Press, 1996), 245.

[18] Daniel Nexon, "What's This Then? 'Romanes Eunt Domus'?," *International Studies Perspectives* 9, no. 3 (2008): 306.

the dominant state still drastically reduces the sovereignty of the subordinate state.[19]

While many forms of informal hierarchy involve direct contracting with central state actors in the subordinate polity, this is not a necessary feature of informal hierarchy. Examining both historical and contemporary examples reveals that dominant actors often negotiated arrangements with subnational actors. These subnational actors because of their effective control over a region were able to render sovereignty to the dominant state. In extreme circumstances, this can mean the establishment of de facto states or the development of frozen conflicts such as those that have appeared in post-Soviet space in Abkhazia, South Ossetia, Transnistria, and the Donbas. De facto states through their external patrons are often able to carve out space for themselves and achieve more autonomy than they would have within the original state, but in doing so they also transfer some sovereignty from their original state to their patron.

Hierarchies demonstrate a persistent and regularized relationship of control by one state over another, not merely high levels of influence. For example, great powers often relied on extraterritoriality to assert control over the legal sovereignty of subordinate states such China, Siam, and the Ottoman Empire.[20] Such arrangements could persist for decades if not centuries. In addition, European powers often established institutions within the subordinate polities to control aspects of the state's revenue-raising capacity.[21] For example, the Ottoman Administration of Public Debt, in effect a European agency within the Ottoman state, at one point in time controlled roughly 27 percent of Ottoman revenue.[22] A similar relationship existed in China through the Chinese Maritime Customs and the Salt Administration.[23] Where such institutions significantly curtail the authority of the subordinate state to act as it ordinarily would, informal empire is present.

---

[19] Jürgen Osterhammel, *Semi-colonialism and Informal Empire in Twentieth-Century China: Towards a Framework of Analysis* (Bibliothek der Universität Konstanz, 1986).

[20] Turan Kayaoglu, *Legal Imperialism: Sovereignty and Extraterritoriality in Japan, the Ottoman Empire, and China* (Cambridge University Press, 2010).

[21] For discussion of such activities in the Ottoman Empire, see Donald Christy Blaisdell, *European Financial Control in the Ottoman Empire: A Study of the Establishment, Activities, and Significance of the Administration of the Ottoman Public Debt* (Columbia University Press, 1929). For examples of similar European actions in China through the Chinese Maritime Customs, see Hans Van de Ven, *Breaking with the Past: The Maritime Customs Service and the Global Origins of Modernity in China* (Columbia University Press, 2014).

[22] M. Sukru Hanioglu, *A Brief History of the Late Ottoman Empire* (Princeton University Press, 2008); Blaisdell, *European Financial Control*.

[23] Albert Feuerwerker, *The Foreign Establishment in China in the Early Twentieth Century* (Center for Chinese Studies, University of Michigan, 1976), 63.

Hierarchical relationships involve the asymmetric surrender of sovereignty. That is, there is a state that clearly is in a dominant position. This means that international organizations or treaties that formally and informally establish symmetric responsibilities are not the object of study. While some international organizations formally or informally provide a privileged position for a dominant actor, status or power hierarchies are not the same as "governance" hierarchy or the surrender of sovereignty.[24] It is important to draw a distinction between states that are purely political clients and those who have established themselves as subordinate actors in a hierarchical relationship. While the former may defer in some areas to a patron, they have not given up their autonomy and may be more prone to shirking.[25] For example, there is something of a *social hierarchy* in NATO, with smaller states deferring to larger states on important matters.[26] Nonetheless, with dominant powers having ostensibly equal rights and more responsibilities, countries like the Baltic states joining NATO, were are not accepting a hierarchical relationship.

Asymmetric institutional reductions of sovereignty are prevalent in the modern era, and many examples can be found in the post-Soviet context. Russia demands the right to police the borders of many states in the Eurasian region, is involved in governing their airspace, and stations military forces on their soil.[27] Russia also seeks to institutionalize a reduction of economic sovereignty through the imposition of a common economic space and a customs union. The former Soviet Republics provide a clear area of interest for those who want to understand the dynamics of hierarchy in the international system.

Theories of Hierarchy

The important role of hierarchy in structuring international politics raises the question of how and why hierarchies develop. Some explanations have attributed the development of these systems to material causes such as power disparities and political efficiencies among unitary state actors.[28] Others have focused on the role that beliefs and identities play in making hierarchical relationships seem

---

[24] McConaughey et al., "Beyond Anarchy."
[25] I thank Reviewer B for pointing out this important distinction.
[26] Vincent Pouliot, *International Pecking Orders: The Politics and Practice of Multilateral Diplomacy* (Cambridge University Press, 2016).
[27] Alexander Cooley, "Imperial Wreckage: Property Rights, Sovereignty, and Security in the Post-Soviet Space," *International Security* 25, no. 3 (2006): 102.
[28] See Jeffry Frieden, "International Investment and Colonial Control: A New Interpretation," *International Organization*, 48, no. 4 (1994); David Lake, "Anarchy, Hierarchy, and the Variety of International Relations," *International Organization*, 50,

Theories of Hierarchy

legitimate.[29] Recently, some attention has been focused on the effects of domestic political institutions.[30] The following section outlines the implications of these approaches, which highlight many of the conditions conducive to informal hierarchy.

Relational contracting offers a principled approach to analyzing actors' choices based on the expected costs of each potential course of action. In this way, the level of hierarchy between two states can be reduced to an equilibrium based on assessments of cost: "the expected costs of opportunism, which decline with relational hierarchy, and governance costs, which rise with relational hierarchy."[31] That is, as the costs to the dominant state of defection by the subordinate rise, so too will the level of hierarchy, as the consequences of opportunism are high. And as the cost of controlling the subordinate state increase, hierarchy will decline. While opportunism and governance costs are undoubtedly important elements of any explanation, they will to a large extent be shaped by the preferences of actors in the subordinate state. The preferences of actors in the subordinate state will explain how much effort and resources the dominant state needs to expend on governance and also the probability of defection. In order to understand the types of hierarchy that have emerged in the international system, these subordinate actors' preferences must be considered in the context of the domestic institutional factors that enable and constrain their choices.

Stephen Krasner has shown that the principles of sovereignty can easily be violated by great powers as they use coercion or its threat to assume control over weaker states.[32] Power is a necessary, but not sufficient, condition for hierarchy. Power disparities can exist between states where no hierarchical relationship occurs. Emphasis on power disparities cannot explain why the Aztecs and Incas crumbled in the face of the advancing conquistadors while the smaller, less differentiated tribes of northern Mexico put up fierce resistance for two generations.[33] Similarly, Russia has possessed a consistent and massive power advantage in relation to Georgia, yet at times Georgian leaders have been prepared to resist Russian hierarchy while at others they have chosen to submit. Alternative

---

no. 1 (1996); Lake, "Beyond Anarchy"; Katja Weber, *Hierarchy Admist Anarchy: Transaction Costs and Institutional Choice* (SUNY Press, 2000).

[29] Sharman, "International Hierarchies."

[30] J. Gerring et al., "An Institutional Theory of Direct and Indirect Rule," *World Politics* 63, no. 3 (2011); Lake, "Legitimating Power."

[31] Lake, "Anarchy, Hierarchy," 2.

[32] Stephen Krasner, *Organized Hypocrisy* (Princeton University Press, 1999).

[33] John Elliot, *Empires of the Atlantic World: Spain and Britain in the Americas 1492–1830* (Yale University Press, 2006), 61–62.

explanations, not rooted in power disparities, must be found to explain this resistance.

Beliefs, historical connections, and culture have been used to explain external patronage and hierarchy.[34] According to these theories, it is legitimacy and an understanding of what is right which drive relationships of hierarchy as much as the material considerations facing each actor. A dominant state may choose to expand due to their beliefs and disposition.[35] However, focusing on the beliefs of the dominant state cannot explain their different treatment of culturally similar subordinate actors during the same period of time. For example, Britain treated Egypt dramatically differently to the Ottoman Empire in the 1880s. Moreover, historians Gallagher and Robinson have shown that Britain's shift to more colonial forms of hierarchy did not occur in the context of changing ideological beliefs.[36] Changes of identity are not necessary for changed practices.

The beliefs and perceptions of legitimacy held by the subordinate actor are also potential mechanisms that might explain the establishment of hierarchy.[37] If the subordinate state sees hierarchy as right, then they may be more inclined to accept external authority. Subordinate identities and beliefs, while important, are not sufficient to determine particular behaviors. Identities interact with the material and institutional contexts in which they are embedded. Nationalist identities can have the paradoxical effect of increasing support for hierarchy if the right domestic environment leads to increased conflict between groups within a polity.[38] In Georgia, the nationalism of the central government and the Abkhaz and Ossetians brought about a reduction in sovereignty. The desire of the Abkhaz and Ossetians to assert their own identities in the face of Georgian nationalism drove them into the arms of Russia. These actors were willing to support Russian incursions and assertions of power, resulting in them

---

[34] Robert Jackson, *Quasi-States: Sovereignty, International Relations and the Third World* (Cambridge University Press, 1990); Wendt and Friedheim, "Hierarchy under Anarchy"; Hobson and Sharman, "Enduring Place of Hierarchy."

[35] Sharman, "International Hierarchies."

[36] John Gallagher and Ronald Robinson, "The Imperialism of Free Trade," *Economic History Review* 6, no. 1 (1953); Ronald Robinson, "Non-European Foundations of European Imperialism: Sketch for a Theory of Collaboration," in *Studies in the Theory of Imperialism* (Longman, 1972).

[37] Wendt and Friedheim, "Hierarchy under Anarchy"; Hobson and Sharman, "Enduring Place of Hierarchy."

[38] Lawrence demonstrates that nationalism does not even require demands for autonomy. Instead she shows that nationalist movements in the French Empire often demanded greater integration, and it was rejection of these initial demands that lead to the pursuit of greater autonomy. Adria Lawrence, *Imperial Rule and the Politics of Nationalism: Anticolonial Protest in the French Empire* (Cambridge University Press, 2013).

rendering parts of Georgian sovereignty to Russia. The cases in this book will show that nationalism and identity are not a sufficient explanation for resistance and, depending on the domestic political situation, can even lead to support for foreign encroachments on sovereignty.

David Lake proposed that political institutions can explain variation in support for hierarchy among states.[39] Where benefits from hierarchy are large, hierarchy will be supported, even by large ruling coalitions such as those under democracy. Where benefits are small, only small ruling coalitions such as authoritarian regimes will support hierarchy. According to this logic, hierarchy is more likely in authoritarian regimes because the benefits do not need to be large to gain support. Lake's work highlights the perspectives and motivations of actors in the subordinate state and draws attention to their agency and the role they play in the establishment of hierarchy. However, this work does not explain what determines the benefits of hierarchy for the subordinate actors, rather the distribution of these benefits. Domestic political institutions can increase the importance of hierarchy as well as alter who benefits. This book, in contrast to Lake's argument concerning *who* benefits from hierarchy, will focus on explaining how institutions can alter the value of those benefits to subordinate actors.

Paul MacDonald is another scholar who has examined how the domestic politics of subordinate states might influence their ability to support hierarchies.[40] He argues that domestic networks make brokers or intermediaries more effective agents for the dominant states. While this is an important insight, he does not fully theorize how or why brokers might be willing to mobilize their resources on the behalf of the dominant state. This work complements the work of MacDonald by showing that certain types of networks – rent-seeking ones in opposition to other groups – are more likely to become intermediaries of the dominant state.

Numerous examples demonstrate that dominant states can establish a level of hierarchy with the support of nonstate or regional actors from within the subordinate state. Russia, for example, was able to increase its level of control in Georgia through the support of the local ruler of Adjara. In Ukraine, Russian support of actors in Eastern Ukraine has acted as a constraint on Ukrainian autonomy. Nonstate actors have often played an important role in the establishment of hierarchy and their choices and behavior remain unexplained by existing theories.

[39] Lake, "Legitimating Power." [40] MacDonald, "Embedded Authority."

International Relations, Domestic Politics, and Support for Hierarchy

All else being equal, great powers prefer informal empire or hierarchy to formal empire because it provides them with a sufficient level of control to achieve their aims without having to pay the cost of formal expansion.[41] Once the great power has made the decision to expand, it is the interaction between the relative cost of formal expansion for the great power and the domestic politics of the subordinate state that explains the type of hierarchy that emerges and if it is stable. Hierarchies are stable when subordinate actors accommodate themselves to the authority relationships. The dominant power does not simply preserve its control through a greater ability to coerce subordinate actors into accepting such arrangements. Accommodation allows hierarchy to exist, persist, and function. Absent some external shock, hierarchy will if met with accommodation persist for a significantly longer period of time than if it is met with resistance.

For example, in the nineteenth century the sovereignty of the Ottoman Empire and China was limited through institutional means such as extraterritoriality and Western control over some government finances. Elements of this informal imperial relationship were to last in both countries for almost a century. This type of relationship only ended in the Ottoman Empire and in China after the exogenous shocks of World War I and World War II respectively.

Empirically, where hierarchy is unstable two possible outcomes are observed. First, agitation against external rule might occur, forcing the great power to seize control using coercion. Second, in the face of such agitation, the external power might simply give up its pretensions to hierarchy. Egypt provides a prime example of a great power being forced to annex the subordinate territory. Initially informal empire was established by the European powers, but in contrast to China and the Ottoman Empire, sufficient numbers of Egyptian elites resisted imperial impositions. The Egyptian ruler, the Khedive Ismail, dismissed his European advisers and Egyptian military officers carried out an uprising against European interests.[42] This led to the British occupation and the establishment of formal empire in 1882. More recently, the overthrow of a local ally in Ukraine and Russia's subsequent annexation of Crimea parallels

---

[41] Lake, "Anarchy, Hierarchy."
[42] Jesse Dillon Savage, "The Stability and Breakdown of Empire: European Informal Empire in China, the Ottoman Empire and Egypt," *European Journal of International Relations* 17, no. 2 (2011): 161.

the processes observed in Egypt as changes in institutions increased resistance and saw a ratcheting up of coercion.

At other times, resistance to an informal hierarchy in the subordinate state has resulted in the great power being forced to retrench. An example can be found in Russia's relationship with Georgia following the breakup of the USSR. Eduard Shevardnadze, once the ruler of Georgia, accepted high levels of Russian hierarchy when faced with significant domestic threats. However, as the regime consolidated he was able to pursue a more independent path as were his successors. While Russia has preserved control in some breakaway regions, steadily, the Georgian government reduced the level of Russian control over its sovereignty.

Support for international hierarchy is critical for great powers seeking to expand. This support can take different forms. One type of support involves groups in charge of the subordinate state directly negotiating away sovereign rights. For example, they can sign treaties that allow the stationing of outside military forces, provide external actors control over economic resources or join or create domestic or international organizations that surrender economic decision-making power to an outside state.[43] These actions result in the establishment of hierarchy.

Hierarchy can also be supported in less direct ways. Nonstate actors can lobby or threaten governments in support of external control. This can be as simple as protesting in favor of a continued military presence, as occurred in the Georgian town of Akhalkalaki.[44] In other cases, it can be more extensive; in Abkhazia local actors established de facto state institutions that were then subordinated to Russian authority. By threatening the central government and making demands, actors who are not part of the central state can impose constraints on central actors in the subordinate state and increase the level of hierarchy.

Elite actors in the subordinate state choose to support great power expansion when their domestic institutions create incentives for them to do so. Subordinate elites will support informal hierarchy where institutions encourage political contestation that then threatens rent-seeking opportunities. In this book, I adopt a broad definition of political contestation. It can occur when outside forces attempt to overthrow regime actors or seize control of formal or informal political institutions; this could be through formal mechanisms such as elections or more informal processes such as protests or coups. It can also occur through informal institutions such as intraregime contestation as regime actors jostle for power. Rent-seeking is the use of political power to increase economic benefits above what an actor would receive in a market relationship. Rent-seeking can be corrupt, using

---

[43] Cooley and Spruyt, *Contracting States*. [44] See Chapter 3.

political positions to demand bribes or engage in criminal activity, or more legal actions such as directing subsidies to clients or the use of unnecessary regulation.

My argument applies to rent-seeking broadly, including both corruption and more formal, institutionalized forms of rent-seeking. Threats result where there are rival actors or government elites who have incentives to seize control of existing political institutions themselves. As a result, rent-seeking links political competition or potential competition to economic competition. Political contestation increases the threat to political survival. In an environment where political competition is tied to rent-seeking, loss of political power means a loss of economic return. Consequently, a threat to political survival combined with rent-seeking creates incentives for groups in the subordinate state to surrender sovereignty to outside powers in order to ensure their political survival.

An example of these dynamics can be found in Georgian region of Javakheti during the 1990s and early 2000s. In this region the ethnic Armenian population saw access to political positions and power as important for their economic life. Political positions such as police chief and customs officials presented an economic advantage by providing opportunities for smuggling or corruption.[45] These actors faced potential threats from other local actors and also from the central regime. Consequently, preserving their political power became paramount. These regional dynamics contributed to the Armenian population seeing Russian intervention in Georgia as a potential source of protection rather than a threat.

However, resources from external actors are only imperfect substitutes for domestic support. Domestic elites need to maintain the support of their own society. If they alienate domestic constituencies and lose the resources of their clients, elites may still lose power even if supported by an external patron. Elites can support hierarchy if it is a choice also favored by their clients and society. Fortunately for elites, the nature of patron–client relationships means that societal actors should be invested in the political survival of their patrons; if institutions create incentives for elites to support hierarchy to facilitate political survival they should also influence the payoffs for societal actors. In other words, high levels of rent-seeking should mean that societal actors accept their patrons trading sovereignty for survival.

Absent support for informal hierarchy, the outcome of a great power's attempts to expand will depend on the costs of conflict for the two states.

---

[45] Ekaterine Metreveli, *The Dynamics of "Frozen Tension": Case of Javakheti* (Georgian Foundation for Strategic and International Studies, 2004), 17.

Formal expansion for the dominant state can be either relatively costly or cheap.[46] Material factors such as the balance of power,[47] technological development,[48] or economic development,[49] can cause the costs of expansion to vary. Alternatively, normative acceptability can also affect costs.[50] When these various factors are configured in such a manner that costs are low, the international system can be said to be permissive.

Assuming perfect information about the costs and incentives of both parties, there are two likely outcomes. Where formal expansion is costly and the domestic institutions are resistant to expansion, the dominant state should accept an anarchic relationship. The dominant and subordinate elites know that it would be too costly to assume formal control through annexation and conquest. The dominant state does not expand or withdraws expecting that they will face resistance that makes hierarchy untenable. On the other hand, if formal expansion is cheap for the dominant state, even if the subordinate institutions create incentives to resist, the subordinate elites should be forced into accepting informal hierarchy as they know the result of resistance would be eventual formal control. Hence, informal hierarchy should always result if it has the support of the elites in the subordinate state or if the costs of formal expansion for the dominant state are sufficiently low.

Resistance to hierarchy is an out-of-equilibrium outcome.[51] However, the empirical record shows that conflict often occurs. Great powers sometimes expand and are forced to retrench; subordinate states sometimes resist and lose sovereignty to a formal hierarchical relationship. I argue that these outcomes can occur when the lack of rent-seeking or contestation creates incentives to resist and there is uncertainty on the part of one state about the costs constraining the other's course of action. That is, one or other side of the potential hierarchical bargain has private information. When the domestic institutions create incentives to resist, for example, the subordinate group may follow through with this resistance if they believe the dominant state will be restricted from expanding and the dominant state will respond with coercion if this is not the case. Hence,

---

[46] H. Spruyt, "The End of Empire and the Extension of the Westphalian System: The Normative Basis of the Modern State Order," *International Studies Review* 2, no. 2 (2000): 65–92.
[47] Michael W. Doyle, *Empires* (Cornell University Press, 1986).
[48] Daniel R. Headrick, *The Tools of Empire: Technology and European Imperialism in the Nineteenth Century* (Oxford University Press, 1981).
[49] Erik Gartzke and Dominic Rohner, "The Political Economy of Imperialism, Decolonization and Development," *British Journal of Political Science* 41, no. 3 (2011).
[50] Tanisha M. Fazal, *State Death: The Politics and Geography of Conquest, Occupation, and Annexation* (Princeton University Press, 2011).
[51] David Lake, *Hierarchy in International Relations* (Cornell University Press, 2009).

violent resistance and formal hierarchy are often the result of incomplete information combined with certain types of domestic institutions.

Cases and Evidence

The project adopts an integrative multimethod design to test the theoretical arguments.[52] The different methods are mostly used to test a variety of different assumptions and portions of the argument, not for triangulation. The post-Soviet region provides the majority of the empirical evidence. The focus on post-Soviet states and their relationship with Russia has several advantages. Crucially, the post-Soviet cases have certain features that help achieve internal validity. The post-Soviet context provides a unique opportunity, somewhat resembling a natural experiment, as these states share the historical and institutional legacies of the Soviet Union.[53] This means that these factors cannot be used to explain the varied outcomes.

Despite their common background, the Soviet states also provide sufficient variation on key variables to allow confidence that arguments will generalize to other parts of the world. Slater and Ziblatt identify factors that provide external validity to studies using relatively small numbers of cases.[54] The first is representative variation. The second is theoretically informed control. The post-Soviet cases provide both.

Representative variation refers to the extent that the cases selected provide variation that is representative of the theoretically expected variation in the population. The theory should be applicable to most states in the world. There is substantial variation in terms of economic development; the Baltic States and Kazakhstan fall into the top third of states by per capita GDP, while states such as Tajikistan and Kyrgyzstan fall in the bottom third; the other states range in between. The economies of these states are dominated by different types of sectoral interests; for example, Ukraine has substantial industrial interests, and in the Caucasus and Central Asia, there are substantial energy producers. In addition, there is substantial variation in terms of ethnic makeup; some states have high levels of ethnic fragmentation, others substantially less. There are different religious identities also represented. The part of the global population

---

[52] Jason Seawright, "Better Multimethod Design: The Promise of Integrative Multimethod Research," *Security Studies* 25, no. 1 (2016); Jason Seawright, *Multi Method Social Science* (Cambridge University Press, 2016).

[53] Keith A. Darden, *Economic Liberalism and Its Rivals: The Formation of International Institutions among the Post-Soviet States* (Cambridge University Press, 2009): 4.

[54] Dan Slater and Daniel Ziblatt, "The Enduring Indispensability of the Controlled Comparison," *Comparative Political Studies* 46, no. 10 (2013).

that the region most obviously fails to capture is the most developed democracies.

In terms of theoretical control, the cases account for rival explanations. Russia has a clear historical and contemporary interest in asserting hierarchy in the region.[55] This means that motives of the dominant state can be held somewhat constant, facilitating a focus on the domestic politics of the subordinate actors. The differing levels of economic development and sectoral interests in the former Soviet Union help dismiss some of the contracting approaches to hierarchy. Different cultural and ideological developments among the countries can also help discount constructivist explanations for hierarchy. Holding constant these alternative explanations should provide a certain degree of external validity.

The study of post-Soviet states draws on several different kinds of evidence. There are two main case studies: Georgia and Ukraine. Leaders in both cases have been deferential to Russian attempts to assert control at various times and resisted Russian overtures at other junctures. Georgia in particular is a useful case because it provides multiple observations and variation in the variables of interest, both at a national and subnational level. It is possible to show that different parts of Georgia had different levels of support for Russian influence and control. Within these cases quantitative analysis examines micro-level variation using survey data; this component provides the clearest test of the societal-level arguments made in the book.

These two cases help rule out several competing explanations. Since they have gained independence, Georgia and Ukraine have both seen their relationship with Russia shift regularly. At times these states have been more willing to acquiesce to Russian impositions on their sovereignty; at others they have been resistant to the point of violent conflict. While culture and history play a large role in determining the predispositions of countries toward resistance,[56] they cannot explain this variation across time. History and culture are often too slow moving to explain rapid shifts in policy. Even when these types of beliefs do change quickly, it is often in response to conflicts over sovereignty and foreign policy outlooks rather than a cause. Instead, factors causing these shifts are located in the changing political environments of these states. These cases provide qualitative evidence for the proposition that competition over rent-seeking in subordinate states partly drives the tendency to support outside intrusions on sovereignty.

[55] A. P. Tsygankov, *Russia's Foreign Policy: Change and Continuity in National Identity* (Rowman and Littlefield, 2010).
[56] Keith Darden, *Resisting Occupation: Mass Literacy and the Creation of Durable National Loyalties* (Cambridge University Press, forthcoming).

As Collier et al. argue, "crucial leverage in testing explanations comes from within-case analysis, and this leverage is valuable irrespective of whether these cases are embedded in a full-variance design or a no variance design."[57] In each of the case studies, process tracing is used. Process tracing involves searching for qualitative observations that are consistent or inconsistent with the proposed theory and its alternatives and using these observations as evidence to confirm or disconfirm the causal arguments.[58] By shifting the level of analysis, process tracing allows additional observations to be made that if implied by the original theory can be used as verification.[59] It is possible to observe the connection between political competition and rent-seeking and for this connection to be tied to the subsequent development of hierarchical institutions. Process tracing thus supplements the testing of theories conducted through cross-case comparison. Comparison across cases synchronically and diachronically allows many potential causes of hierarchy to be discounted.[60]

However, this is not just a story about the legacies of the Soviet Union; its implications are potentially much broader. To test the empirical implications of the book in another historical and geographical context, three cases are analyzed from the nineteenth century. In the nineteenth century, expansion was unconstrained by general normative or international factors, a very different context to the later period of the post-Soviet cases when dominant states were far more constrained. This variation in the international environment provides insight into the relative importance of domestic political variables compared to international factors. If similar domestic factors can explain outcomes across these two very different systems, then it strengthens the case for using domestic political variables to explain international hierarchy.

The persistence and breakdown of informal empire are explored with comparative analysis and examination of within-case evidence from three key examples of nineteenth-century European domination. Focusing on Egypt, the Ottoman Empire, and Qing China allows a clear demonstration

---

[57] David Collier, James Mahoney, and Jason Seawright, "Claiming Too Much: Warnings About Selection Bias," in *Rethinking Social Inquiry: Diverse Tools, Shared Standards*, ed. Henry Brady and David Collier (Rowman and Littlefield, 2004), 101.

[58] J. A. M. Mahoney, "After KKV: The New Methodology of Qualitative Research," *World Politics* 62, no. 1 (2009); D. Collier, "Understanding Process Tracing," *PS Political Science and Politics* 44, no. 4 (2011): 823.

[59] Alexander George and Andrew Bennett, *Case Studies and Theory Development in the Social Sciences* (MIT Press, 2005).

[60] For an example of this method in practice, see Hendrik Spruyt, *Ending Empire: Contested Sovereignty and Territorial Partition*, Cornell Studies in Political Economy (Cornell University Press, 2005); Risa Brooks, *Shaping Strategy: The Civil-Military Politics of Strategic Assessment* (Princeton University Press, 2008).

of how the hypothesized causal mechanisms work in practice.[61] Egypt was originally part of the Ottoman Empire and thus subject to informal imperial control by Britain. After Egypt gained autonomy from its Ottoman rulers, Britain initially established informal control there but had to gradually shift to formal empire. This contrasts with China and the Ottoman Empire, where informal empire persisted for decades longer.

These cases help make the claim that these arguments are applicable beyond the twentieth and twenty-first centuries, and its particular normative and political environments. The three nineteenth-century cases – China, the Ottoman Empire, and Egypt – also help discount alternative explanations. For example, these states all had similar forms of hierarchy at certain times, despite different cultural backgrounds and beliefs, meaning cultural differences could be discounted as a potential cause. In addition, these cases vary in a manner that makes them representative of many similar cases in the nineteenth century.

Finally, we return to the post-Soviet space with a statistical analysis of a data set containing observations from all former Soviet Republics since independence to 2016. This statistical analysis plays an important role in ruling out alternative explanations that might explain the varied success that Russia has had pursuing integration and control over neighboring countries. In addition, this statistical analysis is extended to a global data set to explore generalizability further.

Chapter Outline

Chapter 1 will develop the theory outlined above in more detail and will explain why states choose to expand using informal hierarchy rather than formal empire. It will also explain when subordinate elites choose to accommodate such expansion and when they choose to resist. Resistance is less likely when subordinate elites are competing over rent-seeking opportunities. This changes the relative costs of resistance and accommodation, making accommodation more palatable.

The subsequent three chapters explore the operation of hierarchy in contemporary international politics. Chapter 2 provides case studies of Georgia and Ukraine, exploring the causal processes at the level of national politics. Chapter 3 examines subnational variation in Georgia using the regional cases of Adjara, Abkhazia, Javakheti, and Kvemo Kartli. It explains why some groups seek outside patronage, a variable often believed to exacerbate civil and ethnic conflicts. Chapter 4 uses

---

[61] Collier et al., "Claiming Too Much"; George and Bennett, *Case Studies and Theory Development*.

survey data to demonstrate that the same variables that alter the incentives of national elites to surrender sovereignty also change the preferences of their constituents in society.

The next two chapters demonstrate that the arguments travel beyond the cases of Georgia and Ukraine. The chapters will provide evidence that rent-seeking and contestation are plausible explanatory factors for hierarchy more generally. The two chapters again make use of multiple methods. Chapter 5 analyzes these issues in the context of European expansion and informal empire in the nineteenth century. In particular, the chapter concerns European interactions with China, the Ottoman Empire, and Egypt in the nineteenth and early twentieth centuries. It demonstrates both that European powers preferred informal empire to formal empire and that domestic political institutions can explain the level of support for informal empire by the subordinate state.

Chapter 6 includes an analysis of global data to test the broader generalizability of the argument. It also provides a closer examination of Russia's relationships with all former Soviet states. It makes use of cross-sectional panel data to analyze willingness of these states to surrender sovereignty to Russia. It demonstrates that different regimes with varied political and economic logics are associated with different levels of Russian hierarchy.

Chapter 7 draws out the implications of the book for our understanding of hierarchy in international politics. It reiterates the importance of domestic politics and subnational processes for explaining hierarchy. When domestic politics are considered, it becomes apparent that hierarchy is often a substitute for strong domestic order and not a complement of it.

1 Political Survival and the Surrender of Sovereignty

Why have some attempts by great powers to establish authority over weaker states met with support from actors in these states? Why have some actors within weaker states fiercely resisted giving up their sovereignty? This chapter lays out my theory in detail; I contend that subordinate actors are central to understanding how hierarchies develop in the international system. It is impossible to understand these phenomena without considering political competition within the subordinate state. Only by understanding how politics within the subordinate state creates incentives to resist or support hierarchy is it possible to explain when hierarchy is successful and when great powers must make use of coercion and impose greater levels of control.

Informal forms of hierarchy are of particular importance for understanding international order and conflict in the current era. Norms against territorial annexation and the growth of nationalism have made direct control of foreign states largely redundant. However, it is apparent to scholars of international relations that imperial or empire-like practices continue to play a role in the international politics of the twenty-first century.[1] Given that formal empire, annexation, and territorial expansion are mostly obsolete as strategies, the informal empires of the past have become an important point of comparison for the types of hierarchy we see today.

This chapter situates current practices of hierarchy in the context of past practices of informal empire, demonstrating the importance of domestic politics in subordinate states in establishing hierarchical orders. The interaction of different political incentives in the subordinate state and the hierarchical institutions themselves explain the emergence and stability of hierarchy or resistance to hierarchy and instability. I draw on contracting approaches to explaining hierarchy, proposing that states are

[1] Daniel Nexon, "What's This Then? 'Romanes Eunt Domus'?," *International Studies Perspectives* 9, no. 3 (2008); Stacie E. Goddard and Daniel H. Nexon, "The Dynamics of Global Power Politics: A Framework for Analysis," *Journal of Global Security Studies* 1, no. 1 (2016).

concerned with increasing political efficiencies and control for the minimum possible cost.[2] Hierarchy is more likely to be established in situations when it is less costly for the dominant state; those costs are dramatically lower where the weaker states submit to their authority willingly. To explain the willingness of subordinate actors to surrender sovereignty, I incorporate insights from historical institutionalist approaches to politics.[3] Domestic institutions alter the expected payoffs of giving up sovereignty for subordinate actors and hence are crucial for explaining when they make the choice to do so.

Informal hierarchies and their persistence or breakdown can be explained through the interactions of (1) the dominant state and (2) the elites and society in the subordinate state. Institutions and the preferences they create explain the choices of these actors. Power on its own does little to illuminate these issues. For example, occasionally Georgia resisted Russian encroachment despite great power disparities between the two states, and at other times they accepted a large number of Russian impositions on their sovereignty.

I begin by outlining the preferences and incentives of the dominant state. The core of the argument then explores how domestic institutions in the subordinate state shape the response of actors in that state to outside attempts at establishing hierarchy. Finally, I explain how the interactions between these different actors can lead to the various hierarchical outcomes in the international system. By understanding subordinate actor preferences and the environment that they operate in, we can explain their choice to accommodate informal hierarchy and the resulting stability that accompanies this accommodation.

Preferences and Constraints on Great Powers Seeking to Expand

Informal arrangements can give states an adequate degree of control without the costs of administration and coercion associated with more formal control. Hence, informal hierarchy is often preferable for dominant states. In cases where they fail to establish an informal hierarchy, the costs of formal expansion will determine whether they proceed or accept an anarchical relationship. The international environment plays a crucial role in this – a restrictive

---

[2] Lake, "Anarchy, Hierarchy, and the Variety of International Relations"; Alexander Cooley and Hendrik Spruyt, *Contracting States: Sovereign Transfers in International Relations* (Princeton University Press, 2009).

[3] Kathleen Thelen, "Historical Institutionalism in Comparative Politics," *Annual Review of Political Science* 2, no. 1 (1999); Peter Hall and Rosemary Taylor, "Political Science and the Three Institutionalisms," *Political Studies* 44, no. 4 (1996).

international system that imposes excessive costs on expansion may lead the dominant state to prefer anarchy, while in a more permissive environment, they may choose to expand and establish a formal hierarchy. However, the costs of territorial expansion will also vary based on the characteristics of the states involved and the situation. The following sections outline theoretical reasons why great powers prefer informal hierarchy and show how this preference has been revealed by dominant states throughout history. Constraints imposed by the international system and its implications for states' preferences are then considered.

Why Great Powers Usually Prefer Informal Hierarchy

The support and protection of transnational actors is an essential motivating factor for hierarchy.[4] Through transnational expansion the dominant powers develop an interest in the politics of subordinate states. For example, US imperial ambitions in Latin America were aimed at protecting transnational business interests in the region.[5] In China, Britain enforced unequal treaties to open markets to its merchants and traders.[6] In the Ottoman Empire and Egypt, France, and other European powers often used hierarchy to guarantee loans made by their financiers and protect other business interests.[7] Russia has sought bases for its military in various post-Soviet Republics.[8] As John Darwin put it in explaining the pursuit of empire, "Merchants complained of restraints on trade. Missionaries wanted to win more souls, or to save the souls they had already won. Soldiers wanted a strategic hill, sailors yearned for a deeper anchorage. Proconsuls claimed that a larger colony would mean cheaper rule. Each of these groups could count on lobbies at home to harry its government into intervention or conquest."[9]

---

[4] Michael Doyle, *Empires* (Cornell University Press, 1986), 129–30; Johan Galtung, "A Structural Theory of Imperialism," *Journal of Peace Research* 8, no. 2 (1971).

[5] Warren I. Cohen, *Empire without Tears: America's Foreign Relations, 1921–1933* (Temple University Press, 1987); Noel Maurer, *The Empire Trap: The Rise and Fall of US Intervention to Protect American Property Overseas, 1893–2013* (Princeton University Press, 2013).

[6] Reşat Kasaba, "Treaties and Friendships: British Imperialism, the Ottoman Empire, and China in the Nineteenth Century," *Journal of World History* 4, no. 2 (1993).

[7] M. Şükrü Hanioğlu, *A Brief History of the Late Ottoman Empire* (Princeton University Press, 2010); David Landes, *Bankers and Pashas: International Finance and Economic Imperialism in Egypt* (Harvard University Press, 1958).

[8] Zdzislaw Lachowski, *Foreign Military Bases in Eurasia* (Stockholm International Peace Research Institute, 2007), http://kms1.isn.ethz.ch/serviceengine/Files/ISN/31819/ipublicationdocument_singledocument/b72b4442-d2b3-4684-af9f-b0b136a4c622/en/Policypaper18.pdf.

[9] John Darwin, *After Tamerlane: The Global History of Empire since 1405* (Bloomsbury Press, 2008), 257.

Whatever the exact nature of these transnational actors, they desire hierarchy. Hierarchy is their guarantee in a foreign land that their practices, persons, and economic transactions will be protected. Both informal and formal hierarchy would satisfy their need for protected access to the subordinate state. As long as there is some form of stable hierarchical relationship, these transnational actors are able to continue about their business unperturbed.

Dominant states that guide the establishment of hierarchy are interested in asserting control while limiting governance costs.[10] The costs of hierarchy are constituted by two elements: the costs of control and the costs of governance.[11] Both of these costs are lower for informal hierarchies compared to formal empire; all things being equal, dominant states prefer informal hierarchy over more coercive and costly forms of control. Empires, in and of themselves, rarely returned a financial profit to the imperial powers,[12] though the benefits they attempted to accrue and the goals these empires were pursuing might not have been purely financial.[13]

The costs of control can be defined as the amount of force or coercion that the dominant state needs to exert in order to maintain order and control over the subordinate state. Coercion is a costly method for securing control.[14] The issue is not only whether the dominant state must use force but also how consistently it must be used and the duration of these violent events. The mobilization of the military is expensive and dangerous, requiring the expenditure of both revenue and manpower. The second element of hierarchical costs is the cost of administration or how much direct control the dominant state must take over the subordinate institutions. The greater the number of issue areas that the core or its intermediaries need to administer, the greater the costs become. Where greater levels of control are adopted, greater effort must be placed into administering the subordinate polity.

The stark difference in costs between informal and formal empire was illustrated by the relationship between Britain and Egypt in the nineteenth century. Prior to Britain's intervention in 1882, Egypt was

---

[10] Lake, "Anarchy, Hierarchy."
[11] Both of these costs are implicitly subsumed under the notion of governance costs in the contracting approach.
[12] This is particularly true outside of the mercantilist era of the fifteenth through the seventeenth centuries. Patrick Karl O'Brien and Leandro Prados de la Escosura, "Balance Sheets for the Acquisition, Retention and Loss of European Empires Overseas," *Itinerario* 23, no. 3–4 (1999).
[13] Part of the issue is that the costs of rule increased over time with the imposition of more intensive forms of hierarchy. O'Brien and de la Escosura, 34.
[14] Margaret Levi, *Of Rule and Revenue*, California Series on Social Choice and Political Economy 9 (University of California Press, 1988).

controlled through informal imperial arrangements with certain institutionalized reductions of sovereignty, but overall, administration was still in the hands of Egypt. Informal empire operated through reductions in Egypt's legal authority over European actors and monitoring of financial institutions but was nonexistent in other spheres.[15]

After the occupation, Britain's involvement in all aspects of Egypt's governance expanded, and consequently, empire became more costly. Advisers were forced to monitor the various ministries and the army of Egypt. All in all, the effective sovereignty of the Egyptian state was reduced to almost nothing when faced with the veto of British colonial intermediaries.[16] The British were forced to station up to 30,000 soldiers in Egypt at times.[17] Under these arrangements, the cost of control increased dramatically compared to Britain's earlier informal empire. The increased costs make it apparent why dominant states prefer to avoid asserting direct control.

Across time, dominant states able to establish informal hierarchy have preferred that strategy. Expanding powers have generally adopted informal control before direct control. The long-run origins of European global domination have been well documented.[18] In the late fifteenth century, the European powers began their outward expansion, increasing their contacts with the outside world through trade, exploration, and conquest.[19] Where possible, these relationships began as informal empire before resistance in the subordinate state forced them to impose formal empire.[20] While some of these initial engagements occurred when power favored the empires in Asia,[21] Europeans persisted with such arrangements as their predominance developed. That this occurred when formal

---

[15] Juan Cole, *Colonialism and Revolution in the Middle East* (Princeton University Press, 1993); Afaf Lufti Al-Sayyid-Marsot, "The British Occupation of Egypt from 1882," in *The Oxford History of the British Empire: The Nineteenth Century*, ed. Andrew Porter, vol. 3 (Oxford University Press, 1999).
[16] Al-Sayyid-Marsot.
[17] David M. Edelstein, *Occupational Hazards: Success and Failure in Military Occupation*, Cornell Studies in Security Affairs (Cornell University Press, 2008), 177.
[18] Michael Doyle, *Empires* (Cornell University Press, 1986); P. J. Cain and A. G. Hopkins, *British Imperialism 1688–2000* (Longman, 2002); Ronald Findlay and Kevin H. O'Rourke, *Power and Plenty: Trade, War, and the World Economy in the Second Millennium*, Princeton Economic History of the Western World (Princeton University Press, 2007); Darwin, *After Tamerlane*; David Abernathy, *The Dynamics of Global Dominance: European Overseas Empires 1415–1980* (Yale University Press, 2000); Jane Burbank, *Empires in World History: Power and the Politics of Difference* (Princeton University Press, 2010).
[19] Abernathy, *Dynamics of Global Dominance*.
[20] Gallagher and Robinson, "Imperialism of Free Trade."
[21] Jason Sharman, *Empires of the Weak: The Real Story of European Expansion and the Creation of the New World Order* (Princeton University Press, 2019).

imperial control was comparatively cheap demonstrates the strong preference that dominant states have for informal arrangements.

For example, before the French began their colonial enterprise in North Africa, they had a centuries-long diplomatic and economic engagement with the states of the Maghreb that reduced these states' independence.[22] It was only in the nineteenth century that the French moved to incorporate these states into their colonial empire. Moreover, despite informal European control over many non-European states, the European powers colonized few of the states they dominated. Kayoglu identifies in the secondary literature fourteen cases in which the European powers made use of extraterritoriality, reducing those states' sovereignty.[23] Of these states, the great powers formally occupied only six. The others were able to negotiate the end of these semi-sovereign relations at some point.

Even in cases where one might assume that formal empire was both desirable and inevitable, the European powers initially aimed for informal forms of control. The Berlin Conference, which is often considered to be the starting point of Europe's "scramble for Africa," aimed to establish spheres of influence for the different European powers and their right to trade in different areas; it was not intended to lay the groundwork for territorial partition.[24] While these aims may ultimately have been frustrated by developments on the ground, even in this least likely case, the European powers' immediate preference was seemingly not for direct imperial control.

At the time, there were few norms against international expansion. It is telling regarding their preferences that the European powers opted for informal empire so frequently when the international system imposed few if any costs on their colonial ambitions. The Europeans possessed a technological and power advantage by the mid-nineteenth century.[25] They came up against numerous opponents and defeated them. The British without much difficulty had occupied the remnants of the Mughal Empire in the eighteenth century; they defeated the Chinese in

---

[22] Christian Windler, "Representing the State in a Segmentary Society: French Consuls in Tunis from the Ancien Regime to the Restoration," *Journal of Modern History* 73 (2001); Christian Windler, "Diplomatic History as a Field for Cultural Analysis: Muslim-Christian Relations in Tunis, 1700–1840," *Historical Journal* 44, no. 1 (2001).

[23] Turan Kayaoglu, "The Extension of Westphalian Sovereignty: State Building and the Abolition of Extraterritoriality," *International Studies Quarterly* 51, no. 3 (2007); Turan Kayaoglu, *Legal Imperialism: Sovereignty and Extraterritoriality in Japan, the Ottoman Empire, and China* (Cambridge University Press, 2010).

[24] Ronald Robinson, "The Conference in Berlin and the Future in Africa, 1884–1885," in *Bismark, Europe, and Africa: The Berlin Africa Conference 1884–1885 and the Onset of Partion*, ed. Stig Forster, Wolfgang J. Mommsen, and Ronald Robinson (Oxford University Press, 1988).

[25] D. R. Headrick, *The Tools of Empire: Technology and European Imperialism in the Nineteenth Century* (Oxford University Press, 1981).

Opium Wars; and similarly, the French easily occupied Algiers in 1830. Moreover, theoretically, a multipolar international system should prompt colonization because of the commitment problems it creates.[26] With more great powers competing for influence, there is greater risk that another power will seize direct control. If the European powers possessed a preference for colonialism over informal empire, there was little to stop them acting on it, and there were ample reasons for them to engage in territorial expansion.

Costs of Expansion and Preferences for Hierarchy

When trying to establish an informal hierarchy, first and foremost, the dominant state requires cooperation from actors in the subordinate state. Without their support, this form of control is simply not possible. Absent such support, the dominant state's options are constrained by the cost of formal expansion. In other words, they are constrained by their ability to make use of their coercive capacity in an effective manner and take direct control over the subordinate polity. This capacity is important both for convincing resistant subordinate actors to surrender sovereignty through the threat of formal expansion and for following through with this threat and establishing formal control when faced with resistance. The cost of formal expansion will therefore dictate the dominant state's choices when the subordinate actors are uncooperative.

The cost of formal expansion can change due to either broad systemic factors or more contingent rivalries and interests of great powers. For example, in the late twentieth and early twenty-first centuries, factors such as the cold war, norms against territorial expansion, the technological capacity of developing countries to wage counterimperial insurgencies, and widespread nationalism resulted in a generally restrictive international environment.[27] At other times, the costs of expansion can depend on the willingness of other actors to oppose expansion.[28] These costs can depend on the local priorities of other great powers and their interest in preventing such expansion. Additionally, specific state-level characteristics, such as resolve of the target, will influence choices in the bargaining.[29] Whether or not great powers are restricted by the costs of

---

[26] Doyle, *Empires*: 255.
[27] Jackson, *Quasi-States*; Tanisha M. Fazal, *State Death: The Politics and Geography of Conquest, Occupation, and Annexation* (Princeton University Press, 2007).
[28] Kenneth Waltz, *Theory of International Politics* (McGraw-Hill, 1979): 164–65; Doyle, *Empires*: 255.
[29] Dan Reiter, "Exploring the Bargaining Model of War," *Perspectives on Politics* 1, no. 1 (2003).

Table 1.1 *Preference ranking of the dominant unit conditional on costs of formal expansion*

	Formal expansion cheap	Formal expansion costly
1	Informal hierarchy	Informal hierarchy
2	Formal hierarchy	No expansion
3	No expansion	Formal hierarchy
4	Expansion, resistance, and retrenchment	Expansion, resistance, and retrenchment

territorial expansion, the dominant state's last preference is always for facing resistance and being forced to retrench. This would produce an outcome equivalent to not expanding to begin with, but at a higher cost.

Given these constraints, it is possible to derive preference rankings for a dominant state with interests in expansion. Table 1.1 spells out preferences for outcomes both on and off the equilibrium path to help understand the choices that are made. Regardless of the costs of expansion, their first preference will be establishing a viable informal hierarchical arrangement. Where the costs of territorial expansion are low, their second preference will be for expansion and establishing hierarchy that results in formal control. Following this, no expansion is preferable to expansion resulting in retrenchment. On the other hand, where the costs of expansion are high, no expansion is preferable to incurring the costs of establishing a formal hierarchy, with expansion and retrenchment again being the least favorable outcome. These preferences will inform the analysis of hierarchical outcomes when the dominant state interacts with a subordinate actor.

Preferences in the Subordinate State and Support for Hierarchy

For an informal hierarchy to be established it must be supported, however grudgingly, by elite actors in the subordinate state. The nature of domestic politics determines the preferences of subordinate elites for informal hierarchy or independence. In contrast to previous approaches that treat hierarchy as a relationship between the dominant state and a unified subordinate states, I argue that international hierarchy relations can emerge out of a multiparty relationship involving the external power, societal groups or regional elites, and the central authorities of the subordinate state.[30]

---

[30] Because my focus is on variation within subordinate states, the interests of the external power are considered a constant.

Preferences in the Subordinate State and Support for Hierarchy   29

The search for political survival has been shown to be a strong motivating factor for political elites. Without access to domestic political power, many other goals are unachievable. Elites, therefore, will welcome informal hierarchy to ensure their political survival when the value of that survival is greater than the costs associated with surrendering sovereignty. However, their behavior is also constrained by society – elites will find it difficult to give up sovereignty to an external power if they risk losing the support of their followers. Additionally, if the external actor needs to compensate elites for this lost support, then hierarchy becomes more costly for them too, reducing its benefit to the dominant state and their desire to impose it. Considering these factors, political survival offers a plausible reason why hierarchies emerge or persist.

The prevalence of rent-seeking and political contestation strongly influences the dynamics underlying whether elites can support external hierarchy, and whether the benefits of doing so exceed the costs of surrendering sovereignty. Rent-seeking involves actors using political, legal, or institutional power to extract economic resources, usually by excluding others from free participation in economic relations.[31] Rent-seeking ties political power to economic life such that elites who lose control of political power or lack access also lose economically.[32] This increases the value of political survival because it directly and immediately affects the elite's ability to extract economic resources. When facing a threat or potential threat to political survival, rent-seeking increases the value of the protection that an external patron can provide.

Political actors can engage in rent-seeking using different methods. Corruption is an extreme version of rent-seeking and can occur through a variety of forms.[33] Corruption involves exploiting political power and privilege to gain economic welfare through violation of the law. However, there are legal forms of rent-seeking as well. The government can provide subsidies or regulate competition in a manner that benefits certain groups. Engvall, working the context of Kyrgyzstan, provides a fairly typical list of opportunities that elites can take advantage of including: the sale of public offices, appropriation of public funds, subsidies, procurement of public contracts and kickbacks from privatization.[34] Another

---

[31] Mushtaq H. Khan, "Rent-Seeking as Process," in *Rents, Rent-Seeking and Economic Development: Theory and Evidence in Asia*, ed. Mushtaq H. Khan and K. S. Jomo (Cambridge University Press, 2000), 70–71.

[32] A. Grzymala-Busse, "Beyond Clientelism: Incumbent State Capture and State Formation," *Comparative Political Studies* 41, no. 4–5 (2008): 638.

[33] Jennifer Bussell, "Typologies of Corruption: A Pragmatic Approach," in *Greed, Corruption, and the Modern State Essays in Political Economy* (Edward Elgar, 2015).

[34] Johan Engvall, "From Monopoly to Competition," *Problems of Post-Communism* 65, no. 4 (2018): 272.

example of rent-seeking that directly involves Russia comes from Ukraine. In this example, Russia setting the gas price allowed those with political influence to take advantage of arbitrage opportunities. When Russia set the gas price low, those with political access to the Ukrainian gas industry could purchase gas at low price and sell it at a higher price on the world market.[35] When Russia later raised prices, there were still opportunities as those with access to state companies could purchase Ukrainian gas and sell it at the price set by Russia.[36] All of these techniques translate access to political power into greater economic resources than would be otherwise available to the individuals receiving these benefits.

While both forms of rent-seeking link political power to economic life, it may be that the more extreme forms increase the incentives to pursue political survival to a greater extent given that they occur in a more predatory environment. However, even legally sanctioned forms of rent-seeking can have profound effects on the actors' interests and beliefs. Yuri Zhukov, for example, has demonstrated that the desire to protect access to state subsidies and protectionism drove some regions in Eastern Ukraine to be more supportive of Russian-backed insurgents than others.[37] In other words, all forms of rent-seeking should connect political power and economic welfare and increase the value of political survival and subsequent support for hierarchy.

Political contestation occurs when actors attempt to assert control or authority over institutions controlled by others. These institutions can be both formal and informal.[38] Henry Hale in his magisterial work on "patronal" politics in Eurasia has demonstrated that competition among patronage networks is the driver behind many important political outcomes such as revolution and regime change.[39] Political contestation can operate through formal mechanisms such as elections or informal mechanisms such as protests, threats, or the cooptation of supporters.

[35] Magarita M. Balmaceda, *Politics of Energy Dependency: Ukraine, Belarus and Lithuania between Domestic Oligarchs and Russian Pressure* (Toronto: Toronto University Press, 2013), 107–16.
[36] Anders Åslund, "Oligarchs, Corruption, and European Integration," *Journal of Democracy* 25, no. 3 (2014).
[37] Yuri M. Zhukov, "Trading Hard Hats for Combat Helmets: The Economics of Rebellion in Eastern Ukraine," *Journal of Comparative Economics* 44, no. 1 (2015).
[38] For general discussion, see G. Helmke and S. Levitsky, "Informal Institutions and Comparative Politics: A Research Agenda," *Perspectives on Politics* 2, no. 4 (2004); for discussion in the post-Soviet context, see H. E. Hale, "Formal Constitutions in Informal Politics: Institutions and Democratization in Post-Soviet Eurasia," *World Politics* 63, no. 4 (2011).
[39] Henry E. Hale, *Patronal Politics: Eurasian Regime Dynamics in Comparative Perspective* (Cambridge University Press, 2014).

Contestation is not limited to actors outside of the regime. The role that militias and warlords played in the Georgian regime during the early 1990s provides a good example of how this might work. While they were formally or informally incorporated into regime structures, they often threatened other members of the leadership and competed with each other for access to rents.[40] Intraregime contestation can also create threats to political survival if not properly institutionalized. In other words, political contestation and threats to political survival occur through both *the selectorate* – groups or individuals institutionally empowered to select leaders – and what Zimmerman terms the *ejectorate* – individuals or groups who can seize power through protests and coups rather than formal mechanisms.[41]

Rent-seeking and contestation have a direct influence on elite preferences and also indirectly change their incentives by influencing their supporters in society. The following argument explains how rent-seeking and political contestation influence elite support for informal hierarchy, and the implications for elite–societal relations. Considering these dynamics, the preferences of elite actors faced with a dominant state's designs on expansion are explored.

Elites and the Surrender of Sovereignty

Elites are individuals who can regularly influence political outcomes.[42] Such influence can be gained through prominent positions in formal institutions or their involvement in informal networks of power or both.[43] Elites engaging in rent-seeking use their positions of power to gain an unfair advantage over others. For example, in the early 1990s, ethnic Armenians who had a large presence and some access to power in the Javakheti region of Georgia used their position to avoid customs and smuggle timber into Armenia across the border they were supposed to be

---

[40] Jesse Driscoll, *Warlords and Coalition Politics in Post-Soviet States* (Cambridge University Press, 2015).
[41] William Zimmerman, *Ruling Russia: Authoritarianism from the Revolution to Putin* (Princeton University Press, 2014); see also Mary E. Gallagher and Jonathan K. Hanson, "Power Tool or Dull Blade? Selectorate Theory for Autocracies," *Political Science* 18 (2015).
[42] John Higley and Michael G. Burton, "The Elite Variable in Democratic Transitions and Breakdowns," *American Sociological Review* 54, no. 1 (1989).
[43] Helmke and Levitsky, "Informal Institutions"; Anna Grzymala-Busse and Pauline Jones Luong, "Reconceptualizing the State: Lessons from Post-Communism," *Politics and Society* 30, no. 4 (2002); Michael Bratton, "Formal versus Informal Institutions in Africa," *Journal of Democracy* 18, no. 3 (2007); Hale, "Formal Constitutions in Informal Politics."

protecting.[44] Rent-seeking is a targeted or private good, not a public one, with some individuals benefiting and others not.

The rule of law and open political institutions can protect individuals from rent-seeking, making it more difficult to exploit political power for economic advantage.[45] The prevalence of such institutions can vary widely within states.[46] Thus, the level of rent-seeking can be highly dependent on the local, regional political environments as well institutions nationwide. Elites can be a unified bloc or fragmented into groups. Even authoritarian regimes that may seem dominated by a single group are more often in fact mediating the interests of multiple potentially competing groups.[47]

By giving up sovereignty to an external power, elites can gain resources in exchange.[48] For example, Russian military resources and support were crucial for guaranteeing Shevardnadze's political survival when faced with a Zviadist uprising, and by providing them Russia increased its foothold in Georgia.[49] More mundanely, Russia provided millions of dollars to fund Yanukovych's 2004 electoral campaign in Ukraine in an attempt to keep his pro-Russian faction in power.[50] In both these situations, the political threat was obvious and eminent; in Shevardnadze's case they provided him with space to consolidate power, while being less successful for Yanukovych.

Beyond these one-off provisions of resources in extreme situations, relationships with an external power can provide resources on a more everyday basis. Elites can then use these resources for personal profit and to increase their domestic strength. One clear example of this was Yanukovych and his family and clan's ability to profit from the gas trade

---

[44] Ekaterine Metreveli, *The Dynamics of "Frozen Tension": Case of Javakheti* (Georgian Foundation for Strategic and International Studies, 2004), 17.

[45] Douglass Cecil North, *Violence and Social Orders: A Conceptual Framework for Interpreting Recorded Human History* (Cambridge University Press, 2009), 19; S. Haggard, A. MacIntyre, and L. Tiede, "The Rule of Law and Economic Development," *Annual Review of Political Science* 11 (2008).

[46] C. Gervasoni, "A Rentier Theory of Subnational Regimes: Fiscal Federalism, Democracy, and Authoritarianism in the Argentine Provinces," *World Politics* 62, no. 2 (2010).

[47] Beatriz Magaloni, "Credible Power-Sharing and the Longevity of Authoritarian Rule," *Comparative Political Studies* 41, no. 4–5 (2008).

[48] Dillon Savage, "The Stability and Breakdown of Empire: European Informal Empire in China, the Ottoman Empire and Egypt," *European Journal of International Relations* 17, no. 2 (2011).

[49] Vicken Cheterian, *War and Peace in the Caucasus: Ethnic Conflict and the New Geopolitics* (Columbia University Press, 2008), 203–8.

[50] P. D'Anieri, "The Last Hurrah: The 2004 Ukrainian Presidential Elections and the Limits of Machine Politics," *Communist and Post-Communist Studies* 38, no. 2 (2005): 246.

between Russia and Ukraine. The Yanukovych clan was able to monopolize a large proportion of the profits from this trade and personally profit; the ability to distribute access to these resources consolidated his relationship with important elite actors.[51] In Kyrgyzstan, Russia has used multiple instruments to provide resources to Kyrgyz elites. Russia has directly funded the government through aid and debt write offs, but also provisioning politicians with financing for elections.[52] Another mechanism of providing support and resources has been allowing relatively free migration within the CIS, the remittances sent back to the sending country have provided additional resources.[53] Looking further afield, Russia's engagement with the Venezuelan government of Maduro enabled elites in that country to siphon off resources from weapons sales and aid projects.[54] We also find many analogous processes in cases of nineteenth-century imperialism. European trade and imperialism in places like the Ottoman Empire and China fostered and empowered local actors who then became invested in a European presence.[55] These more everyday provisions of resources and advantages could be used to shore up political positions in less extreme circumstances.

Despite these apparent advantages, there are significant downsides to giving up sovereignty; subordinate elites lose political and cultural autonomy and risk potential exploitation. Elite incentives are strongly influenced by rent-seeking and political contestation, factors that alter both the stakes and the likelihood of losing political power. When rent-seeking is high, elites who lose control of or lack access to political power lose economically, increasing the value of political survival.[56] Political contestation threatens an elite's hold on political power. Where both are present, some elite actors will surrender sovereignty, trading it for resources to aid political survival and continued access to rents.

---

[51] Serhy Yekelchyk, *The Conflict in Ukraine: What Everyone Needs to Know* (Oxford University Press, 2015), 84.

[52] David Lewis, "Reasserting Hegemony in Central Asia: Russian Policy in Post-2010 Kyrgyzstan," *Comillas Journal of International Relations* 1, no. 31 (2015).

[53] Alexander Libman and Anastassia V. Obydenkova, "Understanding Authoritarian Regionalism," *Journal of Democracy* 29, no. 4 (2018). Remittances such as these have been shown to increase regime survival; see Faisal Z. Ahmed, "The Perils of Unearned Foreign Income: Aid, Remittances, and Government Survival," *American Political Science Review* 106, no. 1 (2012).

[54] "Russia in Venezuela: Geopolitical Boon or Economic Misadventure?," Foreign Policy Research Institute, accessed May 30, 2019, www.fpri.org/article/2019/01/russia-in-venezuela-geopolitical-boon-or-economic-misadventure/.

[55] Dillon Savage, "Stability and Breakdown of Empire".

[56] Grzymala-Busse, "Beyond Clientelism,": 640.

If the level of either rent-seeking or contestation is low, elites have fewer incentives to surrender sovereignty. Loss of political power does not have the same negative economic consequences when rent-seeking is low. For example, in a democracy there is political contestation, but elites are institutionally more constrained from exploiting their position. In the absence of rent-seeking, the threat of losing power is not sufficient incentive to risk the costs imposed by surrendering sovereignty. Similarly, where rent-seeking is high and political contestation is low hierarchy will be resisted. Russian influence is rejected in highly centralized regimes such as Turkmenistan where competition is low and elites are coopted into a single ruling party.[57] It is also limited where elites share access to resources cooperatively as seen in the relationship between the Georgian president Saakashvili and local elites in Adjara after the Rose Revolution.[58] Giving up sovereignty can disrupt domestic power and rent-seeking, an unattractive proposition for elites who are unconcerned about losing power and access to rents.

Why do elites within subordinate states not come to terms with each other, rather than inviting in a foreign power? Elites within the subordinate states often face commitment problems if they are competing over rents and autonomy. As various authors have demonstrated, stable bargains are hard to reach when the object of contention can influence the future distribution of power.[59] This is true of bargains struck in a rent-seeking environment. Once elites give up independent control over rent-seeking or their patronage networks it is difficult for their rivals, who now have access to more resources, to commit to avoiding further encroachment. As Hale has convincingly demonstrated, patronal regimes are subject to unstable bargains and cycles of centralization and breakdown.[60] An example of this can be found in the bargains between the central government and elites in Adjara following the Rose Revolution. While central and regional elites came to terms after the Rose Revolution, in the years following the initial bargain there was a continuing reduction in Adjaran independence.

---

[57] K. Collins, "Economic and Security Regionalism among Patrimonial Authoritarian Regimes: The Case of Central Asia," *Europe-Asia Studies* 61, no. 2 (2009).
[58] Kimberly Marten, *Warlords: Strong-Arm Brokers in Weak States* (Cornell University Press, 2012).
[59] James Fearon, "Rationalist Explanations for War," *International Organization* 49, no. 3 (1995); Robert Powell, *In the Shadow of Power: States and Strategies in International Politics* (Princeton University Press, 1999); Powell, "The Inefficient Use of Power: Costly Conflict with Complete Information," *American Political Science Review* 98, no. 2 (2004); Barbara F. Walter, *Committing to Peace: The Successful Settlement of Civil Wars* (Princeton University Press, 2002); Walter, "The Critical Barrier to Civil War Settlement," *International Organization* 51, no. 3 (2003).
[60] H. E. Hale, "Regime Cycles," *World Politics* 58, no. 1 (2005); Hale, *Patronal Politics*.

The argument so far has emphasized a "greed" motive for giving up hierarchy. An alternative possible mechanism is to focus solely on elites' fear of losing political power – and in some contexts such as authoritarian regimes their lives and freedom. In extreme circumstances, this is a likely motivating factor and should not be completely discounted. However, there are a lot of circumstances when threats exist, but sovereignty is not traded. Or alternatively, there are situations where threats are not so extreme that death or imprisonment are likely but sovereignty is traded. For these reasons, focusing on the interaction between rent-seeking and contestation provides more explanatory value than focusing on fear alone.

Elite–Societal Relations and Hierarchy

To offer a more complete account of how domestic politics influences hierarchy it is necessary to consider the role of society, not just elites. Elites guarantee their political position with resources, which come in large part from society. There is plenty of evidence that elites rely on the ability to mobilize societal support to achieve their aims and keep themselves in power. If the same variables that shift elite preferences also influence societal actors, then this will remove a potential constraint on elites and reinforce the effects of these variables. In other words, if rent-seeking or contestation or both influence the preferences of societal actors in the same way as elites, we should expect the effects of these variables on hierarchy to be substantial.

That elites rely on mass support is uncontroversial in democratic systems. However, even in authoritarian regimes elites cannot ignore the interests of their constituents.[61] Magalioni, for example, has shown that authoritarian regimes are most stable when they can rely on mass support.[62] In contrast, when regime elites lose support from society they become more vulnerable.[63] In more specific forms of political contestation, Kaufmann has shown that when competing with other ethnic groups elites need to mobilize the masses.[64] Hale has demonstrated that elite

---

[61] Joel S. Migdal, *Strong Societies and Weak States: State-Society Relations and State Capabilities in the Third World* (Princeton University Press, 1988), 22–23; Jason Brownlee, *Authoritarianism in an Age of Democratization* (Cambridge University Press, 2007), 38–39.

[62] Beatriz Magaloni, *Voting for Autocracy: Hegemonic Party Survival and Its Demise in Mexico* (Cambridge University Press, 2006); Magaloni, "Credible Power-Sharing"; Beatriz Magaloni and Ruth Kricheli, "Political Order and One-Party Rule," *Annual Review of Political Science* 13 (2010).

[63] Magaloni and Kricheli, "Political Order and One-Party Rule."

[64] Stuart J. Kaufman, "Spiraling to Ethnic War: Elites, Masses, and Moscow in Moldova's Civil War," *International Security* 21, no. 2 (1996); Stuart J. Kaufman, *Modern Hatreds: The Symbolic Politics of Ethnic War* (Cornell University Press, 2001).

ability to mobilize mass politics in the competition over political power was a crucial aspect of the Colored Revolutions and hence essential to political survival.[65] Similarly, Scott Radnitz's research in Central Asia has revealed that the ability of local elites to mobilize societal supporters was a critical element of political competition and survival in "predatory regimes."[66] Elites cannot ignore the interests of their supporters in society even in authoritarian contexts.

Due to this reliance on societal resources, in the face of significant domestic opposition, elites' ability to give up sovereign rights will be constrained. Domestic and international sources of support are imperfect substitutes. Elites must therefore consider the interests of their supporters – they cannot surrender sovereignty to gain resources from another state if they risk losing too much domestic support and the resources this support provides. If rent-seeking and contestation are to have a substantial influence on elite choices, then they should also have an effect on the attitudes of society.

There are theoretical reasons to believe that rent-seeking should change the interests of societal actors as well as elites. Rent-seeking can alter the nature of elite–societal relations, creating close ties between elites and the individuals they rely on in society. Rent-seeking often forces individuals to depend on elite protection to secure their economic livelihood.[67] Furthermore, it creates opportunities for these individuals to benefit from patronage and resources from the state.[68] Individuals have an interest in ensuring the political survival of their patrons, which is magnified in a high-rent-seeking environment.[69]

Rent-seeking increases some individuals' investment in the political survival of elites. Without elite sponsors in power, those individuals would lose the benefits of patronage. If these individuals perceive high levels of rent-seeking, they should support the choice to surrender sovereignty for the same reason elites will – doing so improves a potential

---

[65] H. E. Hale, "Democracy or Autocracy on the March? The Colored Revolutions as Normal Dynamics of Patronal Presidentialism," *Communist and Post-Communist Studies* 39, no. 3 (2006); Hale, "Formal Constitutions in Informal Politics"; Henry E. Hale, "Regime Change Cascades: What We Have Learned from the 1848 Revolutions to the 2011 Arab Uprisings," *Annual Review of Political Science* 16 (2013).

[66] Scott Radnitz, *Weapons of the Wealthy: Predatory Regimes and Elite-Led Protests in Central Asia* (Cornell University Press, 2010).

[67] T. Frye and E. Zhuravskaya, "Rackets, Regulation, and the Rule of Law," *Journal of Law, Economics, and Organization* 16, no. 2 (2000).

[68] A. Hicken, "Clientelism," *Annual Review of Political Science*, 14 (2011): 303.

[69] Clientelism and patronage are targeted goods. Some individuals are the beneficiaries or victims, while others are not. Thus access to rent-seeking and awareness will vary at an individual level even when rent-seeking is high in the aggregate. Hicken, "Clientelism"; P. Keefer "Clientelism, Credibility, and the Policy Choices of Young Democracies," *American Journal of Political Science* 51 no 4 (2007).

patron's prospects for political survival. In this way, if individuals perceive rent-seeking and a potential threat from elites outside their network, the patrons of these individuals will be more able to support the external actors' demand for hierarchy.

Such patronage networks do not necessarily remain static. Over time they can change character, widening or narrowing, and these changes will affect the stability and viability of hierarchical bargains. When the network is wider leaders will be able to mobilize sufficient support to undergird hierarchy. Where they dispense fewer benefits in terms of patronage, and the network is narrower, leaders will be less able to provide support to the external power as they can mobilize smaller numbers of elites and societal actors. In other words, focusing too much on retaining benefits for themselves will lead to instability of hierarchical regimes.

These rent-seeking networks will in part be based on particularistic forms of trust. That is, a belief that the elite will provide benefits to societal actor in return for support. While corruption and rent-seeking have been shown to undermine broader forms of social trust, the relationships through which these behaviors operate do constitute a form of "direct protective trust."[70] And in these situations it is often the lack of alternatives that creates dependency and trust.

People make their choices constrained by the institutions and context in which they find themselves. None of the above discussion should suggest that individuals in society, even some of those currently benefiting from patronage, would not be better off under a system where economic transactions were conducted more freely. Indeed, the distribution of benefits in less democratic states are in many ways used as coercive tools aimed at locking in support from society.[71] That said, where individuals do find themselves constrained or operating in system where corruption and patronage are widespread, they will make their decisions according to the incentives of that system.

Subordinate Actor Preferences

The preferences of elite actors in the subordinate state will depend on the level of rent-seeking and political contestation (Table 1.2). High levels of political contestation and rent-seeking will encourage subordinate actors to support informal hierarchy. Regardless of these factors, they will always prefer anarchy and no expansion by the dominant state over resistance because of the costs

---

[70] Warren, "Trust and Democracy," in *The Oxford Handbook of Social and Political Trust*, ed. Eric M. Uslaner (Oxford University Press, 2018).
[71] Michael Albertus, Sofia Fenner, and Dan Slater, *Coercive Distribution* (Cambridge University Press, 2018).

Table 1.2 *Preference ranking of subordinate groups conditional on domestic institutions*

	Rent-seeking and contestation	No rent-seeking or no contestation
1	Informal hierarchy	No expansion by great power
2	No expansion by great power	Great power expansion, resistance, and retrenchment
3	Great power expansion, resistance, and retrenchment	Informal hierarchy
4	Formal hierarchy	Formal hierarchy

involved. Resistance is risky and costly. Furthermore, subordinate elites should never prefer formal hierarchy to any of the other options. Direct control using techniques such as colonialism or annexation results in high levels of exploitation and high levels of insecurity as the dominant state can easily threaten local elites. Absent contestation or rent-seeking in the subordinate state, if the dominant state is determined to expand, subordinate elites prefer first resistance and retrenchment and second informal hierarchy to the dominant state taking direct control, as the latter would result in their autonomy being even more circumscribed.[72]

One caveat to make is that this is a marginal argument. Where actors place an extraordinary value on sovereignty or autonomy, rent-seeking and contestation are unlikely to induce them to give up sovereignty, simply because the costs are not worth paying. For example, the high levels of corruption and contestation in early 1990s Georgia were not sufficient to convince the ardent nationalist Zviad Gamsakhurdia to engage extensively with Russia.[73] Nor are these factors likely to convince the right-wing nationalists in Ukraine, such as Svoboda.[74] However, on average, potentially subordinate actors will be more willing to give up sovereignty when faced with these conditions than when they are not.

Dominant and Subordinate Interaction

Hierarchical outcomes in the international system can be explained by exploring the interactions between the dominant state and those of

---

[72] J. Gerring, D. Ziblatt, J. Van Gorp, and J. Arévalo, "An Institutional Theory of Direct and Indirect Rule," *World Politics* 63, no. 3 (2011).

[73] Zviad Gamsakhurdia paid the price for obduracy and was overthrown shortly into his rule by political actors not so keen on confronting Russia and bearing the costs of resistance.

[74] Andreas Umland, "Starting Post-Soviet Ukrainian Right-Wing Extremism Studies from Scratch," *Russian Politics and Law* 51, no. 5 (2013).

subordinate elites. Given the established preference rankings for each, the possible outcomes are considered in the context of the constraints imposed on dominant and subordinate actors in terms of the costs of formal expansion and domestic institutions respectively (Figure 1.1). This discussion makes the following assumptions, based on the preceding analysis. First, dominant states prefer informal hierarchy to formal empire as it provides them with control while they sustain fewer costs. Second, subordinate actors always prefer informal hierarchy to formal empire as it leaves them with greater autonomy. Finally, both expansion and resistance are costly. The following analysis applies to any elite group in society that could plausibly interact with the dominant state.

The following discussion and the hypotheses drawn from it are derived from a broadly materialist and rationalist framework. Scholars, such as Elster,[75] have offered convincing criticisms of these types of approaches to history and social phenomena. Elster argues that actors' ability to make complex strategic decision is constrained and limited by their mental capacity, that treating aggregate social actors like an individual is problematic, that too often preferences and beliefs are assumed and do not correspond to reality, and that assumptions of perfect information are problematic. These are all potential problems with applying rational choice approaches to historical and social outcomes.

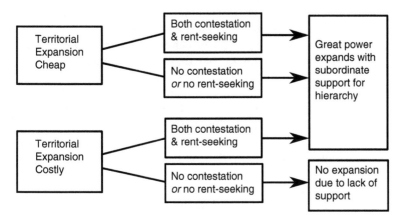

Figure 1.1 Causal process and predicted outcomes with perfect information.

---

[75] Jon Elster, "Rational Choice History: A Case of Excessive Ambition," ed. Robert H. Bates et al., *American Political Science Review* 94, no. 3 (2000).

However, the approach taken is a general one, positing a feedback loop. There may be "off the equilibrium" path decisions, but elites, such as Gamsakhurdia, who make such decisions should suffer consequences. Second, where possible preferences and beliefs are described rather than imputed. And finally, as Elster acknowledges where the consequences are high, historical actors have adopted more materialist and rational approaches.[76] The nature of the study, touching on issues of political survival and sovereignty, means that it is dealing with a high-stakes question. In this context the assumption of rationality is less fraught.

Preferred Outcomes Based on Domestic Institutions and External Constraints

With contestation over rent-seeking in the subordinate state, the preferences of all the important actors align and informal hierarchy should result no matter what type of international environment prevails or what the costs of expansion are for the dominant state. The dominant state chooses to expand by imposing an informal hierarchical arrangement. The subordinate elites, because of the threat posed to them by their domestic institutions, choose to support this form of hierarchy in return for protection. This is the preferred outcome of both the dominant state and subordinate elites. Consequently, the result should be stable informal hierarchy, absent exogenous changes in the subordinate state's domestic institutions and the perceived costs of formal expansion.

The dominant state should provide just enough resources to keep their clients in power, but not enough that they can eliminate their rivals, upsetting the equilibrium of support. This should mean that hierarchy is stable over time. In addition, the dominant state often contracts with multiple actors simultaneously. For example, Russia aided Shervadnadze when dealing with some internal threats such as the Zviadist uprising, while preserving relationships with various subnational actors in Georgia such as in Abkhazia, South Ossetia, and Adjara. However, in some circumstances due to miscalculation and uncertainty over the strength and resolve of their clients, great powers might provide too many resources, and this could allow local actors to consolidate their power. This miscalculation could then lead to long-run instability of hierarchal institutions.

Even when the subordinate institutions encourage elite resistance to informal hierarchy, they are likely to accept it when the costs of formal expansion to the dominant state are low. The benefits to the subordinate

---

[76] Elster, 692.

elites of supporting hierarchy do not have to be greater than those of the anarchic status quo to gain support. As resistance is costly – resources need to be mobilized, money spent, people potentially killed – this can reduce the benefits of resistance to the point that the subordinate actor would rather support informal hierarchy than resist. Conflict is a negative sum.[77] In a situation of perfect information the dominant state will be aware of this fact and expand, forcing the subordinate state to support an informal hierarchy.

Because the dominant state would prefer to colonize the periphery than forgo expansion and the subordinate state prefers informal hierarchy to formal control, the dominant state will succeed in establishing an informal hierarchy. If the subordinate actors believe that the costs of taking formal control are low for the dominant state, they have no incentive to resist informal hierarchy. As long as formal control imposes more costs on the subordinate actor than informal hierarchy and the benefits of expansion are greater than those of the status quo, the result should be the establishment of a stable informal hierarchy.

What are the options of the dominant state when the subordinate actors resist and the costs are restrictive? Subordinate actors can be convinced to accept hierarchy in return for political survival in a rent-seeking environment, but why does the dominant state not simply buy off elites even in other contexts? One reason the dominant state is unlikely to do this is that this will be more costly for the dominant state and will reduce the overall benefit of hierarchy to them. In other words, buying off subordinate actors in the absence of contestation and rent-seeking is rarely a feasible strategy.

Furthermore, as Slater notes in another context, protection pacts are more stable than pure patronage.[78] If subordinate actors rely on the dominant state for protection they are less likely to demand more or renegotiate deals because of the risk that doing so might undermine their source of security. This is likely to be particularly salient in the context of hierarchy where the "contracts" are very often incomplete, leaving many opportunities for such renegotiation and demands from the subordinate state.[79] Evidence that simply trying to buy support may be unstable can be found in the relationship of the United States and Russia with Kyrgyzstan. While both these states were competing to gain authority over aspects of Kyrgyz sovereignty using monetary incentives, the

---

[77] James Fearon, "Rationalist Explanations for War."
[78] Dan Slater, *Ordering Power: Contentious Politics and Authoritarian Leviathans in Southeast Asia* (Cambridge University Press, 2010), 59.
[79] Cooley and Spruyt, *Contracting States*.

Kyrgyz government was able to continually renegotiate the terms of its deals, particularly in relation to Manas Airbase.[80]

Where resistance is high and formal expansion is costly, informal hierarchy is unviable. While the dominant state's first preference is for informal hierarchy, it prefers to forgo expansion rather than assume formal control over the subordinate state or expand and be forced to retrench. The subordinate state, through its choice of resistance, can force the dominant state to either colonize or retrench. Hence, the dominant state should opt for its second preference and accept anarchic relations with the subordinate state.

Supportive subordinate institutions or subordinate beliefs that the dominant state has a low cost of expansion, then, are sufficient for informal hierarchy. In other words, if either of these conditions exists the expected outcome is hierarchy, and otherwise the dominant state will not expand. At this juncture, it is important to emphasize that many of these bargains occur under the shadow of threatened coercion, and many of the relationships can be considered voluntary only in a narrow sense. This account is, in some ways, a rather bloodless way of understanding the development of empires and hierarchy. Doubtless, absent the threat of coercion and violence there would be substantially less hierarchy. Notwithstanding this, when all parties have perfect information, none of the possible outcomes predicted by the theory include conflict. This raises an empirical and theoretical puzzle: why has resistance such as Egypt's resistance to informal empire and Georgia and Ukraine's resistance to Russia's expansion developed?

Coercion and Resistance

The straightforward strategic interactions in the above analysis do not explain when subordinate elites will resist coercion. As David Lake has pointed out, given the power dynamics and potential for coercion, resistance is an "out of equilibrium" outcome when explaining hierarchies and their failure.[81] The reason for this is that conflict is costly and inefficient in almost all circumstances.[82] Both weaker and more powerful states should prefer a bargain over authority and hierarchy to the use of coercion. While descriptively coercion or its threat may provide the groundwork for many

---

[80] Alexander Cooley, *Great Games, Local Rules: The New Power Contest in Central Asia* (Oxford University Press, 2012).
[81] David A. Lake, *Hierarchy in International Relations* (Cornell University Press, 2009).
[82] Fearon, "Rationalist Explanations for War"; Robert Powell, "The Inefficient Use of Power: Costly Conflict with Complete Information," *American Political Science Review* 98, no. 2 (2004).

instances of hierarchy,[83] the actual use of coercion remains difficult to explain from a theoretical perspective.

Given these problems, conflict is likely the result of incomplete information.[84] Even if subordinate institutions create incentives to resist informal hierarchy, a great power can expand in an environment where territorial expansion is cheap, which forces the subordinate elites to concede knowing that they will be formally controlled if they resist. However, there might be uncertainty about the resolve of states to expand in the face of resistance.

If for some reason the domestic elites in the subordinate state believe that expansion is too costly for the dominant state to pay or that they lack resolve then violent resistance can emerge. An example of this was during the Opium wars between England and China, when the Chinese Daoguang Emperor, operating in an information-scarce environment was misled by local officials and believed in China's capacity to defeat the British militarily, fought Britain's initial expansion and attempts at control.[85] In other words, false beliefs regarding the relative power and resolve of the two states resulted in conflict. Alternatively, great powers can expand in a costly environment, thinking that the subordinate state has institutions that will create incentives for them to support informal hierarchy. If this belief is incorrect, then the subordinate state may resist. In this case, it is the dominant state possessing incorrect beliefs regarding the subordinate state's resolve or willingness to fight.

Consequently, for resistance to emerge, the subordinate actors must believe that there is some probability that the cost of formal empire is greater than the cost of retrenchment for the dominant state. Given these beliefs, the expected utility of resistance can outweigh the utility of supporting informal hierarchy. Resistance will in part occur because of some uncertainty on the part of the subordinate state about the costs of expansion for the dominant state and the preferences of the dominant state. Resistance should be accompanied by some sort of assessment that the dominant state would prefer not to expand further.

Egypt provides an example of these sorts of dynamics. In the early period of expansion, European powers were able to operate using informal empire. The Egyptian leaders, embedded in competition with their nominal rulers in Constantinople, saw benefits in surrendering

---

[83] See Alexander Lanoszka, "Beyond Consent and Coercion: Using Republican Political Theory to Understand International Hierarchies," *International Theory* 5, no. 3 (2013).
[84] Fearon, "Rationalist Explanations for War."
[85] Fredric Wakeman, "The Canton Trade and the Opium Wars," in *The Cambridge History of China: Vol. 2. Late Ch'ing 1800–1911* (Cambridge University Press, 1978).

sovereignty in return for financing and support from the European powers. However, once they gained greater autonomy the institutional incentives changed, pushing them toward resistance. These institutional incentives combined with uncertainty over Gladstone's motives, the preferences of the French to block expansion, Britain's recognition of Ottoman sovereignty and support of Ottoman control over Egypt created a situation where Egyptian elites thought they could resist the dominant state. In a more contemporary setting, a similar chain of events occurred in Georgia. After the Rose Revolution, political institutions created incentives to resist Russian control. This combined with a belief that Russia was constrained from expanding led to the violent conflict of August 2008.[86]

Empirical Implications

The theory makes several empirical predictions about the political dynamics of hierarchy that can be used to test the argument in the qualitative case studies and these predictions distinguish the theory from alternative explanations. Dominant states should attempt informal hierarchy before other options. Polities with contestation that could affect rent-seeking opportunities should be subject to long-run, informal domination. In cases with contestation and rent-seeking, informal hierarchy should persist for longer than those with centralized or non-rent-seeking regimes. This should not be simply due to a greater ability to coerce the subordinate elites in decentralized regimes; there should be evidence of accommodation to the practices of informal hierarchy in these cases. Where these arrangements do finally break down, as they did in the Ottoman Empire and China, it should be due to factors exogenous to the theory such as a great power war or shifts in domestic politics unrelated to hierarchy.

In contrast, the failure of hierarchy in noncompetitive or non-rent-seeking cases should occur due to resistance from actors in the subordinate state. However, this breakdown needs to be accompanied by the belief on the part of the subordinate state that the dominant state is constrained by the international system from expanding further. If this belief is correct the outcome will be retrenchment. If this belief is false there should be an increase in the level of empire and hierarchy as the dominant state takes more coercive measures to maintain control.

The theory predicts that the same elite or leader can change their opinion regarding hierarchy based on material incentives, particularly

---

[86] These events are discussed in greater detail in subsequent chapters.

the levels of political threat and rent-seeking. That is, the same individual's preferences can change depending on the political environment. In contrast, if constructivist variables were dominating the process we would expect to see less within-individual variation, or at the minimum some explanation for a normative shift. Similarly, if power differences were explaining choices to support or oppose hierarchy, we would not expect substantial within-individual variation. Changing domestic conditions will often have only a very marginal effect on the relative power between states, but can dramatically change the prospects of individual politicians domestically.

Regime type influences both rent-seeking and political competition. If my theory is correct, there should be observable differences in the acceptance of hierarchy among regime types including different types of authoritarian regimes. The institutions that define the regime type determine the nature and the consequences of political contestation. Some authoritarian regime types manage conflict more poorly than others, are more likely to collapse, and their fallen leaders suffer more extreme consequences. The theory predicts that authoritarian contexts in which losing power has greater consequences for rent-seeking, or institutions encourage greater levels of contestation, should create more support for hierarchy.

Another implication of the argument is that hierarchy can decline from high levels as institutions change. This prediction distinguishes the theory from theories based on divide and rule dynamics, in which the external actor fosters divisions within the subordinate state. While these theories would predict a similar correlation between contestation and the outcome of hierarchy, divide and rule would also predict greater levels of stability as the dominant state manipulates the subordinate institutions for their benefit. If such dynamics were leading to an increase in contestation domestically, we would not expect change in institutions while the level of hierarchy is high. If the external actor were easily able to create new institutions or structure competition in the subordinate state, we would also expect greater levels of stability in hierarchy. In contrast, my theory predicts that external powers take advantage of opportunities provided by domestic institutions in the target state, and may increase their stability somewhat, but great powers have limited capacity to wholesale create competition, and thus as political institutions change in the subordinate state to reduce conflict over rent-seeking opportunities, hierarchy will decline.

Alternative explanations that focus on the supply side of hierarchy, or the dominant state, would predict convergence between small states. If great powers could easily manipulate domestic conditions to facilitate control, then states moving in and out of their orbit would be relatively rare. We would not expect the institutional variation observed among small states to occur. For example, following the collapse of the Soviet Union, Russian interest in control was fairly constant among most of the post-Soviet states, particularly in Ukraine, Belarus, Moldova, the Caucasus, and Central Asia. If Russian interests alone were driving hierarchy, then we would see consistently high levels of control in all these countries, but we do not. Additionally, if the great power were easily able to alter domestic institutions in these states, we would expect them to look more similar than they do.

The theory also predicts that mass politics should play a role in the strategic assessment of both elites in the subordinate state and from the dominant state. Societal interests should be something of a constraint on elite choices. Moreover, the dominant state should pay attention to whether or not elites in the subordinate state can mobilize support for hierarchy as this will affect the viability of informal hierarchy. Finally, if elites act against the interests of society to too great a degree a cost should be imposed on them by societal actors.

Scope Conditions for the Argument

This study deals primarily with relationships between a dominant and subordinate state, including subnational actors within these states where appropriate. I adopt a broad definition of state in order to include polities such as the Ottoman Empire and China that share many but not all the features of the modern state.[87] For example, the Ottoman Empire had regions that were partially autonomous and could engage in their own foreign policy to an extent, but were still part of the Ottoman domains. My definition of state includes political units such as these where the ruled and the ruler believe that they are part of the same polity, whatever rights exist regarding the conduct of internal and external relations. Such a definition can include both modern national states and empires such as China and the Ottoman Empire in the nineteenth century. It would exclude informal empires where there is no explicit or implicit belief that the units involved form one polity.[88]

---

[87] Charles Tilly, *Coercion, Capital and European States AD 990–1992* (Blackwell, 1992); Hendrik Spruyt, *The Sovereign State and Its Competitors: An Analysis of Systems Change*, Princeton Studies in International History and Politics (Princeton University Press, 1994).

[88] In other words, while multiple states can wield authority over one subordinate unit, informal empire exists horizontally and authority is not layered. Simply put, informal empire can exist with multiple external imperial powers exercising some measure of hierarchy over the same polity, as occurred in China.

There must be a clear power disparity between the potentially dominant and potentially subordinate state. It is difficult to imagine a situation where hierarchy emerges without the dominant state being more powerful, at least across some dimension. The great power needs to be able to offer the subordinate state something in return for the surrender of sovereignty, and so must possess some sort of power or resource advantage over the subordinate actor.[89] Furthermore, there must exist a set of institutional compatibilities between the societies that form the hierarchical relationship.[90] For informal hierarchy to be viable it must be possible for one state to conduct its business in and through the other state without completely transforming the subordinate state's political, legal, and economic institutions.

For instance, it was possible for economic actors from the European powers to operate and pursue their interests in the Ottoman Empire and China. Trade was possible because the economic activities of these regions complemented those of Europe and the political and legal institutions allowed such actions to be carried out, even if they required the extra guarantee of informal empire. In contrast, informal hierarchy is not possible in areas that significantly lag in economic development or lack the legal and political institutions to provide surety to transnational actors from the dominant state. For these reasons the scope of this analysis is limited to states that have reached the level of political and economic development that allows transnational actors from the dominant state to operate comfortably within the institutions of the subordinate state with only informal control in place.

Conclusion

How can we explain the variation of hierarchical outcomes seen in the international system? In some cases, states resist great powers' encroachments on their sovereignty, often violently, resulting in the great power either retrenching or escalating the expansion and taking formal control. At other times an informal hierarchical relationship is established with minimal conflict. Great powers with the will to expand, seeking to minimize the costs of governance and control, will always prefer an informal hierarchical relationship where they can achieve their goals by working through actors in the subordinate state. For such relationships to be established, the willingness of these subordinate actors is paramount.

[89] Lake, *Hierarchy in International Relations*.
[90] Gerring et al., "An Institutional Theory of Direct and Indirect Rule."

Elites and their supporters in subordinate states will surrender sovereignty when they place a high value on protection from the dominant state. This protection is most valuable to elites if they are benefiting from rent-seeking activity, tying their sustained economic success to their political survival, and if political contestation threatens their continued access to these rents. Therefore, when there is political contestation and rent-seeking in a subordinate state, an informal hierarchical arrangement is likely to be welcomed.

An informal hierarchy will be established when it is in the best interest of both parties and will generally remain stable unless a change in the domestic institutions of the subordinate state alters their incentives. To explain the other possible outcomes, in which the subordinate actors would prefer not to surrender sovereignty, both the expected costs of conflict for each party and their beliefs about the other's constraints must be considered. If the cost of formal control is greater than the benefits of the status quo and they believe the costs of informal hierarchy outweigh the costs of resistance for the subordinate state, then the dominant state will not expand at all. However, where the costs of assuming formal control are lower, the subordinate state can be forced into an informal hierarchical relationship, which is less costly to them than resistance.

Uncertainty about the costs of formal control on the behalf of either party can result in conflict. For example, where subordinate actors overestimate the constraints on great power expansion from the international system, violent resistance and an ultimate loss of sovereignty can result when the great power assumes formal control. Resistance by subordinate elites can result in either formal control or withdrawal, and they will only resist if they believe the latter is more likely and worth the costs of the conflict.

The above theory can explain why groups at different levels support the surrender of sovereignty. It can help explain why leaders at a national level support the formal surrender of sovereignty and why groups below the national level will lobby or threaten the government in support of outside intervention, or just de facto facilitate the surrender of sovereignty. Moreover, the theory is applicable across different time periods; it can help explain outcomes such as nineteenth-century informal empire as well as more contemporary cases of hierarchy.

The theory explains why informal empire functioned in China and the Ottoman Empire and not Egypt. It explains why some leaders in Ukraine and Georgia were more inclined to support Russian influence than others. Finally, it helps explain why some groups within Georgia, such as the Abkhaz and Armenians, were prepared to support Russian expansion.

2 Submission, Resistance, and War
National Politics and Russian Hierarchy in Georgia and Ukraine since Independence

On August 7, 2008, the Georgian army advanced into South Ossetia with the aim of reuniting the secessionist region with Georgia. This triggered a conflict with the Russian client controlling the region and their Russian patrons. The result of the conflict was not greater independence for Georgia but Russia ratcheting up its control in Abkhazia and South Ossetia. Russia officially recognized these regions' independence, increased its military presence in them, and began greater direct relations with the two breakaway Republics. In this manner, Georgian resistance to Russian authority resulted not in greater independence but further reduced sovereignty. Russia paid substantial direct costs in the conflict but also indirect diplomatic costs from a Western audience that was pro-Georgian. The result was suboptimal for both sets of actors.

In February 2014, Russian soldiers occupied Crimea, an autonomous region of Ukraine. This move was in response to the toppling of Ukrainian leader Yanukovych and his replacement by leaders opposed to Russian hierarchy. While this has shifted and hardened attitudes toward in Russia in Ukraine, in the short-term this resistance resulted in an increase in Russian intervention and control over parts of Ukrainian sovereignty as Russia continued to incorporate Crimea and manufactured a frozen conflict in the Donbas through the use of proxies.

These outcomes are puzzling. Georgia and some actors in Ukraine in an attempt to regain sovereignty resisted Russian demands for hierarchy, ultimately resulting in further loss of sovereignty. When the costs of control increased for Russia, they responded by simply paying more to avoid losing influence over the breakaway regions. What caused the resistance despite adverse outcomes? The following chapter will analyze how national politics in two countries – Georgia and Ukraine – influenced the preparedness of ruling elites to surrender sovereignty. The chapter begins with a general overview of Russia's influence in the former Soviet Republics since independence and the international context within which this has occurred. This overview will provide an understanding of some alternative explanations for varied patterns of integration and Russian hierarchy in the region. This is followed by a detailed exploration of the developments in Georgian politics and Georgia's relationship with Russia. The chapter concludes with an analysis of how domestic politics have influenced Ukraine's relationship with Russia across time.

Russia is a prime example of a state that has attempted to establish informal hierarchical relationships over weaker states with mixed success. The geographic proximity of the post-Soviet states combined with their historical, economic, and military importance to Russia have created incentives for Russia to assert control in an international environment that makes territorial annexation exceedingly difficult. This desire for control and influence in the region is in some ways an end in itself.[1] The former Soviet Republics have responded in strikingly different ways to Russian attempts to maintain influence and control. Some of these states have cautiously welcomed renewed integration with Russia, while others have rejected Russia's demands outright.

Looking at the qualitative data in a controlled comparison provides a means to disprove alternative arguments and mechanisms.[2] By looking at the changing policies and rhetoric adopted by the same politicians across time, individual beliefs and norms that would be expected to remain constant can be somewhat discounted as underlying causes. This chapter demonstrates that political competition, particularly when combined with rent-seeking, explains much of the within-case variation in responses to Russian hierarchy.

Russian Hierarchy in the Wake of the Soviet Collapse

Since the collapse of the Soviet Union, Russia has attempted to maintain its influence over the "near abroad" that formerly constituted the USSR. Organized around different titular minorities and with local political institutions providing incentives and opportunities to mobilize politically, the fifteen Soviet Republics were the natural loci of demands for independence and the formation of new states as Soviet power declined.[3] The openings created by Gorbachev's reforms allowed for greater nationalist mobilization and ultimately independence for the former Soviet

---

[1] Seva Gunitsky and Andrei P. Tsygankov, "The Wilsonian Bias in the Study of Russian Foreign Policy," *Problems of Post-Communism* 65, no. 6 (2018).

[2] David Collier, "Understanding Process Tracing," *PS Political Science and Politics* 44, no. 4 (2011): 823; James Mahoney, "After KKV: The New Methodology of Qualitative Research," *World Politics* 62, no. 1 (2009).

[3] Philip G. Roeder, *Where Nation-States Come From: Institutional Change in the Age of Nationalism* (Princeton University Press, 2007); Valerie Bunce, *Subversive Institutions: The Design and the Destruction of Socialism and the State*, Cambridge Studies in Comparative Politics (Cambridge University Press, 1999).

Republics, all of which have attempted to build new states with varying degrees of success.[4]

Once independence had been achieved, leaders faced multiple challenges. They had to establish new regimes and deal with the political legacies of the Soviet Union, manage economic transitions, and deal with ethnic and national differences within their new borders. In extreme cases, some states such as Georgia, Moldova, and Azerbaijan have seen their state-building efforts result in their sovereignty being riven due to ethnic conflicts.[5] Others such as Tajikistan also fell into civil war, but resulting from regional and religious differences as much as ethnic ones. Meanwhile, other states were able to avoid violent conflict despite ethnic differences.

Some state-building projects have been remarkably successful. The most obvious of these are the Baltic States, who have achieved relatively stable democratic systems, and well-functioning economies. A contrasting successful example is Turkmenistan, which established a relatively stable authoritarian regime. Some states established institutions to manage the problems they faced and did so successfully, though the form of this success varied dramatically.

In this context, Russia has maintained a certain level of hierarchy throughout the region, preserving a network of military bases that existed during the Soviet Union and supplementing these with others.[6] Russia has also constructed a series of regional organizations that attempt to organize economic and security activity under Russia's aegis, providing them authority and power over a range of issues normally associated with the sovereign rights of states. What is more, Russia has constructed these hierarchical relationships in an environment inimical to territorial expansion.

In recent decades, the international environment has been more hostile than ever to imperial expansion by great powers such as Russia. International norms regarding self-determination and sovereignty since World War II have raised the cost of formal empire.[7] These norms make it

---

[4] Gorbachev's reforms were one of the causes of this nationalist mobilization. However, the process of mobilization itself had its own causal effect. See Mark R. Beissinger, *Nationalist Mobilization and the Collapse of the Soviet State* (Cambridge University Press, 2002), 8.

[5] Stuart J. Kaufman, *Modern Hatreds: The Symbolic Politics of Ethnic War* (Cornell University Press, 2001); Christoph Zurcher, *Post-Soviet Wars: Rebellion, Ethnic Conflict, and Nationhood in the Caucasus* (New York University Press, 2007).

[6] A. Cooley, "Imperial Wreckage: Property Rights, Sovereignty, and Security in the Post-Soviet Space," *International Security* 25, no. 3 (2001); Alexander Cooley Hendrik Spruyt, *Contracting States: Sovereign Transfers in International Relations* (Princeton University Press, 2009).

[7] Robert Jackson, *Quasi-States: Sovereignty, International Relations and the Third World* (Cambridge University Press, 1990); Robert Jackson, "The Weight of Ideas in

both morally costly to expand territorially and perhaps, if these norms were internalized, unthinkable on the part of the great powers themselves. In this normative environment, territorial expansion has diminished dramatically.[8] Instances where one state has conquered and removed another's sovereignty have all but ceased since 1945.[9] In the modern era, a state choosing to expand territorially faces moral and political costs.

Modern technological developments have also contributed to this change in the international environment. During the nineteenth century the European powers enjoyed a clear technological advantage, both in terms of military and organizational capacity. These advantages made it relatively cheap for great powers to expand when the need or want arose. However, many of these technologies diffused to the peripheries and colonies, and control of these societies became more difficult. This increased the costs of formal empire, reducing its viability as a form of political organization.[10] This spread of technology has remained central to the ability of smaller states to fight guerrilla insurgencies up to the present day. The ability of smaller powers to gain access to cheap, effective weapons and fight against occupation has greatly increased the costs of direct territorial control of other states by great powers.

Since the collapse of the Soviet Union, Russia and the former Soviet Republics have struggled to define a new regional order in a situation where Russia is highly constrained from expanding formally. Russia has sought control over states in the region largely due to internal pressure of culture, ideology, and history.[11] Some of the post-Soviet states have sought alignment with the West; others have continued their close relationship with Russia; others still, such as Turkmenistan, pursued more autarkic policies. There have been several accounts to explain the responses of different former Soviet Republics to Russian expansion. The following discussion of these accounts will provide the context to consider alternative explanations to the theory of the book that is tested

---

Decolonization," in *Ideas and Foreign Policy*, ed. Judith Goldstein and Robert Keohane (Cornell University Press, 1993).

[8] Tanisha M. Fazal, *State Death: The Politics and Geography of Conquest, Occupation, and Annexation* (Princeton University Press, 2007); B. Atzili, "When Good Fences Make Bad Neighbors: Fixed Borders, State Weakness, and International Conflict," *International Security* 31, no. 3 (2007).

[9] Fazal, *State Death*.

[10] D. R. Headrick, *The Tools of Empire: Technology and European Imperialism in the Nineteenth Century* (Oxford University Press, 1981).

[11] A. P. Tsygankov, "Mastering Space in Eurasia: Russia's Geopolitical Thinking After the Soviet Break-Up," *Communist and Post-Communist Studies* 36, no. 1 (2003); A. P. Tsygankov, *Russia's Foreign Policy: Change and Continuity in National Identity* (Rowman and Littlefield, 2010); D. C. B. Lieven, *Empire: The Russian Empire and Its Rivals* (John Murray, 2000).

through the cases of Georgia and Ukraine and provide a baseline to assess the success of the theory.

Explanations for the Variation in Levels of Russian Hierarchy

A large body of research on what can be considered Russian hierarchy or attempts to assert such influence in the region have approached the issue through a macro-lens. This work has focused on large-scale phenomena such as national identity, culture, civilization, and state-building.[12] These are undoubtedly important factors shaping the international environment and relationships between states in the region that cannot be dismissed out of hand. However, as this book will demonstrate, they cannot explain all the variation that we observe.

The variation in responses to Russian expansion has been attributed by some to the ideas or ideology held by different states. These accounts have focused predominately on economic integration in the region.[13] For example, Darden, rather than ascribing outcomes to international norms, focused on the ideas held by individual decision makers.[14] The ideas held by individuals about the efficacy of particular policies determine what policies leaders adopt. Some ideas drive leaders to pursue integration with Russia, others with the world economy, and others still to pursue autarkic-type arrangements. However, while someone might believe that an idea, all things being equal, is the best way to proceed, all things are rarely equal – especially for political actors in a dangerous, unstable region of the world. Economic and political policies need to be weighed against the other considerations and imperatives politicians face. Ideas and beliefs undoubtedly influence outcomes, but even ideologues cannot ignore the imperatives of political survival.[15]

A second explanation for integration with Russia focuses on efficiency.[16] Integration comes with benefits such as economies of scale

---

[12] Ronald Grigor Suny, "Provisional Stabilities: The Politics of Identities in Post-Soviet Eurasia," *International Security* 24, no. 3 (1999); R. Abdelal, *National Purpose in the World Economy: Post-Soviet States in Comparative Perspective* (Cornell University Press, 2001).
[13] Abdelal, *National Purpose in the World Economy*; Keith A. Darden, *Economic Liberalism and Its Rivals: The Formation of International Institutions among the Post-Soviet States* (Cambridge University Press, 2009).
[14] Darden, *Economic Liberalism and Its Rivals*.
[15] Political elites face a trade-off between office seeking and policy seeking; see Kaare Strom, "A Behavioral Theory of Competitive Political Parties," *American Journal of Political Science* 34, no. 2 (1990).
[16] Cooley and Spruyt, *Contracting States*; Henry E. Hale, *The Foundations of Ethnic Politics: Separatism of States and Nations in Eurasia and the World*, Cambridge Studies in Comparative Politics (Cambridge University Press, 2008).

and reduced transaction costs.[17] These accounts propose that what limits integration is the ability of the dominant state to make credible commitments to the weaker groups. Where these groups can make credible commitments to each other, integration should occur. Where they cannot do so, integration should fail. During the Soviet Union all the republics were built around a titular minority. When the Soviet Union collapsed, new states were organized around ethnic identities. Hale suggested that whether or not integration occurred depended on the relationships between different ethnic groups.[18] These theories provide convincing, but highly abstract accounts of integration and hierarchy. In this book I seek to explain what makes commitments credible and worthwhile, which requires understanding the institutional context.[19]

Another way of explaining integration and hierarchy in the region is more systemic, focusing on competing states and power disparities.[20] In one such account the threat of a subregional hegemon, for instance Uzbekistan in Central Asia, drives states to integrate with Russia to gain security and balance against the local power. While this is a compelling account it does not fully explain the variation in the region. For example, it cannot explain why some regions which lack a potential hegemon still see states prepared to integrate with Russia. Alternatively, it has been claimed that Russia's natural resources, particularly in the energy domain, have increased Russian power and leverage. Even in regions where such theories should hold, such as Central Asia, there is variation that a systemic theory cannot explain. States have changed their policies across time, and some states such as Turkmenistan have not viewed the international system as threatening enough to prompt integration.

Gerard Toal has integrated many of these approaches in his book.[21] The critical geopolitics approach that Toal develops provides a very useful means of organizing our understanding of geopolitics in region and Russian reactions to developments such as NATO expansion. Similar to the approach adopted in this book, Toal highlights the important role played by local and subnational actors. This book complements Toal's work by providing

---

[17] Hale, *Foundations of Ethnic Politics.*   [18] Hale.
[19] Helen V. Milner, *Interests, Institutions, and Information: Domestic Politics and International Relations* (Princeton University Press, 1997); Michaela Mattes and Mariana Rodríguez, "Autocracies and International Cooperation," *International Studies Quarterly* 58, no. 3 (2014); Scott Gehlbach and Philip Keefer, "Investment without Democracy: Ruling-Party Institutionalization and Credible Commitment in Autocracies," *Journal of Comparative Economics* 39, no. 2 (2011).
[20] R. Deyermond, "Matrioshka Hegemony? Multi-levelled Hegemonic Competition and Security in Post-Soviet Central Asia," *Review of International Studies* 35, no. 1 (2009).
[21] Gerard Toal, *Near Abroad: Putin, the West, and the Contest over Ukraine and the Caucasus* (Oxford University Press, 2017).

a theoretical explanation for the choices made by national and subnational actors. In this way, the book provides some *causal* explanations for many of the building blocks that form part of Toal's broader account.

Most great powers have reasons to expand and control. These imperatives can arise due to the international system, contingent security and economic concerns, and because of domestic political competition and ideologies. For this reason, a focus on the domestic institutions of the target state is a potentially revealing way to understand differing levels of hierarchy in the international system. While culture and history and the broader structures of geopolitics are important for shaping the attitudes of political actors, elites, and masses also make decisions influenced by material and strategic concerns rooted in domestic politics. The strategic choices made by both elites and masses as they weigh the costs and benefits of surrendering sovereignty to the external actor must also be studied. One contribution of this book is to show how domestic political threats and rent-seeking can blunt or channel the effects of these macrovariables. Second, the theory and findings of this book push us to consider developments and crises in the region not solely as a product of grand geopolitics but also of local, sometimes very local, political events. All these themes become apparent in the cases of Georgia and Ukraine.

Why Georgia and Ukraine?

Since they have gained independence, Georgia and Ukraine have both seen their relationship with Russia shift regularly. At times these states have been more willing to acquiesce to Russian impositions on their sovereignty; at others they have been resistant to the point of violent conflict. While culture and history play a large role in determining the predispositions of countries toward resistance,[22] they cannot explain all variation across time. History and culture are often too slow moving to independently explain rapid shifts in policy. When culture or normative beliefs do change rapidly, it is often the result of international and political events, not a cause.[23] Factors causing these shifts in foreign policy need to be located in the changing political environments of these states as well as culture and identity. The following chapter provides qualitative evidence for the proposition that competition over rent-seeking in subordinate states partly drives the tendency to support outside intrusions on sovereignty.

---

[22] See for example Darden, *Resisting Occupation*.
[23] See, e.g., the changes in professed Ukrainian identity in the aftermath of the Euromaidan protests in Grigore Pop-Eleches and Graeme B. Robertson, "Identity and Political Preferences in Ukraine – before and after the Euromaidan," *Post-Soviet Affairs* 34, no. 2–3 (2018).

Georgia and Ukraine are similar in many ways that make them interesting comparative cases. Both countries were relatively privileged Republics during the Soviet period, with opportunities for local elites to reach high ranks in the central organs of authority.[24] Similarly, both are multiethnic nations.[25] There is a tendency to view the foreign policy of these countries as driven by slowly changing cultural, historical, and ideological factors. Both had high precommunist rates of literacy and national curricula, which can be used as a proxy for nationalism in the post-Soviet region.[26] Hence, the strong historical and culturally determined predispositions of actors in these states might be expected to swamp the effects of institutional variables. For this reason, both countries can be considered to be hard cases for an institutional or political explanation, such as the one presented here.

Nonetheless, this analysis finds a strong case for the importance of institutions in determining willingness to surrender sovereignty. Despite these strong historical and cultural factors in both Georgia and Ukraine, shifts in political competition and the content of the competition are correlated with shifts in the willingness to surrender sovereignty. When competition over rents was high, both states, or at least important actors within these states, were more accommodating of Russian attempts to curtail their sovereignty. As either the level of competition or rent-seeking diminished so too did the tendency to support Russian expansion.

Russian Hierarchy and Georgian National Politics

Immediately following the collapse of the Soviet Union, Georgia was among the most anti-Russian of the former Soviet Republics. Following the removal of Gamsakhurdia, the more pragmatic Shevardnadze took control of the country. At this point competition over material and rent-seeking opportunities was high, and Shevardnaze accepted high levels of Russian control of Georgian sovereignty. In the early 1990s, Georgia was involved in most of Russia's attempts at regional organization, however half-heartedly, as well as hosting a substantial Russian military presence.[27] As time progressed, however, Georgia abjured joining new organizations as they emerged or developed under Russian guidance.

---

[24] Laitin refers to this as most favored lord status; see David D. Laitin, "Review: The National Uprisings in the Soviet Union," *World Politics* 44, no. 1 (1991): 143.

[25] The Ethnic Power Relations data set shows that Ukraine has five politically relevant ethnic groups, while Georgia has seven.

[26] K. Darden and A. Grzymala-Busse, "The Great Divide: Literacy, Nationalism, and the Communist Collapse," *World Politics* 59, no. 1 (2006).

[27] R. L. Larsson, "The Enemy Within: Russia's Military Withdrawal from Georgia," *Journal of Slavic Military Studies* 17, no. 3 (2004): 410–11.

Furthermore, Georgia negotiated the removal of Russian military bases, and in 1999 did not renew its membership in the Collective Security Treaty Organization (CSTO).[28] By the late 1990s Russian hierarchy had reduced substantially to the extent that Georgia was instrumental in setting up the GUAM (Georgia, Ukraine, Azerbaijan, and Moldova) Organization for Democracy and Economic Development as a counterweight to Russian influence in the region.[29] Shevardnadze even discussed removing Georgia from the Commonwealth of Independent States (CIS).

In 2003, Georgia underwent a democratic transition, the Rose Revolution. After the Rose Revolution, the level of rent-seeking dropped and political competition remained minimal, despite some increase in democratic freedoms. During this period the new president of Georgia Mikhail Saakashvili adopted even more confrontational policies. Saakashvili demanded and eventually achieved the removal of all Russian military forces outside of the breakaway regions of Abkhazia and South Ossetia.[30] Saakashvili removed Georgia from the CIS.[31] He even engaged in military confrontations with Russian clients, first in Adjara,[32] and later in South Ossetia.[33]

Russia had a series of security and ideological reasons to pursue its control over Georgia. Russia was interested in its perceived status in the region, and also in excluding other great powers from involvement in the region.[34] Russian politicians identified the importance of relying on local actors to achieve these goals. For example, in 2010, Boris Gryszlov, the head of United Russia and speaker of the Duma, stated while meeting Zurab Noghaideli, a Georgian opposition leader, that "they perfectly understand the need to find 'healthy forces' in Georgia."[35]

---

[28] Hooman Peimani, *Conflict and Security in Central Asia and the Caucasus* (ABC-CLIO, 2009), 313.
[29] T. Kuzio, "Geopolitical Pluralism in the CIS: The Emergence of GUUAM," *European Security* 9, no. 2 (2000): 102.
[30] Theresa Freese, "Russia's Troop Withdrawal from Georgia: The Start of a New Friendship?," *EurasiaNet*, August 9, 2005, www.eurasianet.org/departments/insight/articles/eav081005.shtml.
[31] "Georgia Finalizes Withdrawal from CIS," *RadioFreeEurope/RadioLiberty*, August 18, 2009, sec. News, www.rferl.org/content/Georgia_Finalizes_Withdrawal_From_CIS/1802284.html.
[32] Kimberly Marten, *Warlords: Strong-Arm Brokers in Weak States* (Cornell University Press, 2012), 74.
[33] Vicken Cheterian, "The August 2008 War in Georgia: From Ethnic Conflict to Border Wars," in *War and Revolution in the Caucasus*, ed. Stephen F. Jones (Routledge, 2010).
[34] Andrei P. Tsygankov and Matthew Tarver-Wahlquist, "Duelling Honors: Power, Identity and the Russia–Georgia Divide," *Foreign Policy Analysis* 5, no. 4 (2009): 319.
[35] V. Vyzhutovich, "Ot nashego ctola-vashemu stolu," *Rossisskaya Gazeta*, February 2, 2019.

Georgia's and Russia's Historical Relationship

Georgia's historical incorporation into the Russian sphere occurred gradually. In the eighteenth and nineteenth centuries, trapped between the expanding Muscovite empire in the West and the Persians and Ottomans in the East, Georgia's kingdoms were forced to contend with one empire or another. Given their limited size, this forced the Georgians to pick a side and find allies. Russia's common Christian identity made them the more palatable option, though they were not reliable allies. Russia on several occasions failed to meet their commitments to their Georgian allies as the Georgians were threatened by the other expanding powers in the region. Eventually, Russia incorporated, in part by invitation and in part through force, Georgia into the empire. The last King of Eastern Georgia, competing with his brothers for control of the kingdom, invited the Russians to take control, and they seized this opportunity.[36] Over the next few decades, Russia took over the remainder of Georgian territory.[37]

The incorporation of Georgia into the Russian Empire happened on fairly generous terms. The various social classes of Georgia were allowed to maintain their existing privileges.[38] The Georgian nobility were treated in a similar manner to Russia's existing noble class. Merchants were allowed trade access. While there were real costs involved, there were also new opportunities. This situation was to continue until the empire collapsed under the dual pressures of World War I and the Russian Revolution.

Following the collapse of the Russian Empire, Georgia experienced a short-lived republic.[39] However, by 1921 Georgia had been reconquered by the Bolsheviks and was governed as part of the Transcaucasian Republic until 1937. Georgia suffered as most of the USSR did under the tyranny of the Soviet and Stalinist systems, though less than some regions, and was relatively privileged under Stalin.[40] The Soviet nationality policy allowed Georgia to retain much of its own identity. Georgian persisted as the dominant language and Russian,

---

[36] While not a direct test of the theory, this does demonstrate one of the core principles of the argument – domestic or internal competition led to a greater willingness to support hierarchy.

[37] See for discussion of these issues Ronald Grigor Suny, *The Making of the Georgian Nation* (Indiana University Press, 1994), chapter 3; Donald Rayfield, *Edge of Empires: A History of Georgia* (Reaktion Books, 2013), chapters 16 and 17.

[38] Suny, *Making of the Georgian Nation*, 64–65.

[39] Stephen F. Jones, *The Making of Modern Georgia, 1918–2012: The First Georgian Republic and Its Successors* (Routledge, 2014); Eric Lee, *The Experiment: Georgia's Forgotten Revolution 1918–1921* (Zed Books, 2017).

[40] Timothy Blauvelt, "Status Shift and Ethnic Mobilisation in the March 1956 Events in Georgia," *Europe-Asia Studies* 61, no. 4 (2009).

while widely spoken, had limited influence. However, despite these opportunities, Soviet policies created problems that would haunt Georgia during its independence. In particular, the creation of autonomous republics and regions within the Georgian Republic, led to political entities where some groups had rights and privileges that they wanted to protect, exacerbating conflict latter on.

Following Stalin's death, the local Georgian authorities were able to carve out a reasonable amount of autonomy. The result was a highly corrupt local administration and limited development. Eventually, Eduard Shevardnadze was placed in power to attempt reforms. In this context, an organized anti-Soviet Georgian nationalist movement grew in prominence in the 1970s. Led in part by future president of Georgia Zviad Gamsakhurdia, this movement was to forcefully protest against efforts to increase the status of Russian language and culture in the republic and against the rights of minorities in the autonomous republics. The nationalist mobilization of Georgian society during the 1970s and 1980s positioned its leader Zviad Gamsakhurdia to take power as the centripetal forces unleashed by Gorbachev's reforms tore the Soviet Union apart.

Civil War, State Weakness, and the Development of Russian Dominance

Russia's relationship with Georgia, particularly in the years that immediately followed Georgia achieving statehood, was indelibly marked by the politics of Georgia's independence movement. The political institutions and arrangements that followed independence were strongly influenced by the fractious politics of the Georgian nationalist and first President Zviad Gamsakhurdia.

Like other nationalist or local leaders, Zviad Gamsakhurdia increased his influence as Soviet power waned. Nationalist leaders in Georgia organized protests to promote the position of Georgian independence but also the dominance of ethnic Georgians within the country.[41] However, the Georgian nationalist movement was not unified; there was fierce contestation among the leaders like Gamsakhurdia and Gia Chanturia.[42] The promotion of nationalism allowed Gamsakhurdia to defeat the Communist rulers of Georgia. Delegitimized by their repression of pro-independence protesters in 1989, the Communist leadership

---

[41] Stephen Francis Jones, *Georgia: A Political History since Independence* (IB Tauris, 2013), 30–32.
[42] Jones, 38–39.

opened up the political system in 1990 allowing elections for the Supreme Council that Gamsakhurdia's Round Table-Free Georgia bloc won comfortably.[43] Shortly afterward, the Supreme Council elected Gamsakhurdia Chairman. Gamsakhurdia's victory came while Georgia was still formally part of the Soviet Union.

This anti-Russian and nationalist environment persisted throughout the short rule of the erratic Gamsakhurdia. Georgia did not join the Commonwealth of Independent States. Gamsakhurdia argued against Soviet military presence on Georgian soil.[44] After losing power, Gamsakhurdia even went as far as issuing a supporting statement for the breakaway Chechen republic.[45]

The political choices made by Gamsakhurdia in the pursuit of independence created high levels of contestation within the country. Gamsakhurdia's rhetoric created tensions with the minority groups in the country.[46] The secessionist movements in Abkhazia and South Ossetia were in part motivated by Gamsakhurdia's nationalist policies, which had created unease among the national elites of these regions. This incipient nationalism posed a threat to the institutional and economic privileges they had carved out for themselves.[47] While the USSR was crumbling the minorities of Abkhazia and South Ossetia had already been agitating for their continued autonomy.[48] Gamsakhurdia responded by trying to reunite Georgia by force.[49] So began the first of Georgia's wars between the South Ossetians and the central government of Georgia.

Throughout the rule of Gamsakhurdia, institutional and political and social divisions were widespread in Georgia. At the formal institutional level, political authority in Georgia was fragmented because of the separation of the country into autonomous Republics and the central authorities.[50] Informally, the central government was chaotic and divided as the rule of Gamsakhurdia was propped up by an uneasy alliance of warlords. Socially, the state was riven by ethnic conflict; the Abkhaz, the Ossetians and Armenians were all in positions of competition with the Georgian state that was seen as representing the interests of the majority Georgian population and not their interests.[51]

---

[43] Jones, 49–50. [44] Jones, 68. [45] *Izvestia*, February 20, 1992.
[46] Jones, *Georgia*, 64. [47] Zurcher, *Post-Soviet Wars*, chapter 5.
[48] Georgi Derluguian, "The Tale of Two Resorts: Abkhazia and Ajaria before and since the Soviet Collapse," in *The Myth of "Ethnic Conflict": Politics, Economics, and "Cultural" Violence*, ed. Beverly Crawford and Ronnie Lipschutz (University of California Press, 1998).
[49] Miriam Lanskoy and Giorgi Areshidze, "Georgia's Year of Turmoil," *Journal of Democracy* 19, no. 4 (2008): 154.
[50] Bunce, *Subversive Institutions*, 1999; Zurcher, *Post-Soviet Wars*, 35.
[51] M. D. Toft, "Multinationality, Regions and State-Building: The Failed Transition in Georgia," *Regional and Federal Studies* 11, no. 3 (2001).

While Gamsakhurdia adopted anti-Russian policies and rhetoric, those that saw political outcomes in terms of rent-seeking opportunities were less inclined to resistance than Gamsakhurdia. Gamsakhurdia stressed cultural, national, and ethnic issues.[52] Despite the high level of competition he faced, the extreme value that Gamsakhurdia placed on sovereignty meant that the marginal effect of contestation and rent-seeking was insufficient to drive him to support hierarchy. Nonetheless, political and institutional variables played an important role in determining attitudes toward Russia. Paradoxically, the highly nationalist rhetoric and policies that Gamsakhurdia adopted drove competition between ethnic groups over control of rent-seeking and forced many of these groups into the arms of Russia. In the end, elites concerned with rent-seeking were prepared to come to an arrangement with Russia.

The conflict between the central government and ethnic minorities increased the power of the militias that Gamsakhurdia was forced to rely on. The breakdown of state authority in Georgia and ethnic violence that occurred provided opportunities for a group of warlords and militias to develop. From independence in 1991 to 1992, during Gamsakhurdia's presidency and its immediate aftermath, the Georgian state was highly fragmented and the economy highly politicized. This enabled militia leaders to parlay their coercive capacity into political influence and authority within the state, and to exploit economic actors for their own benefit.[53] Militia leaders like Jaba Ioseliani initially provided support to Gamsakhurdia, and propped up his regime.[54] These militia leaders proved far more willing to countenance Russian intrusions into Georgian sovereignty in their pursuit of material wealth and political survival.

The relationship between the warlords and Gamsakhurdia soon fell apart. The militias were more concerned about material gain and less about removing the Russians from Georgia. Ioseliani stated that "I still cannot believe that Russia not only agreed to our independence but also left us arms and technology."[55] Gamsakhurdia made moves to reduce their power. Gamsakhurdia tried to assert his control, attempting to ban the armed organizations or remove their leadership from positions of authority. First, Gamsakhurdia went after Ioseliani and the Mkhedrioni, and then Kitovani's control of the National Guard.[56] With the

---

[52] G. O. Nodia, "Georgia's Identity Crisis," *Journal of Democracy* 6, no. 1 (1995): 109–11.
[53] Jonathan Wheatley, *Georgia from National Awakening to Rose Revolution: Delayed Transition in the Former Soviet Union*, Post-Soviet Politics (Ashgate, 2005), 78.
[54] Aleksander Krilov, "Zabiti uroki Jaba Iosiliani," *Novaya Politika*, 2006.
[55] Quoted in Krilov.
[56] Vicken Cheterian, *War and Peace in the Caucasus: Ethnic Conflict and the New Geopolitics* (Columbia University Press, 2008), 177–78.

destabilizing and aggressively nationalist leadership of Gamsakhurdia threatening their interests, the warlords moved into outright opposition to Gamsakhurdia.

At this point the threat to his political survival was great enough that even Gamsakhurdia turned to Moscow for aid. In 1991, he used Soviet soldiers to attack the Mkhedrioni forces of Ioseliani.[57] Following the defection of Kitovani from the government, there was a brief period of conflict between the opposition and forces still loyal to Gamsakhurdia. Later, after the defection of Kitovani, Gamsakhurdia asked the "Transcaucus" Soviet troops still situated in Tbilisi to intervene on his behalf.[58] Favoring the opposition, they refused Gamsakhurdia's request. In January 1992, these warlords overthrew Gamsakhurdia armed with weapons supplied by the Russian military in Georgia.[59] They then formed the Military Council to rule the country. The Military Council chose to replace the anti-Russian Gamsakhurdia with the seemingly more pro-Russian and pragmatic Eduard Shevardnadze.[60]

Kitovani following his defection from Gamsakhurdia's government was also able to maintain close relationships and access to power partly through cooperation with Russian defense minister Pavel Grachev.[61] In 2008, Kitovani was directly accused by the then president of Georgia Saakashvili of having been a Russian agent.[62] This is backed up somewhat by the fact that following his release from prison in 1999, he fled to Russia. While in Russia, Kitovani continued to make comments critical of the Georgian government and supporting Russian propaganda claims.[63]

During the pursuit of independence, Georgian leaders adopted a highly nationalistic set of policies, which continued into the postindependence era. However, those political leaders and groups that felt that their rent-seeking opportunities were threatened by the political competition occurring in Georgia were more inclined to support Russia. In other words, the institutional conditions, competition over rent-seeking, that defined politics for the many of the key actors in the country, eventually trumped the cultural concerns of the president and he was removed from power. The events of

---

[57] Wheatley, *Georgia from National Awakening to Rose Revolution*, 55.
[58] Cheterian, *War and Peace in the Caucasus*, 179.   [59] Jones, *Georgia*, 71.
[60] Zurab Chiaberashvili and Gigi Tevzadze, "Power Elites in Georgia: Old and New," in *From Revolution to Reform: Georgia's Struggle with Democratic Institution Building and Security Sector Reform* (National Defense Academy, 2005); D. Aphrasidze and D. Siroky, "Frozen Transitions and Unfrozen Conflicts, or What Went Wrong in Georgia?," *Yale Journal of International Affairs* 121 (2010): 130.
[61] Trenin, Russia's Security Interests and Policies in the Caucasus Region.
[62] Civil.ge, "Saakashvili Says No to Treaty on Non-use of Force," March 15, 2008.
[63] See, e.g., "Interview with Tengiz Kitovani," accessed May 16, 2014, http://rt.com/politics/interview-with-tengiz-kitovani/.

this period also demonstrate that external actors can gain a degree of hierarchy and control even when opposed by the central government. The contestation and rent-seeking among elites within Georgia created incentives for certain actors among ethnic minorities and violent entrepreneurs to support Russian claims.

Shevardnadze, State Weakness, and the Zenith of Russian Hierarchy, 1992–95

Once installed in power, Shevardnadze's rule was a fragile balancing act. He faced divisions within Georgia proper and, like his predecessor, was reliant on warlords and paramilitaries to maintain control. He also needed to respond to uprisings from supporters of the former leader Gamsakhurdia and violent secessionist movements among the minorities of Georgia. Despite this perilous situation, Shevardnadze was not initially prepared to surrender much Georgian sovereignty to Russian authority. However, as his situation became more precarious, this changed. Shevardnadze's political sensibility was pragmatic and flexible, rather than ideological.[64] At this point the secessionists and the central state were closer in strength than at any other time during independence. The weakness of the central authorities meant that threats from the regions were significant.[65] This created an incentive for the central government to surrender power to the Russians in order to ensure their political survival.

One Russian newspaper described the economic system in Georgia as almost completely dominated by the militias. "Everyone from money changers to directors and owners of powerful companies had to pay up to 50% of their profits in tribute."[66] Here we see the role played by political power and force in the economy of Georgia at this time. In other words, along with high levels of political contestation, there were extreme levels of corruption and rent-seeking.

The fractures in Georgian society, most notably those between the majority and minorities, enabled Russia to find an opening and to establish bridgeheads on Georgian territory. These divisions were not limited to those between the ethnic majority and minorities; divisions among ethnically Georgian political actors played a role as well. Shevardnadze needed the support of Russia to defeat the Zviadists, supporters of the

---

[64] Carolyn Ekedahl and Melvin A. Goodman, *Wars of Eduard Shevardnadze* (Penn State Press, 2010), xxii.
[65] Cheterian, *War and Peace in the Caucasus*, 209–11.
[66] Situatsiya v Gruzii: Shevardnadze poshol va bank, *Kommersant*, October 6, 1995.

former president Zviad Gamsakhurdia.[67] It was Russian battalions that occupied and pacified western Georgia for Shevardnadze.[68] This in turn forced Shevardnadze to submit to Russian authority.

The events of this period demonstrate Russia's ability to manipulate contestation and threats to political survival for their own ends. During ceasefire negotiations involving the Abkhaz, Georgians, and Russians, the Russians included conditions requiring Georgia to host military installations and join the CIS.[69] While the Georgian government initially rejected these demands, the war's persistence and the growing threat in Mingrelia forced Shevardnadze to turn to Russia for help.[70] By the end of this period Georgia was involved in the CIS and the extra security treaty, the CSTO, which many other former Soviet countries did not join.[71] Moreover, at the end of this period, Georgia signed an agreement to host Russian military bases for twenty-five years.[72]

One significant example of Russia control over Georgian sovereignty in this period was the appointment of Georgia's minister of defense, Vardiko Nadibaidze. Appointed, in part at the behest of the Russian authorities, to this post in 1994, Nadibaidze was still a serving Russian military officer and deputy commander of Russian forces in the Transcaucasus region.[73] This appointment was made to help Georgia gain the time and space to stabilize the country and as a reassurance to the leaders of pro-Russian Abkhazia about the future. The appointment was also in part explained by the politicized state of the Georgian military forces at this time; Nadibaidze tried to reduce the influence of militias such as the Mkhedrioni as well as factionalism in the armed forces.[74] Along with this link to contestation, Nadibaidze's role also demonstrates the importance of rent-seeking, he allowed practices of Georgian military elites personally benefiting from the military budget.[75]

Russia had other possible agents in prominent positions. Igor Giorgadze, state security minister from 1993 to 1995, is another example. Allegedly, Giorgadze benefited from his Russian connection by using it to

---

[67] S. E. Cornell, *Small Nations and Great Powers: A Study of Ethnopolitical Conflict in the Caucasus* (RoutledgeCurzon, 2001), 173.
[68] Pavel Baev, "Civil Wars in Georgia," in *Potentials of Disorder*, ed. Jan Koehler and Christoph Zurcher (Manchester University Press, 2003), 133.
[69] Cheterian, *War and Peace in the Caucasus*, 200.   [70] Cheterian, 207.
[71] Peimani, *Conflict and Security in Central Asia and the Caucasus*.
[72] Larsson, "Enemy Within."
[73] Ilya Bulavinov, "Rossiskii general v minobroni gruzii," *Kommersant*, April 28, 1994.
[74] David Darchiashvili, "Georgia: A Hostage to Arms," in *The Caucasus: Armed and Divided* (SaferWorld, 2003), 12.
[75] Davit Darchiashvili, "Georgian Defense Policy and Military Reform," in *Statehood and Security: Georgia after the Rose Revolution*, ed. Bruno Coppieters and Robert Levgold (MIT Press, 2005), 136.

engage in smuggling.[76] Giorgadze then used these resources from corruption and rent-seeking to create a patronage network within the security forces, paying his supporters above standard wages.[77] Russian control helped place Giorgadze into a position of power, which he then used to pursue his rent-seeking aims.

Georgia maintained some distance from the formal institutional apparatus that Russia established in the former Soviet States, but still surrendered an increasing number of sovereign rights. Given the right political environment hierarchy can emerge because the costs of resistance outweigh the benefits, not because hierarchy is authoritative or legitimate. As Wheatley argues: "it would appear evident that if Shevardnadze had not acted as he had in the autumn of 1993, no further progress would have been made towards the building of a viable state."[78] A most important element of this was Shevardnadze's submission to Russian authority. This action provided Shevardnadze with crucial resources in his fight with the Zviadists. Shevardnadze stated that joining the CIS to gain time and support to fight the Zviadists in Western Georgia was the "only true solution, which life will prove."[79]

The changed political preferences of the relevant leaders combined with rent-seeking and contestation during this period increased the willingness of Georgia to surrender its sovereignty. In contrast to the earlier period where the central leadership had been strongly nationalistic and defined its political interests in these national-cultural terms, Shevardnadze was more pragmatic and materialist. In a situation where conflict between the regions and the center was prevalent and there was informal fragmentation within the central government, Shevardnadze's preferences drove him to surrender sovereignty to Russia. Russia in turn provided support to help Shevardnadze defeat rivals threatening his political survival.

Shevardnaze's Consolidation of Power, Reduced Competition, and the Diminishment of Russian Hierarchy, 1995–2003

During the years from 1995 to 1999, the level of Russian hierarchy that resulted from Shevardnadze bowing his head in the early 1990s began to

---

[76] Darchiashvili, 129.
[77] Charles H. Fairbanks, "II. The Postcommunist Wars," *Journal of Democracy* 6, no. 4 (1995): 27.
[78] Wheatley, *Georgia from National Awakening to Rose Revolution*, 91; see also Cornell, *Small Nations and Great Powers*, 173.
[79] Dmitri Kamishev, "Reshen vopros vistuplenii Gruzii v SNG," *Kommersant*, October 10, 1993.

decline. The regime stabilized, representing an increasingly narrow elite, and the level of hierarchy began to drop. While the level of rent-seeking remained high, the level of political competition was far below that of the previous era. Numerous examples of Georgia's changed relationship with Russia during this period exist. Georgia was involved in the creation of the GUAM Organization for Democracy and Economic Cooperation.[80] This organization was seen as a counterweight to the Russian-led CIS.[81] They failed to renew their membership in the CSTO – now a stand-alone treaty.[82] They negotiated the removal of some, though not all, of Russia's military bases in the country.[83] All in all, the level of Russia's influence over Georgia experienced a steady decline during this period.

Consistent with the theoretical predictions, Russia resorted to greater coercion, reportedly backing attempted assassinations of Shevardnadze in 1995 and 1998.[84] In response, Shevardnadze continued his renewed assertion of Georgian sovereignty. First, Giorgadze fled to Moscow, and his allies left their positions.[85] In 1998, he took control over the Ministry of Defence, removing the Russian military officer Nadibaidze from the post of minister and appointed Davit Tevzadze, a pro-Western military officer who had started his career in a Georgian militia rather than the Soviet or Russian armies.[86] This removed a further source of Russian hierarchy.

Shevardnadze's ability to reduce Russian control over Georgian sovereignty can partly be attributed to change in the political environment. Shevardnadze consolidated his position and Russia became a less valuable source of resources to achieve his political survival. Nodia and Scholtbach describe the regime that Shevardnadze constructed in this era as one where "the real levers of power remained in the hands of a small elite that did not allow other groups to enjoy effective means of political competition."[87] Wheatley supports this assertion, arguing that by 1995 Shevardnadze had managed to reestablish the demarcation between state and society that broken down in the early 1990s.[88] No longer could social actors such as paramilitaries significantly influence political outcomes.

[80] GUAM is an acronym based on the members of the organization: Georgia, Ukraine, Azerbaijan, and Moldova.
[81] Kuzio, "Geopolitical Pluralism," 86.   [82] www.dkb.gov.ru/a/a.htm.
[83] Larsson, "Enemy Within," 409.
[84] Georgie Anne Geyer, "Conversations with Eduard Shevardnadze," *Washington Quarterly* 23, no. 2 (2000): 60–61.
[85] Jesse Driscoll, *Warlords and Coalition Politics in Post-Soviet States* (Cambridge University Press, 2015), 118–19.
[86] Darchiashvili, "Georgian Defense Policy and Military Reform," 132.
[87] G. Nodia and Á. P Scholtbach, *The Political Landscape of Georgia: Political Parties: Achievements, Challenges and Prospects* (Eburon, 2006), 14.
[88] Wheatley, *Georgia from National Awakening to Rose Revolution*, 93.

In order to achieve this level of stability Shevardnadze needed to accomplish two things. First, Shevardnadze needed to sideline the paramilitaries that had, up until this point, played a pivotal role in Georgia's postindependence politics. Second, he needed to build a secure base of control over other political actors. By 1995, the ethnic separatism had settled into two frozen conflicts.[89] Shevardnadze with Russia's aid had also defeated the supporters of Zviad Gamsakhurdia. This provided Shevardnadze with an opportunity to defeat the militias which still influenced Georgian politics in 1995, coercing a role for themselves in appointing ministers and intimidating local governors.[90] In the middle of 1995, Shevardnadze gave the order to outlaw and disarm the armed criminal group led by Ioseliani, the Mkhedrioni. After the Mkhedrioni had failed in an attempt to assassinate Shevadnadze, its leaders were arrested, and they ceased to be a real force in Georgian politics.[91]

Igor Giorgadze, the state security minister and a possible Russian agent, was also accused of being involved in an assassination attempt on Shevardnadze and was removed from his position.[92] He fled to Russia for protection.[93] This was one of the first moves Shevardnadze made to reclaim control over important security ministries in Georgia. The case of Giorgadze again highlights the role political fragmentation and contestation combined with rent-seeking plays in facilitating hierarchy. Similarly, Kitovani's political influence was destroyed when, disobeying orders, he marched on Abkhazia.[94] On the road to Abkhazia, Kitovani was arrested and imprisoned until 1999. These actions effectively marked the end of the warlords as a political force in Georgia, with the possible exception of Abashidze in Adjara.

Giorgadze's attempts to act as a Russian agent and his failure demonstrate the importance of mass support. From Russia, Giorgadze continued to try to influence Georgian politics in Russia's favor, establishing a political party to compete in Georgian elections.[95] Once removed from his position of power, his attempts to influence Georgian politics were highly ineffective. Unable to find support in Georgia, his political interventions did little for Russia's goals to influence Georgian policy.

---

[89] C. King, "The Benefits of Ethnic War: Understanding Eurasia's Unrecognized States," *World Politics* 53, no. 4 (2001): 525.
[90] "Situatsiya v Gruzii: Shevardnadze poshol va bank," *Kommersant*, October 6, 1995.
[91] Krilov, "Zabiti uroki Jaba Iosiliani."   [92] Baev, "Civil Wars in Georgia," 133.
[93] Thornike Gordadze, "Georgia-Russia Conflict in August 2008: War as a Continuation of Politics," in *Reassessing Security in the South Caucasus: Regional Conflicts and Transformation* (Ashgate, 2011), 16.
[94] Baev, "Civil Wars in Georgia," 133.
[95] Civil.ge, "Giorgadze threatens Revolution of Nettles," Civil Georgia, May 26, 2006, www.civil.ge/eng/article.php?id=12637.

Similarly, in later periods, support from politicians such Burjanadze and Noghaideli was of limited effect as they failed to mobilize sufficient mass support.

Even after the marginalization of militias and warlords, a high level of corruption and rent-seeking persisted in the Georgian economy.[96] There were close connections between political and economic elites. Political elites provided protection to economic elites, who were able to amass wealth through these connections. Georgia during the 1990s was rated among the most corrupt countries.

Several power centers operated in Georgia during this period: Shevardnadze and the State Chancellery, the Ministry of Internal Affairs, Abashidze in the autonomous region of Adjara, the parliament, and a group of selected businessmen.[97] Hence, there existed a certain level of political competition and pluralism within the state structures but ultimate power resided with Shevardnadze. While some political competition continued in this period it was diminished compared to that which had prevailed in the early period of Shevardnaze's rule. It is notable that it is around these conflict points that the Russian hierarchy that remained in Georgia was based. This contestation was often built around control of rents, with one such example resulting in a budget war between central government and Abashidze, the strong man of Adjara.[98] One source of Russian hierarchy in Georgia in this period was the divisions between the central government and local power brokers such as Abashidze. Abashidze lobbied against Shevardnadze's attempts to reduce Russia's influence in Georgia.[99]

Other potential sources of conflict were managed. While the governors of important regions of Georgia such as Kvemo Kartli and Imereti were able to gain control of important political and economic resources, they remained loyal to Shevardnadze.[100] This means that a potential source of political competition was present but not particularly salient during this period.

Despite the high levels of corruption and rent-seeking, the reduction of political competition during this period and Shevardnadze's greater assuredness of survival meant that there was less incentive to surrender sovereignty to Russia. As a consequence, during this period, Shevardnadze

---

[96] Nina Dadalauri, "Political Corruption in Georgia," in *Corruption and Development*, ed. Sarah Hacking (Palgrave Macmillan, 2007), 155.
[97] Wheatley, *Georgia from National Awakening to Rose Revolution*, 110.
[98] Vladimer Papava, "The Political Economy of Georgia's Rose Revolution," *Orbis* 50, no. 4 (2006): 660.
[99] See Chapter 3.
[100] L. Mitchell, "Georgia's Rose Revolution," *Current History—New York Then Philadelphia* 103 (2004): 348.

reversed his former policies. He ended Georgia's relationship with an organization that he had previously agreed to join and demanded that the military bases he agreed to host be removed. Shevardnadze succeeded in significantly reducing Russian influence in Georgia.

The Rose Revolution and Resistance to Russian Hierarchy, 2003–8

In 2003 the Georgian political scene underwent a massive transformation. In the early 2000s, after a period of consolidation, opposition again emerged to Shevardnadze. This time it was not violent conflict, but a reform movement. A former minister in Shevardnadze's government, Mikhail Saakashvili, led the opposition to him. Saakashvili left the government, resigning as justice minister, citing the high levels of corruption. He immediately set about organizing an opposition party, the National Movement.[101] This new political movement constituted the first genuine threat to Shevardnadze's control over the central Georgian government since the mid-1990s.

The political threat to Shevardnadze was associated with a slight reorientation of Georgia's foreign policy, giving up a certain degree of sovereign control, seeking an improved relationship with Russia. As this opposition threatened Shevardnadze's position, he spoke of détente with Russia.[102] He also surrendered some sovereignty regarding Georgia's borders, agreeing to allow Russian border patrols around the Pankisi Gorge in pursuit of Chechen terrorists.[103] In addition, Shevardnadze appointed the very pro-Russian leader, Aslan Abashdize, to negotiate with Russia over Abkhazia. Notably, during the Rose Revolution itself, Shevardnadze turned to Russia and Vladimir Putin for support.[104]

After a year of opposition, a rigged election was enough to prompt tens of thousands of protesters onto the street forcing Shevardnadze to step down.[105] Having lost mass and elite support Shevardnadze was unable to

---

[101] Lincoln Mitchell, *Uncertain Democracy: US Foreign Policy and Georgia's Rose Revolution* (University of Pennsylvania Press, 2008), 36–37.
[102] Sergei Blagov, "Military Issues Block Russia-Georgia Detente," *EurasiaNet*, January 5, 2003, www.eurasianet.org/departments/insight/articles/eav010603.shtml.
[103] Giorgi Kandelaki, "Shevardnadze's Chisinau Concessions Shatter Georgia's Political Unity," *EurasiaNet*, October 8, 2002, www.eurasianet.org/departments/insight/articles/eav100902.shtml.
[104] David L. Phillips, "Shevardnadze under Fire: Pulling Georgia from the Brink," *New York Times*, November 12, 2003, sec. Opinion, www.nytimes.com/2003/11/12/o pinion/12iht-edphillips_ed3_.html.
[105] J. A. Tucker, "Enough! Electoral Fraud, Collective Action Problems, and Post-communist Colored Revolutions," *Perspectives on Politics* 5, no. 3 (2007): 538; Lucan Way, "The Real Causes of the Color Revolutions," *Journal of Democracy* 19, no. 3

hold on to power. The overthrow of Shevardnadze's regime by the Rose Revolution resulted in dramatic changes to the institutions governing Georgian political life.

The period following the Rose Revolution saw a further consolidation of the state and reduction in rent-seeking behavior and corruption. That Georgia transformed from one of the most corrupt regimes in the world to a country that within 6 years was ranked as one of the most business friendly in the world by the World Bank demonstrates the dramatic shift in Georgia's institutional structures.[106] Moreover, the dominance of the ruling United National Movement across several elections demonstrates the limited level of competition within the country between 2004 and 2011. The Rose Revolution restructured Georgian politics in variety of different ways.

The United National Movement (UNM) was able to cement its power to an extent that previous ruling party had not, while the state increased its control over the regions. From the moment he took power, Saakashvili established his power with an extraordinary mandate. The elections that followed the Rose Revolution saw Saakashvili win the presidency with 96 percent of the vote.[107] While observers discovered some irregularities, there is little reason to doubt Saakashvili's strong political position. Moreover, he was more or less unopposed by other serious political figures. Prominent politicians such as Zurab Zhvania, who had been Speaker, and Nino Burjanadze, who had been acting prime minister, became part of Saakashvili's government, indicating a relatively unified elite.[108] In the 2008 parliamentary elections, UNM won close to 60 percent of the votes.[109] Saakashvili governed with a larger majority than Shevardnadze's party was able to achieve.

Some of these elites, such as Burjanadze, were to defect later and begin opposing Saakashvili over the next half decade.[110] Nonetheless, these defections did little to undermine his and his party's strong position in Georgia. The UNM continued to dominate elections at all levels, both national and local. This situation contrasts to the earlier period where certain regions, such as Adjara, were dominated by local leaders and parties. During the period between the Rose Revolution and the rise of Georgian Dream, there was limited opposition, democratic or otherwise. Through interviews with party officials and groups such as National

(2008): 59; S. Radnitz, "The Color of Money Privatization, Economic Dispersion, and the Post-Soviet Revolutions," *Comparative Politics* 42, no. 2 (2010): 136.
[106] www.doingbusiness.org/data/exploreeconomies/georgia (last accessed July 1, 2011).
[107] www.civil.ge/eng/article.php?id=5968&search=.
[108] Civil.ge, November 27, 2003; February 28, 2004.
[109] www.electionguide.org/results.php?ID=1412.   [110] Civil.ge, October 27, 2008.

Democratic Institute and International Republican Institute that work in training and developing parties in the region, it was clear the UNM was the only party with significant presence around the country. UNM claimed more organization nationwide.[111] UNM themselves, other parties, and observers acknowledged the party's dominant position when it came to resources as well.[112]

Beyond Saakashvili and UNM's dominance of the formal political scene, Saakashvili also managed to rein in the independence of many of the regions. The most notable instance of this increasing centralization is the reincorporation of Adjara.[113] Another example was the removal and arrest of high-profile regional leaders such as Levan Mamaladze, the governor of Kvemo Kartli.[114] This increased control of the regions and reduced competition from the perspective of the central state reduced incentives to align with Russia. An interesting corollary of this observation is that one of the points of closest cooperation between the Saakashvili government and Russia occurred when he was trying to reincorporate Adjara.[115] That is, Saakashvili seemed most pliable when he was engaged in direct competition with regional rivals.

Saakashvili moved quickly to curb corruption. He began massive anticorruption campaigns shortly after taking power. Though arguably aimed more at low-level corruption, the campaigns made a significant difference to life in Georgia. The reduction of rent-seeking and corruption was indicated by a variety of different measures. First, the World Bank development indicator of Control of Corruption shows a dramatic increase in government control over corruption following the Rose Revolution, with Georgia moving from being in the twenty-first percentile to the fifty-second.[116] Other measures such as Transparency International perceptions of corruption index also show a dramatic reduction in corruption.[117] Similarly, even some opposition politicians acknowledge the success that Saakashvili's regime has had when trying to reduce corruption, at least in the broader society. One opposition party activist said that a sign of the change was that even in a corrupt institution like the courts it was more expensive to buy a judge.[118] While corruption remains problematic in the country, and is still widespread among elites, it has been substantially reduced.

[111] Author interviews, July/August 2010.
[112] Party officials, author interviews, July/August 2010.
[113] This will be discussed in greater detail in Chapter 3.   [114] Civil.ge, January 18, 2004.
[115] Charles King, "A Rose among Thorns: Georgia Makes Good," *Foreign Affairs* 83, no. 2 (2004): 16.
[116] http://info.worldbank.org/governance/wgi/sc_chart.asp (last accessed July 4, 2011).
[117] www.transparency.org/policy_research/surveys_indices/gcb (last accessed July 4, 2011).
[118] Author interview with opposition party activist, July 2010.

The government and leadership asserted its independence following Georgia's democratic transition. Georgian elites increased their resistance, which led to an even lower level of Russian hierarchy and influence in some areas, though in others such as Abkhazia and South Ossetia Russia increased its control. Regions such as Adjara lost their pro-Russian leadership, military bases were removed, and Georgia withdrew from the CIS. Rather than seeking compromise with Russia, the government built state capacity and independence. Saakashvili asserted Georgian sovereignty over areas where previous Georgian regimes had surrendered sovereignty.

The changes in Russian influence in Georgia must be located in the changing political environment after regime change. The limited political competition created incentives for the governing elites within the central government of Georgia to engage in state-building exercises.[119] Rather than surrender sovereignty for political survival as Shevardnadze had done, Saakashvili resisted. However, the result of this resistance was ambiguous for Georgia. While some of it resulted in a more unified, stronger state, the most obvious act of resistance was the conflict fought between Georgia and Russia in 2008, which resulted in Georgian sovereignty being further diminished.

Resistance, Ambiguity, and Violence

Georgia's conflict with South Ossetia and Russia in 2008 can be related to the changes in political competition and rent-seeking. The lack of political competition in this case altered the incentives for Georgia's rulers. Instead of focusing on their own political survival they now had incentives to engage in state-building and assert their autonomy, creating greater levels of conflict with Russia. However, it is clear that they did not expect such a forceful response from Russia, which ultimately resulted in a net loss of Georgian sovereignty. Georgia engaged in resistance because their incentives had changed, but also because of this ambiguity about how Russia would react; Georgia had a number of reasons to believe that Russia's response would be more restrained.

South Ossetia, as with Abkhazia, has been closely aligned with Russia since the demise of the Soviet Union. South Ossetia has hosted a Russian military presence in the form of peacekeepers, its primary currency is the Russian ruble, and one of its primary sources of income is smuggling from

---

[119] S. Neil MacFarlane, "Colliding State-Building Projects and Regional Insecurity in Post-Soviet Space: Georgia versus Russia in South Ossetia," in *Troubled Regions and Failing States: The Clustering and Contagion of Armed Conflicts* (Emerald, 2010), 113–15.

Russia.[120] The former president of South Ossetia Eduard Kokoity captured Ossetian perceptions of the relationship between Russia and Ossetia when he declared: "We are obliged and grateful to the Russian Federation. Russia is our main strategic partner and this has been the case for many centuries."[121]

The establishment of South Ossetia as a de facto state within Georgia in the early 1990s created opportunities for rent-seeking by the South Ossetians. South Ossetia's geographic location provided it with a singular opportunity for smuggling Russian goods.[122] The Transcaucasian Highway, the road that connects Russia and Georgia, passes through South Ossetia. At the end of this highway, in a stretch of land between South Ossetia and Georgia, sat the Ergneti Market.[123] This market was shut down in 2004 following the Rose Revolution, as part of Saakashvili's anticorruption campaign. The International Crisis Group (ICG) estimates that several hundred million dollars' worth of goods were sold in this market.[124] The Organization for Cooperation and Security in Europe estimated that some US$60–70 million worth of goods passed through South Ossetia each year, much of this coming from Russia through the Roki Tunnel from North Ossetia.[125] The ICG also argues that when the Georgian government shut down the market the South Ossetians lost almost half their income.[126] This loss of income was also borne by the Russia's "men on the spot." Russia's military leadership in the region had been benefiting from illegal trade and smuggling.[127]

Saakashvili, confident in his new position, proceeded to engage in activities that brought him into conflict with Russia. His desire to increase state capacity and to limit outside impediments to Georgian sovereignty led the Georgian government to attempt to remove Russia's proxies in South Ossetia. This required building up military forces and supporting political actors in the region.[128] Ultimately, the government initiated a conflict with South Ossetia in early

---

[120] Pal Kolstø and Helge Blakkisrud, "Living with Non-recognition: State-and Nation-Building in South Caucasian Quasi-States," *Europe-Asia Studies* 60, no. 3 (2008): 497.
[121] RFE/RL, February 24, 2010.
[122] Kolstø and Blakkisrud, "Living with Non-recognition," 497.
[123] Alexandre Kukhianidze, "Corruption and Organized Crime in Georgia before and after the 'Rose Revolution,'" *Central Asian Survey* 28, no. 2 (2009): 223–24.
[124] International Crisis Group, "Avoiding War in South Ossetia," Europe Report (2004), 159.
[125] King, "Benefits of Ethnic War," 537.
[126] International Crisis Group, "Georgia: Avoiding War in South Ossetia," 2004, 11.
[127] International Crisis Group.
[128] Julie A. George, *The Politics of Ethnic Separatism in Russia and Georgia* (Palgrave Macmillan, 2009), 181.

August 2008.[129] This conflict, because of the presence of Russian peacekeepers, South Ossetia's allies, also meant conflict with Russia. Indeed, in the first days of the war Russian soldiers were killed. Moreover, as attested to by one of the negotiators in earlier peace talks with the South Ossetians, opportunities to compromise with Russia and the South Ossetian authorities were ignored by Saakashvili so that he could pursue his nation-building policies.[130]

Whereas Shevardnadze had carved an uneasy peace with Russia, involving some compromises of sovereignty, Saakashvili openly fought to remove Russian influences. The reasons for this resistance to Russia can be found in Georgia's changed domestic political sphere. Other external factors cannot explain the change. While Georgia was stronger than before, it was still so much weaker than Russia that its relative gains made no significant difference to the balance of power. Furthermore, the financial support of the United States for Georgia predates Saakashvili and did not lead to aggression on the part of previous governments.[131]

These events also demonstrate the role of ambiguity and incomplete information in causing conflict. One source of ambiguity was Russia's past actions. A second source was the increased role of the United States in Georgia in the aftermath of September 11, 2001. These two factors may have influenced Saakashvili's beliefs regarding how constrained Russia was to respond violently to any resistance.

Ultimately, resistance did not increase autonomy for Georgia. Instead, within certain bounds, Russia was prepared to pay a higher cost and ratchet up its control and the level of coercion over Georgia. However, there was clearly enough doubt about Russia's response in Saakashvili's mind to justify an attack. The first source of ambiguity may have come from the reputation effects that Russia had developed over the previous four years. In 2004, Saakashvili twice engaged in militaristic behavior. In both instances Saakashvili challenged Russian clients, first in Adjara where he mobilized the military to remove Aslan Abashidze the local strong man and an ally to Russia.[132] In this case, Russia negotiated his exile without conflict. The second instance was the anticorruption

[129] Independent International Fact-Finding Mission on the Conflict in Georgia, "Report" (European Union, September 2009).
[130] Victor Dolidze, former OCSE ambassador from Georgia, author interview, August 23, 2010.
[131] The US provided Shevardnadze's regime with US$1.3 billion in aid. Eric A. Miller, "Smelling the Roses: Eduard Shevardnadze's End and Georgia's Future," *Problems of Post-Communism* 51, no. 2 (2004): 13.
[132] L. A. Mitchell, "Democracy in Georgia since the Rose Revolution," *Orbis* 50, no. 4 (2006).

campaign that Saakashvili undertook around the South Ossetian boarder.[133] Again this brought him into conflict with Russian clients and again the Russian reaction was relatively mild as they did not respond with force.

Furthermore, Georgia possessed a close relationship with the US government, which may have provided Saakashvili with a false sense of security. Indeed, it has been claimed that Georgian leadership interpreted Condoleezza Rice's visit to Georgia a month before the conflict as a demonstration of support.[134] Given this potential deterrent, and the influence of past behavior in shaping reputation and for reputation to shape beliefs about future behavior,[135] it is plausible to assume that Russia's response to resistance might have been more restrained. Without this belief, resistance would not make sense.

In addition, the action of the Bush administration after the conflict is evidence that Saakashvili may have been subject to a situation of moral hazard. The United States promised additional resources to Georgia. The United States pledged almost US$1 billion to Georgia for postconflict reconstruction, with US$570 million to be disbursed in 2008.[136] In this way, the United States rewarded Georgia's aggression and decision to gamble under uncertainty.

However, Georgia underestimated the costs that Russia was willing to pay to maintain their control over South Ossetia. After the 2008 conflict, Russia increased the numbers of soldiers it had stationed in Georgia, increased its investment in infrastructure and was also prepared to pay diplomatic costs in terms of its actions and its recognition of Abkhazian and South Ossetian sovereignty.[137] Georgian sovereignty in these regions was further diminished. In addition to these costs, while there was a short-run payoff from the Bush administration, the Obama administration downgraded Georgia's importance. While it maintained support for Georgia in general, the United States under Obama was more equivocal both in support for the Georgian government and its NATO aspirations.[138]

---

[133] Vicken Cheterian, "The August 2008 War in Georgia: From Ethnic Conflict to Border Wars," *Central Asian Survey* 28, no. 2 (2009): 165.
[134] Cheterian, "August 2008 War in Georgia," 72.
[135] J. Mercer, *Reputation and International Politics* (Cornell University Press, 2009); A. E. Sartori, "The Might of the Pen: A Reputational Theory of Communication in International Disputes," *International Organization* 56, no. 1 (2002).
[136] Alexander Cooley and Lincoln A. Mitchell, "No Way to Treat Our Friends: Recasting Recent US–Georgian Relations," *Washington Quarterly* 32, no. 1 (2009): 37.
[137] A. Cooley and L. Mitchell, "Abkhazia on Three Wheels," *World Policy Journal* 27, no. 2 (2010), 78.
[138] Ruth Deyermond, "Assessing the Reset: Successes and Failures in the Obama Administration's Russia Policy, 2009–2012," *European Security* 22, no. 4 (2013); Lincoln A. Mitchell and Alexander A. Cooley, "After the August War: A New

Post-2008 Politics and the Rise of Georgian Dream

While the war and its aftermath may have damaged some of Saakashvili and UNM's credibility, the ruling party managed to preserve, even strengthen, its hold over Georgian politics. After the Rose Revolution, in 2004, Saakashvili had increased the power of the presidency through a constitutional reform. Saakashvili's reforms that strengthened the presidency by giving the president the right to dismiss parliament if the parliament refused to support cabinet appointments, budgets, and legislation.[139] The result was a hyperpresidential system. This weakening of the parliament further reduced competition at that time. However, in the build up to the 2012 elections, Saakashvili was confident enough that he could change the constitution again, making it more of parliamentary system, with the aim of emulating Putin and changing roles from president to Prime Minster.[140]

The political dominance of Saakashvili and UNM persisted until 2011. However, in 2011, Georgia's richest person, Bidzina Ivanishvili entered the political contest.[141] Using his wealth and connections, Ivanishvili was able to cobble together a coalition of antigovernment parties.[142] The resources and political organization that Ivanishvili brought to the coalition introduced a level of democratic competition into the political system that had not been witnessed previously. Combined with various political scandals, for the first time UNM's electoral dominance was threatened.[143] These events culminated in the Georgian Dream coalition comfortably winning the 2012 parliamentary elections, winning eighty-five seats to UNM's sixty-five.[144] Saakashvili ceded control of government to the new parliament, despite the hyperpresidentialism of the constitution. UNM's dominance of the political landscape was finally broken.

In addition, Georgian political institutions underwent a further change. The reforms that increased the power of the parliament relative to the president, enacted in 2010, meant that the hyperpresidentialism of the system changed following the 2013 presidential elections.[145] This change increased the power of parliament relative to the president.

Strategy for US Engagement with Georgia," 2010, 14–15; S. Neil MacFarlane, "Georgia: National Security Concept versus National Security," *Caucasus Social Science Review* 1 (2013): 29.

[139] Civil.ge, "New Constitution Boosts President's Powers," February 7, 2004, www.civil.ge/eng/article.php?id=6172 (last accessed March 3, 2011).

[140] Charles H. Fairbanks Jr. and Alexi Gugushvili, "A New Chance for Georgian Democracy," *Journal of Democracy* 24, no. 1 (2013): 119.

[141] Lincoln Mitchell, "What's Next for Georgia?," *World Affairs* 175, no. 5 (2013): 76–77.

[142] Fairbanks and Gugushvili, "A New Chance for Georgian Democracy," 119–20.

[143] Mitchell, "What's Next for Georgia?," 79.

[144] "Elections," http://civil.ge/eng/category.php?id=32.

[145] Fairbanks and Gugushvili, "A New Chance for Georgian Democracy," 119.

The new political environment has been accompanied by a moderation of Georgia's previous bellicose attitude toward Russia.[146] A special envoy was sent to Moscow.[147] However, it has not resulted in a substantial shift from Georgia's previous policy of pursuing integration with Western international organizations such as NATO and the EU.[148] Nor has it resulted in much willingness to surrender sovereignty to Russia in the region. In 2013, the PM, Ivanishvili, stated,

We have gotten rid of masters once and for all. We want freedom, the respect of all human rights, equality, democracy, and the formation of democratic institutions. Therefore we are watching what principles the Eurasian Union will choose. If it turns out to be what you describe [dominated by Russia], then, of course, we will not join it.[149]

Effectively, the emergence of Georgian Dream, and the persistence of UNM, meant that there was more political contestation in the system. However, in a historical context, corruption and rent-seeking remained comparatively low. Transparency International has found little change in the perception of corruption between Georgia under Saakashvili and Georgia ruled by Georgian Dream.[150] In addition, Ivanishvili's large personal wealth probably means that he is less reliant on state power for economic welfare. While there was increased contestation during this period, rent-seeking had not increased. For these reasons, there was little change in the incentives to give up sovereignty to Russia.

Independent Ukraine and Russian Hierarchy

Following independence and prior to the Orange Revolution, Ukraine pursued an autarchic path. Across two different presidential administrations Ukraine did not engage significantly with Russia, but nor did they pursue integration with the West. Ukraine made some concessions to Russian demands for control such as agreeing to 25-year lease over Sevastopol, the port that hosts the Black Sea fleet. Following the Orange Revolution, Yushchenko the new president, adopted a more nationalist stance, but this was not mirrored by society at large or by the

---

[146] "Ivanishvili on Foreign Policy, Territorial Integrity," accessed May 14, 2014, www.geotimes.ge/index.php?m=home&newsid=26072.
[147] Civil.ge, "PM Appoints Special Envoy for Relations with Russia," November 1, 2012.
[148] Helena Bedwell and Henry Meyer, "Georgia Pushes for Fast-Track NATO Entry to Ward Off Russia," *BusinessWeek*, April 30, 2014, www.businessweek.com/news/2014-04-29/georgia-pushes-for-fast-track-nato-membership-to-ward-off-russia.
[149] www.eurasianet.org/node/67485.
[150] Corruption Barometer 2013, Transparency International, http://transparency.ge/en/corruptionbarometer2013.

78 Submission, Resistance, and War

political opposition. After the 2010 election, Ukraine became more pro-Russian than in previous years following independence. Yanukovych agreed to host the Black Sea fleet for a further twenty-five years.[151]

Ukraine's foreign policy has been, on average, neither Russian nor Western in its orientation. However, at times of heightened political competition there has been a tendency for certain factions in Ukraine to pursue a more pro-Russian line and make deals that surrender sovereignty to Russia. For example, the arrangements regarding the right of Russia to station its Black Sea fleet in Ukraine occurred at a time of high political competition. The following sections begin with an overview of the countries' historical relationship and then chronicle the development of Ukrainian foreign policy in more detail across two decades of independence. The analysis demonstrates that competition over access to the central government has been associated with a greater willingness to surrender sovereignty to Russia.

Russia and Ukraine's Historical Relationship

The incorporation of what is now Ukraine into the Russian Empire arguably began in the seventeenth century. The process of drawing Ukraine into Russia and the Soviet Union took place over many centuries. What we now think of as the Russian state grew out of Muscovy. As Mongol power in the region collapsed in the fourteenth century, various polities, Muscovy among them, saw an opportunity to expand their power and influence.[152] However, the first power to extend their control into Ukraine was the Grand Duchy of Lithuania.[153] It was with this polity that Muscovy was to compete with initially over the territory that is now Ukraine.

Competition between the Grand Duchy and Muscovy was first concentrated on control of the Baltic regions and what is now Belarus and Russia.[154] It was not until roughly the seventeenth century that the focus of their competition became the region now that is Ukraine.[155] By the 1650s, Muscovy had a weak form of control or influence over "Sloboda

---

[151] *Kyiv Post*, April 27, 2010.
[152] Valerie A. Kivelson and Ronald Suny, *Russia's Empires* (Oxford University Press, 2017), 42–43; Nancy Shields Kollmann, *The Russian Empire 1450–1801* (Oxford University Press, 2016), 45–48.
[153] Paul R. Magocsi, *A History of Ukraine: The Land and Its Peoples* (University of Toronto Press, 2010), 127.
[154] Kollmann, *The Russian Empire*, 51–52.
[155] That is not to say that there was no engagement with the region prior to this; both Moscow and the Grand Duchy formed alliances at different stages with the Crimean Tatars. Kollmann, 51.

Ukraine," the areas of Ukraine located east of Kyiv.[156] Russia extended control over Cossack groups in 1650s, when they signed a treat of protection with the Hetmanate on the Dnieper.

The imperial center of the Russian Empire was to gradually increase its control over the region of Ukraine.[157] The autonomy and rights of the Cossacks, who the Russians had wielded influence through, were downgraded. While this process of centralization was occurring, Russia was also extending the reach of its territorial control. Eventually the partitions of Poland beginning in the late eighteenth century allowed the Russian Empire to claim dominion over nearly all of what is now Ukraine, with the Austro-Hungarian Empire taking control over the most western provinces of Ukraine.[158] The Russians also pursued policies of Russification, privileging the Russian language in a variety of ways.[159]

When the Russian Empire fell, Ukraine was able to enjoy a brief period of independence. The Rada they established refused to support the broader revolution that was ongoing in Russia, and claimed independence. Ukraine became a point of competition between Russia and countries to the West. Germany provided Ukraine military support.[160] Eventually, the Germans overthrew the government and installed another government in its place.[161] The far western areas of Ukraine, which had mostly been part of the Austro-Hungarian Empire were incorporated into the Second Polish Republic and the bulk of Ukraine became one of the Soviet Socialist Republics. Ukraine suffered greatly under Stalinist rule. Most obviously the *holodomor* or famine that was the result of Stalinist policies was responsible for the deaths of millions.[162] Two decades after the Bolsheviks reclaimed Eastern Ukraine, the Molotov-Ribbentrop pact allowed the Soviets to annex Eastern Galicia.[163]

As in Georgia, following the death of Stalin, Ukraine had greater autonomy, though the degree oscillated depending on the policies of the CPSU. And, again similar to Georgia a dissident nationalist movement emerged or increased its prominence. The political and economic liberalization processes of *Glasnost* and *Perestroika* played out in Ukraine as

---

[156] Kollmann, 68; Magocsi, *A History of Ukraine*, 212–13.
[157] Zenon E. Kohut, *Russian Centralism and Ukrainian Autonomy: Imperial Absorption of the Hetmanate, 1760s–1830s*, vol. 66 (Harvard Ukrainian, 1988).
[158] Serhy Yekelchyk, *Ukraine: Birth of a Modern Nation* (Oxford University Press, 2007), 34.
[159] Yekelchyk, 56–57.
[160] Joshua A. Sanborn, *Imperial Apocalypse: The Great War and the Destruction of the Russian Empire* (Oxford University Press, 2014), 229–30.
[161] Magocsi, *A History of Ukraine*, 488–89.
[162] Andrew Wilson, *The Ukrainians: Unexpected Nation* (Yale University Press, 2015), 144.
[163] Yekelchyk, *Ukraine*, 2007, 132.

well.[164] The liberalization of politics allowed opposition movements and civil society to develop, and nationalist groupings such Rukh mobilized substantial support. However, unlike in Georgia where the nationalist leaders positioned themselves to take control, it was a Communist party official, Leonid Kravchuk, who seized the opportunities provided by the weakening authority of the Soviet Union and positioned himself to govern Ukraine during the first years of its independence.

Kravchuk and the Origins of Ukrainian Neutrality

In the earliest period after independence, Ukraine steered an independent path. While Ukraine was heavily involved in founding the CIS, they never officially ratified. Moreover, they focused mainly on economic not political issues and did not join many other agreements related to regional organizations. Ukraine sought to maximize its political autonomy despite its economic dependence on Russia and other CIS countries.[165]

The rule of Ukraine's first president, Kravchuk, was relatively short-lived, from 1990 to 1994. During this period Ukraine was swept up in the cultural politics of independence. Initially, elite coalitions remained relatively stable. A neutral path and the attempts to preserve Ukraine's newfound sovereignty were motivated by elites whose position in the initial years after independence was threatened mainly by competition from Russia and not from domestic sources.[166] Kravchuk won his initial election by a landslide based on a "Grand Bargain" between different political factions representing both nationalists and the existing political elites.[167] Political competition in Ukraine was for the first two years after independence relatively low; elites could be sure of their position in the power structures.

From 1991 to 1992, the Verkhovhna Rada, the Ukrainian parliament, operated under the Soviet Constitution. This initially preserved the unity and power of Ukrainian elites during the early period of transition.[168] According to D'anieri it was the desire to preserve economic and political privileges that prompted Ukrainian elites to pursue independence at this point.[169] Gorbachev and later Yeltsin were pursuing reforms that would undermine the economic and political interests

---

[164] Yekelchyk, chapter 9; Magocsi, *A History of Ukraine*, chapter 49.
[165] Kuzio, "Geopolitical Pluralism," 85–86; Hale, *Foundations of Ethnic Politcs*, 199–200.
[166] Abdelal, *National Purpose in the World Economy*, 117–18.
[167] Wilson, *The Ukrainians*, 183.
[168] Paul J D'Anieri, *Understanding Ukrainian Politics: Power, Politics, and Institutional Design* (M. E. Sharpe, 2007), 75.
[169] D'Anieri, *Understanding Ukrainian Politics*, 77–78.

of these actors by removing price controls, and instituting ownership laws that would have reduced the rent-seeking capabilities of Ukrainian elites. Kravchuk was president and his ally, Fokin, served as the prime minister.[170] This stable political environment provided a basis for Kravchuk to adopt an autonomous position in regard to Russia. Kravchuk had a relatively firm grip on power.

Meanwhile, the Ukrainian economy remained dominated by political influence. Government ownership of property remained ubiquitous, and rent-seeking was widespread. Following the partial liberalization of the economy and the transition to capitalism, corruption was rampant in Ukrainian society, including at the highest levels.[171]

This political stability was short-lived, however. Rivals in other branches of government emerged. Politics during the period from 1992 to 1994 became fiercely contested. Leonid Kuchma emerged as a political rival to Kravchuk as financial crisis caused a breakdown of elite unity.[172] Kuchma, a member of the Rada, had strong links with industry in Eastern Ukraine. In 1992, Prime Minister Fokin was forced from the office and Kuchma was installed in the position.[173] During the period of Kuchma's rivalry with Kravchuk, Kuchma adopted a pro-Russian stance.[174] For example, he arranged meetings between Russian and Ukrainian business leaders seeking to promote integration of Eastern Ukraine and Russia.[175]

Kuchma was seen as a pro-Russia candidate both in Ukraine and in Russia. The presidential election of 1994 was closely contested. Kuchma began to appeal to the more Russo-centric east and Kravchuk to the west.[176] Kuchma promised a pro-Russian foreign policy. In the end Kuchma was to win a closely fought election in the second round, by primarily gaining support from Eastern Ukraine.[177]

Kuchma and a Surprising Continuance of Neutrality

In his inauguration speech, Kuchma stated "Ukraine's self-isolation and its voluntary refusal to campaign vigorously for its own interests in the Eurasian space was a serious political mistake, which caused great

---

[170] D'Anieri, *Understanding Ukrainian Politics*, 81.
[171] D'Anieri, *Understanding Ukrainian Politics*, 64–65.
[172] H. E. Hale, "Regime Cycles," *World Politics* 58, no. 1 (2005): 148–49.
[173] D'Anieri, *Understanding Ukrainian Politics*, 81.   [174] Wilson, *The Ukrainians*, 193.
[175] "Vestrecha promeshlennikov Rossii i Ukraini," *Kommersant*, June 16, 1994.
[176] Wilson, *The Ukrainians*, 193–94.
[177] Central Election Commission of Ukraine, www.cvk.gov.ua/pls/vp1999/webproc0 (last accessed May 25, 2011).

damage, above all to the national economy."[178] He went on to argue for close economic and political relationships with Russia.[179] However, this was not the path that was ultimately pursued by Kuchma. Kuchma quickly established his authority and power in the domestic sphere, and shifted away from his earlier pro-Russian position.[180] While Kuchma made a few concessions to Russia, such as giving up Ukraine's nuclear arsenal and formally agreeing to Russian control over the Black Sea fleet, he mostly continued a relatively autarchic path.

Kuchma united the competing factions within Ukraine, in part through economic and political patronage. He provided opportunities for his former political rivals. For example, Kravchuk was able to join the pro-Kuchma business and political grouping the Social Democratic Party, led by Kuchma's ally and former prime minister Medvedchuk.[181] Kuchma was quick to appoint regional leaders and governors who were his clients, further cementing political control and stability.[182] Kuchma concentrated more power in the hands of the president.[183] On top of this formal institutional centralization, informal institutions were also increasingly centralized. Way identifies multiple sources of regime strength and weakness, and along all the dimensions – including control of elections, the media, strength of the executive and strength of the opposition – Kuchma was in a stronger position and faced less competition than the president had in the earlier period.[184]

Evidence for the consolidation of political power is found when examining the regions that Kuchma won in the 1999 presidential election. During this election Kuchma won in places that would later be strongholds of the Orange Revolution such as Ivano-Frankivsk (92.3 percent of vote in second round) and in Lviv (91.6 percent of the votes in the second

---

[178] Leonid Kuchma, quoted in Zbigniew Brzezinski and Paige Sullivan, *Russia and the Commonwealth of Independent States: Documents, Data, and Analysis* (M. E. Sharpe, 1997), 273.
[179] Brzezinski and Sullivan, 273.
[180] Richard Sakwa and Mark Webber, "The Commonwealth of Independent States, 1991–1998: Stagnation and Survival," *Europe-Asia Studies* 51, no. 3 (1999): 402.
[181] A. Wilson, *Virtual Politics: Faking Democracy in the Post-Soviet World* (Yale University Press, 2005), 136.
[182] Kimitaka Matsuzato, "All Kuchma's Men; The Reshuffling of Ukrainian Governors and the Presidential Election of 1999," *Post-Soviet Geography and Economics* 42, no. 6 (2001); Hale, "Regime Cycles," 150.
[183] R. K. Christensen, E. R. Rakhimkulov, and C. R. Wise, "The Ukrainian Orange Revolution Brought More Than a New President: What Kind of Democracy Will the Institutional Changes Bring?," *Communist and Post-Communist Studies* 38, no. 2 (2005): 213.
[184] L. Way, "Authoritarian State Building and the Sources of Regime Competitiveness in the Fourth Wave: The Cases of Belarus, Moldova, Russia, and Ukraine," *World Politics* 57, no. 2 (2005): 242.

round), but also in what were strongholds of pro-Russian parties such as Donetsk (52.9 percent of vote in second round) and Dnipropetrovsk (56.35 percent of the vote in second round).[185]

Kuchma maintained or intensified the link between the economy and political power in a variety of ways. Kuchma also made use of political and economic patronage to reduce conflict and foster elite cooperation among oligarchs and politicians.[186] He extended the privatization process in a very untransparent manner, which allowed him to buy off rivals. Another tool Kuchma often used was blackmail.[187] The use of these tools also had the effect of reducing the level of competition, culminating with the reform of the constitution to give Kuchma greater powers.

The oil and gas industry also directly implicated Russia in the processes of elite rent-seeking. The gas industry provided multiple avenues for rents: elites could engage in arbitrage because Russia set the prices; they could take advantage of selective payments and liabilities, with private companies gaining access to lucrative clients and leaving the least profitable to the state or gaining state guarantees; engage in barter and price manipulations; and they could outright steal Russian gas.[188] Rent-seeking was central part of the political system in Ukraine at this point, and Russia played an important role here.

The developments in this period strongly indicate that there is a political, as well as an ideological component, that explains shifts in Ukrainian elite policies toward Russia. Kuchma was pro-Russian while he was caught up in political competition with Kravchuk. After he established a dominant and relatively secure position in Ukrainian political scene, he moved away from his previous integrationist stance.

Breakdown of the Elite Alliance and the Return to Russia's Sphere

The appointment of Victor Yushchenko, former Head of the Central Bank, as prime minister in 1999 marked the beginning of the end for the coalition that Kuchma had constructed. As prime minister, Yushchenko adopted the stance of a reformer and began to enact policies that undermined rent-seeking opportunities for the industrial oligarchs.

---

[185] Central Election Commission of Ukraine, www.cvk.gov.ua/pls/vp1999/webproc0 (last accessed May 25, 2011).

[186] Lucan Way, "Kuchma's Failed Authoritarianism," *Journal of Democracy* 16, no. 2 (2005): 135–37.

[187] K. A. Darden, "Blackmail as a Tool of State Domination: Ukraine under Kuchma," *East European Constitutional Review* 10, no. 2/3 (2001): 67–71.

[188] Margarita Mercedes Balmaceda, *The Politics of Energy Dependency: Ukraine, Belarus, and Lithuania between Domestic Oligarchs and Russian Pressure*, vol. 40 (University of Toronto Press, 2013), 109.

He removed subsidies and began to open up the privatization process, including to foreign, particularly Russian, investors.[189] This triggered opposition from elites who benefited from the existing structures, and felt threatened by the reforms. Once opposition developed, the fate of Yushchenko as PM was quickly decided. In 2001 he faced a vote of no confidence that he lost overwhelmingly.[190] However, the outcome was not Yushchenko's isolation, but a split in the ruling elite. Yushchenko, who had in the past been happy to rise through the ranks, was now cast as an outsider; his dismissal was a catalyst for overt opposition to the existing regime.

The split in the regime had immediate electoral impacts. Yushchenko formed a temporary alliance with his deputy prime minister and oligarch Yulia Tymoshenko.[191] Yushchenko became head of the Nasha Ukraina Party and Tymoshenko continued her leadership of the Batkivshchyna Party. In the 2002 Rada elections, the pro-Kuchma parties struggled to return a pro-presidential majority. The opposition led by Yushchenko received a plurality of votes but failed to form a majority coalition and control the Rada.[192]

Seeing the elite alliance that he had constructed fall apart, Kuchma turned to a new, more pro-Russian policy. He supported the Common Economic Space, hoping to win the support of Russia and the pro-Russian population in Eastern Ukraine with the aim of securing victory for his anointed successor, Yanukovych, in the 2004 presidential elections.[193] Guaranteeing his political position and ensuring that his successor won were of vital importance to Kuchma because of the threat of prosecution from the political opposition.[194] In other words, he moved away from his and Ukraine's previous stance of neutrality to a "multivectored," but in reality pro-Russian, position.[195]

Kuchma changed his general policy toward Russia three times over the course of a decade. This variation is a good indicator that a relatively fast moving process played a role in determining his political attitudes rather

---

[189] A. Åslund and M. McFaul, *Revolution in Orange: The Origins of Ukraine's Democratic Breakthrough* (Carnegie Endowment for International Peace, 2006), 14.
[190] T. Kuzio, "From Kuchma to Yushchenko Ukraine's 2004 Presidential Elections and the Orange Revolution," *Problems of Post-Communism* 52, no. 2 (2005): 29.
[191] Steven Levitsky and Lucan Way, *Competitive Authoritarianism: Hybrid Regimes after the Cold War* (Cambridge University Press, 2010), 217–18.
[192] S. Birch, "The Parliamentary Elections in Ukraine, March 2002," *Electoral Studies* 22, no. 3 (2003): 528–30.
[193] Tor Bukkvoll, "Private Interests, Public Policy: Ukraine and the Common Economic Space Agreement," *Problems of Post-Communism* 51, no. 5 (2004): 20.
[194] T. Kuzio, "Regime Type and Politics in Ukraine under Kuchma," *Communist and Post-Communist Studies* 38, no. 2 (2005): 176.
[195] Hale, *Foundations of Ethnic Politics*, 204–5.

than ideology and personal beliefs alone. While the historical and cultural and normative development of Ukraine obviously played a powerful part in determining Ukraine's course, the more medium-term variation that surrounds politics are also influencing outcomes. When these leaders were faced with political threat in an environment where rent-seeking was rampant they became more willing to surrender sovereignty.

The Orange Revolution

As in Georgia, Ukraine was to undergo a rapid and somewhat unexpected democratic transition. The initial process evolved similarly to events in Georgia. A rigged presidential election trigged mass protests, demanding the removal of the government.[196] Eventually this mass pressure forced Kuchma's successor Yanukovych to hold new, fairer elections. The result, this time, was a narrow victory for Yushchenko over his rival for the presidency and Kuchma's appointed successor – Yanukovych.[197]

During the second 2004 election campaign between Yanukovych and Yushchenko, Russia provided resources to Yanukovych to improve his electoral prospects. Some have estimated that Russia provided him with financial support of roughly US$300 million.[198] Russian "political technologists" associated with the Kremlin, such as Gleb Pavlovsky, provided political support and advice to Yanukovych.[199] In addition, the Russian media, widely viewed in parts of Ukraine, provided a pro-Yanukovych spin on events.[200] This election is a clear demonstration of the role external actors can play to improve the chances of political survival of an elite actor.

After the Orange Revolution, the elites of Ukraine were split between those who supported either Yushchenko or Tymoshenko and those that supported Yanukovych.[201] Tymoshenko was initially appointed as acting prime minister by Yushchenko. Henry Hale accurately describes the period as being characterized by multiple competing patronage

---

[196] Tucker, "Enough!," 538.   [197] www.cvk.gov.ua/postanovy/2005/p0015_2005.htm.
[198] P. D'Anieri, "The Last Hurrah: The 2004 Ukrainian Presidential Elections and the Limits of Machine Politics," *Communist and Post-Communist Studies* 38, no. 2 (2005), 535.
[199] Alexander Etkind and Andrei Shcherbak, "The Double Monopoly and Its Technologists: The Russian Preemptive Counterrevolution," *Demokratizatsiya* 16, no. 3 (2008): 234; A. Wilson, *Ukraine's Orange Revolution* (Yale University Press, 2005), 100.
[200] Etkind and Shcherbak, "Double Monopoly," 234.
[201] In contrast to Georgia, where only UNM had widespread support, all three major politicians in the post-Kuchma era were able to establish successful political parties, as can be seen by electoral results see Central Election Commission of Ukraine: www.cvk.gov.ua.

blocs.[202] During this process there were also intense efforts to change the institutional structure of Ukrainian politics. The result was to weaken the presidency and strengthen the parliament; both sides had incentives to do so. The intense divisions between the groups meant that increasing the number of veto points was a potential protection against their opponents, as it could prevent rivals from consolidating power.[203] Both sides agreed to further weaken institutions, effectively increasingly factional competition.

During and immediately following the Orange Revolution, Tymoshenko became a symbol of Ukrainian nationalism, characterized by the traditional peasant braids in her hair and her stories and beliefs about the importance of learning and using the Ukrainian language. Coming from a Russian speaking family, she recounted how she realized the importance of learning Ukrainian and using it in everyday life.[204] However, her ability to maintain this strongly nationalist stance consistently was undermined by the competition among different elite groups. In the Rada elections of 2006 and 2007, Tymoshenko was competing for the nationalist vote with her rival among the Orange factions associated with President Yushchenko. In this situation to win a nationwide vote she also had to appeal to nonnationalist sentiments in Eastern Ukraine. At times her rivalry with Yushchenko led Tymoshenko to change tack, adopting a more pro-Russian stance. As Prime Minister Tymoshenko made jokes at the expense of her president while signing a new oil deal with Russia and Vladimir Putin.[205] Tymoshenko's bloc was in part responsible for preventing a resolution being passed condemning Russian intervention in Georgia in 2008, and adopted rhetoric that emphasized a degree of compromise with Russia.[206]

Furthermore, the competition between the various factions led Tymoshenko to informally undermine the institutions that had already been formally weakened. Tymoshenko took advantage of her position as prime minister to weaken the opposition. She did this through patronage, but in manner that further split the elite in Ukraine.[207] The previous

---

[202] Hale, *Patronal Politics*, 325–31.
[203] Robert K. Christensen, Edward R. Rakhimkulov, and Charles R. Wise, "The Ukrainian Orange Revolution Brought More Than a New President: What Kind of Democracy Will the Institutional Changes Bring?," *Communist and Post-Communist Studies* 38, no. 2 (2005): 216–17.
[204] Yulia Tymoshenko, "Yuliya Tymoshenko: pust kazhdii lubit rodnoi yazik nashego gosudarstvo," www.tymoshenko.ua/ru/article/yulia_tymoshenko_mova.
[205] Pavel Korduban, "Putin, Tymoshenko Agree on Gas and Deride Yushchenko, Saakashvili," *Jamestown Foundation Eurasia Monitor*, 6, 220.
[206] Taras Kuzio, "Strident, Ambiguous and Duplicitous," *Demokratizatsiya: The Journal of Post-Soviet Democratization* 17, no. 4 (2009): 363–67; Hale, *Patronal Politics*, 337–39.
[207] Serhiy Kudelia, "The Sources of Continuity and Change of Ukraine's Incomplete State," *Communist and Post-Communist Studies* 45, no. 3 (2012): 425.

Kuchma regime was able to use blackmail and patronage to construct a system that was relatively controlled and unitary.[208] However, under the new conditions of competition such techniques served to further exacerbate divisions and reduce the strength and structures of the state. For patronage politics to function there has to be credible commitments from both sides of the relationship. Given the behavior of both sides of the elite divide such trust was hard to establish.

The legacy of this competition was that Ukraine, in 2010, had moved away from its tendency to pursue autarchic relationships with both Russia and the EU to one that was seeking accommodation. The major leader who most consistently identified with the nationalist aspirations – Yushchenko – was quickly isolated by the majority of political forces in Ukraine. His ostensible ally Tymoshenko abandoned him.[209] In the first round of the 2010 presidential election, Yushchenko finished fifth with a little over 5 percent of the vote.[210] The winner after two rounds was pro-Russian Yanukovych winning 48.85 percent to Tymoshenko's 45.47 percent.[211] The nature of the Ukrainian regime had changed again.

Yanukovych, 2010–13

After the election, Yanukovych quickly moved to alter parliamentary procedure and then the constitution itself to increase his power and eliminate some forms of conflict. Yanukovych and his allies altered the rules surrounding the formation of governments, allowing individuals to change their political faction within the Rada.[212] By coopting individuals from other parties, Yanukovych's party, the Party of Regions, was able to form a coalition with a political majority. This cooptation was achieved in part through the use of bribery and corruption; the Party of Regions offered bribes to members of the opposition faction to defect.[213] The 2004 constitution, which had weakened the presidency, returned to its previous form.[214] Yanukovych consolidated his position.

---

[208] Darden, "Blackmail as a Tool of State Domination"; K. Darden, "The Integrity of Corrupt States: Graft as an Informal State Institution," *Politics and Society* 36, no. 1 (2008): 35.
[209] Henry E. Hale, "The Uses of Divided Power," *Journal of Democracy* 21, no. 3 (2010): 85–87.
[210] Ofitsiini Resultati Vibiriv 2010, Pershii Tur, *Ukrainska Pravda*, accessed May 20, 2014, www.pravda.com.ua/articles/2010/01/18/4630133/.
[211] Central Election Commision of Ukraine, accessed May 20, 2014, www.cvk.gov.ua/pls/vp2010/WP0011.
[212] "Rada razreshila koalitsiyu tushek," *Ukrainska Pravda*, March 9, 2010.
[213] Author interview, Member of Parliament (Batkivshchyna), October 2, 2010.
[214] Serhiy Kudelia, "Maidan and Beyond: The House That Yanukovych Built," *Journal of Democracy* 25, no. 3 (2014): 21.

Institutionally, Yanukovych was arguably in a stronger position than his predecessor. However, underlying contestation persisted. Yanukovych used administrative and legal techniques to attack the opposition, particularly opposition leaders such as Tymoshenko and Lutsenko.[215] However, the strength of the Party of Regions was not dramatically increased, and in the 2012 parliamentary elections their support dropped.[216] The threat to Yanukovych's political survival was ever present.

In 2010, some polling suggested that more Ukrainians preferred closer relations with Russia than they had previously.[217] These preferences were reflected in the policies of the new president, Yanukovych. Where he had previously served in a government that had aimed to preserve Ukraine's independence, Yanukovych, as leader, was comfortable pursuing policies that preserved limitations on Ukrainian sovereignty such as re-signing leases giving Russia control over the Black Sea fleet.[218] That said, he demanded better terms on the gas deal with Russia, and at the height of his strength refused to join the Customs Union.[219] The final result of the process was a country that asserted itself in the international sphere even less than it had in the past.

Euromaidan, Resistance, and Russian Intervention

The state of affairs that developed early in Yanukovych's rule could not continue indefinitely as many of the underlying fractures in Ukrainian society and political institutions persisted.[220] As Yanukovych's rule proceeded, he directed the benefits of his power to a narrower set of actors.[221] This contrasts with the less targeted patronage networks that existed under Yuschchenko.[222] The narrow clan around Yanukovych was able to extract billions from the Ukrainian economy. Much of this was related

---

[215] Serhiy Kudelia, "When External Leverage Fails," *Problems of Post-Communism* 60, no. 1 (2013): 33–36.
[216] Election results 2012, *Ukrainska Pravda*, www.pravda.com.ua/articles/2012/10/29/6975859/.
[217] Razumkov Center, www.uceps.org/eng/poll.php?poll_id=305.
[218] "Factbox: Russia's Black Sea Fleet in Ukraine," *KyivPost*, accessed May 16, 2014, www.kyivpost.com/content/ukraine/factbox-russias-black-sea-fleet-in-ukraine-65036.html.
[219] Balmaceda, *Politics of Energy Dependency*, 40:148.
[220] Serhiy Kudelia, "The House That Yanukovych Built," *Journal of Democracy* 25, no. 3 (2014); Serhiy Kudelia, "The Sources of Continuity and Change of Ukraine's Incomplete State," *Communist and Post-Communist Studies* 45, no. 3 (2012).
[221] Svitlana Tuchynska, "All in the Family," *KyivPost*, March 2, 2012, www.kyivpost.com/content/ukraine/all-in-the-family-123517.html.
[222] Serhiy Kudelia, "The Sources of Continuity and Change of Ukraine's Incomplete State," *Communist and Post-Communist Studies* 45, no. 3 (2012): 425.

to the gas trade, creating a symbiotic relationship with Russia who was a major player in this area. Yanukovych continued rent-seeking practices that developed in Ukraine since independence, some of these were particularly related to the gas industry. Russia's ability to set gas prices allowed local actors with the correct political connections to benefit from buying or selling gas either at a low or high price.[223]

The narrowing of support resulted in the collapse of his regime, ultimately. Oligarchs crucial for mobilizing political support defected as they no longer benefited from Yanukovych's rule.[224] While this is an "off-the-equilibrium-path" outcome – Yanukovych should have maintained a broad enough patronage network to preserve his position – it serves to demonstrate how essential it is for elites and rulers to maintain their patronage network and support. These fractures came to a head in late 2013 when Yanukovych rejected an EU association agreement in favor of a closer relationship with Russia.[225] This was something of a reversal of his previous position. This rejection can again be directly tied to the economic leverage and rent-seeking opportunities provided by Russia, as they offered Yanukovych a better gas deal and to purchase Eurobonds.[226] The response was immediate; pro-European forces began protests in Kyiv.[227]

The government tried to repress these protests, and in response to this repression, the protests shifted from pro-EU to an antigovernment movement. However, the repression did not end the protests and, eventually, Yanukovych was removed from power. Shortly after coming to an agreement with leading opposition politicians to loosen his control on the apparatus of power, Yanukovych fled Kyiv.[228] First, Yanukovych ran first to his hometown of Donetsk and from there eventually made his way to Russia.[229] This marked the end of the Yanukovych regime.

---

[223] Åslund, "Oligarchs, Corruption, and European Integration," 65.
[224] Andrew Wilson, *Ukraine Crisis: What It Means for the West* (Yale University Press, 2014), 53; Thomas Ambrosio, "The Fall of Yanukovych: Structural and Political Constraints to Implementing Authoritarian Learning," *East European Politics* 33, no. 2 (2017): 203.
[225] David M. Herszenhorn, "Facing Russian Threat, Ukraine Halts Plans for Deals with EU," *New York Times*, November 21, 2013, sec. World / Europe, www.nytimes.com/2013/11/22/world/europe/ukraine-refuses-to-free-ex-leader-raising-concerns-over-eu-talks.html; "Azarov Otkazalsya Ot Coglasheniya Ob Assotsiatsii s ES," *Ukrainska Pravda*, November 23, 2013, www.pravda.com.ua/rus/news/2013/11/21/7002657/.
[226] Samuel Charap and Timothy J. Colton, *Everyone Loses: The Ukraine Crisis and the Ruinous Contest for Post-Soviet Eurasia* (Routledge, 2018), 121.
[227] "Ukraintsi samoogranizovalis, shtobi podderzhat kurs na Evropu," *Ukrainska Pravda*, November 22, 2013.
[228] "Yanukovych velitil v Kharkov," *Ukrainska Pravda*, February 21, 2014.
[229] "Yanukovych: Moego vnuka xoteli lustripovat," *Ukrainska Pravda*, February 28, 2014.

In the first weeks and months after the Yanukovych regime ended, the new ruling faction had to deal with little formal political contestation over the control of the central government. After the ousting of Yanukovych, the opposition members of the Verkhovna Rada voted for a new government. There was little or no opposition. The Verkhovna Rada voted for Arseniy Yatsenyuk as prime minister with a record total of 371 vote in favor.[230] This included support from many members of the Party of Regions. Some former members of the Party of Regions had formed a new bloc, the Group for Economic Development, supporting the government.[231] Remaining members of the Party of Regions accused the new ruling coalition of using patronage techniques, offering economic and material incentives, to achieve this.[232] The short-run dominance of the new ruling party was demonstrated as Poroshenko, a prominent businessman and politician, easily won the subsequent presidential election, without the necessity of a run-off.[233]

In late February 2014 a series of protests in Crimea called for secession from Ukraine.[234] Russia responded with a surreptitious military intervention.[235] In a February press conference in Russia, Yanukovych claimed that Russia had the "right" to intervene due to historical connections and agreements, but also that Russia "should and is obliged to act."[236] Russia also presented to the UN Security Council a letter from Yanukovych requesting Russian military intervention.[237] Russian forces with local support spread their influence and control throughout Crimea. Russia preserved the support of actors on the ground in Crimea. Local leaders supported Russian intervention and worked to legitimate it, organizing a referendum

[230] "Rada naznachila Yatsenyuka premerom," *Ukrainska Pravda*, February 27, 2014.
[231] "Kinakh anosiruet novuyu fraktsiyu v Rade uzhe v ponedelnik," *Ukrainska Pravda*, February 24, 2014.
[232] "Efremov obyavil o perexode regionalov v oppozitsiyu," *Ukrainska Pravda*, February 24, 2014.
[233] Shaun Walker, "Petro Poroshenko Wins Ukraine Presidency, According to Exit Polls," *Guardian*, May 26, 2014, sec. World news, www.theguardian.com/world/2014/may/25/petro-poroshenko-ukraine-president-wins-election.
[234] "V Sevastopole Russkii blok formiruyet Otryadi samooboroni, pod gorodom-protivotankovie ezhi," *Ukrainska Pravda*, February 23, 2014; Howard Amos, "Ukraine Crisis Fuels Secession Calls in Pro-Russian South," *Guardian*, February 24, 2014, sec. World news, www.theguardian.com/world/2014/feb/23/ukraine-crisis-secession-russian-crimea.
[235] Andrew Higgins and Steven Erlanger, "Gunmen Seize Government Buildings in Crimea," *New York Times*, February 27, 2014, www.nytimes.com/2014/02/28/world/europe/crimea-ukraine.html.
[236] "Yanukovych vyletil v Kharkov," *Ukrainska Pravda*, February 21, 2014.
[237] "Putin poluchil prosbu Yanukovych ob ispolzovanii VC RF na Ukraine," *Ria Novosti*, March 4, 2014.

for independence.[238] Finally, the referendum voted 95 percent in favor of secession from Ukraine.[239] Shortly after the referendum, Russia formally annexed the region.[240] This referendum was likely influenced by fraud, with claims of premarked ballots being used.[241] However, polls from the region show widespread support for Russian action, and little opposition.[242] Russian actions and presence emboldened and increase support from locals in Crimea.[243] It is undoubted that Russia achieved its goals with reasonable support from the local population.

During these events local actors constrained the ability of central politicians to assert their authority in the region, thus further inhibiting the ability of the government to maintain authority. Local actors removed recalcitrant politicians from political authority, such as Prime Minister of the Region Anatolii Mohyliov and his government.[244] Mohyliov was replaced with an even more pro-Russian politician Sergey Aksyonov, with a reputed past as an extortionist and criminal.[245] Local politicians switched their support from Kyiv to Russia because, in the words of one politician: "When instead of talks, Kiev launched criminal investigations (against Crimea's new leaders) . . . That is when it became clear: how long can we live in isolation?"[246] Local actors played a crucial role in the establishment of hierarchy. These actors were motivated to do this because of fear of what the central authorities would do. They facilitated the surrender of sovereign rights and acted as a constraint on other political actors, reducing their ability to choose complete sovereign independence.

[238] "RPT-INSIGHT-How the Separatists Delivered Crimea to Moscow," March 13, 2014, http://in.reuters.com/article/2014/03/13/ukraine-crisis-russia-aksyonov-idINL6N0M93AH20140313.
[239] Chris Morris, BBC News, and Kiev, "Crimea 'Votes for Russia Union,'" BBC News, accessed November 3, 2014, www.bbc.com/news/world-europe-26606097.
[240] "Putin Signs Laws on Reunification of Republic of Crimea and Sevastopol with Russia," TASS, accessed November 3, 2014, http://en.itar-tass.com/russia/724785.
[241] Aleksandar Vasovic and Adrian Croft, "US, EU Set Sanctions as Putin Recognises Crimea Sovereignty," March 17, 2014, http://in.reuters.com/article/2014/03/17/ukraine-crisis-crimea-referendum-idINDEEA2G00620140317.
[242] Pew Research Center, "Despite Concern about Governance, Ukrainians Want to Remain One Country," www.pewglobal.org/files/2014/05/Pew_Global_Attitudes_Ukraine-Russia_Report_FINAL_May_8_2014.pdf.
[243] Charap and Colton, *Everyone Loses*, 127–31.
[244] RFE/RL's Ukrainian Service, "Crimean Parliament Fires Government, Sets Autonomy Referendum," *RadioFreeEurope/RadioLiberty*, February 27, 2014, sec. Ukraine, www.rferl.org/content/ukraine-turchynov-appeal-calm-crimea-buildings-seized/25278931.html.
[245] Tim Sullivan and Yaras Karmanau, "Crimea's New Leader, a Man with a Murky Past," Associated Press, March 8, 2014.
[246] "RPT-INSIGHT – How the Separatists Delivered Crimea to Moscow."

Russia has suffered costs for annexing Crimea. The West has placed economic and political sanctions on Russia.[247] Russia will also need to foot the bill of incorporating Crimea into the Russian Federation.[248] However unsuccessfully, Russia went to great lengths to co-opt norms of self-determination by staging a referendum in the region.[249] This indicates an awareness of the normative constraints placed on territorial expansion, even if these norms have not been internalized. Russia expanded in an environment that placed strong normative restrictions on territorial expansion, which the response from the Western powers demonstrates. Arguably Russia was prepared to pay this high price despite a restrictive international environment. Crimea and the Black Sea fleet are important for Russia's security.

Outside of Crimea, Russia interfered in other parts of Eastern Ukraine.[250] Pro-Russian local actors seized government buildings in cities in the Donbas region of Ukraine.[251] In other parts of the country, there were protests and violent clashes between pro-Russian or secessionist groups and groups supporting the central government in Ukraine. This was followed by the declaration of a separatist People's Republic in Donetsk.[252] Russia was able to manipulate subnational actors in attempt to maintain control of Ukrainian sovereignty.

As the separatist movement spread, the importance of rent-seeking as well as patronage can be inferred from the actions of the new Ukrainian government. Oligarchs Ihor Kolomoyskiy and Serhiy Taruta were sent to control potentially secessionist or unstable regions of the country.[253] The purpose of doing so was revealed by a pro-Maidan politician and presidential adviser Yuri Lutsenko who claimed that the purpose of

---

[247] Mark Landler, Annie Lowrey, and Steven Lee Myers, "Obama Steps Up Russia Sanctions in Ukraine Crisis," *New York Times*, March 20, 2014, www.nytimes.com/2014/03/21/us/politics/us-expanding-sanctions-against-russia-over-ukraine.html.

[248] Illan Berman, "How Russia Is Paying for the Crimean Annexation," *Foreign Affairs*, accessed September 7, 2016, www.foreignaffairs.com/articles/ukraine/2015-09-08/paradise-lost-crimea.

[249] William W. Burke-White, "Crimea and the International Legal Order," *Survival* 56, no. 4 (2014).

[250] Bureau of Public Affairs Department of State, Office of Website Management, "Evidence of Russian Support for Destabilization of Ukraine," Press Release|Media Note, US Department of State, April 13, 2014, www.state.gov/r/pa/prs/ps/2014/04/224762.htm.

[251] Bridget Kendall, diplomatic correspondent, and BBC News, "Pro-Russians Storm Ukraine Buildings," BBC News, accessed November 7, 2014, www.bbc.com/news/world-europe-26910210.

[252] Andrew Higgins, "In Eastern Ukraine, a One-Building, Pro-Russia Realm Persists Despite Criticism," *New York Times*, April 9, 2014, www.nytimes.com/2014/04/10/world/europe/ukraine-russia.html.

[253] Maria Danilova, "Ukrainian Oligarchs Get Key Posts in Bid for Unity," Associated Press, March 7, 2014.

appointing oligarchs to positions of power was "to stabilize the situation in regions using not only state resources, but also private resources for the integrity of Ukraine."[254] Taruta stated on accepting the position of Governor of Donetsk that "My decision is a desire to protect our country. We Ukrainians have the right to a strong and united Ukraine."[255] In Dnipropetrovsk, Kolomoyskiy offered a cash reward for turning in "foreigners" engaging in subversive acts.[256]

Kolomoyskiy's political trajectory is revealing. Initially, upon gaining control of Dnipropetrovsk, Kolomoyskiy was fiercely anti-Russian, funding militias to fight Russian-backed rebels and engaging in a slanging match with the Kremlin, calling Putin a "schizophrenic of short stature."[257] However, as events progressed, his relationship with the government in Kyiv deteriorated. At one point, militias associated with Kolomoyskiy even seized buildings belonging to state-run energy company in an attempt to secure his economic interests and was eventually dismissed from his post as governor.[258] At the same time, Kolomoyskiy began advocating for compromise with the breakaway regions and Russian proxies, stating in a television interview, "We have two subjects that we do not recognize, but that have achieved a certain success, unfortunately. They exist."[259] Kolomoyskiy, when aligned with the central authorities, resisted Russia's control over Ukraine. When he was competing with them for the control of economic rents, Kolomoyskiy was more accepting of Russian control in the region.[260]

Taruta, seemingly, had little success in Donetsk. Donetsk remained the most unstable region in Ukraine, with the strongest pro-Russian separatist movement, the Donetsk People's Republic. Eventually, however, another oligarch, Rinat Akhmetov, stepped in; using factory workers employed by his factories he managed to restore some control over the

---

[254] Andrew Cramer, "Ukraine Turns to Its Oligarchs for Political Help," *New York Times*, March 2, 2014.
[255] Maria Danilova, "Ukrainian Oligarchs Get Key Posts in Bid for Unity," Associated Press, March 7, 2014.
[256] Carol Matlack, "In this Ukrainian Region, an Oligarch Governor Pays to Keep Peace," *Businessweek Bloomberg,* May 6, 2014.
[257] "Ukraine: An Oligarch Brought to Heel," *Financial Times*, accessed September 14, 2016, www.ft.com/cms/s/0/b0b04474-d232-11e4-a225-00144feab7de.html.
[258] "Ukraine Leader Fires Powerful Oligarch Kolomoisky as Regional Chief," Reuters, March 25, 2015, www.reuters.com/article/us-ukraine-crisis-oligarch-idUSKBN0ML0CG20150325.
[259] "Internal Rifts in Ukraine Play in Russia's Favor – Analysts," accessed September 14, 2016, https://themoscowtimes.com/articles/internal-rifts-in-ukraine-play-in-russias-favor-analysts-45110.
[260] Kolomoisky is also rumored to have been an important backer of Zelenskiy the television celebrity turned politician who defeated Poroshenko in 2019.

city of Mariupol.[261] This is despite earlier accusations of Akhmetov supporting the separatists. While Taruta was wealthy, his political network, being affiliated with Batkivshchyna, in Donetsk was much weaker than Akhmetov, who had strong past links with the Party of Regions. Politics and patronage remain important for elites to be able to mobilize and guarantee mass support; they cannot simply coerce such support.

In an excellent study of the Ukrainian civil war, Yuri Zhukov has documented the importance of rent-seeking and economic factors for increasing support for the Moscow backed rebels.[262] Consistent with the more general argument presented here, Zhukov finds that regions that were most economically dependent on subsides and other forms of rent-seeking displayed substantially stronger support for rebels and connections to Russia.

The military campaign that Ukraine waged against Russian-backed separatists has up to this point resulted in a stalemate. Russia provoked and provided backing to the separatist forces in the Donbas region. However, the Ukrainian military seemed to be progressing until they suffered a catastrophic defeat in August 2014. In the buildup to the parliamentary election, Poroshenko pursued a peace deal with Russia. In 2014, the September 5 peace deal was favorable to the Russian-backed separatists, and may provide a means for Russia to control aspects of policy in that region at least.[263] Since 2014, little has changed, and the Donbas now resembles other de facto states or frozen conflicts.[264]

Fluctuations in Ukrainian policy have been revealing. Ukrainian sovereignty was drastically reduced in some areas, most notably Crimea. Russia paid higher costs of control, too. Russia will be forced to pay the costs of incorporating Crimea. Russian leadership and elites faced sanctions from Western governments. In addition, there are probably reputational costs to be paid. With Russia's client removed from power and a government resistant to Russian influence in place, the results echo those of other cases. Greater resistance resulted in greater reliance on coercion from Russia, and a further reduction of Ukrainian sovereignty. Rent-seeking and competition played an important role in how events played out. The changing nature of Yanukovych's patronage network

---

[261] Stepan Kravchenko and Henry Meyer, "Ukraine's Top Oligarch Walks a Fine Line," *BusinessWeek*, July 10, 2014, www.businessweek.com/articles/2014-07-10/in-ukraine-separatist-war-rinat-akhmetov-walks-fine-line.
[262] Yuri M. Zhukov, "Trading Hard Hats for Combat Helmets: The Economics of Rebellion in Eastern Ukraine," *Journal of Comparative Economics* 44, no. 1 (2016).
[263] "Ukraine's Unhappy Ceasefire," *Economist*, September 7, 2014, www.economist.com/blogs/easternapproaches/2014/09/war-ukraine.
[264] Tetyana Malyarenko and Stefan Wolff, *The Dynamics of Emerging De-Facto States: Eastern Ukraine in the Post-Soviet Space* (Routledge, 2019).

plausibly contributed to his downfall, while the desire to hold on to power and access to rents drove certain actors to provide greater support to Russian intervention than they had previously.

Conclusion

The above analysis has shown that elite policy toward sovereignty has varied depending on the nature of political competition. When there has been a high level of competition between elite factions, some elites have been more inclined to give in to the demands of the outside power, in this case, Russia. This finding offers something of a counter to those that see the policies of these countries being driven exclusively by long-run cultural and historical variables. The fluctuations in policy in both countries demonstrate that more proximate causes and motivations play an important role in explaining the emergence of hierarchy.

Moreover, the same leader often opted for different approaches to Russia depending on his political situation, helping further discount cultural or ideational factors. Both Kuchma and Shevardnadze changed their policies toward Russian hierarchy. In Kuchma's case, he oscillated from pro-Russian to anti-Russia to pro-Russian again, all in correspondence with the level of political competition he faced from other elites in Ukraine. It would be difficult to attribute these changes over the space of a decade to sudden change in ideological predilection.

The preceding chapter has shown that even in cases with strong historical and cultural variables determining attitudes to sovereignty, the policies of leaders can vary with the political climate. A key factor was the ability of nonstate and subnational actors to play an important role in the manifestation of hierarchy. In both Georgia and Ukraine, the external power – Russia – was also able to bargain with actors outside of the central state apparatus. The next chapter will build off these initial findings, demonstrating in greater detail that competition and rent-seeking can influence subnational actors as well, and these subnational actors will contribute to reduced sovereignty either by pressuring the central government or allying themselves directly with the external power. Explicitly incorporating subnational actors into an explanation of hierarchy is a significant departure of existing theoretical explanations that have focused on unitary actors or central governments.

This chapter also demonstrated the importance of mass politics. Protests and uprisings in various forms foiled the ability of elites to act freely. Governments fell in Georgia during the Rose Revolution and twice in Ukraine. The changes of ruler or regimes altered the relationship with Russia. These events help demonstrate that external support is often insufficient to guarantee political survival, even if it can often help. Instead, the bargains struck with external actors and the benefits that accrue from them are likely to stable and persistent if they also have the support from a significant portion of society. This raises the question of what, then, leads societal actors to support elites trading away sovereignty. A subsequent chapter will demonstrate that not only does political competition tied to rent-seeking change the incentives of elites, it also changes the incentives of their constituents. This provides an additional impetus or at least removes a constraint on elites opting to surrender sovereignty.

3 Subnational Politics and Sovereignty in Post-Soviet Georgia

In 2005, in Akhalkalaki, a Georgian town on the mountainous Armenian border, the ethnically Armenian population staged a protest against the removal of the local Russian military base. While Georgia has had problems with ethnic secessionism, the protest was not about secession; protesters demanded Russian involvement in the region and in Georgia, but also affirmed their commitment to a territorially unified Georgia.[1] In contrast, when similar bases were removed from other regions in Georgia, there was little or no political action by the inhabitants. Indeed, other regions of Georgia were actively hostile to a Russian military presence. While unusual in the Georgian context, the Akhalkalaki protest was not a random event. Local actors had an interest in maintaining a Russian presence in Georgia.

This chapter explains why some groups in Georgia supported Russian interventions and diminishment of Georgian sovereignty and why others did not. The variation in attitudes and actions toward Russia in Georgia is reflective of the varied attitudes in other regions within post-Soviet states. For example, residents of Eastern Ukraine have, on average, a more positive view of Russia than other regions of the country. As has been demonstrated in earlier chapters, subnational or regional actors often played a central role in the surrender of sovereignty, either by acting as a constraint on the choices of the central government or serving as a direct bridgehead for the external power. This chapter aims to demonstrate the reasons for their actions and how these might be tied to rent-seeking and political contestation. Understanding the actions and choices of subnational actors and social groups is important for understanding instances when states surrender sovereignty in former Soviet countries and in other regions of the world.

Highlighting the role of subnational actors is a major departure from theories of hierarchy that emphasized either unitary state actors or central governments. The focus on political competition and rent-seeking is also

[1] Civil.ge, March 13, 2005.

different from the literature on post-Soviet integration, which, while it often highlights regional differences within countries, tends to emphasize cultural, identity, and historical differences. The cultural and historical variables are important, but they miss the role that the distribution of power and resources can play in actor choices and preferences even at the subnational level. Overall, this chapter demonstrates that we cannot just focus on central governments when attempting to understand the development and functioning of hierarchy, as subnational actors in certain circumstances are able to contract directly with outside actors or influence the types of relationships central governments establish.

Russia had ample reason to want closer integration with Georgia and reasons to meddle in the subnational regions of the country. Interference with these regions allowed Russia to pressure the central Georgian authorities. As discussed in previous chapters, Russia had an incentive to maintain control over Georgia because Georgia's position in the Southern Caucasus and on Russia's borders makes it important for its broader security interests in the region. However, Russia also had direct interests in most of the subnational regions in Georgia, and Georgia contains several regions that for institutional or demographic reasons might be vulnerable to outside manipulation. Among these are the autonomous regions Abkhazia and Adjara, in which Russia has security interests due to their access to the Black Sea. Kvemo Kartli and Samtskhe Javakheti, regions with territorially concentrated minorities, are also actual or potential transport hubs. We can safely assume that all these regions would be subject to Russian interventions if possible.

This chapter explores the nature of domestic politics and how it shaped elite responses to Russia in these four regions. A cross-case analysis is combined with within-case observation and narratives, drawing on secondary and primary sources such as contemporary media reports and interviews conducted in Georgia. In weaker states, external actors are sometimes supported by the central government elites. In other instances, external actors are supported by the subnational actors who seek allies against their own central governments. In regions where local elites saw themselves as competing with the center over rents, they supported Russian intervention and the subordination of Georgia to Russian authority in certain spheres. In contrast, where elites were not competing over rents, either because of the absence of rent-seeking or because of cooperation among elites, then there was little support for Russia.

The cases below highlight that there were two moments – critical junctures – when the Georgian state had the opportunity to reorganize its relationship with subnational actors. During the period of Soviet collapse, relationships with the center were structured in particular ways that then determined the nature of political competition that followed. The second moment was following the Rose Revolution, a time of political upheaval which also provided opportunities to renegotiate relationships between the center and different regions.

Subnational Variation and Georgia

Georgia provides a rich set of cases for controlled comparison, allowing an in-depth examination of the factors that lead to subnational support for hierarchy. This chapter will explore variation among four regions to test the relevance of political autonomy, secessionism, possessing an ethnicity different from the majority of Georgians, the level of economic development relative to one another and the type of political competition. Such subnational analysis allows the researcher to relax the assumption that variables equally affect all parts of a country.[2] The variation between different regions within Georgia provides strong evidence about the origins of hierarchy that could not be captured in a national-level analysis.

Two of the regions under study possessed autonomous status during the Soviet period – Adjara and Abkhazia. The autonomous political institutions of these regions marked them as somewhat separate from the rest of the country and created clear political identities for the regions. The institutional dynamics of these regions made them prone to separatism and provided an institutional base for political elites to elicit support from outside powers.[3] Following the collapse of the Soviet Union, both Adjara and Abkhazia displayed high levels of support for a Russian presence in Georgia. However, after the Rose Revolution, Adjara displayed little interest in supporting Russia while Abkhazia remained hostile to Georgia and supportive of Russia. Institutional autonomy, then, is neither necessary nor sufficient to account for high levels of support for Russia. We can gain insight into the source of this support by comparing these regions over the two time periods.

In both Kvemo Kartli and Javakheti, non-Georgian ethnics are demographically dominant. Kvemo Kartli has a high concentration of Azerbaijanis, while Javakheti has a high concentration of Armenians. Ethnicity can demarcate groups, making them political relevant units of

---

[2] Richard Snyder, "Scaling Down: The Subnational Comparative Method," *Studies in Comparative International Development* 36, no. 1 (2001).

[3] Steven Lee Solnick, *Stealing the State: Control and Collapse in Soviet Institutions*, Russian Research Center Studies 89 (Harvard University Press, 1998); Philip G. Roeder, *Where Nation-States Come From: Institutional Change in the Age of Nationalism* (Princeton University Press, 2007); B. Coggins, "Friends in High Places: International Politics and the Emergence of States from Secessionism," *International Organization* 65, no. 3 (2011).

analysis.[4] It does so in multiple ways: ethnicity tends to be correlated with common symbolic understandings that create perceptions of a common fate; ethnicity is often associated with linguistic differences that create barriers to communication with other groups; there are often visible physical differences; and ethnicity tends to be correlated with other important factors such as social status and economic well-being.[5] The general effect of ethnicity is compounded in Georgia by the territorial concentration of ethnic minorities. Territorial concentration increases both an ethnic group's organizational capabilities and their sense that such mobilization is legitimate.[6] For these reasons, the Armenian and Azerbaijani populations of these two regions are potentially important political actors in their own right.

An explanation for hierarchy based on ethnicity might suggest that these non-Georgian groups would both seek external support as protection against the Georgian majority. However, the responses of these two groups have differed substantially. In Javakheti the Armenians have been particularly supportive of Russian involvement in Georgian politics. Meanwhile, the Azerbaijanis of Kvemo Kartli have been more inclined to support Georgian sovereignty. This chapter leverages this variation to explore the determinants of support for hierarchy at a subnational level.

Beyond ethnic identity and institutional autonomy, it is possible to discount further potential causes of support for Russia using both sets of cases together (Table 3.1). Of the three cases that have supported Russia, only Abkhazia has secessionist tendencies. While economic development was lower in Javakheti, it was relatively high in both Abkhazia and Adjara. Political competition over rent-seeking is the only variable that cannot be discounted as potentially causing support for an outside patron in all cases.

In the cases under study competition over rents emerged from a variety of contexts, making it unlikely that the effect was caused by some other unobserved variable. In the case of Abkhazia, it was a product of institutional autonomy and the ethnic structure of the Soviet Union. In Adjara, competition developed from institutional autonomy and the ambitions of the local strongman. In Javakheti, competition resulted from geographic isolation and ethnic difference. In Kvemo Kartli, despite ethnic difference and suffering at the hands of Georgian militias in the early 1990s, competition was absent, as was support for Russia. The ability of the Georgian leadership to remove

---

[4] Henry E. Hale, *The Foundations of Ethnic Politics: Separatism of States and Nations in Eurasia and the World*, Cambridge Studies in Comparative Politics (Cambridge University Press, 2008), 42–44.
[5] Hale.
[6] Monica Duffy Toft, "Indivisible Territory, Geographic Concentration, and Ethnic War," *Security Studies* 12, no. 2 (2002).

Table 3.1 *Comparison of Adjara, Abkhazia, Javakheti, and Kvemo Kartli, 1991–2012*

	Ethnic differences	Secession	Autonomy	Competition over rents	Support for Russia
1991–2004					
Abkhazia	Yes	Yes	Yes	High	Yes
Adjara	No	No	Yes	High	Yes
Javakheti	Yes	No	No	Moderate	Yes
Kvemo Kartli	Yes	No	No	Low	No
2004 to present					
Abkhazia	Yes	Yes	Yes	High	Yes
Adjara	No	No	Yes	Low	No
Javakheti	Yes	No	No	Moderate	Yes
Kvemo Kartli	Yes	No	No	Low	No

Azerbaijanis from positions of authority before the fall of the Soviet Union meant that they could be coopted into a patronage network, removing competition.[7] These differences make it possible to focus on competition and its interaction with rent-seeking to explain support for hierarchy.

Two Autonomous Regions: Adjara and Abkahazia

The federal political structures of the Soviet Union have had a significant effect on how political competition and conflict have developed in the post-Soviet states.[8] The Soviet Union generally based its subnational organization around ethnic groups.[9] The Soviet Union constructed a system of federal political units with differing degrees of authority and autonomy. By allowing regions to form their own governments and perform other governance functions, the autonomous political structures of the Soviet Union provided a basis for political and economic organization. These structures created incentives to secede or make moves to preserve autonomy when the opportunity arose.[10]

---

[7] J. Wheatley, "Managing Ethnic Diversity in Georgia: One Step Forward, Two Steps Back," *Central Asian Survey* 28, no. 2 (2009): 126.
[8] Christoph Zurcher, *Post-Soviet Wars: Rebellion, Ethnic Conflict, and Nationhood in the Caucasus* (New York University Press, 2007); Valerie Bunce, *Subversive Institutions: The Design and the Destruction of Socialism and the State*, Cambridge Studies in Comparative Politics (Cambridge University Press, 1999).
[9] Rogers Brubaker, "Nationhood and the National Question in the Soviet Union and Post-Soviet Eurasia: An Institutionalist Account," *Theory and Society* 23, no. 1 (1994).
[10] Bunce, *Subversive Institutions*.

Autonomous political institutions have the potential to create a high level of political competition with central authorities.[11] Autonomy can create incentives to resist other political centers in order to preserve freedom of action. Autonomy also created structures that constituted a separate identity and increased organizational capacity, further raising the level political competition. Central governments often possess incentives to try to remove autonomy from regions, which can exacerbate tensions and competition.[12]

Adjara and Abkhazia are similar in many ways. Both were among the more prosperous regions of Georgia in the Soviet period.[13] They both relied on a mixture of tourism and agriculture. Both are border regions situated on the Black Sea. Both had populations of several hundred thousand. These similarities hold many potential causes of support for hierarchy constant across the two cases.

However, Adjara is unusual because it was one of the few autonomous republics in the Soviet Union that lacked a titular minority. The lack of a titular minority in Adjara provides the opportunity to assess the effects of political autonomy absent ethnic differences. These republics with titular minorities were more separatist and more vulnerable to Russian manipulation, as ethnic identity and nationalism worked to exacerbate political competition and the perception that political power was tied to economic outcomes. However, the effect is a matter of degree. Adjara, where the ethnic majority was Georgian and politically dominant, was supportive of Russia during the 1990s as well. The variation within Adjara across time helps discount ethnicity as a primary cause of local elites supporting hierarchy.

Adjara: A Case of Shifting Support

During the 1990s and early 2000s, Adjaran elites aligned themselves with Russia. After the opening of Georgian society and its economy following the Rose Revolution, Russian influence diminished, culminating with the removal of the Russian military base from Batumi in 2006. Adjara is predominantly made up of ethnic Georgians and not secessionist, helping

---

[11] Bunce; Roeder, *Where Nation-States Come From*; David S. Siroky and John Cuffe, "Lost Autonomy, Nationalism and Separatism," *Comparative Political Studies* 48, no. 1 (2014); Zurcher, *Post-Soviet Wars*.
[12] Siroky and Cuffe, "Lost Autonomy."
[13] Daur Bargandzhia, "The Economy: Traditional and Modern," in *The Abkhazians: A Handbook*, ed. Brian Hewitt (Curzon Press, 1998); Georgi Derluguian, "The Tale of Two Resorts: Abkhazia and Ajaria before and since the Soviet Collapse," in *The Myth of "Ethnic Conflict": Politics, Economics, and "Cultural" Violence*, ed. Beverly Crawford and Ronnie Lipschutz, 261–92 (University of California Press, 1998).

to discount two alternative factors that could explain why groups surrender sovereignty to an outside power. The changes in relation to Russia were accompanied by lower levels of contestation over rent-seeking between the regional elites and the central government.

Before the Rose Revolution, political conflict for the ruling elite in Adjara was highly linked to economic factors. There was conflict between the central authorities of Georgia and Adjara over tax revenue, rents, and institutional autonomy.[14] Culturally, Adjarans had ceased to be so differentiated from the center. While in the past they had been Muslim, by the 1990s Adjarans in the political and urban centers of lower Adjara were increasingly orthodox Christians.[15] Many Muslims today have or talk of converting to the religion of their ancestors – Christianity. Nor is there a history of conflict between the region and other parts of Georgia. If anything, potential historical resentment should have motivated Adjarans away from Russia and toward Georgia.[16] It was the Russian Empire that had in conflict in the region which had largely sided with the Ottoman Empire and later the Soviet Union that imposed collectivization and other forms of oppression. Adjara's support for Russia in this period was clearly motivated by concerns regarding political survival and rent-seeking opportunities.

Abashidze's Rule and Support for Russia, 1991–2003   During the 1990s, the ruler of Adjara, Aslan Abashidze lobbied the central government to adopt policies that reduced Georgian sovereignty. While this was consistent with President Shevardnadze's policy preferences during the early or mid-1990s, by the late 1990s or early 2000s, it conflicted with many of the positions adopted by the central government. Abashidze provided support for Russian control over Georgian sovereignty throughout his rule, and by doing so hindered the government's desired policy evolution during this later period.

Abashidze directly and indirectly supported Russian control over Georgian sovereignty. While Shevardnadze worked to remove Russian military forces from Georgia, Abashidze even provided Russian forces with a building free of charge.[17] On numerous occasions, Abashidze used his power to lobby on behalf of Russia. During the late 1990s he called the policies of Shevardnadze "irresponsible" in response to Shevardnadze's

---

[14] Ghia Nodia, "Georgia: Dimensions of Insecurity," in *Statehood and Security: Georgia after the Rose Revolution*, ed. Robert Legvold and Bruno Coppieters (MIT Press, 2005), 54.
[15] Mathijs Pelkmans, *Defending the Border: Identity, Religion, and Modernity in the Republic of Georgia* (Cornell University Press, 2006), 113–20.
[16] T. De Waal, *The Caucasus: An Introduction* (Oxford University Press, 2010), 146.
[17] "Rossiya-Gruziya. Premier Sdaet Armiyu," *Pravda*, May 23, 1998.

criticism of the role of the Russian military in Georgia.[18] Abashidze also expressed his support of Russian leadership when the Georgian parliament formed a committee to discuss leaving the Commonwealth of Independent States, referring to this as an "unconstructive position."[19] In 1998, as Shevardnadze attempted to reassert Georgian sovereignty over its borders, Abashidze threatened to mobilize his own border guard if Russian forces were removed as border guards.[20] Abashidze also negotiated with Russia a visa regime for the region, more flexible than that enjoyed by other Georgians, described by the central government as a "violation of Georgian sovereignty."[21] By supporting Russian claims, Abashidze increased Russian control over some areas of Georgian sovereignty.

Abashidze's support for Russian hierarchy developed in an environment where there was both contestation with the central government in Tbilisi and high levels of rent-seeking. Abashidze was a prominent local figure in the early 1990s when Gamsakhurdia, the first president of Georgia, tasked him with restoring order to Adjara.[22] However, once Abashidze had disposed of his local rivals, he worked to preserve his and the region's independence from central government control.[23] He took control of the local military forces, declared a state of emergency, and formed militias that he used to control the region.[24] Abashidze's growing power in the region provided a base for contestation between the Georgian government and Abashidze and his supporters.

Control over Adjara allowed Abashidze to become one of the most powerful politicians in the country, viewed as a potential successor to Shevardnadze.[25] Abashidze competed for control over institutions with Shevardnadze. He established the political party Revival which became the second largest in the country. While the party was initially prepared to form a coalition with Shevardnadze, this relationship soon broke down.[26] Despite flaws in Georgian elections, political contestation was very real. The Commission for Security and Cooperation in Europe described the

---

[18] "Alsan Abashidze 'Igrayet v Otkrituyu,'" *Chernomorskaya Pressa*, April 8, 1998.
[19] E. Krutikov, "Lider Adzharii Obvinayet Tbilisi v Provakastiach," *Segodnia*, December 17, 1997.
[20] Y. Golotyuk, "Russia Retreats from First Frontier," *Current Digest of the Post-Soviet Press* 51, no. 4 (1999).
[21] "Uneasy Neighbors Watchful at Each Other," Civil.ge, December 18, 2003.
[22] Elizabeth Fuller, "Aslan Abashidze: Georgia's Next Leader?," *RFE/RL Research Report* 2, no. 44 (1993).
[23] Fuller. [24] Zurcher, *Post-Soviet Wars*, 203–4.
[25] Fuller, "Aslan Abashidze: Georgia's Next Leader?"; Jonathan Wheatley, *Georgia from National Awakening to Rose Revolution: Delayed Transition in the Former Soviet Union*, Post-Soviet Politics (Ashgate, 2005).
[26] Wheatley, *Georgia from National Awakening to Rose Revolution*, 124.

1999 parliamentary election, contested primarily by Shevardnadze's Citizen Union of Georgia (CUG) party and Abashidze's Revival party, as "open but bruising."[27] Abashidze prevented the CUG from advertising in Adjara, organizing hostile crowds, and even blocking high-ranking officials from visiting the region, while the CUG responded in kind.[28] Abashidze was in frequent opposition to the central government through formal avenues of political contestation.

Informal political contestation was also rife as both the central government and Adjaran elites tried to assert authority over institutions controlled by the other. In 1997, Abashidze accused Tbilisi of multiple assassination attempts.[29] In 1999, Adjaran elites declared important political positions such as the mayor of Batumi, the regional capital, to be locally elected officials, no longer appointed by Tbilisi.[30] Tbilisi and Adjara also contested control of tax and customs revenue from the region.[31] For example, in 2003, the government of Shevardnadze criticized the Adjaran government's refusal to transfer taxes from the region to the central government budget.[32] In response, Abashidze complained that Adjara had "received [in transfers] much less from the central government than had been approved by budget documents."[33] Tax revenue was also a source of conflict between Adjara and the center after Saakashvili took control of Georgia in 2003.[34] These examples demonstrate that control over institutions was fiercely contested by elites.

When compromises were made between the center and the region they were as much indicative of informal solutions to political contestation as genuine cooperation. In other words, they can better be understood as bargains rather than collaborations. For instance, in return for Abashidze pulling out of the 2000 presidential elections, Adjara was granted more autonomy.[35] Shevardnadze would not have made this concession if

---

[27] Commission on Security and Cooperation in Europe, "Georgia's Parliamentary Election," October 31, 1999, 5.
[28] Commission on Security and Cooperation in Europe, 5–6.
[29] E. Krutikov, "Lider Adzharii Obvinayet Tbilisi v Provakastiach," *Segodnia*, December 17, 1997.
[30] David Losaberidze, Konstantine Kandelaki, and Niko Orvelashvili, "Local Government in Georgia," in *Developing New Rules in the Old Environment*, OSI/LGI, 2001, 309.
[31] Ghia Nodia, "Georgia: Dimensions of Insecurity," in Legvold and Coppieters, *Statehood and Security*, 54.
[32] "Prezident Shevardnadze podverg kritike vlasti Adzharii," *KavkazskiiUzel*, March 12, 2003.
[33] V. Janashia, "Prezident Adzharii Opustoshaet Gruzinskuyu Kaznu," *Kommersant*, May 19, 2003.
[34] Civil.ge, "Tbilisi, Batumi Discuss Financial Problems," January 22, 2004, www.civil.ge/eng/article.php?id=6069.
[35] Darrell Slider, "Recent Elections in Georgia: At Long Last, Stability?," *Demokratizatsiya* 8, no. 4 (2000): 517.

contestation were not an issue. Supporting this assertion is the fact that Abashidze made minimal effort to help get Shevardnadze elected; indeed, the Adjaran media controlled by Abashdize continued to report negatively about Shevardnadze and his policies during the election.[36] In addition, Adjara was the only region where the ruling party did not control local election officials.[37] What support Abashidze provided was bought somewhat grudgingly.

These moments of compromise and bargaining may have been signs of a client-patron relationship between Shevardnadze and Abashidze.[38] However, the relationship was as competitive as clientelistic. Abashadize saw as threatening, and directly refused, many of Shevardnadze's blandishments and attempts to co-opt him. When offered the position of prime minister, Abashidze explained his rejection of this proposal by stating that he "was not the type to dive into an empty swimming pool."[39] This behavior stood in contrast with Shevardnadze's relationship with other powerful elites. For example, Levan Mamaladze, the governor of Kvemo Kartli, was a member of Shevardnadze's political party CUG and preferred to operate "under Shevardnadze's umbrella."[40] This sort of relationship was clearly absent in Abashidze's case. The time when cooperation was highest was in 2003, when both sides were threatened by Saakashvili's movement.[41] A strong or clear example of a patron-client relationship with Shevardnadze across Abashidze's tenure is not clearly discernable.

Numerous opportunities existed for the ruler of Adjara to engage in rent-seeking. Adjara is a hub for transporting goods from Turkey into Georgia, and rent-seeking was widespread. One estimate is that customs officials could make US$2,000 a day through corruption.[42] In addition to the customs revenue, those who controlled the political apparatus restricted free access to the economic market; any substantial business operating in the region had to get approval from Abashidze.[43] Local elites transferred little of the taxes and customs gained to the central government. When Abashidze was removed from power he was charged with

---

[36] ODHIR, Georgia: Presidential Election Final Report, April 9, 2000, 14.
[37] ODHIR, Georgia: Presidential Election Final Report, 9.
[38] Julie A. George, "The Dangers of Reform: State Building and National Minorities in Georgia," *Central Asian Survey* 28, no. 2 (2009): 141.
[39] Quoted in Fuller, "Aslan Abashidze: Georgia's Next Leader?," 26.
[40] Wheatley, *Georgia from National Awakening to Rose Revolution*, 120.
[41] Marten, *Warlords*, 74.
[42] Mathijs Pelkmans, *Defending the Border: Identity, Religion, and Modernity in the Republic of Georgia* (Cornell University Press, 2006), 180.
[43] International Crisis Group, "Saakashvili's Ajara Success: Repeatable Elsewhere in Georgia?," August 18, 2004.

embezzling 98 million lari or roughly US$57.6 million.[44] Rent-seeking was highly profitable for elites in Adjara.

The benefits of Abashidze's relationship with Russia were clear. Political power allowed Abashidze to control rents from the region. He believed that by supporting the Russian presence in Georgia he was securing a guarantee of his continued control of the region's institutions.[45] The potential that Russia might support Abashidze deterred Shevardnadze from attempting to force Abashidze from power. Russia provided direct material support as well. When Tengiz Kitovani, a warlord associated with the central government, threatened to intervene in Adjara and remove Abashidze, the Russian military backed Abashidze, and this action was deterred.[46] Some of his militia, which formed the base of Abashidze's power, received Russian training.[47] Russian protection consolidated Abashidze's position in Adjara and his continued access to rents.

The nature of Georgian-Adjaran relations changed dramatically in 2003 when Georgia underwent a regime transition, the Rose Revolution. Contestation between Adjara and the central authorities was initially exacerbated as Saakashvili attempted to reassert control over Georgia's regions. Saakashvili mobilized the military at the border of the Adjaran Republic. Abashidze responded with resistance, destroying the bridges into the Republic.[48] Abashidze visited Moscow seeking protection from his patron.[49] He also visited Yerevan at the same time as Russian defense minister Sergei Ivanov.[50] Anti-Abashidze activists feared that Russia would intervene on his behalf.[51] In response to his visit to Yerevan, Saakashvili stated that Shevardnadze and Abashidze "might use the Russian military forces deployed in Armenia and Batumi [Adjarian capital] to provoke civil confrontation in Georgia."[52] Ultimately, Russia

---

[44] Civil.ge, "Ex-Adjaran Leader Sentenced to Prison in Absentia," January, 22, 2007, www.civil.ge/eng/article.php?id=14486; Ria Novosti, "Georgia Sentences Ex-Adjaran Leader to Prison Term in Absentia," January 22, 2007.

[45] Jonathan Aves, *Georgia, from Chaos to Stability?* (Royal Institute of International Affairs Russia and Eurasia Programme, 1996), 42; Nodia, "Georgia: Dimensions of Insecurity," 51.

[46] Fuller, "Aslan Abashidze: Georgia's Next Leader?"; Georgi Derluguian, *Bourdieu's Secret Admirer in the Caucasus: A World-System Biography* (University of Chicago Press, 2005), 232.

[47] Civil.ge, "46 of Abashidze's Elite troops flee Adjara," Civil Georgia, April 27, 2004.

[48] EurasiaNet.org, "Georgia: Popular Protest Topples Ajarian Leader," 2004, www.eurasianet.org/departments/insight/articles/eav050504.shtml.

[49] "Saakashvili's Ajara Success: Repeatable Elsewhere in Georgia?"

[50] Civil.ge, "Abashidze's visit to Armenia increases oppositions fear," November 11, 2003, www.civil.ge/eng/article.php?id=5479.

[51] "Our Adjaria to Fight against Aslan Abashidze till 'Victorious End,'" *Caucasian Knot*, accessed May 21, 2014, http://eng.kavkaz-uzel.ru/articles/2446/.

[52] Civil.ge, "Abashidze's Visit to Armenia Increases Oppositions Fear."

did not preserve Abashidze's position but secured his safe passage to Moscow.[53] His actions clearly demonstrate Abashidze's belief that Russia could play the role of protector.

Abashidze's overthrow provides a further demonstration of the importance of maintaining mass support. After the Rose Revolution, society in Adjara saw changes in the rest of the country which, combined with Abashidze's increasingly narrow distribution of benefits to Adjaran society, further alienated them from Abashidze's patronage network.[54] Large-scale protests by locals against Abashidze developed.[55] These protests ultimately played a large role in Abashidze's downfall. Elites rely on mass support to sustain their power. Without such support, protection derived from an external relationship was not enough to preserve Abashidze's position.

Diminished Support for Russia after the Rose Revolution, 2004–10
After the removal of Abashidze, the Georgian government transformed Adjara's relationship with the center. The region's autonomy was curtailed; Adjara was governed by members of Saakashvili's ruling United National Movement (UNM) party, and the central government could legally appoint the leader of the region and disband the region's parliament. Contestation between the center and the region declined dramatically.

The Adjaran economy benefited from transfers from the center, and foreign investment and tourism increased.[56] Saakashvili made the region a development priority of the government, and there has been cooperation between the region and the center in pursuing these aims.[57] The elite in Adjara possess a sense of similar purpose and belief about the pursuit of development through a constructive relationship with the central government. Local UNM elites saw the central government as a source of opportunities, and claimed they shared a common purpose with the center.[58]

After the Rose Revolution, Adjaran elites were unconcerned about contestation with the center.[59] While the Adjaran budget is partially funded by local revenue-raising activities it is also funded by the central

[53] Nodia, "Georgia: Dimensions of Insecurity," 56.
[54] Mitchell, "Georgia's Rose Revolution," 2004, 6.
[55] "15,000 Protestors Demand Abashidze's Resignation," Civil Georgia, May 5, 2004.
[56] Joshua Kucera, "Batumi: Making a Break for the West," *Eurasia Insight*, May 17, 2007.
[57] Author interviews with head of UNM in Adjara Gela Dekanidze; Chair of Legal Affairs, Supreme Council of Adjara Petre Zambakhidze; and Chairman Batumi City Council Giorgi Kirtadze, Batumi, August 2010.
[58] Author interviews with Gela Dekanidze; Chair of Legal Affairs, Supreme Council of Adjara Petre Zambakhidze; and Chairman Batumi City Council Giorgi Kirtadze, Batumi, August 2010.
[59] J. A. George, "Minority Political Inclusion in Mikheil Saakashvili's Georgia," *Europe-Asia Studies* 60, no. 7 (2008).

government. There have been accusations that a development fund set up by Saakashvili for use by certain elites in the region was being mismanaged.[60] While rent-seeking and corruption clearly remained, contestation between Adjara and Tbilisi over these rent-seeking opportunities was low.

The lack of political contestation meant that elites in the region no longer needed Russian support to maintain their economic position, and they began to resist Russian encroachment on Georgian sovereignty along with the center. For example, two Russian officers were arrested in Batumi for espionage.[61] The negotiation and ultimate withdrawal of the Russian military base in 2006 produced little response, where previously the threat of its removal, or discussion of withdrawing from the Commonwealth of Independent States, had produced an outcry from Abashidze.[62] Russian influence diminished substantially after the Rose Revolution.

Early during Georgian independence, Adjaran society faced the choice of being robbed by the center or the local strong man. The choice of the local strong man came with the possibility of Russian protection in domestic contestation for elites and their clients. Following the Rose Revolution, Saakashvili presented a new opportunity for prosperity to the Adjarans, who gave up support of a Russian presence and the corrupt local potentate Abashidze.

Abkhazia: Consistent Support for Russia

In Abkhazia the ethnic Abkhaz supported Russia out of a desire to preserve the privileges they had enjoyed during the Soviet Union. The potential move from an autonomous republic where the Abkhaz dominated political power and the corresponding economic benefits to, at best, a republic defined in civic terms providing equal access to residents of other ethnicities threatened the position of local political elites. This threat continues to exist, creating a high level of support for Russian involvement in Abkhazia and Georgia.

In some ways, Abkhazia's close relationship with Russia is surprising. For much of the Soviet period Abkhazia was subjected to a program of Georgianization and anti-Abkhazian policies.[63] Abkhazians had for long

---

[60] Eter Turadze, "Ajaria: Concern over Missing Funds," *Caucasus Reporting Service* 263 (2004).
[61] Civil.ge, "Georgia Arrests Russian Intelligence Operatives," September 26, 2006, www.civil.ge/eng/article.php?id=13657.
[62] This contrasts with Abashidze's response to earlier proposals to remove the base and the reaction in other regions of Georgia such as Javakheti.
[63] Timothy Blauvelt, "Abkhazia: Patronage and Power in the Stalin Era," *Nationalities Papers* 35, no. 2 (2007).

periods of time been opposed to rule from Russia.[64] In addition, it has been demonstrated that attitudes toward Russia vary along with attitudes to political elites and the economy.[65] This fluctuating relationship points to the difficulty in tying Abkhazia's current relationship to historical and cultural trends, though these do play a role.

Russia's influence over Abkhazia has been high since the collapse of the Soviet Union. Abkhazia has relied on the Russian ruble as its primary currency.[66] This weakens Georgian sovereignty, as adopting another country's currency reduces the capacity of the subordinate state to set its own monetary policy.[67] A Russian military presence has been a feature of life in Abkhazia since the end of the Soviet Union. Russia has kept a permanent peacekeeping force there since the civil war between Georgia and Abkhazia.[68] In 2008, Russia began construction of permanent military installations in the region.[69] Furthermore, large numbers of Abkhazians have accepted Russian citizenship; since 2000 Russia has issued passports to Abkhazian citizens.[70] Following the 2008 conflict in South Ossetia, Russian presence in the region has increased dramatically.[71]

Origins of the Relationship The cooperative relationship between Russia and the Abkhaz elite that exists today has its origins in the Soviet period. As the Soviet state weakened in the late 1970s and 1980s, the constituent parts of the USSR gained more autonomy.[72] Political contestation within constitutive units of the Soviet Union emerged. In this environment, the Georgian leadership, not the central Soviet authorities, were the more immediate threat to the Abkhaz.

Being the titular minority with its own republic meant that the Abkhaz had high levels of influence over the political life in the region, despite being a minority of the citizens within the Republic. The Abkhaz used their political power to increase their economic resources; they

---

[64] Stanislav Lakoba, "History: 18th Century–1917," in *The Abkhazians: A Handbook*, ed. Brian Hewitt (Curzon, 1999), 69.
[65] Kristin M. Bakke et al., "Dynamics of State-Building after War: External-Internal Relations in Eurasian de Facto States," *Political Geography* 63 (2018): 165–67.
[66] International Crisis Group, "Abkhazia Today," *Europe Report* 176 (2006).
[67] David Lake, *Hierarchy in International Relations* (Cornell University Press, 2009), 73–74.
[68] Dov Lynch and Royal Institute of International Affairs, *Russian Peacekeeping Strategies in the CIS: The Cases of Moldova, Georgia and Tajikistan* (Macmillan, 2000).
[69] International Crisis Group, "Abkhazia: Deepening Dependence," February 26, 2010.
[70] International Crisis Group, "Abkhazia Today."
[71] A. Cooley and L. Mitchell, "Abkhazia on Three Wheels," *World Policy Journal* 27, no. 2 (2010): 73–81.
[72] See Steven Lee Solnick, *Stealing the State: Control and Collapse in Soviet Institutions*, Russian Research Center Studies 89 (Harvard University Press, 1998).

monopolized political and bureaucratic positions in the Republic and dominated the police force.[73] During the Soviet period, Abkhazia's economy largely relied on tourism, the production of tobacco, wine and sugar, and the black market. The Abkhazians were able to use state power to preserve their position and limit competition from other ethnic groups such as the Georgians.[74]

Through much of the Soviet period, the government had pursued a policy of Georgianization of Abkhazia.[75] The transformation of the region's demographics threatened the political position of the Abkhaz. The Abkhaz had made up a minority of the population since 1945. The last Soviet Census conducted in 1989 showed the composition of the Republic to be 45 percent Georgian, 17 percent Abkhaz, with Russians and Armenians making up the bulk of the remainder of the population, each constituting around 14 percent.[76] In this environment, the connection between the Abkhaz ethnic identity and political power was a necessary condition of their continued economic welfare; loss of political power or even the opening up of the political process to ethnic Georgians would have resulted in a loss of rent-seeking opportunities as other groups increased their political power in the region.

In 1978, the Georgian nationalist opposition organized a series of protests demanding a privileged position for the Georgian language within the Republic and emphasizing Georgian nationalism.[77] This threat increased the Abkhaz elite's awareness of their vulnerability and reliance on external support and aid. Perceiving these protests as a threat to their position, the Abkhaz elites organized a series of counterprotests coupled with violent skirmishes with local Georgians.[78] These protests, in contrast to those of the Georgians, adopted a pro-Soviet stance.[79] The central authorities of the Soviet Union intervened on behalf of the Abkhaz. While Russia did not incorporate Abkhazia into Russia as the Abkhaz elites wished, they provided the Abkhaz with extra support, increased funding for the region, and appointed a Russian minister of the interior.[80]

During the 1980s, Zviad Gamsakhurdia began to direct his nationalism at ethnic minorities such as the Abkhaz, as much as the Soviet authorities.[81]

---

[73] Derluguian, "Tale of Two Resorts," 279.   [74] Derluguian, 269.
[75] Blauvelt, "Abkhazia."
[76] R. Clogg, "The Politics of Identity in Post-Soviet Abkhazia: Managing Diversity and Unresolved Conflict," *Nationalities Papers* 36, no. 2 (2008): 308.
[77] Jones, *Georgia*, 221.   [78] Derluguian, "Tale of Two Resorts," 270–71.
[79] D. Slider, "Crisis and Response in Soviet Nationality Policy: The Case of Abkhazia," *Central Asian Survey* 4, no. 4 (1985).
[80] Vicken Cheterian, *War and Peace in the Caucasus: Ethnic Conflict and the New Geopolitics* (Columbia University Press, 2008), 61.
[81] Jones, *Georgia*, 32.

In 1989, again responding from a perceived threat to their interests, the Abkhaz mobilized to demand improved political status within the Soviet Union as a Union Republic.[82] Georgian nationalist leaders responded with a counterdemonstration.[83] In an attempt to maintain order, the Soviet authorities resorted to violence to disperse the protests. The repression of the protesters resulted in 19 dead and 427 injured.[84] From this point on, Communist leaders in Georgia adopted more pro-independence and nationalistic policies. Elections were called in which participation was restricted to groups that had nationwide representation, effectively excluding ethnic minorities.[85] As described in the previous chapter, these elections brought Zviad Gamsakhurdia to power, as his Round table bloc won convincingly.

Soon after, Georgia achieved independence from the Soviet Union. The Abkhaz adopted a power-sharing arrangement within the Abkhazian parliament, reserving twenty-eight seats for the Abkhaz, twenty-six for Georgians, and eleven each for Russians and Armenians.[86] Such an arrangement would preserve a relatively privileged position for the Abkhaz.

After the warlords Kitovani, Sigua, and Ioseliani forced Gamsakhurdia from power, state authority continued to deteriorate, and outside of the capital the new rulers of Georgia had very little control. The central Georgian authorities responded by abolishing Abkhaz autonomy, reintroducing the 1921 Constitution. This action drove the Abkhaz into outright rebellion.[87] In Mingrelia, the region that borders Abkhazia and the homeland of the ousted Gamsakhurdia, supporters of Gamsakhurdia had begun an armed uprising. In August 1992, the Zviadists took Deputy Prime Minister Alexander Kavsadze hostage. After a failed attempt at negotiation one which involved Interior Minister Roman Guentsadze being kidnapped as well, Shevardnadze sent an armed force to resolve the situation.[88] The Abkhaz permitted the National Guard to enter Abkhazia with certain restrictions.[89] However, the National Guard violated the agreement and seized Sukhumi, the capital of the region.

It was at this point that Russia actively intervened. With Russia now providing military support, the Abkhaz were able to push the Georgian

---

[82] Cheterian, *War and Peace in the Caucasus*, 83–84; Stuart J. Kaufman, *Modern Hatreds: The Symbolic Politics of Ethnic War* (Cornell University Press, 2001), 103.
[83] Wheatley, *Georgia from National Awakening to Rose Revolution*, 43.
[84] Jones, *Georgia*, 32.   [85] Jones; Cheterian, *War and Peace in the Caucasus*.
[86] De Waal, *Caucasus*, 152.
[87] John Cuffe and David S. Siroky, "Paradise Lost," in *Secessionism and Separatism in Europe and Asia: To Have a State of One's Own* (Routledge, 2012), 45–46.
[88] Cheterian, *War and Peace in the Caucasus*, 186–87.
[89] Kaufman, *Modern Hatreds*, 119.

forces back. As they advanced, the Abkhaz engaged in attacks on local Georgians, resulting in 250,000 refugees fleeing the region.[90] As described earlier, the threat of military defeat combined with growing threat of the Zviadists forced Shevardnadze to come to terms with Russia. A peace deal was signed in April 1994. In late 1993, shortly prior to this deal being signed, Russian forces intervened on behalf of Shevardnadze against the Zviadists. Georgia then agreed to host Russian military forces.[91] They also joined the CIS. Ethnic conflict and rebellion had resulted in Russia gaining greater levels of hierarchy.

After the Civil War Following the civil war, the Abkhaz elites with the aid of Russia constructed what amounted to a de facto state.[92] The Abkhaz political elite continued to derive income from their political position. While the Abkhaz improved their demographic position in the region, making up a plurality, they are not a majority and are hardly more demographically secure in their position now than in 1989.[93] There is a perception that ethnicity and connections are an important part of economic life in Abkhazia.[94] The Abkhaz perpetuated a situation where their political and economic well-being were linked.

Another factor tying the political situation to rent-seeking and economic life is the position of Georgian internally displaced people (IDPs). The Abkhaz elite used their privileged position to seize property of non-Abkhaz citizens after the war.[95] The return of these IDPs with equal rights within the Republic was a nonnegotiable condition of the Georgian government as part of any peace agreement. According to the former minister for reintegration, Temuri Yakobashvili, agreement without this right would be "impossible" and that it would not be right for the Abkhaz to benefit from their human rights violations.[96]

In 2010, the government was prepared to offer continuing autonomy to the region, but this autonomy and political identity must be defined in civic not ethnic terms and allow for the return of Georgian refugees.[97]

[90] Dov Lynch, "Separatist States and Post–Soviet Conflicts," *International Affairs* 78, no. 4 (2002): 863.
[91] R. L. Larsson, "The Enemy Within: Russia's Military Withdrawal from Georgia," Journal of Slavic Military Studies 17, no. 3 (2004): 406.
[92] Charles King, "The Benefits of Ethnic War: Understanding Eurasia's Unrecognized States," *World Politics* 53, no. 4 (2001).
[93] Clogg, "Politics of Identity in Post-Soviet Abkhazia," 308.
[94] John O'Loughlin, Vladimir Kolossov, and Gerard Toal, "Inside Abkhazia," *Post-Soviet Affairs* 27, no. 1 (2011): 23; Clogg, "Politics of Identity in Post-Soviet Abkhazia," 317.
[95] T. Trier, H. Lohm, and D. Szakonyi, *Under Siege: Inter-ethnic Relations in Abkhazia* (Columbia University Press, 2009), 96.
[96] Yakobashvili, author interview, July 29, 2010.   [97] Yakobashvili.

However, much of the Abkhaz population views this as impossible.[98] Sergei Shamba, the prime minister of Abkhazia, stated, "Returning to Abkhazia Georgian refugees would inevitably create a new conflict situation, bringing a new war. With the development of such events we cannot agree."[99] The Georgian government insists on the return of IDPs and their property and equal rights for people of all ethnicities;[100] this creates a situation where the incentives of the Abkhaz to support Russia are perpetuated.

Abkhazia's elite behaved in a way consistent with the idea that contestation combined with rent-seeking creates incentives to surrender sovereignty.[101] Russia has been a bulwark to Georgian encroachment. The Abkhaz elite have remained throughout the post-Soviet period in a situation where economics and politics were highly linked. For this reason the Abkhaz have been prepared to surrender sovereignty to Russia to maintain their protection. The Abkhaz acted to prevent the loss of their existing position and the rent-seeking opportunities they held during the Soviet era.

Two Minorities: Samtshke Javakheti and Kvemo Kartli

Javakheti and Kvemo Kartli are two regions in Georgia where ethnic minorities are demographically dominant. These areas, despite not being formally autonomous, are seen as potentially separatist at worst and a problem for political integration of the country at best. Ethnic minorities in these regions, along with Ossetia and Abkhazia, were subject to the State Ministry of Reintegration.[102] The fact they are subject to governmental control in this way shows that they are in a practical sense different from the rest of the country. In the Javakheti region as a whole Armenians make up 54 percent of the population, and in two districts – Ninotsminda and Akhalkalaki – they make up more than 90 percent of the population.[103] In Kvemo Kartli, Azerbaijanis are 45 percent of the

[98] O'Loughlin et al., "Inside Abkhazia," 29.
[99] A. Kuchuberia, "Shamba: 'bistro reshet vopros sobstvennosti rocciyan v Abkazii nevozmozhno,'" *Kavkazskii Uzel*, August 25, 2010, http://georgia.kavkaz-uzel.ru/articles/17 3368/.
[100] Government of Georgia, 2010.
[101] Since achieving de facto state status, the Abkhaz have made limited attempts to preserve their language. Russian is more prestigious in the region, and education is primarily in Russian. While laws exist to promote the Abkhaz language, elites in the region do not assign many resources to this task. This indicates little practical concern with cultural factors. See Anahid Gogorian, "Abkhaz Worried by Language Law," *CRS* 424 (December 21, 2007).
[102] See www.smr.gov.ge/en/home.
[103] www.ecmicaucasus.org/upload/stats/Census%202002.pdf.

population but in several districts – Dmanisi, Marnueli, and Bolnisi – they are above 60 percent and up to 83 percent.[104]

Of these groups, the Armenians of Javakheti preserved a desire for Russian involvement in the region for most of the postindependence period. They are less concerned with violations of Georgian sovereignty than the Azerbaijanis. Azerbaijanis, on the other hand, respond to issues regarding sovereignty in a manner similar to ethnic Georgians. They care about territorial integrity and resisting outside influence, as will be demonstrated by the later statistical analysis.[105]

A note should be made regarding culture and history. It could plausibly be argued that Armenians are culturally and historically closer to Russia than the Azerbaijanis. However, while this might be true in general it is not a historically universal relationship. In the conflict between Azerbaijan and Armenia, the Soviet/Russian metropole continually shifted sides depending on its interests. For instance, during the early periods the Soviet center was far more supportive of the Azerbaijani side of the Nagorno-Karabagh conflict than the Armenian.[106] The shifting nature of such relationships of patronage and support demonstrates the difficulty in attributing these outcomes to history or culture. Culture, history, and national identity do play a role, but political conflicts and competition and the interests of the central and peripheral elites ultimately determine whether historical connections are mobilized or not.

Javakheti: Support for Russia

The primary center of Armenian political activism in Georgia was the town of Akhalkalaki, in the region of Javakheti. The hill outside the town is marked by a large military base, which until 2007 was occupied by the Russian Army. During this period, Javakheti was among the poorer regions of Georgia, with few economic opportunities. The primary industry was agriculture and the primary crop is the potato. Most farming is for subsistence, and only a limited amount is commercial.[107] The region is mountainous and isolated; for most of the post-Communist period both transport and communications within the region were of poor quality.

Support for Russia in this region was apparent across the period of observation. While the region was never actively secessionist, the Armenian population supported the subordination of Georgian sovereignty

---

[104] www.ecmicaucasus.org/upload/stats/Census%202002.pdf.   [105] See Chapter 4.
[106] Cheterian, *War and Peace in the Caucasus*, 121–22.
[107] Jonathan Wheatley and European Centre for Minority Issues, *Obstacles Impeding the Regional Integration of the Javakheti Region of Georgia*, ECMI Working Paper 22, European Centre for Minority Issues, 2004, 9.

to Russian control in some areas. For instance, when the Georgian government attempted the removal of Russian military forces from Georgia these actions were met by protests among the Armenian community in Javakheti.[108] According to Ghia Nodia, a political analyst and a former minister in the Georgian government, this level of support was so apparent that some Georgian elites associated with the government saw the region as potentially going the way of South Ossetia.[109] While agitation has died down since the removal of the Russian military base, there persists a belief among both Armenian and Georgian government officials that Russia could stoke anti-Georgian forces in the region.[110] In 2013, while still president, Mikhail Saakashvili compared a local nationalist leader Vahagn Chakhalyan to the Abkhazian separatist leader Vladislav Ardzinba, and called Chakhalyan an "emissary of the Russian military."[111]

The Armenians of Javakheti had a long-standing connection and cooperative relationship with Russia. This makes it more difficult to rule out historical and cultural affinities as a cause of cooperation between Russia and the Armenians in the region.[112] The majority of the Armenian population came to the region fleeing wars in the Ottoman Empire in the 1820s and 1830s, partially seeking Russian protection. Events following the collapse of the Russian Empire further fostered the perception that the Russians or the Soviet Union could offer political protection. During the brief period of independence there was a war between Georgia and Armenia in 1918. As a consequence, the Armenians in Georgia suffered a series of depredations and ethnic violence. Even today there are people in the region that still hold a belief that Russia could have acted as a potential protector against Turkish or Georgian aggression.[113]

The benefits of Russian intervention for the region of Javakheti are immediately apparent in the town of Akhalkalaki. A Russian military base

---

[108] Civil.ge, March 13, 2005.
[109] Ghia Nodia, former minister of education and professor at Illia Chavchavadze State University, author interview, September 2009.
[110] See International Crisis Group, "Abkhazia: Deepening Dependence." According to this report, these government officials are also of the opinion that potential activists are motivated by material and economic goals not nationalistic ones.
[111] "Saakashvili Condemns Chakhalyan's Release," Civil.ge, www.civil.ge/eng/article.php?id=25681.
[112] While Armenians are often perceived as having a close relationship with Russia, they are also one of the nationalities that voted to reject the continuation of the Soviet Union. Furthermore, at times, the Soviet leadership supported Azerbaijani interests over Armenian interests in the Nagorno–Karabagh conflict. The Armenian state has also rejected economic integration with Russia since the demise of the USSR. In contrast, Armenia developed a close security relationship with Russia following the collapse of the USSR. Given these mixed relationships, it is difficult to draw strong inferences about any cultural or historical connection between Armenians and Russians.
[113] Author interviews, September/October 2009, July/August 2010.

employed a large number of locals directly and many more gained their income from servicing the base.[114] In the early 1990s, local actors were able to block the appointments of prefects from the central government.[115] They also prevented the Georgian militias from entering the region.[116] In 1998, protests by the local population prevented Georgian military exercises in the region.[117] The ability of the Armenians to do this was in part a function of their relationship with the Russian military base.[118]

Armenians in the region blamed the central government for the lack of services and opportunities. A survey conducted by the Georgian government found that "there is a perception among the local population of Akhalkalaki and Ninotsminda that the insufficient allocation of resources was a purpose oriented move."[119] Though there may not be much systematic difference between Javakheti and many other regions of Georgia, in some ways this perception is borne out.

Even after the anticorruption campaign associated with the Rose Revolution, Javakheti remained affected by everyday corruption and political exploitation by local officials and police. For example, the locals claim that the chief of police has been engaged in conflicts with local Armenians over money.[120] The central government attempted to remove Armenians from important economic positions including their roles as customs officials on the Armenian border.[121] However, "clans" managed to preserve control over many of the important government institutions in the region.[122] Control over local political positions and law enforcement in the region were essential for the facilitation of smuggling over the border from Georgia into Armenia.[123] In this way, political power was an important source of economic advantage and a source of contention in

---

[114] Kornely Kakachia, "The End of Russian Military Bases in Georgia: Social, Political and Security Implications of Withdrawal," in *Military Bases: Historical Perspectives, Contemporary Challenges* (IOS Press, 2009), 200.

[115] Wheatley, *Georgia from National Awakening to Rose Revolution*, 150; S. E. Cornell, "Autonomy as a Source of Conflict: Caucasian Conflicts in Theoretical Perspective," *World Politics* 54, no. 2 (2002).

[116] Voitsekh Guretski, "The Question of Javakheti," *Caucasian Regional Studies* 3, no. 1 (1998); H. Lohm, "Javakheti after the Rose Revolution: Progress and Regress in the Pursuit of National Unity in Georgia," ECMI Working Paper, 2007.

[117] Anatol Lieven, "Imperial Outpost and Social Provider: The Russians and Akhalkalaki," *EurasiaNet*, February 19, 2001, www.eurasianet.org/departments/insight/articles/ea v022001.shtml.

[118] Cornell, "Autonomy as a Source of Conflict," 69; Guretski, "Question of Javakheti."

[119] Government of Georgia, *National Integration and Tolerance in Georgia*, 2008, 68.

[120] Political activist, author interview, July 2010.

[121] Regnum.ru, "Naseliniye Samtskhe-Javakheti razgromilo tamozhni na Armyano-Gruzinkskoi granitse," December 12, 2005.

[122] International Crisis Group, "Abkhazia: Deepening Dependence."

[123] Metreveli, *The Dynamics of "Frozen Tension": Case of Javakheti*, 17.

the region, in contrast to other parts of Georgia where government reforms had been more successful. The lack of economic alternatives made access to local political power and resources of central importance in Javakheti.

During elections, the ruling party has tended to be successful in the minority areas by coopting voters and engaging in fraud.[124] These effects may be somewhat overstated, but opposition political parties engage in little contestation in the minority dominated regions.[125] While there is limited formal political competition in the region, despite appearances, much political competition takes place informally or through nongovernmental groups. There are a large number of active political and social organizations; Wheatley states that there were more than one hundred NGOs nominally existing within the Javakheti region.[126] While the Armenian population voted for the ruling party out of fear that the alternatives were more nationalist and antiminority, and did so since the collapse of the Soviet Union, the population often demanded ethnically Armenian representatives and local officials.[127] This contrasts with the Azerbaijani population in Kvemo Kartli that accepted ethnic Georgians in these roles.[128]

Armenians in Javakheti continued to face problems of integration into Georgian political and civic life.[129] The Armenian population in the region was prone to protests and opposition for a variety of reasons.[130] Past protests have ranged from a few hundred demonstrators to several thousand, such as the one that protested the removal of the Russian military.[131] All in all, political competition with the central authorities was relatively strong and sometimes violent.

The competition in Javakheti occurred across multiple dimensions. While cultural factors mattered, particularly issues regarding language and assimilation, economic factors partly structured responses to cultural issues. For instance, very few of the Armenian population in Javakheti spoke Georgian, relying on Armenian and Russian to a greater extent.[132] The government introduced and started enforcing laws regarding the use

---

[124] J. Wheatley, "The Integration of National Minorities in the Samtskhe-Javakheti and Kvemo Kartli Provinces of Georgia," European Center for Minority Issues, 2009; Miriam Lanskoy and Giorgi Areshidze, "Georgia's Year of Turmoil," *Journal of Democracy* 19, no. 4 (2008): 164.
[125] Julie A. George, "Can Hybrid Regimes Foster Constituencies? Ethnic Minorities in Georgian Elections, 1992–2012," *Electoral Studies*, 2014, 331.
[126] Wheatley, "Managing Ethnic Diversity in Georgia."
[127] H. Lohm, "Javakheti after the Rose Revolution," 23.   [128] Lohm.
[129] George, "Minority Political Inclusion," 1170–72.   [130] George.
[131] Civil.ge, October 9, 2005; Civil.ge, March 11, 2006.
[132] George, "Dangers of Reform," 145.

of the Georgian language in public institutions such as universities and courts. The enforcement of language laws regarding the bureaucracy and education concerns Armenians because it relates to their access to jobs and ability to appeal against government decisions.[133]

The Armenian enclave of Javakheti has supported Russian control of Georgian sovereignty. In particular, they lobbied to keep a Russian military base in the town of Akalkalakhai. In part, the Armenian population was motivated by the direct material benefits they received from a Russian presence in the region. This support developed and was sustained in a context where contestation and rent-seeking were prevalent.

Kvemo Kartli: Support for Georgian Sovereignty

The Azerbaijanis residing in Kvemo Kartli are in many ways in a similar position to the Armenians in Javakheti. Yet Kvemo Kartli, of all the potential trouble areas in Georgia, has remained the quietest. Neither Russia nor Azerbaijan has played much of a role in provoking unrest in this region of the country. This is despite the fact that there has historically been a territorial dispute over the status of the region between the Azerbaijanis and Georgia.[134] Azerbaijani leaders in Kvemo Kartli indicated commitment to Georgian sovereignty. Some Azerbaijanis rejected involvement by outside actors, including the Azerbaijani state, because they feared it might prompt a hostile reaction from the Georgian government.[135]

Moreover, even if efforts to manipulate the Azerbaijani population in Kvemo Kartli have been more limited than those in other regions, the Azerbaijani elites tended to express beliefs about issues that approximate those of the broader Georgian population. Some Azerbaijani leaders disapproved of Russian attempts to violate Georgia's sovereignty and aid separatist movements.[136] The survey analysis in the following chapter shows that Azerbaijani respondents were not significantly different from Georgian respondents. There are lower levels of support for an external actor to play a substantial role in Georgian politics.

The Azerbaijani leadership in Georgia was removed from positions of power during the last years of the Soviet Union and the early 1990s. In 1990, the first secretary of the Georgian Communist Party stated that in

---

[133] Nodia, former minister for education, author interview, September 2009.
[134] Jonathan Aves, *Georgia, from Chaos to Stability?* (Royal Institute of International Affairs Russia and Eurasia Programme, 1996), 46.
[135] International Crisis Group, "Georgia's Armenia and Azeri Minorities," November 2006, 20.
[136] Author interviews, August 2010.

the Kvemo Kartli region "that not one Azerbaijani remains in their post."[137] This meant that the Azerbaijani elite had little access to political power and rent-seeking opportunities and relied on the patronage of the central Georgia authorities.

Unlike in Javakheti, access to Tbilisi and the rest of Georgia is relatively easy from Kvemo Kartli. This has allowed the development of tight economic linkages and interaction with the central economic markets. Kvemo Kartli supplies 40 percent of Georgia's agricultural products. They also have the economic option of trading with Azerbaijan and Russia if necessary. According to official statistics, Kvemo Kartli was the third most prosperous region in the country after Adjara and Tbilisi.[138]

During the period before the Rose Revolution, Kvemo Kartli as with all other regions of Georgia was subject to corruption and rent-seeking. What makes this region different from the others discussed is that Azerbaijani and Georgian elites were not competing over the rent-seeking opportunities. Instead, there was a lack of political mobilization among the Azerbaijani population, partly due to the more successful cooption of Azerbaijani leaders, and close cooperation between the Shevardnadze regime and his protégé, and governor of the region Levan Mamaladze.[139]

Politically, the Azerbaijanis are less organized than Armenians in Javakheti. The Azerbaijanis do not appear to demand that their local representatives be Azerbaijani. They are, if not content, then at least less prepared to challenge the imposition of Georgian representatives.[140] Moreover, they are far less organized outside of the formal party politics of the state, with fewer and less active NGOs whose purpose it is to protect Azerbaijani rights.[141] Local governments at the district and regional level are also dominated by ethnic Georgians in contrast to those in Javakheti. One Georgian municipal figure stated that Azerbaijanis are allowed to run the "village" level.[142] Though even in local politics Azeribaijanis are more underrepresented than Armenians.[143]

What Azerbaijani political organization did exist in the region during the 1990s was largely supportive of Georgian power. The primary Azerbaijani nationalist organization in Georgia, Geryat, acted as a mediator between Azerbaijanis and the local and central Georgian authorities.

---

[137] Quoted in Ibrahimli Khaladdin, *Azerbaijdzhantsy Gruzii: Istoriko-etnograficheskii i Sotsialno-politicheskii Kommentarii* (Evropa, 2006), 54.
[138] Wheatley, "Integration of National Minorities," 8.
[139] Aves, *Georgia, from Chaos to Stability?*, 46. [140] George, "Dangers of Reform," 145.
[141] Wheatley, "Integration of National Minorities."
[142] Marneuli local official, author interview, August 18, 2010.
[143] Daniel Zollinger and Daniel Bochsler, "Minority Representation in a Semi-Democratic Regime: The Georgian Case," *Democratization* 19, no. 4 (2012): 638–39.

Rather than contest problems through political confrontation this group tended to engage in negotiation.[144] Leaders of the group were allowed to engage in their own rent-seeking in exchange for cooperation with higher levels of government dominated by Georgians.[145]

An example of the general attitude held by the Azerbaijanis to social and political problems in Georgia can be found in this statement made by Alibala Askerov, the leader of the Azerbaijani Nationalist group Geyrat, in response to Armenian protests of the limited water supply in the Tsalka region:

> Armenians want to be at the center of the anniversary of the August events. They think that the Azerbaijani-Georgian unity is strengthened and force Armenians out the territory. It is a lie. It is typical Armenian illness. Provocation runs in their blood. Armenian provocation is a protest against the Georgian-Azerbaijani solidarity ... Roughly 55 of 60 villages of Marneuli region where Azerbaijanis live are short of drinking water. We do not apply to official agencies, because global warming is the cause. We do not politicize this problem.[146]

Other representatives of Azerbaijanis in Georgia express similar sentiments. Comparing the Azerbaijani attitude to that of the Armenians in Georgia one Azerbaijani leader stated that the Armenians in Georgia are "too political."[147] Azerbaijani leaders believe that the lack of economic development and opportunity is not a political issue unique to Kvemo Kartli but a problem common to the whole of Georgia. A leader of one Azerbaijani group claimed that there is a problem of economic development, but this a problem for everyone in Georgia not just Azerbaijanis.[148] These answers are echoed by the finding of the United Nations Development Program that Azerbaijani populations were more critical of privately provided services than public services, and that the local population was not prepared to be critical of the government for the lack of provided services.[149] The Azerbaijanis are more eager to place their children into Georgian language schools.[150] The head of an umbrella organization representing different minorities in Georgia commented that the Armenians were "angry," while Azerbaijanis were more afraid than angry.[151]

---

[144] Wheatley, *Georgia from National Awakening to Rose Revolution*, 151–52.
[145] Wheatley, "Managing Ethnic Diversity in Georgia," 126.
[146] "Azerbaijanis in Georgia Say Armenians Resort to Provocation," Trend Azerbaijani News Service, August 7, 2009.
[147] Author interview, August 16, 2010. [148] Author interview.
[149] UNDP, Institutional Baseline Mapping report for the Kvemo Kartli region of Georgia, 2008, 47–48.
[150] Rusudan Chanturia, coordinator of civil integration programs, Ministry of Education and Science, author interview, July 20, 2010.
[151] Author interview, July 21, 2010.

For the Armenian population of Javakheti, political competition strongly affected their economic situation. In contrast to the Azerbaijani's, their geographic isolation and relative poverty, combined with a more activist and demanding political environment, allowed the local Armenian population to hold on to political power. Local leaders in the region have from an early period often been of Armenian origin. Armenians feared the loss of what income they could derive from the Russian presence and from their limited access to government posts. The fear of losing their economic position and not having it replaced led them to defend the Russian presence. This fear was derived from a belief that their poor position in Georgian society was the result of political maneuvering.

In Kvemo Kartli, there were lower levels of political competition and what political competition existed was less concerned with economic matters. Azerbaijani leaders were closely connected to Tbilisi and benefited from the patronage networks of the Georgian state. The Azerbaijanis were more concerned about Russian interventions, violation of Georgian sovereignty, and the risks these posed. There has been little political engagement with Russia or even patronage from the Azerbaijani government.[152]

Conclusion

The comparison of these four Georgian regions reveals that competition over rents is an important factor driving elites to surrender sovereignty. Where local elites perceived themselves to be in competition with the center over rents, they were inclined to support the subordination of Georgian sovereignty to Russian interests. In this situation local elites saw Russia as a protector and means to preserve their access to rents. When such competition was absent leaders were less inclined to support Russia. Leaders would gain little from support of Russia and risk much. They would risk losing whatever secure position they had gained for themselves.

Elite actors in these regions had differing effects on the level of hierarchy. In Abkhazia, local elites were able to directly facilitate the surrender of Georgian sovereignty. In Adjara, Abashidze acted as a constraint on the choices of the central government, increasing Russian control over the country. In Javakheti, they may have slowed the removal of a Russian

---

[152] One interesting side note is that the one group in Kvemo Kartli that has sought outside protection is the dwindling Greek minority. Threatened by internal Georgian migration, they sought help from the Greek government: Jonathan Wheatley and European Centre for Minority Issues, *Defusing Conflict in Tsalka District of Georgia: Migration, International Intervention and the Role of the State* (European Centre for Minority Issues, 2006).

Conclusion

military base slightly. These different effects may be explained by the greater or lesser resources possessed by the various groups, and geographical factors. What is consistent, however, is that groups that felt threatened by political contestation and engaged in rent-seeking were more inclined to support Russia.

The comparison at a macro or meso level rules out several possible causes of Russian influence in Georgia. Regions where elites had a separate ethnic identity from the majority do not exhibit greater levels of support for outside powers. Adjarans, who at most are only nominally ethnically separate, and in practice Georgian, have at times displayed a large inclination to support Russia. In contrast, the Azerbaijanis in Georgia have shown no inclination at all to support Russia or even the Azerbaijani government.

Institutional autonomy played a role to the extent that it fostered greater political competition. Despite preserving formal autonomy, Adjara in the later period under observation lost its close relationship with Russia, while Javakheti, which has no formal independence, has shown high levels of support for Russia. Finally, as both Javakheti and Adjara have supported Russian domination it is possible to rule out secessionism as a cause, as neither of these regions was secessionist.

It is also possible to dismiss cultural or historical factors as direct causes, though they may influence the outcome indirectly by contributing to political competition. Almost all the groups in the region have suffered at the hands of the Russian metropole. At various times these groups have also engaged in serious resistance to Russian advances. The Abkhaz for instance faced deportation at the hands of the Russians; similarly the Adjars suffered from repression during the Soviet period. Yet both these groups at various stages became Russian proxies.

More contemporary political developments, then, provoked these elites to surrender sovereignty. While the type of political competition present in these regions may have its origins in long-run cultural and institutional development, these processes vary from region to region. The reason for political competition in Adjara in the 1990s was different to the reasons for such competition in Javakheti. Therefore it is possible to focus on the existence of competition over rents as the cause, rather than competition as an intervening factor.

The cases here show the importance of examining subnational actors when attempting to explain the development of hierarchy at a more aggregate level. These groups have at various stages provided a foothold for Russia and made it difficult for the central government of Georgia to assert its autonomy. The support for Russia from elites in Javakheti and Adjara made it difficult for Shevardnadze to remove Russian military from Georgia. Elites in Abkhazia and South Ossetia continue to provide Russia with control over parts of Georgian sovereignty to this day. A failure to address the interests, preferences, and actions of elites in these subnational regions would leave the reason for Russia's role in Georgia largely unexplained.

4 Mass Politics and the Surrender of Sovereignty

In Ukraine in late 2013 and 2014, Ukrainian opposition movements mobilized, launching mass protests that eventually overthrew President Viktor Yanukovych. This is one of many incidents during the post-Soviet period that demonstrate the importance of societal support to elites in competitive authoritarian regimes. In the period leading up to his overthrow, Yanukovych lost support from fellow elites but also saw a dramatic diminishment in support from society. Despite turning to Russia for aid, Yanukovych could not maintain his hold on political power. In contrast, in an earlier period, Yanukovych had been able to preserve a strong political position receiving backing from both Russia and large parts of society. Similarly, Abashidze in Adjara was able to compete politically when he combined the ability to mobilize elements of Adjaran society along with Russian backing. When this societal support was lost, Abashidze was unable to hold on to power. A combination of resources is clearly important for elites to guarantee political survival, and external support alone is rarely sufficient.

The case studies in the previous chapters demonstrated that rent-seeking and contestation among elites could drive them to give up sovereignty, and that elites lost power in part due to lack of societal support. The cases could not demonstrate an association between societal attitudes toward sovereignty and rent-seeking and contestation among elites. The purpose of this chapter is to provide a test of one of the structural conditions of the argument. That mass support for sovereignty will vary along with perceptions of elite–societal relations and corruption. By analyzing survey data, it is possible to show how mass attitudes to sovereignty might be influenced by political dynamics and consequently remove or place a constraint on elite actors and great powers.

The following quantitative analysis is conceptually integrated with the preceding qualitative chapters. Rather than performing "triangulation," where the same argument is tested using different methods,[1] the methods complement one another by performing different tasks.[2] The analyses can be thought of as hoop tests, rather than direct tests of the broader argument.[3] In other words, they are not meant to demonstrate that society plays a role in the formation of hierarchy; rather, it is a test that can falsify my argument that societal preferences concerning sovereignty are influenced by elite–society relations and rent-seeking. If the tests are passed, confidence in the overall argument should increase. Combined with the other evidence presented in the book, a strong case will have been made for society's role in the formation of hierarchy.

The effects of mass politics on the formation of international hierarchies have received little attention in the literature because of a focus on states as unitary actors. Yet elites are not operating in a vacuum and cannot adopt policies based solely on their personal material well-being if they expect to gain or hold on to power. Elites must consider their supporters' interests, and this consideration can be an important factor in the formation of hierarchy. Even in authoritarian regimes, political leaders must consider the interests of groups within society who provide them with power and resources, or alternatively can threaten their survival.[4] For these reasons, the preferences of societal groups become constraints on the ability of the leaders to make choices.

In the case of competitive authoritarian regimes such as Ukraine and Georgia, the number of groups and individuals that influence elite political survival and policies, though smaller than that in a democracy, includes large parts of society. Loss of societal support has contributed to leaders losing power in many instances.[5] The interests of society play a role either as a direct source of pressure on the decisions of elites or as a constraint on the choices available to elites as they struggle for political survival. For example, Tymoshenko, after the Orange Revolution in Ukraine, moderated her overtly nationalist stance in order to compete politically. Yanukovych adopted an overtly pro-Russian position but was unable to mobilize sufficient domestic resources to stay in power. It

---

[1] J. D. Fearon, D. D. Laitin, and J. M. Box-Steffensmeier, "Integrating Qualitative and Quantitative Methods," in *The Oxford Handbook of Political Methodology* (Oxford University Press, 2008), 200.
[2] Jason Seawright, *Multi Method Social Science* (Cambridge University Press, 2016).
[3] David Collier, "Understanding Process Tracing," *Political Science and Politics* 44, no. 4 (2011); J. A. M. Mahoney, "After KKV: The New Methodology of Qualitative Research," *World Politics* 62, no. 1 (2009).
[4] B. B De Mesquita et al., *The Logic of Political Survival* (MIT Press, 2005); Jessica L. P. Weeks, *Dictators at War and Peace* (Cornell University Press, 2014).
[5] H. E. Hale, *Patronal Politics: Eurasian Regime Dynamics in Comparative Perspective* (Cambridge University Press, 2014).

makes no sense for elites to gain external resources only to lose domestic supporters.

Individuals who are connected to elites in patronage-based societies should be invested in the political survival of those elites. Rent-seeking and patronage have a distorting effect on both economic and political life. Patronage allows elites to provide economic and other material benefits to portions of society in return for their political support. When rent-seeking and patronage practices are prevalent, individuals should be invested in the political survival of the elites they feel represent their interests. If a patron loses power, their clients or constituents also lose access to resources. While high levels of corruption and rent-seeking undermine generalized trust, they create and rely on particularized forms of trust.[6] That is, groups or individuals develop expectations that goods will be provided to them in return for support. This structures the relationship between elites and certain people in society altering incentives regarding politics, foreign policy, and international hierarchy.

If surrendering sovereignty increases the chances of elite political survival then societal actors should support their patron doing so when the benefits outweigh the costs. If individuals feel that their interests are represented by one set of elites and that they are threatened by a different group, they should show less commitment to preserving their state's sovereignty if they believe rent-seeking is also prevalent. If this is the case, then elites who are threatened by political contestation and engage in rent-seeking and patronage should be able to give up sovereignty to guarantee their survival without having to worry about losing support from their constituents.

Mass support will influence the emergence of hierarchy for a second reason. Support from society is going to influence the choices of the dominant state, not just elites within the subordinate state. Where mass support is present, the dominant state will need to provide fewer resources to keep their elite clients in power. This increases the value of hierarchy for the dominant state, making them more likely to establish it.

This chapter tests two separate hypotheses to demonstrate that mass political opinion about hierarchical relationships varies according to individual beliefs concerning elite interactions and rent-seeking. First, it tests the hypothesis that individuals' increased perception of rent-seeking should reduce commitment to state sovereignty and autonomy. Second, it explores if individuals who are invested in one group of elites but threatened by another are more prepared to surrender sovereignty when

---

[6] Warren, "Trust and Democracy," in *The Oxford Handbook of Social and Political Trust*, ed. Eric M. Uslaner (Oxford University Press, 2018): 84.

they also perceive high levels of corruption and rent-seeking. If rent-seeking and different patterns of elite–societal relations change the beliefs of societal actors in this way, elites can respond to their incentives to surrender sovereignty stemming from political competition without risking the loss of domestic support. The analysis thus tests a mechanism through which institutional factors such as rent-seeking and threats to political survival might influence hierarchy.

The hypotheses are tested through examination of survey data from Georgia and Ukraine. The two surveys were used because of their availability and their suitableness; both surveys asked detailed questions about political and social institutions as well as foreign policy. The data are from very different contexts, postconflict in Georgia and prior to armed conflict in Ukraine. This difference potentially undermines some of the comparability of the results in the two countries. However, the similar results found in both samples show that the dynamics of rent-seeking and contestation play a role in diverse contexts.

Statistical analysis demonstrates a significant and substantive association between concern about the rule of law and the willingness to surrender sovereignty when individuals also perceive a potential political threat or rivalry. This finding calls our attention to how the nature of political competition or institutions in a state can limit demands for autonomy among the population and affect the state-building projects of leaders in former Soviet space.

The Georgia data come from the 2009 Caucasus Barometer, a nationally representative survey excluding Abkhazia and South Ossetia.[7] The period of this survey, shortly after the 2008 conflict with Russia, provides a hard test for an explanation based on domestic political variation.[8] During this period anti-Russian sentiment and security concerns would have been at their highest and thus might swamp the effects of other variables.

The Ukraine data are from a nationally representative survey conducted in 2000 to gather information about attitudes toward foreign policy.[9] It was useful to analyze results from this period before the Orange Revolution made issues such as Ukraine's relationship with Russia even more highly politicized and more controversial. In this way

---

[7] The data and documentation are publicly available from http://crrccenters.org/caucasus barometer/datasets/, Caucasus Barometer 2009, Caucasus Research Resource Center, Tbilisi, Georgia.

[8] Unfortunately, earlier and later iterations of the Caucasus Barometer do not ask detailed questions regarding Russia's relationship with Georgia.

[9] S. White, M. Light, and J. Lowenhardt, "Outsiders: Russia, Ukraine, Belarus, Moldova and the New Europe, 1999–2001," UK Data Archive, November 2003, SN: 4747.

it is possible to analyze the different effects of attitudes toward corruption without it being confounded with broader political trends.

Test 1: Rent-Seeking and Sovereignty

Individuals can constrain elites' ability to make certain policy choices, including giving up sovereignty and establishing hierarchy. The aim here is to demonstrate that rent-seeking and corruption loosen a potential constraint on elites. This means that if the same variables change both societal and elite preferences, elites should be inclined to surrender sovereignty if rent-seeking and political threat are combined. Perceptions of rent-seeking should lower an individual's commitment to sovereignty. This is because individuals in such environments may also see external actors as a means to guarantee access to rents if the external actor can keep their patrons in power. More generally, where rent-seeking is perceived as high, individuals will see sovereignty as less valuable. Then, given a rent-seeking environment, elites will be able to surrender sovereignty with less fear that they will be punished by society.

Georgian Survey Data, 2009

Protect from Russia From the Georgian data, *Protect from Russia* was the main dependent variable, capturing concern about Russian influence within the country. This question asked, "To what extent do you believe our way of life needs to be protected from Russian influences?" The potential responses were: (1) strongly disagree; (2) disagree; (3) agree; and (4) strongly agree. Those who strongly agree with this statement are more likely to want to resist Russian encroachment on Georgian sovereignty.[10]

The belief that Georgia should be protected from Russian influence is strongly related to the outcome of interest. Giving up sovereignty entails a large amount of Russian influence. At a minimum, this variable can falsify my argument if the individuals predicted to be affected by the independent variable are unaffected on average, as limiting Russian influence would naturally limit Russian control over sovereignty.

Moreover, there is a convincing argument that this variable will directly measure the outcome of interest. Individuals are unlikely to make academic distinctions between sovereignty and influence. This is particularly true when considering that Russia, the former imperial metropole, has helped breakaway regions of Georgia and has made the many other

---

[10] Agree was the most frequent response, while respondents were least likely to strongly disagree.

impositions on Georgian sovereignty described in previous chapters. It is unlikely that individuals could compartmentalize a question concerning Russian influence from Russia's historical role in the country.

The Rule of Law Where individuals perceive high levels of rent-seeking, they should be less inclined to resist outside powers. Rule of Law measures perceptions that the country is governed by the rule of law. It asked whether the respondent agreed that "The country is governed by the Rule of Law?" The rule of law has been used to measure rent-seeking and clientelism in other studies.[11] The responses ranged on a four point scale from strongly disagree to strongly agree. Low rule of law provides elites opportunities to target goods to clients and exploit others. Low rule of law allows elites to use power for personal economic gain.[12] Limited rule of law forces businesses to rely on patronage and protection, further increasing rent-seeking.[13] In contrast, high rule of law reduces rent-seeking by limiting the ability of elites to use power arbitrarily.[14]

If individuals believe that the rule of law is limited, then they will believe that rent-seeking is prevalent. Rent-seeking and clientelism are private or club goods,[15] meaning awareness of them and their effects will vary at an individual level. As some individuals are excluded or included in rent-seeking processes, some will be more affected by rent-seeking than others. Therefore, there will be substantial variation in individual-level perceptions, even within a community.

Control Variables Alternative explanations for individuals' attitudes toward Russian influence were accounted for using a number of control variables. *Ethnic Identity* was included as a control because conflicts between certain ethnic groups and the majority have helped loosen

---

[11] P. Keefer, "Clientelism, Credibility, and the Policy Choices of Young Democracies," *American Journal of Political Science* 51, no. 4 (2007).
[12] T. Frye and E. Zhuravskaya, "Rackets, Regulation, and the Rule of Law," *Journal of Law, Economics, and Organization* 16, no. 2 (2000); J. E. Alt and D. D. Lassen, "The Political Economy of Institutions and Corruption in American States," *Journal of Theoretical Politics* 15, no. 3 (2003); I. Slinko, E. Yakovlev, and E. Zhuravskaya, "Laws for Sale: Evidence from Russia," *American Law and Economics Review* 7, no. 1 (2005); R. Fisman and R. Gatti, "Decentralization and Corruption: Evidence across Countries," *Journal of Public Economics* 83, no. 3 (2002); S. Haggard, A. MacIntyre, and L. Tiede, "The Rule of Law and Economic Development," *Annual Review of Political Science* 11 (2008).
[13] Frye and Zhuravskaya, "Rackets, Regulation, and the Rule of Law."
[14] Douglass North, *Institutions, Institutional Change, and Economic Performance* (Cambridge University Press, 1990); North, *Violence and Social Orders*.
[15] Herbert Kitschelt and Steven I. Wilkinson, "Citizen-Politician Linkages: An Introduction," in *Patrons, Clients, and Policies: Patterns of Democratic Accountability and Political Competition* (Cambridge University Press, 2007).

ties of minorities to Georgian sovereignty.[16] For example, Armenians in Georgia see their deprived position as being a result of political decisions.[17] This variable also helped control for arguments based on culture.

Age was included as older people had lived under the Soviet Union and could be more sympathetic to Russia. *Income* controlled for the fact that wealthier individuals may be affected more by corrupt elites. *Education* was included as it has been found to be correlated with level of nationalism.[18] *Sex* was also included; the patriarchal structures of Georgia mean gender differences may play a role.

Friends with Russian controlled for prejudice, which could increase resistance to Russian influence. A dummy variable measured if the respondent disapproved of being friends with a Russian. *Family in Local Government* and *Family in National Government* measured if the individual had family working for local or national governments. Family in government increases access to rents and might be related to the outcome; connection to the government could change preferences regarding giving up power.

Analysis and Results An ordered logistic regression was used to estimate the effect of Rule of Law on Protect from Russia.[19] The analysis found a significant relationship between Rule of Law and the dependent variable. Coefficients in models with limited dependent variables, such as ordered logistic models as well as binary dependent variable models, are difficult to interpret. To aid interpretation, I calculated predicted probabilities for different values of Protect from Russia using simulation. Control variables were set to their mean or mode and the level of the independent variable was varied.

Figure 4.1a shows the effects of increasing belief in the rule of law from its minimum to maximum value. That is, it shows the difference in attitudes for the average case varying if they strongly disagree that the country is governed by the rule of law or strongly believe the country is governed by the rule of law. The results show that an individual is significantly more likely to strongly agree that Russian influence should be resisted if they believe the rule of law is strong and significantly less

---

[16] The variable categories were Georgian, Armenian, Azerbaijani, Russian, and Other Caucasus Ethnicity.
[17] Government of Georgia, *National Integration and Tolerance in Georgia*, 2008, 68.
[18] M. Coenders and P. Scheepers, "The Effect of Education on Nationalism and Ethnic Exclusionism: An International Comparison," *Political Psychology* 24, no. 2 (2003).
[19] Running a logistic regression on a dichotomized dependent variable also provides support for the hypothesis.

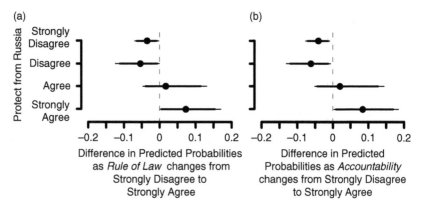

Figure 4.1 Change in predicted probabilities on Russian influence as (a) belief in the rule of law and (b) accountability vary from strongly disagree to strongly agree. Thick lines represent 90% CIs, thin lines 95% CIs.

likely to disagree with the Protect from Russia Statement. This size of this effect is an increase of 8 percent in the probability that the respondent will want to resist Russia.

As an additional test, the response to "Are Politicians punished for their crimes?" was substituted for belief in the rule of law. The results are very similar. As individuals' belief that leaders are held accountable for violating the law increases so does belief that Russia should be resisted (see Figure 4.1b).

Ethnic Identity and Friends with a Russian also had a significant effect on Protect from Russia. As shown by the qualitative research in the previous chapter, Armenians are a group likely to see political contestation in terms of competition over rents, and Armenians are significantly less likely to view Russian influence as a threat when compared to Georgians. Ethnic Azerbaijanis residing in Georgia were not significantly different from ethnic Georgians. There was also a significant effect for the gender variable, with women being less likely to believe that Russian influence needs to be resisted.

Ukrainian Survey Data, 2000

The results from Georgia support the argument that an individual's preferences regarding sovereignty will vary based on their beliefs about rent-seeking. The following analysis explores whether similar processes can explain variation in a different context. Specifically, the analysis in this section demonstrates that in Ukraine, as in Georgia, individual-level beliefs about corruption are associated with variation in attitudes toward sovereignty.

Attitudes toward Russia The question providing the dependent variable asked "What kind of relationship would you like to see between Russia and Ukraine? (1) It should be as they are, different states with closed borders, visas and customs; (2) They should be independent states but friendly, with open borders, no customs and visas; (3) They should be united into one state." This variable captures how much sovereignty individuals think should be surrendered to Russia. The higher levels indicate a reduced commitment to Ukrainian independence.

Corruption Rent-seeking was measured with a question that asks about the level of corruption in government. The independent variable asked: "In your opinion, how widespread is bribe taking and corruption in the central organs of authority in Kiev? (1) Hardly anyone is involved; (2) Some people are involved; (3) The majority of people are involved; (4) Everyone is involved."

Controlling for Alternative Explanations Once again, a number of control variables were included in the model to account for alternative explanations. The east and west of Ukraine had very different historical trajectories. Eastern Ukraine was part of the Russian Empire and consequently was more culturally Russified. It was also part of the Soviet Union much earlier, creating different attitudes. The west was part of the Austro-Hungarian Empire which allowed a stronger Ukrainian identity to develop and was not incorporated into the Soviet Union until the World War II. Consequently, it is argued that the west is more nationalistic.[20] This would lead to a greater commitment to Ukrainian sovereignty and more anti-Russian attitudes.[21] For this reason, a *Region* dummy was included in the model.

Ethnicity was the second control variable. The majority of respondents were ethnic Ukrainian, the next largest group was Russian, followed by much lower numbers of Belarusians and Moldovans. Ethnicity has been

---

[20] Darden, *Resisting Occupation*.
[21] L. W. Barrington and E. S. Herron, "One Ukraine or Many? Regionalism in Ukraine and Its Political Consequences," *Nationalities Papers* 32, no. 1 (2004); O. Malanchuk, "Social Identification versus Regionalism in Contemporary Ukraine," *Nationalities Papers* 33, no. 3 (2005); P. Rodgers, "Understanding Regionalism and the Politics of Identity in Ukraine's Eastern Borderlands," *Nationalities Papers* 34, no. 2 (2006); G. Sasse, "The Role of Regionalism," *Journal of Democracy* 21, no. 3 (2010).

found to play a role in Ukrainian politics.[22] Though policy preferences are arguably more important.[23] Therefore, a control was included for ethnicity, indicating whether the respondent was Ukrainian or from some other ethnic group.

Language was also used as a control variable in these models. Some Ukrainians might use Russian creating a closer affinity with Russia, despite being of a different ethnicity.[24] Alternatively, people of other groups who use Ukrainian may be better assimilated. Therefore, a control variable for the first language of the respondent was included.

Employment was also included as a control variable. Whether or not an individual works for the government could influence access to rent-seeking and attitudes toward sovereignty. A dummy variable was used that indicated whether or not the individual was employed by any of the federal government, the local government, or the security services. The other controls were a battery of demographic variables: *Age, Education, Income,* and *Sex*. These variables could for different reasons be correlated with preferences regarding sovereignty and politics. Education can lead to greater levels of nationalism.[25] Income creates incentives to preserve autonomy, or might make someone a target for corrupted practices. Gender has played a large role in the construction of Ukrainian nationalism and state.[26]

Analysis and Results As with the previous analysis, the dependent variable was an ordered, categorical variable, so an ordered logistic regression was used. Following the procedure above, predicted probabilities are reported because interpreting a regression coefficient from a response model provides little information. Using the same simulation method described earlier, the independent variables were varied while the control variables were held at their mode or mean, the predicted probabilities for the different responses were generated. As with the analysis in Georgia, I find that as belief that corruption is widespread increases, desire for autonomy drops. Individuals in Ukraine become more likely

---

[22] J. George, R. G. Moser, and M. Papic, "The Impact of Minority-Majority Districts: Evidence from Ukraine," *Post-Soviet Affairs* 26, no. 1 (2010).

[23] Timothy Frye, "What Do Voters in Ukraine Want? A Survey Experiment on Candidate Ethnicity, Language, and Policy Orientation," *Problems of Post-Communism* 62, no. 5 (2015).

[24] Volodymyr Kulyk, "Language Identity, Linguistic Diversity and Political Cleavages: Evidence from Ukraine," *Nations and Nationalism* 17, no. 3 (2011).

[25] M. Coenders and P. Scheepers, "The Effect of Education on Nationalism and Ethnic Exclusionism: An International Comparison," *Political Psychology* 24, no. 2 (2003).

[26] Tatiana Zhurenko, "Gendernii rinki Ukraini: Politicheskaya Ekonomiya Natsionalnogo Stroitilstvo," EGU, Vilnius, 2008.

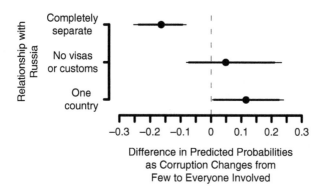

Figure 4.2 Change in predicted probabilities for relationship with Russia as Attitudes to Corruption changes from few involved to everyone involved. Thick lines represent 90 percent CIs, thin lines 95 percent CIs.

to believe that Russia and Ukraine should form one country (see Figure 4.2).

Along with the rent-seeking variable, several of the cultural or historical variables had an effect: Region, Ethnicity, and Language. People from Western Ukraine were less likely to support close relations with Russia. As would be expected, ethnic Russians and those who speak Russian as a first language had a higher probability of wanting to give up sovereignty.

Test 2: Elite–Societal Relations and Rent-Seeking

The above analysis provides strong support for the argument that perceptions of rent-seeking should reduce overall support for autonomy and desire to resist external actors' demands for hierarchy. The next step tests whether the effects of rent-seeking are more pronounced for those that perceive their interests as bound up with particular elites while viewing some other elites as a potential threats. This is important as what should concern elite–societal calculations is not just the overall attitudes of individuals in society, though this undoubtedly matters, but particularly those individuals from whom they could extract resources and support if necessary.

Elite–Societal Relations in Georgia

The Elite–Societal Relations variable was constructed with the aim of measuring how individuals viewed the consequences of different elites holding power. In the survey, respondents separately rated their trust in local government and the executive on a scale of 1 (fully distrust) to 5 (fully trust). Using these variables I constructed a new variable with four categories: (1) *Trust Local Officials*, those who trust local government and distrust the executive; (2) *Trust Executive*, those who trust the executive and not local government; (3) *Trust Neither*, those who distrust both; (4) *Trust Both*, those who trust both. Different combinations of trust reflect different relationships with elites and capture some of an individual's beliefs about the consequences or potential consequences of their interactions with these elites.

The variable facilitates the examination of how the attitudes toward sovereignty held by individuals who might support one set of elites against another changes along with attitudes toward rule of law. It also enables the examination of differences among individuals who perceive their interests represented by elites in different ways. The constructed variable is similar to that used by Nilson and Nilson to predict political protest behavior.[27] They found that a "trust differential" was an important predictor of political mobilization in opposition to the government. That is, individuals who trusted one set of elites but not another were more likely to be mobilized for protests than others.

Trust has important political and social consequences that make it appropriate for measuring the investment or lack of investment individuals have in an elite's political survival. A substantial literature has developed in sociology concerning trust.[28] Trust develops out of continued interaction and measures a relationship between individuals that can be understood as "encapsulated interest."[29] Trust is related to informal and formal political relationships that are the basis of political interaction and contestation. Furthermore, trust is correlated with partisan attitudes. Individuals claim higher levels of trust when members of their political party are in power in a variety of contexts such as in the United States,[30] Western Europe,[31] the Baltic States,[32] and political trust is correlated with forms of partisanship in other postcommunist countries.[33]

---

[27] Douglas C. Nilson and Linda Burzotta Nilson, "Trust in Elites and Protest Orientation: An Integrative Approach," *Political Behavior* 2, no. 4 (1980).

[28] N. Luhmann, *Trust and Power* (John Wiley, 1979); Russell Hardin, *Trust* (Polity, 2006).

[29] Hardin, *Trust*, 18–20.

[30] J. Citrin, "Comment: The Political Relevance of Trust in Government," *American Political Science Review* 68, no. 3 (1974); L. Keele, "The Authorities Really Do Matter: Party Control and Trust in Government," *Journal of Politics* 67, no. 3 (2005).

[31] Ola Listhaug, "The Dynamics of Trust in Politicians," in *Citizens and the State*, ed. Hans-Dieter Klingmann and Dieter Fuchs (Oxford University Press, 1995).

[32] K. Lühiste, "Explaining Trust in Political Institutions: Some Illustrations from the Baltic States," *Communist and Post-Communist Studies* 39, no. 4 (2006).

[33] R. Rose and W. Mishler, "Negative and Positive Party Identification in Post-Communist Countries," *Electoral Studies* 17, no. 2 (1998).

Even in societies where general levels of trust may be low, trust can play important political and social roles. In their seminal comparative historical study of patronage networks, Eisenstadt and Roniger drew attention to the importance of trust.[34] While patronage societies may have an ambivalent relationship to institutions and society at large, the interpersonal relationships that constitute patron–client relations are predicated on trust to a large extent.[35] This is true even in extreme circumstances, such as individuals dealing with Mafiosi in Sicily.[36] Indeed, trust in a patron often compensates for the individual's inability to trust others.[37] The reason for this becomes apparent when we consider that clientelism and patronage are built on the notion of reciprocity, and the beliefs of both the patron and the client that the other will fulfill their part of the exchange.[38] As Granovetter has pointed out, large-scale economic malfeasance is highly dependent on networks where the individuals trust one another.[39] Empirically, studies in a diverse set of contexts such as South East Asia, Latin America and Central Asia have shown that those who are part of patronage network express higher levels of trust for their patrons.[40]

Trust enables political mobilization. Tilly has shown how trust networks have been both important sources of opposition to government and resources for government to mobilize. "Trust networks ... consist of ramified interpersonal connections within which people set valued, consequential, long-term resources and enterprises at risk to the malfeasance of others."[41] According to Tilly, while patronage networks do rely in part on coercion they also use trust and commitment-based techniques of mobilization.[42] The ability to mobilize supporters in political contests has been crucial for elites trying to ensure their survival. Yanukovych was

---

[34] Shmuel Noah Eisenstadt and Luis Roniger, *Patrons, Clients and Friends: Interpersonal Relations and the Structure of Trust in Society* (Cambridge University Press, 1984).
[35] Eisenstadt and Roniger.
[36] Diego Gambetta, "Fragments of an Economic Theory of the Mafia," *European Journal of Sociology/Archives Européennes de Sociologie* 29, no. 1 (1988).
[37] Gambetta.   [38] Kitschelt and Wilkinson, "Citizen-Politician Linkages."
[39] Mark Granovetter, "Economic Action and Social Structure: The Problem of Embeddedness," *American Journal of Sociology* 91, no. 3 (1985): 491–92.
[40] James C. Scott, "Patron-Client Politics and Political Change in Southeast Asia," *American Political Science Review* 66, no. 1 (1972); Larissa Adler Lomnitz, "Informal Exchange Networks in Formal Systems: A Theoretical Model," *American Anthropologist* 90, no. 1 (1988); J. Auyero, "'From the Client's Point (s) of View': How Poor People Perceive and Evaluate Political Clientelism," *Theory and Society* 28, no. 2 (1999); Brent Hierman, "What Use Was the Election to Us? Clientelism and Political Trust amongst Ethnic Uzbeks in Kyrgyzstan and Tajikistan," *Nationalities Papers* 38, no. 2 (2010).
[41] Charles Tilly, "Trust and Rule," *Theory and Society* 33, no. 1 (2004): 5.
[42] Charles Tilly, *Trust and Rule* (Cambridge University Press, 2005), 110–11.

toppled by protesters and Abashidze fell when his supporters defected. Elites can mobilize societal actors due to a common set of interests built on relationships of trust.

Trust measures an individual's belief that an elite represents their interests and their fear of those they distrust. Individuals expect something from those they trust and fear the actions of those they do not. An individual who trusts only local officials feels represented by the local officials and threatened by the executive. The reverse is also true. An individual that trusts neither feels their interests are potentially threatened by both sets of elites but that their interests are represented by neither set of elites. An individual who trusts both has no perception of threat.

Large-scale competition occurs when coalitions develop; these competitive coalitions are dependent on interpersonal relationships and expectations of reciprocity within one group and a lack of ties to another.[43] For the purpose of this analysis, it is not important that the Elite–Societal Relations variable measures actual political contestation. Instead what matters are the individuals' perceptions regarding the consequences of different sets of elites holding power. The effect of a perceived threat to their political interests on an individual's beliefs regarding sovereignty can be evaluated whether or not this threat is actually based in reality.

Empirical Predictions The theory makes the following empirical predictions. For the Trust Local Officials or Trust Executive categories we should observe a significant decrease in them either strongly disagreeing or disagreeing with the Protect from Russia statement as their belief in the rule of law increase. We should also see a significant increase in them either agreeing or strongly agreeing with the Protect from Russia Statement. An individual who trusts local officials and distrusts the executive perceives a difference between local and central elites, is more closely connected to local elites, and fears the central government's policies or intentions. They are also invested in the survival of local elites because of rent-seeking and thus will support Russian involvement to aid their political survival. The reverse is true for those who trust the executive. In both cases, lower levels of Rule of Law will reduce the probability of agreeing with Protect from Russia, while higher levels will increase the probability of either agreeing with the statement.

For the other two categories, those who trust neither and those who trust both, there should be no change in attitudes toward sovereignty no matter their beliefs regarding the rule of law (see Table 4.1 for a summary of predicted effects). If corruption is high, those who trust both will

[43] Granovetter, "Economic Action and Social Structure," 493.

Table 4.1 *Predicted effects as perceptions of rule of law change for Georgia*

	Rule of law	
	Low	High
Trust Local	More support for Russia	Less support for Russia
Trust Executive	More support for Russia	Less support for Russia
Trust Both	No change	No change
Trust Neither	No change	No change

continue to support elites either way and the Trust Neither have no reason to change their attitudes either.

Lack of trust could be associated with a belief that the respondent will be exploited through corruption, suggesting that trust and Rule of Law might measure the same concept. However, trust does not necessarily imply that the trusted party is honest, only that they represent the interests of the one that trusts. For example, members of criminal groups can have high levels of trust despite knowledge that those they are trusting are criminals.[44] Empirically, if these variables measure the same concept there would be an additive or substitutive effect. Those who Trust Both and have a high belief in the rule of law and those that Trust Neither and have a low belief in the rule of law would fall into the extremes. If the variable was to have an effect, the largest observed differences would be between such individuals. Instead of extreme differences between these two categories, I predict that we will see changes in behavior for individuals who trust one set of elites as their belief in the rule of law changes.

Analysis and Results As in the earlier analysis an ordered logistic regression was used. Instead of examining the unmoderated effects of the Rule of Law, I estimated the effect of the interaction between Elite–Societal Relations and Rule of Law on Protect from Russia.[45] This test will look at how Rule of Law changes attitudes toward sovereignty within the different categories of elite–societal relations. The prediction is that there will be a larger and significant effect for those categories that trust one set of elites and distrust another.

---

[44] Diego Gambetta, *Codes of the Underworld: How Criminals Communicate* (Princeton University Press, 2009).
[45] Running a logistic regression on a dichotomized dependent variable also provides support for the hypothesis.

In line with expectations, the analysis using the interaction between the Rule of Law and the Elite–Societal relations variables found a significant relationship between the interaction term of Elite–Societal Relations and the Rule of Law and the dependent variable. Coefficients of interaction terms in models with limited dependent variables are difficult to interpret. The marginal effect can vary depending on the level of the independent variable because it is conditional on the value of other variables in the model.[46] To aid interpretation, I calculated predicted probabilities for different levels of the interaction using simulation. Control variables were set to their mean or mode and the levels of the independent variables were varied.

Consistent with the theoretical predictions, for the trust local category, we see significant reduction in the probability of them strongly disagreeing with the statement and a significant increase in them agreeing that Georgia should be protected from Russia when their belief in the rule of law is high (Figure 4.3a). When an individual trusts only local officials and they strongly disagree that the country is governed by the rule of law the predicted probability of them strongly agreeing that Russian influence should be resisted is 27 percent (22 percent agree); when they strongly agree that the country is governed by the rule of law it is 46 percent (28 percent agree). Separate simulations estimating the first difference between those who strongly agree with Rule of Law and those that strongly disagree estimated an 18 percent (0.002–39 percent, 95% CI) difference in predicted probabilities of strongly agreeing with the Protect from Russia statement (see Figure 4.3a).[47] For individuals who trust only local officials, the predicted probability of strongly agreeing with Protect from Russia increased as belief in Rule of Law increased.

The predicted effects are larger for those who trust only the executive. The predicted probability of strongly agreeing with Protect from Russia for those that strongly disagree that the country is governed by the rule of law is 22 percent (21 percent disagree), increasing to 50 percent (26 percent agree) when they strongly agree the country is governed by the rule of law. Simulations of first differences showed a 28 percent (0.00002–66 percent, 95% CI) difference between those who strongly disagree and strongly agree with Rule of Law (Figure 4.3b).

For individuals that trust both local officials and the executive or distrust both, there is no substantive change. Simulations show no statistically significant changes with an increase in belief in Rule of

---

[46] C. Ai and E. C Norton, "Interaction Terms in Logit and Probit Models," *Economics Letters* 80, no. 1 (2003).

[47] Ninety-five percent confidence intervals were calculated using results from simulations; they represent 2.5 percentiles and 97.5 percentiles of estimates from 10,000 simulations.

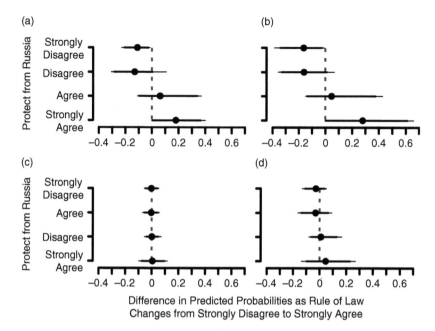

Figure 4.3 Changes in predicted probabilities for (a) Trust Local, (b) Trust Executive, (c) Trust Neither, and (d) Trust Both as Rule of Law changes from strongly disagree to strongly agree. Thick lines represent 90 percent CIs, thin lines 95 percent CIs.

Law. For Trust Neither there is no change in the predicted probabilities (Figure 4.3c). There is a 25–26 percent predicted probability of agreeing and a 32–37 percent chance of strongly agreeing with the Protect from Russia statement, regardless of the value of Rule of Law.

For those who trust both, the probability of strongly agreeing (or agreeing) that Russian influence should be resisted is 25 percent (30 percent) for those who strongly disagree that the country is governed by the rule of law, and 25 percent (31 percent) for those who strongly agree that that the country is governed by the rule of law. The predicted probabilities vary only slightly (Figure 4.3d).

The change in predicted probabilities is consistent with the theory. For individuals in the Trust Local or Trust Executive categories as their perception that the country was governed by the rule of law increased, so too did their belief that Russia should be resisted. High belief in the rule of law meant that they were significantly more likely to strongly believe that Russia should be resisted. In contrast, Rule of Law has no effect for the categories when they Trust Neither or Trust Both.

Elite–Societal Relations in Ukraine

Unlike the survey from Georgia, there are no questions that ask directly about the relationship between individuals and local officials or the executive. However, there are questions that ask about whether individuals trust the president and whether they trust the parliament. The parliament in Ukraine was partly elected from single member districts, which gains some leverage over these issues as members of parliament potentially represent interests different from the president.[48] Moreover, the issues of interest are not confined to local and central elites. Splits within elites at different levels can have similar effects. If levels of trust differ between the executive and the parliament then the individuals could be incorporated into different political networks.

Following the same procedure as that in the previous survey a variable was constructed containing four categories: those who trust parliament and distrust the president; those who trust the president and distrust the parliament; those who trust neither; and those who trust both. Trust was again used to measure elite–societal relations for the reasons outlined in the analysis of Georgia.

As in the earlier analysis, rent-seeking was measured with a question that asks about the level of corruption in government. The theory predicts that this variable will be positively correlated with the belief that more sovereignty should be surrendered to Russia when interacted with the Trust Parliament and Trust President categories.

As with the previous analysis, the dependent variable was an ordered, categorical variable, so an ordered logistic regression was used. Following the procedure above, predicted probabilities are reported because interpreting a regression coefficient from a response model provides little

Table 4.2 *Predicted effects as perceptions of corruption change for Ukraine*

	Extent of corruption	
	Low	High
Trust Parliament	Less support for Russia	More support for Russia
Trust President	Less support for Russia	More support for Russia
Trust Both	No change	No change
Trust Neither	No change	No change

---

[48] Erik S. Herron, "Electoral Influences on Legislative Behavior in Mixed-Member Systems: Evidence from Ukraine's Verkhovna Rada," *Legislative Studies Quarterly* 27, no. 3 (2002).

information. Using the same simulation method described earlier, the predicted probabilities for the different responses were generated for all levels of the interaction. These predicted probabilities showed a clear relationship between a desire to surrender sovereignty and the interaction of Trust Parliament and rent-seeking.

The association between rent-seeking and perceived threat was most clearly demonstrated in the case of those who only trust the parliament (Figure 4.4a). In this case, when they believed few people were involved in corruption, the probability of them wanting to form one country with Russia was only 7 percent; when they believed everyone was involved the predicted probability of them wanting to form one country with Russia was 33 percent. In this category, the probability of those who believed that corruption was limited wanting to be completely independent was 46 percent; for those who believed that everyone was involved in it was only 8 percent. The intermediate category of shared borders showed an increase from 45 percent to 58 percent. Overall, there was a large increase in the probability of wanting to give up sovereignty for those who believed that corruption was widespread.

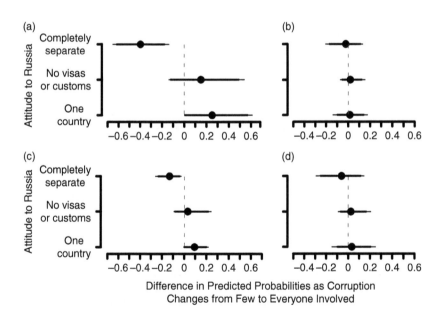

Figure 4.4 Changes in predicted probabilities for (a) Trust Parliament, (b) Trust President, (c) Trust Neither, and (d) Trust Both as Attitudes to Corruption changes from few involved to everyone involved. Thick lines represent 90 percent CIs, thin lines 95 percent CIs.

For all the other categories there was also a slight increase of willingness to give up sovereignty with belief in the prevalence of corruption (Figures 4.4b–4.4d). However, this change was only statistically significant for the category of Trust neither (Figure 4.4c). In this case, the probability of wanting to form one country with Russia changed from 17.5 percent to 27.5 percent, and the first difference between these values was statistically significant. For the other categories, the changes were small and not statistically significant.

Discussion

The results demonstrate the importance of taking into account individual perceptions of political institutions and the economy when assessing attitudes toward sovereignty. Individual-level preferences regarding sovereignty vary substantially. There is evidence across both cases that some of this variation is explained by perceptions of corruption and the rule of law. As perceptions of corruption increase or faith in the rule of law decreases, commitment to sovereignty drops.

Additionally, rent-seeking and corruption seemed to have a larger effect on individuals connected to elites who perceived a threat from other groups than individuals who had no connection or did not feel threatened by elites. That this held in a state as anti-Russian as Georgia, shortly after a violent conflict with the outside state, demonstrates the power of political contestation and institutions in driving attitudes toward sovereignty.

If we assume that the elites who are the focus of these networks share similar preferences and interpretations of the strategic situation to the respondents then the implication is clear; they will also want to pursue closer relationships with Russia if they perceive a situation of domestic political competition and rent-seeking behavior. This assumption is supported by evidence from the case studies. Where they perceive political contestation to be a threat to their economic lives, elites will accommodate Russian demands over sovereignty.

However, even if the interests of elites and society are not in alignment, elites are still constrained by their constituents. Elites must mobilize domestic resources if they are to ensure their political survival. While it might be in the interests of elites to pursue rent-seeking arrangements with the external power for their own sake in the absence of contestation or threat, their constituents' disapproval would limit elites' capacity to pursue such strategies successfully.

The findings have implications for understanding the establishment of hierarchy. Lake has claimed that subordinate states benefit from hierarchy because "their security and territorial integrity are enhanced" and "property rights at home and more so abroad are clearly defined and protected."[49] However, in practice Russia has increased disorder and supported separatists, reducing Georgia's territorial control and capacity. Some of Russia's interventions led to reduced order and rule of law through the promotion of corruption. For example, Russia's control over South Ossetia and Abkhazia has contributed to smuggling and the drug trade around those regions.[50] Russia has not supplied domestic order in return for authority, but a means of political survival in the absence of true order.[51] Those who perceived political contestation and rent-seeking are less likely to want to resist Russia, despite these effects on Georgian society. If the provision of domestic order and protection of property rights was a primary motivating factor then Russia is an odd source from which to expect such outcomes.

The results from Georgia are just a snapshot of micro-level variation. That said, they do reflect what was observed in the case studies. In Georgia in 2009, elites were unified, competition was minimal, and rent-seeking was lower than it had been in the past. In the sample, most individuals either felt no connection to elites, trusting neither, or they trusted both the executive and local authorities. Meanwhile, the Georgian Government adopted a fiercely anti-Russian stance. Nonetheless, it still seems that perceptions of threat from some elites combined with perceptions of rent-seeking reduced commitments to sovereignty.

The results from the Ukrainian survey also provide evidence, if not as strong as in Georgia, that rent-seeking opportunities and different patterns of elite–societal relations explain some of the variation in attitudes toward sovereignty. It is those who trust the parliament but not the president and believe that corruption is widespread who are most likely to support giving up sovereignty in a relationship with Russia. The other competitive category, Trust President, shows a slight increase which, somewhat against expectations, was not significant. However, the fact that it was not significantly correlated with changes in attitudes to sovereignty might reflect President Kuchma's dominance over the Ukrainian

---

[49] David Lake, *Hierarchy in International Relations* (Cornell University Press, 2009), 8–9.
[50] Alexandre Kukhianidze, "Corruption and Organized Crime in Georgia before and after the 'Rose Revolution,'" *Central Asian Survey* 28, no. 2 (2009); Kukhianidze, "Organized Crime and Smuggling through Abkhazia and South Ossetia," *Abkhazia*, July 3, 2007, 87.
[51] The analysis also supports the political survival theory better than an account based on actor beliefs or culture, as rent-seeking and political competition explain willingness to support actors as diverse as Russia, the EU, and the United States. Despite very different identities and historical relationships with Georgia, political competition and rent-seeking was correlated with a greater willingness to surrender sovereignty to these three very different actors. See Appendix A for these additional results.

political landscape at this time, meaning the threat from parliament was minimal.[52] There is no consistent evidence that the noncompetitive categories change much in response to changes in the perceived level of corruption. While for those who trust neither the parliament nor the president there was a slight increase in willingness to surrender sovereignty to Russia, this was not consistently significant across other models (see Appendix A). Furthermore, when it was significant, the effect size was much smaller than that for the Trust Parliament category.

While the result is not robust to alternative measurement strategies, one deviation from the predictions is that those who trust neither and view high levels of rent-seeking are also less inclined to support sovereignty. This is demonstrated by the models that show that individuals who trust neither have weaker support for sovereignty than individuals who trust both sets of elites. There are several reasons why this might be the case. First, the original predictions were made under the default assumption that individuals should prefer autonomy to other outcomes. This effect might be weaker than assumed, and demand for autonomy may be a weaker preference in some circumstances. A second possibility is that these individuals are incorporated into other networks, not represented in the survey, and perceive a threat. Finally, they might see the external actor as a means to gain access to rents and reverse their exclusion. It should be noted that the change in attitude in this category is smaller than those observed among the individuals who trust one set of elites.

In both countries, there were variables such as ethnic identity or region that predicted changes in attitudes toward sovereignty. These findings confirm many of the broader findings about attitudes toward Russia and sovereignty. In Georgia, Armenians who have long-run historical connections with Russia and a generally considered more predisposed to Russia and less assertive of Georgian sovereignty. In Ukraine, ethnic Ukrainians, those who speak Ukrainian, and those from the west of the country are all more likely.

The results are from the period prior to the conflict with Russia that began in the wake of the Euromaidan protests. Historical and cultural variables set people's baseline attitudes; culture and identity clearly matter, but they can change slowly or unpredictably. Moreover, they do not come with clear set of incentives. When they do change, in the face of large exogenous shocks, identity can be shaped more by politics and political economy variables than vice versa. For example, the Euromaidan

---

[52] This was discussed in detail in Chapter 2; see also Steven Levitsky and Lucan Way, *Competitive Authoritarianism: Hybrid Regimes after the Cold War* (Cambridge University Press, 2010).

revolution and the war with Russian-backed rebels have altered the nature of Ukrainian nationalism and identity and its salience.[53] However, along with these changes others have shown important continuities in how identity affects attitudes.[54] Due to these complexities, identity variables on their own cannot completely explain outcomes that vary rapidly or within groups with similar cultural or historical backgrounds or who have experienced similar shocks. Indeed, this study has found an independent effect of perceptions of rent-seeking and elites while controlling for variables that proxy for identity.

However, there has been an observable decline in support for integration with Russia. When Yanukovych took power in 2010, a plurality of people surveyed in Ukraine favored integration with the Russian-led Customs Union. By 2019, this had declined to around 23 percent of the population.[55] Meanwhile, support for joining western institutions such as NATO has also increased compared to past periods. Confidence in the government improved in the immediate aftermath of Yanukovych's ouster, but has declined subsequently.

Looking only at the period after Euromaidan, it is possible to observe a slight softening of anti-Russian sentiments, as we move further away from these events. Over the period between 2014 and 2017 there was surge in the popularity of western organizations and in anti-Russian sentiments. By February 2019, the strength of opposition had declined in the population.[56] Overall, this demonstrates that while the war with Russian-backed forces has shifted opinions this effect, at least for some of the population, has not been a persistent one.

In terms of corruption, there has been little change in how the population of Ukraine has experienced corruption.[57] It is possible that a larger number of Ukrainians now believe corruption is widespread than in the past.[58] Neither is there much of a perception that the new regime leaders

---

[53] Volodymyr Kulyk, "Shedding Russianness, Recasting Ukrainianness: The Post-Euromaidan Dynamics of Ethnonational Identifications in Ukraine," *Post-Soviet Affairs* 34, no. 2–3 (2018); Kulyk, "Identity in Transformation: Russian-Speakers in Post-Soviet Ukraine," *Europe-Asia Studies* 71, no. 1 (2019).

[54] Grigore Pop-Eleches and Graeme E. Robertson, "Identity and Political Preferences in Ukraine – before and after the Euromaidan," *Post-Soviet Affairs* 34, no. 2–3 (2018).

[55] "Press Releases and Reports – Geopolitical Orientations of the Residents of Ukraine: February 2019," accessed May 16, 2019, www.kiis.com.ua/?lang=eng&cat=reports&id=827&page=4&t=3.

[56] "Press Releases and Reports – Geopolitical Orientations of the Residents of Ukraine: February 2019."

[57] "Corruption in Ukraine 2015," 41, accessed May 16, 2019, https://kiis.com.ua/materials/pr/20161602_corruption/Corruption%20in%20Ukraine%202015%20ENG.pdf.

[58] Gallup Inc., "World-Low 9% of Ukrainians Confident in Government," accessed May 16, 2019, https://news.gallup.com/poll/247976/world-low-ukrainians-confident-government.aspx.

are particularly invested in fighting corruption. Overall, Ukrainians believe that involvement in corruption is high and that they are affected by it on a regular basis. Little has changed on this front.

While potentially risky, it is possible to draw a few plausible inferences based on mass political behavior about opinions. One fact worth noting, is that in contrast to the presidential and parliamentary elections of 2014, anti-Russian sentiment was less effective in the 2019 presidential elections and pro-Russian candidates have done somewhat better.[59] This does not indicate that there is same strength of support for Russia in Ukraine as has existed in the past, but that there has been a tempering of opinion. The election was won by Zelenskiy, who while not pro-Russian has not adopted the same aggressive stance as Poroshenko. Zelenskiy is purportedly supported by former Poroshenko ally Kolomoyskiy and unlike Poroshenko's rivals in 2014 was a far more effective political opponent. In addition, this has all occurred in a context where confidence and trust in Poroshenko had collapsed from highs of 47 percent to levels equivalent to the lack of confidence in Yanukovych at the time of his ouster.[60] The correlation between the renewed political contestation and developments in public opinion are partly consistent with the theory outlined in the book.

As detailed in the previous chapter, Ukraine has shown variation across time in how its leadership has managed its relationship with Russia; of all the significant variables, the competition variable is the one most theoretically likely to account for these changes. This is supported here by showing that at least cross-sectionally and in two different countries political economy and political variables are significantly associated with attitudes toward sovereignty even when controlling for identity variables.

The results from the models indicate that we need to have a more complicated understanding of politics and political economy when trying to assess individuals' attitudes toward foreign policy and sovereignty. Just controlling for demographic variables such as income or education will not capture all of how these opinions are shaped. The perceived benefits of different foreign policy choices in general, and choices about sovereignty in particular are going to be affected by more specific relationships such as how an individual perceives themselves benefiting or being threatened by elites or rent-seeking.

---

[59] Emmanuel Dreyfus, "Expectations for Kyiv-Moscow Relations After Ukraine's Presidential Election," *PonarsEuarasia – Policy Memos*, May 13, 2019, www.ponarseurasia.org/memo/expectations-kyiv-moscow-relations-after-ukraines-presidential-election.

[60] Gallup Inc., "World-Low 9% of Ukrainians Confident in Government."

Future research should aim to disentangle how identity variables and these political economy variables are related and how they might jointly affect the outcomes of interest. Events in Ukraine in 2014 have shown how politics and conflicts over sovereignty can shape understandings of national identity rather than reverse. Understanding how the effects of identity are moderated or reinforced by economic perceptions might shed additional light on regional differences within countries such as Ukraine.

Conclusion

Domestic institutions and politics determine whether elites are willing to surrender sovereignty to another state. Where great powers confront other states with high levels of contestation and rent-seeking, they will find elites with incentives to give up sovereignty in exchange for external aid. Where competition among elites is controlled or rent-seeking is low, elites have more incentive to resist. Elites motivated by their struggle for political survival will find external support more attractive.

However, for elites, turning to external actors for aid is often not sufficient to guarantee political survival. As shown in earlier chapters, despite external backing, elites such as Abashidze at a subnational level in Georgia and Yanukovych at the national level in Ukraine have lost power. Elites need to maintain support from society as well. External patrons can provide some support but rarely enough to counteract the loss or complete erosion of a domestic power base.

This chapter has demonstrated that individuals that distrust one set of elites but trust another have less commitment to sovereignty when they also perceive high levels of rent-seeking. Theoretically, it is probable that individuals will experience higher levels of distrust and perceptions of threat when the elites they feel represent them are engaged in political contestation with other elites. That individuals become less concerned with the preservation of sovereignty under these conditions removes a potential constraint on elite choices. If elites manage their patronage networks appropriately they can surrender sovereignty successfully.

Studying mass politics in countries like Georgia and Ukraine presents many difficulties.[61] Limited data availability and the importance of informal institutions present challenges for good measurement of key concepts. The results presented here are an attempt at determining how mass attitudes toward sovereignty and hierarchy are affected by domestic politics.

---

[61] For a summary of these difficulties, see Hale, *Patronal Politics*, 436.

5 European Informal Empire in China, the Ottoman Empire, and Egypt
Hierarchy and Informal Empire in Historical Context

In 1882 the British colonized Egypt after a combined, but failed, effort with the French to reform Egypt's domestic political and legal institutions. As with China and the Ottoman Empire, Egypt until then had been controlled by European powers through a system of informal empire for much of the nineteenth century. The occupation of Egypt raises a puzzle: why were Britain and the other European powers able to maintain informal empire in the Ottoman Empire and China, while similar arrangements broke down in Egypt leading to formal empire?

The traditional narrative has neatly divided the last two centuries into an era of imperialism and one of national resistance and state sovereignty. The cases in this chapter show that despite the international system being highly permissive of territorial expansion in this era, it was resistance to informal empire that caused great powers to expand territorially using direct means of control. The chapter also addresses the theoretical puzzle of why resistance emerges between groups when the power disparity is great. Why would subordinate actors resist informal empire when, if the great power has the coercive ability to impose formal empire, resistance is more costly than accommodation for all actors involved?

Once an empire is established, its continuity or destabilization depends on the degree to which the incentives and opportunities provided by the domestic political structures of the subordinate state correspond to the incentives and opportunities provided by imperial institutions. The theory developed in this book predicts that the more competitive the political structures of the subordinate state, the more incentive subordinate actors have to support informal empire. This is particularly true when economic welfare is tightly linked to political power. The limited benefits, such as profits from trade or transfers of technology, provided by empire can appeal to them more because they benefit less from autonomy than they would if competition and rent-seeking were absent. Once political institutions create incentives for resistance, subordinate actors will only resist if they believe that the dominant state is not prepared to pay the costs of formal control.

The following chapter proceeds in five parts. It begins by discussing the reasoning behind the case selection, followed by a description of the international system of the time and its permissiveness for imperial expansion. Next, an analysis of China's relationship with the European powers explains the persistence of informal empire. A comparison of informal empire in the Ottoman Empire with that of China then demonstrates its similar origins and dynamics. Finally, the chapter will explain the breakdown of informal empire in Egypt and its subsequent occupation.

Why China, the Ottoman Empire, and Egypt?

The persistence and breakdown of informal empire are explored with comparative analysis and examination of within-case evidence from three key examples of nineteenth-century European domination. Focusing on Egypt, the Ottoman Empire, and Qing China allows a clear demonstration of how the hypothesized causal mechanisms work in practice.[1] Egypt was originally part of the Ottoman Empire and subject to informal imperial control by Britain. After Egypt gained autonomy from its Ottoman rulers, Britain initially established informal control there but had to gradually shift to formal empire. This contrasts with China and the Ottoman Empire, where informal empire persisted for decades longer.

Because Egypt for a time existed within the Ottoman Empire and adopted many of the same institutional structures, it should have been subject to many of the same dynamics as the Ottoman Empire. This makes an institutional explanation for colonialism unlikely, presenting a crucial case of the least likely variety.[2] However, the British established only informal empire over other domains of the Ottoman Empire, whereas it established formal empire in Egypt. By comparing British rule in Egypt with British informal empire over other Ottoman areas and China, it is possible to isolate key causal factors. By tracing developments in Egypt we can see why Britain had to retreat from informal empire and shift to formal empire.

Controlled comparison between cases allows one to dispel rival explanations and provides grounds for generalization.[3] By examining potential

---

[1] David Collier, James Mahoney, and Jason Seawright, "Claiming Too Much: Warnings about Selection Bias," in *Rethinking Social Inquiry* (Rowman and Littlefield, 2004), 96–98; Alexander L. George and Andrew Bennett, *Case Studies and Theory Development in the Social Sciences* (MIT Press, 2004).
[2] John Gerring, "Is There a (Viable) Crucial-Case Method?," *Comparative Political Analysis* 40, no. 3 (2007).
[3] Dan Slater and Daniel Ziblatt, "The Enduring Indispensability of the Controlled Comparison," *Comparative Political Studies* 46, no. 10 (2013).

explanations for resistance in the Ottoman Empire and Egypt, both before and at the time of failure of informal empire in the latter, the more likely causes can be isolated. Regime type can be dismissed as a potential cause given that both Egypt and the Ottoman Empire were patrimonial, while colonialism was established in Egypt and not in the Ottoman Empire. The system was multipolar during periods of informal and formal empire in Egypt; therefore, the involvement of multiple great powers cannot explain the variation. Furthermore, the relative power of the various states involved cannot be the cause, because while European power increased in comparison to both the Ottoman Empire and Egypt, only Egypt was colonized. Additionally, Egypt's power did not significantly vary across time. Economic factors can also be ruled out as the primary cause, as both states were primarily agrarian economies.

The case of China contrasts with that of the Ottoman Empire along a number of dimensions, providing a basis to rule out further explanations as informal empire persisted in both cases. In the Ottoman Empire, Russia was seeking territorial aggrandizement, while there were no states trying to expand territorially into China. Security issues can thus be ruled out as a probable cause. Moreover, cultural factors emanating from the subordinate states can be dismissed, the culture of the Qing Empire and China differed significantly from the identity of the Ottoman Empire. Combined, the cases of China, the Ottoman Empire, and Egypt allow a rough approximation of the method of difference with the method of agreement, which in combination provide a stronger basis for causal inference than either individually.[4]

The level of external validity of the study depends on how representative the selected cases are of a broader population of interest.[5] While this chapter analyzes only three cases in depth, it provides a basis for generalization to other states that had reached a level of development such that there were institutional compatibilities with the nineteenth-century European powers. For instance, informal empire would not be possible in situation where the subordinate polity lacks institutions to protect property or enforce diplomatic agreements, but it was possible in states such as the Ottoman Empire and China where a sufficient set of commercial and legal institutions existed. For informal empire to be viable it

---

[4] James Mahoney, "Strategies of Causal Assessment in Comparative Historical Analysis," in *Comparative Historical Analysis in the Social Sciences*, ed. James Mahoney and Dietrich Rueschmeyer (Cambridge Univesity Press, 2003); Theda Skocpol and Margaret Somers, "The Uses of Comparative History in Macrosocial Inquiry," *Comparative Studies in Society and History* 22 (1980).
[5] Jason Seawright and John Gerring, "Case Selection Techniques in Case Study Research: A Menu of Qualitative and Quantitative Options," *Political Research Quarterly* 61, no. 2 (2008).

must be possible for one state to conduct its business in and through the other state without transforming the subordinate state's political, legal, and economic institutions. It is states with these characteristics that constitute the relevant population.

The three selected cases capture many of the dynamics prominent in the broader population. Egypt was characteristic of the cases in which informal empire became unstable. A duration of thirty or forty years was typical for informal empires that became unstable during the nineteenth century. For example, informal empires established in the early or mid-nineteenth century failed in Tunis in the 1880s and Japan in the 1890s.[6] China and the Ottoman Empire were typical of stable informal empires in their duration and the manner in which informal empire ended in the early to mid-twentieth century; similar cases were Iran where Russia and Britain jointly shared control,[7] and Siam where Britain dominated the finance of the country, while other Western powers staffed other ministries.[8] The failure of informal empire in all of these states was clustered around the exogenous shocks of the world wars.

The Correlates of War data set identifies thirty non-European states in the international system during the nineteenth century.[9] The cases selected provide are representative of many of the characteristics that are present in this population. Most obviously, these states share characteristics with states and polities found in Eurasia and North Africa like Persia/Iran, Siam/Thailand, Tunisia, and Japan. However, in some important theoretical ways Egypt, which was breaking free of Ottoman control and engaging in state-building might reflect patterns elsewhere such as Latin America. The states of Latin America also broke free of imperial control during the nineteenth century and were engaging in independent state-building.[10] While this chapter analyzes only three cases in depth, it provides a basis for generalization to other contexts.

---

[6] Turan Kayaoglu, "The Extension of Westphalian Sovereignty: State Building and the Abolition of Extraterritoriality," *International Studies Quarterly* 51, no. 3 (2007); Kayaoglu, *Legal Imperialism: Sovereignty and Extraterritoriality in Japan, the Ottoman Empire, and China* (Cambridge University Press, 2010).
[7] David Mclean, "Finance and 'Informal Empire' before the First World War," *Economic History Review* 29, no. 2 (1976).
[8] Ian Brown, "British Financial Advisers in Siam in the Reign of King Chulalongkorn," *Modern Asian Studies* 12, no. 2 (1978): 193–94.
[9] Correlates of War Project, "State System Membership List, v2011," 2011, http://correlatesofwar.org/.
[10] Miguel Angel Centeno, *Blood and Debt: War and the Nation-State in Latin America* (Penn State Press, 2002).

Informal Empire and China

The great powers took liberties with China's institutions in the nineteenth century, using to their power advantage, they subordinated Chinese sovereignty to open markets and guarantee the economic and legal security of their citizens operating abroad. This relationship displayed all the elements associated with informal imperialism.[11] Chinese sovereignty was significantly reduced, but without complete control over Chinese territory ever being lost to a dominant state. In the words of Feuerwerker: "Chinese sovereignty might be derogated, but it never came near to being extinguished ... the foreigner in China had always to acknowledge that there was a Chinese authority, central or local ... He might threaten it, defraud it, bribe it, seek to ingratiate himself with it, with greater or lesser success, but he could not avoid taking it into account."[12]

The great powers' relationship with China was clearly marked by institutional reductions of Chinese sovereignty, principally, extraterritoriality, control of administrative bodies, and concessions. Extraterritoriality "embodies certain rights, privileges and immunities which are enjoyed by the citizens, subjects, or protégés of one state within the boundaries of another, and which exempt them from local territorial jurisdiction."[13] Along with these grants of extraterritoriality there were several instances where complete or partial control over government agencies was surrendered to partial European control. Notably, two revenue-raising bodies, the Chinese Maritime Customs Service and the Salt Administration, were used to guarantee Western loans. The concessions were territories surrendered to the control of European powers.[14] At no point, however, did all these privileges ever result in the complete removal of Chinese sovereignty.

The development of informal empire in China clearly demonstrates both that the European powers preferred informal empire to formal empire where possible, and that the acceptance and stability of informal empire was a product of domestic political concerns. The European powers worked through traditional Chinese institutions or created new institutions congruent with old traditions. This arrangement was made possible by China's domestic political environment.

---

[11] J. Osterhammel, "Semi-Colonialism and Informal Empire in 20th Century China," in *Imperialism and After: Continuities and Discontinuities*, ed. W. Mommsen and J. Osterhammel (Allen and Unwin, 1986).

[12] Albert Feuerwerker, *The Foreign Establishment in China in the Early Twentieth Century* (Center for Chinese Studies, University of Michigan, 1976), 1.

[13] Wesley Fishel, *The End of Extraterritoriality in China* (University of California Press, 1952), 2.

[14] Feuerwerker, *Foreign Establishment in China*.

Informal Empire and China 155

Domestic Authority Structures and Political Centralization

Chinese political institutions featured high levels of contestation and fragmentation. China's imperial character, the need to rule a culturally diverse and territorially extensive polity, had necessitated such institutions. The need to incorporate a wide variety of actors over a huge expanse meant that, with limited technological capacity in the early period, the Qing dynasty constructed an ideologically and politically decentralized polity.[15] Up to that point, China was never compelled to undergo a process of political centralization to the degree of the Europeans states.[16] Moreover, domestic legal institutions and political powers were complementary between local authorities and central actors, which allowed the continuation of such institutions.[17]

The history of the Qing dynasty is partly a history of negotiations and conflict between the state, gentry, and the regions over centralization of political authority. Wakeman demonstrates that the Qing dynasty was regularly subject to centripetal and centrifugal forces.[18] The period of European informal imperialism was one where centrifugal forces had led, once again, to a period of increasingly decentralized political authority. China's character as a universal empire, and its non-Western version of modernity, did not demand the centralization of authority.[19] While the attempt to incorporate actors of varying origin and identity and later the internal dynamics of Chinese political institutions meant that "indirect rule and limited formal governance were the preferred form of administration in China."[20]

The Long-Term Process of Informal Empire

In China, European informal empire began in the early to mid-nineteenth century. Over the previous decades European trade with China had

---

[15] Pamela Crossley, *The Translucent Mirror: History and Identity in Qing Imperial Ideology* (University of California Press, 1999).
[16] R. Bin Wong, *China Transformed: Historical Change and the Limits of European Experience* (Cornell University Press, 1997).
[17] R. Bin Wong, "Formal and Informal Mechanisms of Rule and Economic Development: The Qing Empire in Comparative Perspective," *Journal of Early Modern History* 5, no. 4 (2001).
[18] Fredric Wakeman, "Introduction: The Evolution of Local Control in Late Imperial China," in *Conflict and Control in Late Imperial China*, ed. Fredric Wakeman and Carolyn Grant (University of California Press, 1975).
[19] Huri Islamoglu, "Modernities Compared: State Transformations and Constitutions of Property in the Qing and Ottoman Empires," *Journal of Early Modern History* 5, no. 4 (2001).
[20] Melissa Macauley, "A World Made Simple: Law and Property in the Ottoman and Qing Empires," *Journal of Early Modern History* 5, no. 4 (2001): 340.

begun to expand. From the very beginning of the relationship, it was a source of revenue for the Emperor and his officials. The connection between a willingness to accept outside intervention, rent-seeking, and contestation was apparent very early on, when the Emperor and the state used resources from trade with Britain to suppress rebellions.[21] As European power increased, the level of hierarchy began to increase and Chinese autonomy became more curtailed.[22]

While many Chinese actors benefited from the hierarchical relationship, the views of the Chinese toward European encroachments were "ambivalent."[23] On the one hand, there were actors among the Chinese elites who saw benefits from interaction with European powers in terms of technological and economic development. On the other, the exploitative arrangements promulgated by the great powers did something to trigger a nationalistic backlash among certain parts of the elite.[24] Even those who argue that local gentry played a large role in opposing imperialism concede that "the gentry who led the movement were enlightened intellectuals, not traditional local gentry whose concern usually never went beyond the interests of their own areas."[25] Eng describes European preferences in this manner: "Western imperialists generally favored working through indigenous political structures and institutions and superimposing a supervisory agency, rather than restructuring the whole political system."[26] The arrangements of the Europeans and their facilitation of global exports benefited local elites by strengthening their control at a provincial level and providing them with rents.

The initial expansion of Europeans into China was conducted on a rather ad hoc basis but in a manner in accordance with past Chinese practices. The initial institutions that regulated European economic interactions with China had long-standing historical origins.[27] These institutions and regulations originated with the China's dealings with

---

[21] Fredric Wakeman, "The Canton Trade and the Opium Wars," in *The Cambridge History of China: Vol. 2. Late Ch'ing 1800–1911*, ed. John K. Fairbank and Kwang-Ching Liu (Cambridge University Press, 1978): 165.

[22] Informal empire was arguably established in the wake of the Opium Wars. These wars can be attributed to miscalculation on the part of both the British and the Chinese. The Chinese underestimated the relative strengths of both sides, while the British overestimated the willingness of the Chinese to accept their intervention. Wakeman.

[23] Yen-P'ing Hao and Erh-min Wang, "Changing Chinese Views of Western Relations, 1840–95," in Fairbank and Liu, *Cambridge History of China*.

[24] Hao and Wang, 172–81.

[25] Min Tu-Ki, *National Polity and Local Power: The Transformation of Late Imperial China* (Harvard University Press, 1989), 207.

[26] Robert Eng, *Economic Imperialism in China: Silk Production and Exports, 1861–1932*, Chinese Research Monograph 31 (Institute of East Asian Studies, 1986), 189–90.

[27] Kristoffer Cassel, *Grounds of Judgment: Extraterritoriality and Imperial Power in Nineteenth-Century China and Japan* (Oxford University Press, 2012).

foreign actors. For example, the Qing's dealt with the Mongols and attempted to satisfy the Mongol demands while limiting their penetration of the Chinese polity. In Purdue's words: "the Canton trade system known to the Western coastal traders had been anticipated by these regulated trading arrangements on the Russian and Qinghai frontiers."[28]

Extraterritoriality had historically had a place in China proper as well. The Manchus had in establishing their regime granted themselves certain special rights, including the avoidance of certain forms of punishment for their bannermen. In effect they established a form of weak legal pluralism where different types of groups had different legal obligations and rights.[29] These institutions were enough to ensure the protection and distributional advantage of European transnational actors.

Informal imperialism was able to function because there existed a means to ensure the operation of European economic relationships and interests, allowing a commitment to the territorial integrity of China. While this imperialism was to become more competitive and exploitative as power relationships shifted, it never reached the point of territorial partition.[30] In the end European powers were for the most part satisfied with informal control facilitating their economic interests.

Domestic Political Institutions, Subordinate Interests, and the Stability of Informal Empire in China

European trade and institutions brought benefits to the central state by increasing revenue from foreign trade; income from commerce in China increased dramatically from over the second half of the nineteenth century. Moreover, the guarantees of the Maritime Customs allowed the government access to loans necessary to put down rebellions in the north and to build railways.[31] This increased revenue was an important factor in the central state's short-term functioning and reform process.[32]

The processes developed along with Chinese nationalism and modernization programs. Conservative Chinese nationalism was a complex

[28] Peter Purdue, "Empire and Nation in Comparative Perspective: Frontier Administration in Eighteenth-Century China," *Journal of Early Modern History* 5, no. 4 (2001): 295.
[29] Par Cassel, "Excavating Extraterritoriality: The 'Judicial Sub-Prefect' as a Prototype for the Mixed Court in Shanghai," *Late Imperial China* 24, no. 2 (2003).
[30] Robert Lee, *France and the Exploitation of China, 1885–1901: A Study in Economic Imperialism* (Oxford University Press, 1989); Niels Petersson, "Gentlemanly and Not-So-Gentlemanly Imperialism in China before the First World War," in *Gentlemanly Capitalism, Imperialism and Global History*, ed. Shigeru Akita (Palgrave Macmillan, 2002).
[31] Wong, *China Transformed*, 156–57.
[32] Richard Horowitz, "International Law and State Transformation in China, Siam, and the Ottoman Empire during the Nineteenth Century," *Journal of World History* 15, no. 4 (2005): 471.

phenomenon, one which, paradoxically, partially aided the cause of imperialism. Centralization of the government was the aim of nationalist bureaucrats and this was partially supported by the increased administrative capacity that European involvement in Chinese administrative organs brought. Feuerwerker writes of the Salt administration that "the political current of bureaucratic centralization whose interests for a time paralleled those of the foreign syndicate and which gladly made use of such pressure against local, centrifugal forces as foreign pressure might provide."[33] There existed a similar attitude toward the Chinese Maritime Customs.[34] While resenting European imperialism, Chinese leaders gladly made use of the resources they could gain from relationship.

Another example of the Europeans providing resources to facilitate the political survival of Chinese elites is the support provided to the Chinese state during the Taiping Rebellion. According to Phillip Kuhn, the British and French were initially neutral in regards to the conflict.[35] It was only after the signing of additional treaties and a more sympathetic emperor coming to power, that Britain began to provide resources to the Chinese state to suppress the rebellion.[36] Following the suppression of these rebellions, the self-strengthening movement, a set of policies aimed at improving Chinese state and military capacity, developed, which saw accommodation with the Western powers and acceptance of the unequal treaties as integral to strengthening the Chinese state.[37] Chinese officials saw the development of maritime customs, to improve revenue-raising capacity.[38] Chinese engaged with the West to improve their military.[39] And they pursued similar policies in regards to their navy.[40] The fact that external resources could be used to increase the probability of political survival was important for motivating Chinese elites to accept outside authority in certain domains.

The relationship between the Europeans and Chinese political actors of political financing and control occurred at both the central and regional

---

[33] Feuerwerker, *Foreign Establishment in China*, 76.   [34] Feuerwerker, 63.
[35] Philip Kuhn, "The Taiping Rebellion," in Fairbank and Liu, *Cambridge History of China*, 301–2.
[36] Kuhn, 303–4; Ssū-yü Têng, *The Taiping Rebellion and the Western Powers: A Comprehensive Survey* (Clarendon Press, 1971), 289–92.
[37] Ting-Yee Kou and Kwang-Ching Liu, "Self Strengthening: The Pursuit of Western Technology," in Fairbank and Liu, *Cambridge History of China*, 451.
[38] Richard Horowitz, "Politics, Power and the Chinese Maritime Customs: The Qing Restoration and the Ascent of Robert Hart," *Modern Asian Studies* 40, no. 3 (2006): 558.
[39] Richard J. Smith, "Foreign-Training and China's Self-Strengthening: The Case of Feng-Huang-Shan, 1864–1873," *Modern Asian Studies* 10, no. 2 (1976).
[40] Benjamin A. Elman, "Naval Warfare and the Refraction of China's Self-Strengthening Reforms into Scientific and Technological Failure, 1865–1895," *Modern Asian Studies* 38, no. 2 (2004).

levels. Horowitz states that provincial governors had access to loan guarantees, thus benefiting from informal empire and the guarantee of loans to gain financing.[41] The governor of Jiangnan and Jianxi was provided a loan to finance a campaign against Muslim rebels. Another example of European engagement with regional actors began with the Viceroy of Chihli threatening to seize British mining concessions. In the end, an agreement between various governments and interests was struck whereby a Chinese company and the British established a profit sharing relationship.[42] These examples demonstrate that European powers provide resources and protection to political elites outside of the central government in an attempt to maintain control and access.

Informal empire had broad effects on Chinese society, gaining the European powers constituents in numerous spheres. European and international actors dominated finance and foreign trade, but made up only a small proportion of the overall Chinese economy. Relationships with economic and provincial actors were symbiotic and organic. The provinces benefited from European economic penetration beyond the treaty ports, but these benefits were mainly distributed through Chinese actors. Moreover, control of actual production remained in the hands of local gentry who used the rents from their privileged connections to foreign trade to shore up income and power. European entry into Chinese social networks triggered an expanded role for the local gentry in Chinese informal institutions of control.[43]

The Canton delta provides examples of some of the ways that people at the regional level benefited. There, local gentry were able to gain from increased exports of silk and the consequent increased value of land.[44] They were able to use the profits from this increased trade to pay off the peasants, keeping resentment at a minimum when negatively affected by the vagaries of the world market, and increasing local control and stability. The buyers and Chinese merchants also benefited from their comprador relationship with Western factors because it gave them extra bargaining power. The limited penetration of Western economic actors into the hinterland provided opportunities for Chinese actors. Chinese merchants were able to take the imports to the treaty ports and then expand them into regions not dominated by European actors. Using

---

[41] Richard Horowitz, "Politics, Power and the Chinese Maritime Customs: The Qing Restoration and the Ascent of Robert Hart," *Modern Asian Studies* 40, no. 3 (2006): 559–60.

[42] Ian Phimister, "Foreign Devils, Finance and Informal Empire: Britain and China C. 1900–1912," *Modern Asian Studies* 40, no. 3 (2006): 749.

[43] Wong, "Formal and Informal Mechanisms," 403.

[44] Eng, *Economic Imperialism*, 31:190–92.

their local knowledge and connections, Chinese merchants could take advantage of European importers and supply the rural regions.[45]

Overall, European imperialism brought short-term gain to a number of actors both in the central government and the provinces. The decentralization of power and politics was a crucial factor in the persistence of the informal domination because of the effect it had on the distribution of resources and power. The central government's lack of power meant that it was often forced to ally itself with European actors to constrain the centrifugal pressures from the provinces.

The theorized dynamics are visible in this quote from Sir Robert Hart, the head of the Chinese Maritime Customs from the 1860s until the early twentieth century:

Official interference and protection handicap every enterprise and create dead weight that sink almost everything that's launched. The country changes very slowly for the better, and most of what we do is merely to keep the tyre on the wheel! Still we have kept the country on her legs–given time and provided funds for improvement–and thus preserved peace and quiet in everybody's interest.[46]

In this passage Hart makes reference to the rent-seeking behavior in the form of official interference. He also mentions the role that the European powers had in ensuring the survival "keeping the country on her legs." This testimony from a direct participant and observer in these processes supports much of what the theory hypothesizes.

These dynamics held even when this relationship with the central government was threatened. For example, during the Boxer Rebellion when it seemed that European control over China was falling apart, the external actors were still able to find crucial support that facilitated their control. The most notable of supporters was Yuan Shikai, a prominent Chinese general who despite the government's support of the Boxers worked with the Western powers to crush the rebellion. He received external support for his political and military reforms.[47] The Western powers, particularly Britain and Germany, provided support that pressured the Dowager Empress into appointing Shikai Governor of Zhili.[48] Nor was Yuan Shikai the only provincial actor to support the Western powers. Ignoring the declaration of war from the central government, the

---

[45] Albert Feuerwerker, *The Chinese Economy, 1870–1890* (Center for Chinese Studies, University of Michigan, 1995), 67–68.

[46] Sir Robert Hart and James Duncan Campbell, *The I. G. in Peking: Letters of Robert Hart, Chinese Maritime Customs, 1868–1907* (Harvard University Press, 1975), 938.

[47] David Bonavia, *China's Warlords* (Oxford University Press, 1995), 35; Jonathan D. Spence, *The Search for Modern China* (W. W. Norton, 1990), 278.

[48] Stephen R. MacKinnon, *Power and Politics in Late Imperial China: Yuan Shi-Kai in Beijing and Tianjin, 1901–1908* (University of California Press, 1980), 24–26.

governors in Canton, Nanking, and Wuchang, also acted to support foreign interests and repress the Boxer Uprising.[49] These events demonstrate not only the main point that hierarchy will be supported when competition and opportunities for rent-seeking create incentives, but also that it is not sufficient to focus on the interests and choices of the central government if the aim is to explain hierarchy.

The Chinese case demonstrates how the relationship between a hierarchical order and decentralized polity creates both incentives and opportunities for peripheral actors to behave in a manner that leads to the long-term persistence of informal empire. The trappings of informal empire in China were to continue until they failed due to external factors such as the Japanese invasions and World War II.[50] The effects of the Japanese invasion, the war dynamics as well as the Communist revolution centralized authority and removed incentives to support informal empire. Prior to this, internal dynamics had allowed informal empire to persist for close to a century beginning in the mid-nineteenth and ending in the mid-twentieth century.

The Ottomans and Informal Empire

During the nineteenth century, the Ottoman Empire partially succumbed to the pressures of European expansion and an informal imperialism developed.[51] As they did with China, Europeans forced free trade agreements on the Empire.[52] They assumed control of parts of the Ottoman government. European merchants were permitted to operate outside of the Ottoman legal system. The ability of the Ottoman Empire to determine its fate independently of the wishes of the great powers was severely limited due to the extensive hierarchical control that the European powers possessed in the Ottoman Empire during this time. However, the great powers never assumed formal control and the Ottoman government retained a certain amount of authority.

---

[49] Immanuel Hsu, "Late Ch'ing Foreign Relations, 1866–1905," in Fairbank and Liu, *Cambridge History of China*, 123–24.

[50] Nicholas Rowland Clifford, *Spoilt Children of Empire: Westerners in Shanghai and the Chinese Revolution of the 1920s* (Middlebury College Press, 1991), 284.

[51] Sevket Pamuk, *The Ottoman Empire and European Capitalism, 1820–1913: Trade, Investment and Production* (Cambridge University Press, 1987); Ronald Robinson and John Gallagher, *Africa and the Victorians: The Official Mind of Imperialism* (London: Macmillan, 1961), 5.

[52] Patrick K. O'Brien and Geoffrey Allen Pigman, "Free Trade, British Hegemony and the International Economic Order in the Nineteenth Century," *Review of International Studies* 18, no. 2 (1992): 94–95.

Transnational Expansion, the Capitulations, and the Origins of Informal Empire

Following the initial economic expansion of the European powers in the Ottoman Empire, institutions were established or adapted to their presence. These institutions were or became part of a much a broader institutional complex within the Ottoman Empire. The relationship of these institutions with rent-seeking and contestation affected the perception of their benefits and the potential costs of such arrangements for both subordinate and dominant actors. These institutions later became a focal point around which imperial strategies could coalesce.

Trade was crucial for the cohesion of the Ottoman Empire. The institutions and nature of the trade patterns initially established in the seventeenth century positioned European actors to take advantage of Ottoman decline.[53] Of particular importance for European actors in the Ottoman Empire were the capitulations. The capitulations were agreements between various states and the Ottoman Empire which codified the conditions and arrangements that allowed foreign merchants to live and operate in the Ottoman Empire.[54]

The capitulations provided benefits to European actors in three areas: law, economics, and the conditions under which they could reside in the Ottoman Empire.[55] The first two areas with their direct impact on the competitiveness of the European merchants were crucial elements in determining the future development of relations between the European states and the Ottoman Empire. The first privilege related to the jurisdiction under which a citizen of a country with capitulatory rights could be tried or could bring legal action.[56] The advantage of such a condition was that it provided legal protection for the European merchants involved, as they could seek the protection of their consul in legal matters and be tried according to their own legal system.

The second benefit related to issues of taxation. The European merchants of capitulatory countries were exempted from paying certain types of taxes and benefited from a reduction of customs duties.[57] This positioned the European merchants favorably in comparison to the domestic

---

[53] Daniel Panzac, "International and Domestic Maritime Trade in the Ottoman Empire during the 18th Century," *International Journal of Middle East Studies* 24, no. 2 (1992).

[54] Maurits Van Den Boogert, *The Capitulations and the Ottoman Legal System: Qadis, Consuls and Beraths in the 18th Century* (Brill, 2005).

[55] Nasim Susa, *The Capitulatory Regime of Turkey* (The Johns Hopkins University Press, 1933), chapter 4; Maurits Van Den Boogert, *The Capitulations and the Ottoman Legal System: Qadis, Consuls and Beraths in the 18th Century* (Leiden: Brill, 2005), 7–9.

[56] Van Den Boogert, *Capitulations and the Ottoman Legal System*.

[57] Van Den Boogert, 32–33.

merchants in the Ottoman Empire. These benefits were to have long-term influence on the comparative competitiveness of European and Ottoman traders.

The capitulations had a broad influence on Ottoman society. Kuran shows how these institutions had a large effect on the economic structure of Ottoman society.[58] The capitulations not only gave European economic actors a competitive advantage, they also provided benefits to the economic actors among the religious minorities of the Ottoman Empire. The establishment of the protégé system, the extension of capitulatory rights to citizens of the Ottoman Empire, has been described as a "protection racket."[59] The capitulations played an essential role in the form of hierarchy that the Europeans wielded over the Ottoman Empire during the nineteenth century, by providing them with the means to buy support from local actors.

These local actors could acquire capitulatory benefits in two different ways: they could either become official intermediaries, or European states could grant these actors citizenship. Once they had gained capitulatory privileges, they had many of the same economic and legal advantages that the European merchants had under the capitulations.[60] The effects from these benefits were broad; these actors were now able to operate under the same legal and institutional structure that had facilitated rapid European economic growth. Operating under European law, minorities could now form joint-stock companies, providing greater continuity for business; gain adequate insurance, allowing merchants the advantage of not having to remain financially liquid to cover potential losses; and operate under inheritance laws that did not divide the wealth among family members, permitting greater wealth accumulation.[61] The benefits to these actors of the capitulations were manifold.

Ottoman Muslims, however, could not benefit from the capitulations or European legal traditions. This discrimination resulted in part because such actors did not wish to abandon their Islamic legal traditions, but also because of the hesitancy of to grant Muslims the status that would allow them to benefit from such legal innovations.[62] The effect was such that by the nineteenth century the economic equality between the Muslim

---

[58] Timur Kuran, "Why the Middle East Is Economically Underdeveloped: Historical Mechanisms of Institutional Stagnation," *Journal of Economic Perspectives* 18, no. 3; Timur Kuran, "The Economic Assent of the Middle East's Religious Minorities: The Role of Islamic Legal Pluralism," *Journal of Legal Studies* 33 (2004).

[59] Salahi R. Sonyel, "The Protégé System in the Ottoman Empire," *Journal of Islamic Studies* 2, no. 1 (1991): 66.

[60] Kuran, "Economic Assent," 476.   [61] Kuran, 492–93.

[62] Kuran, "Why the Middle East Is Economically Underdeveloped," 85. Muslims were also reluctant to break with their own legal traditions.

majority and non-Muslim economic actors had vanished, while minorities and Europeans dominated international trade and all other nonagriculture sectors of the economy. These groups managed to maintain significant and influential connections to the politics and civil life of the empire.[63]

The result of this development was a "commercial elite – perhaps a would-be bourgeoisie – which chose to disassociate itself from the Ottoman commonwealth through foreign protection, or as in the case of many eighteenth century Greeks and Armenians, through expatriation."[64] This meant that, as disparities of power between the Ottomans and European actors increased, there was a significant and important constituency that supported continued privileges for European actors as a means of benefiting themselves.

State Organizations and Institutional Persistence

The functioning of institutions such as the capitulations was dependent on state organizations. Political competition placed limits on the ability of the Ottoman state to assert its autonomy. This is attested to by a memorandum written by the British ambassador, Sir Henry Elliott, about the Ottoman Sultan:

He deplores his ignorance of the character to those whom he has to entrust administration, for while he is known not to be satisfied with those whom he found in the highest positions, His Majesty does not yet feel sufficient confidence in his own judgment to venture upon making changes.[65]

Sir Henry Elliott was a sympathetic observer of the Ottoman Empire, criticized for being too soft on the Ottoman rulers.[66] In this memorandum he described how Sultan was hamstrung by the Ottoman state and bureaucracy.

Political weakness and contestation were not confined to the central state apparatus. Contestation over control of economic resources occurred between the center and the provinces of the Ottoman Empire.

---

[63] Caglar Keyder, "The Ottoman Empire," in *After Empire*, ed. Karen Barkey and Mark von Hagen (Westview Press, 1997), 34; Ioanna Pepelasis Minoglou, "Ethnic Minority Groups in International Banking: Greek Diaspora Bankers of Constantinople and Ottoman State Finances, C. 1840–81," *Financial History Review* 9, no. 2 (2002).

[64] Edhem Eldem, "Capitulations and Western Trade," in *The Cambridge History of Turkey: The Later Ottoman Empire, 1603–1839*, ed. Suraiya Faroqhi (Cambridge University Press, 2006), 3:335.

[65] British Documents on Foreign Policy: 171.

[66] See, e.g., Sir Henry Elliot – Observations, Hansard C Debate, March 27, 1877, vol. 233 cc568–613.

From its founding, the Ottoman state played a crucial role in training and appointing governors at the highest level of provincial administrations. The appointment of such elites was done through the Sultan's palace, and as the Ottoman Empire progressed, it was less likely to occur on the basis of local experience.[67] The state also provided a source of wealth and identity for local elites who were not at the top through the sale of tax-farming rights. This tax farming, while leading to the Ottomanization of local elites, also led to further decentralization.[68]

However, tax farming became an inadequate and inefficient means of wealth generation for the center. In the face of opposition from the local elites, the Ottoman state struggled and ultimately failed to reform these institutions. The failure to reform the revenue-raising system of the empire in the face of financial necessity in part forced the Ottoman state to rely on finance and loans from Europe.[69] Here the processes triggered by decentralization – the inability to raise adequate resources from the provinces and local tax-farmers – added to the stability of informal imperialism by creating need for the Ottoman state to rely on European support and loans.

European engagement provided benefits to both provincial actors and the center, even if these benefits would not have been accepted ex ante or with foresight of the vulnerabilities that the situation would create. For provincial actors, the benefits came at multiple levels, and while they could not be taxed themselves, the European actors brought wider economic benefits.[70] The effects of this were to increase the tax base, at least in the short-term, as local elites could tax at least some of those who interacted with European merchants. Actors at the provincial level, the center, and important minorities all gained from European trade and thus the institutional relationships that sustained informal imperialism.

---

[67] Karen Barkey, *Bandits and Bureaucrats: The Ottoman Route to State Centralization* (Cornell University Press, 1994), 77–80; Metin Kunt, *The Sultan's Servants: The Transformation of Ottoman Provincial Government, 1550–1650* (Columbia University Press, 1983).

[68] Dina Rizk Khoury, *State and Provincial Society in the Ottoman Empire: 1540–1834* (Cambridge University Press, 1997); Dina Rizk Khoury, "The Ottoman Centre Versus Provincial Power-Holders: An Analysis of the Historiography," in *The Cambridge History of Turkey: The Later Ottoman Empire, 1603–1839*, ed. Suraiya Faroqhi (Cambridge University Press, 2006); Murat Cizaka, *A Comparative Evolution of Business Partnerships: The Islamic World and Europe, with Special Reference to the Ottoman Archives* (Brill, 1996); Ilkay Sunar, "State and Economy in the Ottoman Empire," in *Ottoman Empire and the World Economy*, ed. Huri Islamoglu-Inan (Cambridge University Press, 1987), 74; Ariel Salzmann, *Tocqueville in the Ottoman Empire: Rival Paths to the Modern State* (Brill, 2004).

[69] Karen Barkey, *Empire of Difference: The Ottomans in Comparative Perspective* (Cambridge: Cambridge University Press, 2008), 274–75.

[70] Suraiya Faroqhi, *The Ottoman Empire and the World Around It* (I. B. Tauris, 2004), 159–60.

As in China, the lack of political centralization was further confounded by uprisings in the provinces. The need to repress these movements created further incentives for the Ottoman state to seek European support. For example, the Ottoman Empire relied on European backing to prevent Muhammed Ali expanding his power beyond Egypt.[71] Later, in the 1860s, the Cretan revolt forced the Ottomans to expend large amounts of resources, increasing their indebtedness to European powers.[72] These events provided external actors with opportunities to increase their influence and control.

Institutional Refinement

From the point of view of both the Ottomans and the Europeans "economic and particularly commercial activity was often considered to be subservient or even instrumental to political priorities, a constant interaction between politics and trade was considered rather normal."[73] While persuasion was often necessary for the Europeans to get their way, it was regularly found that "the political economy of the Ottoman state was compatible with – or, at least could be adjusted to – some of their own most basic commercial objectives."[74] Where necessary, the European states could limit themselves and compromise with the Ottomans in order to permit the persistence of these institutions. An example of this was the compromise reached between the European powers and the Ottoman government in the late nineteenth century to limit the number of protégés, once this practice had begun to cause egregious problems for the Ottoman state.[75]

The result of these interactions was that, as Ottoman power waned and the Europeans' power waxed, the Europeans still felt no need to take formal hierarchical control in the bulk of the Ottoman Empire. The legal institutions that the Europeans and Ottomans had established guaranteed the economic benefits the Europeans sought without them having to assume extensive and costly forms of control. European domination persisted because it provided short-term and long-term benefits to important actors

---

[71] John Darwin, *After Tamerlane: The Global History of Empire Since 1405* (Bloomsbury Press, 2008), 288.
[72] Barkey, *Empire of Difference*, 274–75.
[73] Edhem Eldem, *A History of the Ottoman Bank* (Economic and Social History Foundation of Turkey, 1999), 267.
[74] Ibid.
[75] Feroz Ahmad, "Ottoman Perceptions of the Capitulations 1800–1914," *Journal of Islamic Studies* 11, no. 1 (2000); Roderic Davison, "Ottoman Diplomacy and Its Legacy," in *Imperial Legacy: The Ottoman Imprint on the Balkans and the Middle East*, ed. L. Carl Brown (Columbia University Press, 1996), 188.

in the Ottoman Empire. The decentralized and pluralistic politics of the Ottoman Empire allowed broad coalitions to be incorporated and benefit from imperial bargains, increasing its long-term stability.[76]

Ultimately, the various European powers did dismember much of the Ottoman Empire. However, consistent with the empirical expectations of the theory, this happened due to exogenous rather than endogenous processes. The shock of World War I and Ottoman defeat is what brought the empire crashing down the European powers to move into the vacuum left behind.

The Origins of Egypt's Veiled Protectorate

Imperialism in the Egyptian case must be understood in the context of two distinct time periods. In the first period, Egypt was part of the Ottoman Empire and consequently subject to the dynamics of a decentralized, competitive political system. The elites in Egypt had an interest in supporting informal imperialism to counterbalance their rivals in the Empire proper. During the second period, as Egypt reduced Ottoman authority, the system was effectively centralized and consequently became a more unitary system. This resulted in an unstable informal empire that ultimately broke down and transitioned into the occupation by the British in 1882.

Following the British occupation, the governance of Egypt approached that of colonialism. British advisers were placed in all ministries, and attempts by Egyptian ministers to contradict the policies of these advisers would result in the Egyptian minister's dismissal. The British also controlled the Egyptian army and the state's finances.[77] The Egyptian state possessed very little authoritative decision-making capacity. Moreover, at times the British stationed tens of thousands of soldiers in Egypt.[78] The British drastically reduced Egypt's sovereign autonomy.

The occupation was a stark contrast with the informal imperialism that had persisted through much of the nineteenth century, through institutions very similar to those of the Ottoman Empire. As with the Ottoman Empire, the capitulations with their accompanying extraterritoriality and legal benefits were seen as central to the imperialist project. As late as 1908, over a quarter of a century into the British occupation, a British lawyer residing in Egypt commented on the impossibility of Europeans doing business in Egypt without the guarantees of the capitulatory system:

[76] Barkey, *Empire of Difference*.
[77] Al-Sayyid-Marsot, "British Occupation of Egypt from 1882."
[78] David M. Edelstein, *Occupational Hazards: Success and Failure in Military Occupation. Cornell Studies in Security Affairs* (Cornell University Press, 2008), 177.

Although abuses of privileges now occur, and although certain privileges have ceased to be beneficial, there are yet certain very important rights guaranteed by the Capitulations – rights which are essential to the continued residence of Europeans in Egypt – and the well being of the numerous Europeans who have made Egypt their place of residence is indissolubly bound up with the well-being and prosperity of the country.[79]

By this stage the capitulations were being maintained and reformed through direct control of the Egyptian state by the British, but it nevertheless indicates the importance placed on these institutions by European imperialists. This is supported by Cole's assertion that the purpose of the British intervention in Egypt was an attempt "to ensure that a process of state formation did not succeed in creating a new sort of stable order that would end European privileges and threaten European property and investments."[80] The developments that led to the British assumption that colonialism was necessary were part of a long-term process, and cannot be reduced to a discrete moment of debt crisis, minor riots in Alexandria, or phantom French threats to the Suez Canal.[81]

Muhammed Ali and Contestation within the Empire

The beginning of a changed institutional trajectory for Egypt can be located in the growing power and autonomy of Muhammed Ali in the early nineteenth century. The Ottomans had taken control of Egypt in the sixteenth century. During the Napoleonic Wars, Egypt was occupied by the French. The English and Ottomans sent an occupying force to retake control. Muhammed Ali, an Albanian, was an officer in this force.[82] Ali was able to take advantage of the situation to usurp control in Egypt.[83]

While it has become common to see the reign of Muhammed Ali as a distinct break from the past, as the moment of Egypt's birth as a modern nation, this is not the complete story.[84] Muhammed Ali did set Egypt on a particular path toward autonomy, but there remained important connections with the past; a past heavily influenced by institutions of the

---

[79] James Harry Scott, *The Law Affecting Foreigners in Egypt as the Result of the Capitulations, with an Account of Their Origin and Development* (William Green, 1908), xi.
[80] Juan Cole, *Colonialism and Revolution in the Middle East* (Princeton University Press, 1993), 17.
[81] A. G. Hopkins, "The Victorians and Africa: A Reconsideration of the Occupation of Egypt, 1882," *Journal of African History* 27, no. 2 (1986).
[82] Afaf Lufti Al-Sayyid-Marsot, *Egypt in the Reign of Muhammad Ali* (Cambridge University Press, 1984), 32–34.
[83] Khaled Fahmy, *Mehmed Ali: From Ottoman Governor to Ruler of Egypt*, Makers of the Muslim World (Oneworld, 2009), 27–30.
[84] Khaled Fahmy, *All the Pasha's Men: Mehmed Ali, His Army and the Making of Modern Egypt* (Cambridge University Press, 1997), 14–18.

Ottoman Empire.[85] Not only did Ali allow the continuation of institutions such as the capitulations from the Ottoman era; in Egypt the capitulations were even more favorable to the Europeans than in the rest of the Ottoman Empire.[86] Ali needed Western support to preserve his independence from Ottoman encroachment. Moreover, he was politically, economically, and militarily weak when compared to the Sublime Porte. These factors placed Ali in a position of vulnerability. The outcome of this vulnerability was that he had to accept abuses of the capitulations that the rest of the Ottoman Empire did not.

Muhammed Ali's support for the capitulations system was not only a product of his weakness or his socialization as part of the Ottoman Empire. His desires to develop the Egyptian economy and Westernize the country were also important motivations for his decision to continue the capitulatory regime.[87] The capitulations were thus perpetuated for a variety of reasons, and were both beneficial and costly for the ruler of Egypt.

In 1841, this situation led the future British prime minister Palmerston to claim that "we want to trade with Egypt, we want to travel through Egypt, but we do not want the burthen of governing Egypt."[88] During Muhammed Ali's reign, despite his aggressive foreign policy that led to civil war within the Ottoman Empire, despite his attempt to construct state monopolies, the British believed that they could securely do business in Egypt without resorting to colonial control. An important part of this was no doubt due to the commitment shown to the institutions that had regulated European trade and commerce in Egypt in the past. Yet forty years later, the British assumed the burden of governance in Egypt.

Prior to Ali's reign, Egypt had been largely dependent on trade with the rest of the Ottoman Empire. During Ali's tenure his encouragement of international trade led to Egypt's economic activity, primarily reliant on the cotton trade, to be diverted outward, away from the Ottoman Empire.[89] The effect of this was to decouple Egypt from its economic dependence on the Ottoman Empire.

Independence was to increase in the political sphere as well as the economic. Muhammed Ali, through force and diplomacy, had been able to carve a certain degree of autonomy for Egypt during the first half

---

[85] Afaf Lufti Al-Sayyid-Marsot, *Egypt in the Reign of Muhammad Ali* (Cambridge University Press, 1984), 1.
[86] David Landes, *Bankers and Pashas: International Finance and Economic Imperialism in Egypt* (Harvard University Press, 1958), 90.
[87] Landes, 91.
[88] Afaf Lufti Al-Sayyid, *Egypt and Cromer: A Study in Anglo-Egyptian Relations* (John Murray, 1968), 2.
[89] Al-Sayyid-Marsot, *Egypt in the Reign of Muhammad Ali*, 22.

of the nineteenth century. Ali, following the intervention of the European powers and their mediation, came to an agreement with the Sultan on the levels of Ali's power. Ali had basic autonomy, his rule became hereditary, and in return Ali had to pay tribute, limit the size of his army and abide by treaties signed by the Sublime Porte.[90] These conditions were to persist until the 1860s and 1870s when, through negotiation and increasing the size of the tribute, one of Ali's successors, Ismail, was to remove most of the restrictions on his power. Ismail assumed the title of Khedive and near complete independence.[91]

Subsequently, the state structure in Egypt centered on the Khedive. In contrast to the Ottoman Empire where the benefits of the state were somewhat more expansive and its demands less onerous; the Khedive was more authoritarian and exclusive. Social actors depended on him or were excluded from governance structures in a meaningful way. "Promotion in the bureaucratic hierarchy was not based primarily on performance or experience; more decisive were the personal relationships with the dynasty, and – closely connected with this – ethnic origin."[92] This meant that political power and extensive engagement with the institutions in question were limited to the Turko-Circassian elite that was becoming increasingly detached from its Ottoman origins. Meanwhile, the bulk of the Egyptian population, who were not part of the Turko-Circassian elite, was excluded from both the economic and political benefits of power and the potential economic benefits associated with imperialism.

Egypt was largely dependent on the cotton trade and foreign investment activities that were dominated by the Khedive, the land-owning elite and Europeans.[93] These structures excluded the bulk of the Egyptian population, creating frustration and resentment. No significant proportion of the population had reason to support the continuance of institutions such as the capitulations. This stood in contrast with other parts of the Ottoman Empire where the capitulations had established minority merchants who were dependent on the capitulations for their competitive advantage, and where provincial governors gained short-term benefits.

The situation in Egypt had reached a point where both the Europeans and the Egyptian government felt the need for reform of the capitulatory system. Egypt, because of the consular powers and legal authority possessed by various European nations, was faced with up to fifteen different

---

[90] Letitia W. Ufford, *The Pasha: How Mehemet Ali Defied the West, 1839–1841* (McFarland, 2007), 220–24.
[91] Alexander Schölch, *Egypt for the Egyptians: The Socio-political Crisis in Egypt 1818–1882* (Ithaca Press, 1981), 11–12.
[92] Schölch, 10. [93] Cole, *Colonialism and Revolution in the Middle East*, 25, 44.

The Origins of the Egypt's Veiled Protectorate

jurisdictions to navigate. There was no mechanism for dealing with disputes between foreigners from different nations, and the consular jurisdiction had begun to be abused to take advantage of the Khedive's debt.[94] In response to these problems, a process was begun to reform the system, introducing mixed courts involving European and Egyptian actors.[95] These courts provided many of the benefits of the capitulatory system while avoiding many – but not all – of the problems that had developed with capitulatory regime in Egypt.[96] Ultimately the courts were to become self-undermining as they pursued the narrow interests of economic actors without adequate concern for the fiscal requirements of the state. They found in the interest of the European debt holders in the face of the Khedive's financial need, exacerbating problems and leading to political instability.[97]

As Al-Sayyid writes, the European privileges "while designed to remedy local 'deficiencies,' tended to simultaneously unleash a tide of commercial rapacity which seriously exacerbated local problems, hindering development of local industries, destroying the trust, confidence, and sense of proportion essential to sound exchange."[98] State actors and the Khedive had gradually detached themselves from their Ottoman identity, both politically and economically. Initially, local actors of Egyptian origin were largely excluded from the governing structures. However, by the late nineteenth-century divisions between elites of Turkish and Egyptian origin had diminished, aligning preferences of subordinate groups and leading them into opposition with Europeans.[99] Moreover, by the late nineteenth century, the exploitation of Egypt by the Europeans had created resentment in Egyptian society without ever fostering the development of countervailing interests in support of European imperialism.[100] The result was a revolution against informal imperialism by the Egyptians.[101]

The Khedive Ismail's attempted to remove European influence due to domestic pressure and growing debt.[102] In response, Ismail was deposed by the European powers – in favor of his son Tawfiq, a figure more

---

[94] Mark Hoyle, *Mixed Courts of Egypt* (Graham and Trotman, 1991), 7.   [95] Hoyle, 11.
[96] Byron Cannon, "A Reassessment of Judicial Reform in Egypt, 1876–1891," *International Journal of African Historical Studies* 5, no. 1 (1972).
[97] Byron Cannon, *Politics of Law and the Courts in Nineteenth Century Egypt* (University of Utah Press, 1988).
[98] Al-Sayyid-Marsot, "British Occupation of Egypt from 1882," 653.
[99] Ibrahim Abu-Lughod, "The Transformation of the Egyptian Élite: Prelude to the 'Urābī Revolt," *Middle East Journal* 21, no. 3 (1967).
[100] Abu-Lughod; Cole, *Colonialism and Revolution in the Middle East*, 198–99.
[101] Cole, *Colonialism and Revolution in the Middle East*, 199.
[102] A. G. Hopkins, "The Victorians and Africa: A Reconsideration of the Occupation of Egypt, 1882," *Journal of African History* 27, no. 2 (1986): 375.

supportive of European interests.[103] This was followed by a general uprising by members of the Egyptian society, bureaucracy, and army.[104] This uprising was led by an Egyptian military officer, Urabi.[105] Understanding, or fearing, that the strategies and institutions they had been using could no longer guarantee their economic interests, the British intervened.[106] At this point the institutions of informal empire were no longer enough to ensure the benefits that the Europeans wished for, and Britain was forced to bear the greater governance costs associated with colonialism.

Ambiguity, Incomplete Information, and Resistance

While the evidence shows that the British were more likely motivated by developments in the domestic politics of Egypt and that these developments were a product of changing incentives for Egyptian political actors, there remains a puzzle: why would the Egyptians risk a confrontation with the much stronger European powers? A likely explanation is that they did not expect an intervention. There was plenty of ambiguity surrounding whether the British would intervene and how other states, particularly the French, would respond.

The first source of ambiguity can be derived from the past behavior of the British and Europeans. The great powers had demonstrated by their failure to enact full-scale intervention in the past, despite years of disagreements and threats, that they were unlikely to do so in the future. Other sources of ambiguity come from the behavior of the different great powers and their domestic politics. There may have been uncertainty regarding how the actions of the other great powers would affect British decisions. Disagreement between the British and the French and their changing policies must have created uncertainty for Egyptian actors about the likely outcome of any uprising. Indeed, the French tried to use diplomacy to prevent a British intervention.[107]

It is apparent from the accounts of observers that there was great uncertainty about the preferences of Gladstone, the British prime minister. According to Wilfred Blunt an observer and confidant of Urabi, Gladstone at various stages had expressed his opposition to any

[103] Al-Sayyid-Marsot, "British Occupation of Egypt from 1882," 654.
[104] Colin Newbury, "Great Britain and the Partition of Africa," in *The Oxford History of the British Empire: The Nineteenth Century*, ed. Andrew Porter (Oxford University Press, 1999), 3:632–35.
[105] Alexander Schölch, "The 'Men on the Spot' and the English Occupation of Egypt in 1882," *Historical Journal* 19, no. 3 (1976).
[106] P. J. Cain and A. G. Hopkins, *British Imperialism 1688–2000* (Longman, 2002).
[107] Schölch, "Men on the Spot," 775–76.

The Origins of the Egypt's Veiled Protectorate

intervention in Egypt. Indeed Blunt claimed to have passed on to Urabi a letter stating Gladstone's preference of not intervening; in the letter Gladstone stated: "Unless there be a sad failure of sense on one or both, or as I should say, all sides, we shall be enabled to bring this question to a favourable issue."[108] Gladstone was opposed in principle to actions that would undermine the integrity of the Ottoman state, and would have preferred the situation to be resolved by Turkey.[109] Additionally, two years before the intervention he had been elected on an antiexpansionist agenda, otherwise known as the Midlothian campaign.[110] As Schultz has convincingly demonstrated, such domestic politics can influence the beliefs of external actors about a state's resolve.[111] Given direct correspondence and some knowledge of Gladstone's disposition, it is plausible to assume some miscalculation on Urabi's part regarding the probability of British intervention in Egypt.

Furthermore, Gladstone describe British policies toward Egypt in the following manner:

They are well known to consist in the general maintenance of all established rights in Egypt, whether they be those of the Sultan, those of the Khedive, those of the people of Egypt, or those of the foreign bondholders, or whatever they may be – that, in fact, the single phrase, that we seek the maintenance of all established rights, and the provision of due guarantees for those rights, is the description of the policy.[112]

The publicly stated aims of British did not involve removing sovereignty from Egypt.

There is reason to believe that Urabi was uncertain about European intentions. It seems that he correctly predicted that the French would not intervene, as evidenced by their withdrawal. But he drew false conclusions concerning the British. Further evidence of his uncertainty was demonstrated by Urabi's claim in his defense statement at his trial that he had not even sought to repair the defenses of Alexandria.[113] If Urabi had believed that invasion were likely, presumably he would have acted to

---

[108] Wilfrid Scawen Blunt, *Secret History of the English Occupation of Egypt, Being a Personal Narrative of Events* (A. A. Knopf, 1922), 153–55.

[109] David Steele, "Three British Prime Ministers and the Survival of the Ottoman Empire, 1855–1902," *Middle Eastern Studies* 50, no. 1 (2014): 51.

[110] O. MacDonagh, "The Anti-Imperialism of Free Trade," *Economic History Review* 14, no. 3 (1962): 499.

[111] Kenneth A. Schultz, *Democracy and Coercive Diplomacy*, vol. 76 (Cambridge University Press, 2001).

[112] Hansard 3/CCLXX, June 14, 1982.

[113] Aḥmad 'Urābī, *The Defense Statement of Ahmad 'Urabi, the Egyptian: From the Blunt Manuscript at the School of Oriental and African Studies, London* (American University in Cairo Press, 1982), 32.

improve his defenses. There is little evidence that Urabi expected his actions to trigger a full-scale intervention.

The literature provides two primary alternative explanations for the occupation of Egypt. One is economic.[114] The other concerns a state crisis and control over the Suez Canal.[115] Neither type of explanation provides an adequate account of the occupation of Egypt. Krasner presents a fairly standard account of the economic causes of occupation. Foreign lending led to the European powers having an interest in ensuring that the debt be repaid. When a somewhat nationalist government came to power threatening the chance of repayment, Egypt was occupied.[116] The problem with this account is that there is no reason why Egypt should have been occupied once the government had been removed. Debt and default in no way automatically implied occupation or colonialism or even increased coercion.[117] As Frieden has shown, problems surrounding default are just as likely to be solved using more informal methods of domination.[118] Indeed, this is apparent in Krasner's own account where he discusses various cases of default that were not followed by occupation.[119] This is supported by Tomz's finding that gunboat diplomacy was rarely directly caused by default and debt.[120] Moreover, the short time frame fails to account for why European financiers felt that the commitment of the Egyptian Khedive was credible and repayment was likely in the first place.

Hopkins adopts a more sophisticated explanation with economic factors as the primary explanatory variables.[121] Hopkins improves on Krasner's explanation by extensively integrating events in Egypt with the economic motivations of the metropole. Nonetheless, he, too, is unable to explain the occupation in solely economic terms. He never adequately demonstrates why this crisis had the effects it did when previous crisis-like situations did not. Despite examining long-term trends, Hopkins never specifies what made informal empire function in earlier periods, before its breakdown.

---

[114] A. G. Hopkins, "The Victorians and Africa: A Reconsideration of the Occupation of Egypt, 1882," *Journal of African History* 27, no. 2 (1986); Krasner, *Organized Hypocrisy*.
[115] D. K. Fieldhouse, *Economics and Empire: 1830–1914* (Macmillan, 1984); Robinson and Gallagher, *Africa and the Victorians*.
[116] Hopkins, "Victorians and Africa."
[117] M. Tomz, *Reputation and International Cooperation: Sovereign Debt across Three Centuries* (Princeton University Press, 2007).
[118] Jeffry Frieden, "International Investment and Colonial Control: A New Interpretation," *International Organization* 48, no. 4 (1994); Frieden, "The Economics of Intervention: American Overseas Investments and Relations with Underdeveloped Areas, 1890–1950," *Comparative Studies in Society and History* 31, no. 1 (1989).
[119] Krasner, *Organized Hypocrisy*, chapter 4.
[120] Tomz, *Reputation and International Cooperation*, chapter 6.
[121] Hopkins, "Victorians and Africa."

The evidence from the cases shows that balancing does not have much effect on the particular outcome or form of empire. The move to formal empire in Egypt cannot be explained by the Suez Canal, oft cited as the reason for British colonialism.[122] Evidence shows that the British sought to resolve Egypt's domestic political troubles for years, with French cooperation, before intervening. This is not consistent with an immediate concern about protecting the Suez Canal from outside intervention. What is striking is that the British intervened when the French were adopting a more moderate stance than in past.[123] Moreover, statements and evidence are rather mixed regarding whether the canal was a motivating factor or an ad hoc justification.[124] Disraeli made the statement that there was no difference between controlling Egypt or Constantinople, both were potential routes to India.[125]

Hopkins ably disposes of many of the competing explanations for the occupation of Egypt.[126] He shows through examination of the official archives that neither chaos in the periphery, concern about control of the Suez Canal or "contagious Gallic enthusiasms" can explain the British occupation. The Urabi uprising was a response to European intervention, not a cause. The Suez Canal was low on the priorities of the Admiralty, which placed a far larger emphasis on the Cape passage. And the French were not visibly threatening British interests in Egypt; indeed, by the 1880s the French were far less aggressive in their attitudes toward Egypt than the British.

Informal Hierarchy in the Time of Colonialism

The following section discusses alternative explanations for the development of empire by the European powers in the nineteenth century, in the context of the cases of this chapter. Many of the explanations for empire that have been put forward are rooted in the international environment of the time, which was highly permissive for the development of formal empire. While none of these alternative explanations can adequately explain the variation in the level of hierarchy seen in the cases, they serve to illustrate some of the incentives that the European powers had during this period to expand using either formal or informal means. By demonstrating the minimal constraints to formal expansion faced by the great powers and the numerous incentives that these powers possessed to

---

[122] Robinson and Gallagher, *Africa and the Victorians*. [123] Schölch, "Men on the Spot."
[124] Ronald Hyam, *Britain's Imperial Century, 1815–1914: A Study of Empire and Expansion* (Palgrave Macmillan, 2002), 176–83.
[125] Ian St. John, *Disraeli and the Art of Victorian Politics* (Anthem Press, 2005), 168.
[126] Hopkins, "Victorians and Africa."

expand territorially, the section helps demonstrate the strength of my alternative institutional explanation. Finally, the generalization of the theory to a wider set of cases is considered.

International society is a crucial element of the international system.[127] Bull and Watson define an international society as "a group of states (or, more generally, a group of independent political communities) which not merely form a system, in the sense that the behaviour of each is a necessary factor in the calculation of others, but also have established by dialogue and consent common rules and institutions for the conduct of their relations, and recognize their common interest in maintaining those arrangements."[128]

The international system of the nineteenth and early twentieth centuries was highly permissive of imperial expansion, through both informal and formal empire. The international normative environment, at least as defined by the European powers, did not place many restrictions on international expansion. By the middle of the nineteenth century the great powers had begun to expand through much of the world. Great Britain had absorbed much of India and France was moving into North Africa, having colonized Algiers in 1831. Over the next half century, most of the rest of the world was to be divided among the European powers.

The international society in the period, it is often argued, created a system of insiders and outsiders. There were those states, such as the European powers, who could be engaged through state to state interactions using sovereignty as the basis of their interactions. There were those outsiders, not considered part of international society, who could be subjugated and subordinated.[129] In other words, the international society created a series of systemic structures where formal, territorial expansion into outsider states would receive no normative sanction.

There is little in these theories of international society, however, to explain the rapid shift from one form of empire to another that was seen, for example, in Egypt. While international society, as described by the English school, helped set scope conditions for those that could be engaged through informal empire and colonialism, it does not explain the variation between the two forms of empire. Subordinated polities with overlapping, in a very broad sense, historical experiences and cultural

---

[127] Hedley Bull, *The Anarchical Society: A Study of Order in World Politics* (Columbia University Press, 1977); R. J. Vincent, *Nonintervention and International Order* (Princeton University Press, 1974); Martin Wight, *Systems of States* (Leicester University Press for the London School of Economics and Political Science, 1977).

[128] Hedley Bull and Adam Watson, "Introduction," in *The Expansion of International Society*, ed. Hedley Bull and Adam Watson (Clarendon, 1984), 1.

[129] Yongjin Zhang, "China's Entry into International Society: Beyond the Standard of 'Civilization,'" *Review of International Studies* 17, no. 1 (1991).

origins such as the Ottomans and Egypt were treated differently. Despite permissiveness toward formal expansion, informal empire was often preferred by the great powers.

Competition between the European states may have created incentives for formal expansion. Balancing theories posit that states may choose to preserve or dismember other polities to balance against each other.[130] In such a multipolar system, the more states that are potential threats, the greater the number of commitment problems, and the greater the incentive to expand through formal means.[131]

A further argument about the stability of informal empire regards crises and contingencies in the subordinate state.[132] It was systematic crises within the subordinate sphere that led to the assumption of formal control. The argument is that while the subordinate state remained strong, it was able to control its populace. Because the population was under control, the dominant state was able to rule through the subordinate state facilitating informal empire. Where the subordinate state weakened and uprisings against the imperial order manifested, the dominant state needed to take direct colonial control.

Such an approach to explaining the shift between informal and formal empire is unsatisfying because it fails to account for the differences between cases. This is particularly evident in the cases of China and Egypt. China was perhaps the longest run case of informal empire, with aspects of it, such as extraterritoriality, existing well into the twentieth century. In Egypt, on the other hand, informal empire broke down and was replaced by formal control far more rapidly. Both, however, featured nationalist uprisings. In the case of Egypt, the Urabi uprising preceded British occupation, but it is better understood as symptomatic, and part of a long-run failure of informal empire. It followed, and did not precede the removal of the Khedive. China, too, featured numerous rebellions, warlordism, and uprisings, notably the Boxer Rebellion. However, at no point, did these factors lead to removal of Chinese sovereignty much beyond those conditions already in place. The social and political context in which such nationalist uprisings occur determines the response to them.

The international system of the nineteenth century, then, provided both opportunities and incentives to expand using formal control. The norms and international legal and social structures of the era were highly permissive of formal expansion, reducing the costs of territorial

---

[130] Tanisha M. Fazal, *State Death: The Politics and Geography of Conquest, Occupation, and Annexation* (Princeton University Press, 2007).
[131] Michael Doyle, *Empires* (Cornell University Press, 1986), 136.
[132] John Gallagher and Ronald Robinson, "Imperialism of Free Trade," *Economic History Review* 6 (1953).

expansion. The distribution of power within the system meant there were incentives to expand in order to avoid other states taking advantage of such opportunities. Finally, systematic crises spread through the periphery created further incentives for control.

Despite the relative low cost of formal expansion and the possible advantages to such expansion there was notable and important variation. Informal empire was often the first form of empire that was attempted and the European powers seemed to persist with it where that seemed possible. In other words while the international system made formal imperial expansion easy and perhaps even desirable, the great powers actually preferred alternative forms of control such as informal empire. The cases in this chapter demonstrate that only when the domestic political situation was inhospitable for informal empire were the great powers forced to adopt alternative forms.

This institutional explanation plausibly extends to other cases. Three cases that provide an interesting point of comparison are the Beyical states of the Ottoman Empire. The Beyical states of North Africa were semiautonomous states within the Ottoman Empire permitted to conduct foreign policy on limited terms. The historical development of the Maghrebi states was different from that of that of the Ottoman Empire. This development was one that was to result in colonialism in these places while other parts of the Ottoman Empire were left intact if subject to informal forms of domination. The breakdown and unraveling of the institutions of North Africa's Beyical states is attributable to the Napoleonic Wars. Whereas prior to the war the great powers had conducted their interactions with the Barbary States in a manner similar to that seen in the Ottoman Empire,[133] the Napoleonic Wars altered the economic behavior of the North African states. The consequences of this change led to greater conflict with Europe, economic collapse, and eventual colonization.[134] An interesting exception to the colonization of North Africa is the case of Tripoli. The failure of this province to be colonized until 1911 supports the argument being made here. While initially an autonomous province like Algiers and Tunis, Tripoli was incorporated into the Ottoman Empire proper in the mid-nineteenth century, losing its semiautonomous status.[135] In this manner Tripoli become subject to the same institutional dynamics that have

---

[133] Christian Windler, "Diplomatic History as a Field for Cultural Analysis: Muslim-Christian Relations in Tunis, 1700–1840," *Historical Journal* 44, no. 1 (2001); Windler, "Representing the State in a Segmentary Society: French Consuls in Tunis from the Ancien Regime to the Restoration," *Journal of Modern History* 73 (2001).

[134] Daniel Panzac, *Barbary Corsairs: The End of a Legend, 1800–1820* (Brill, 2005).

[135] Lisa Anderson, "Nineteenth-Century Reform in Ottoman Libya," *International Journal of Middle East Studies* 16, no. 3 (1984).

been described in the Ottoman case. This is in stark contrast to the other Maghrebi states and Egypt which retained their autonomy or extended it and were thus subject to a very different set of circumstances.

India provides an additional example of an exogenous shock leading to the breakdown of informal hierarchy. Briefly, in the eighteenth century, the Mughal Empire displayed similar dynamics to the Ottoman Empire and China. The British developed dense social ties with various intermediaries within the Mughal Empire, providing them with resources in return for support.[136] The East India Company was able to take advantage of decentralization in the Mughal Empire to claim privileges for themselves, such as the exemption from customs duties. However, with the breakdown of Mughal authority in the nineteenth century, due to centrifugal as well as exogenous pressures, the British colonized India, piecing together different kingdoms such as the Mughal Delhi, the Mahrattas, and others.[137] This is similar to what occurred in China and the Ottoman Empire where informal empire ended due to exogenous shocks, World War I in the case of the Ottomans and the Japanese invasion in the case of China. In Mysore, once Tippu Sultan centralized the regime there the British colonized.[138] However, they continued to use informal domination of Hyderabad under the Nizams, with its decentralized power centers and powerful landholders.[139] Overall, the various cases that constituted India at that time provide additional evidence for the plausibility of the theory.

Conclusion

Informal empire as established in the Ottoman Empire and China by the European powers demonstrates the importance of institutions and strategic calculation in determining the type of hierarchy that develops. Domestic legal institutions for incorporating foreigners provided transnational actors from the dominant states with the protection that they required to carry out their activities. These were gradually refined to

---

[136] Paul MacDonald, *Networks of Domination: The Social Foundations of Peripheral Conquest in International Politics* (Oxford University Press, 2014), 83–89.
[137] C. A. Bayly, *Indian Society and the Making of the British Empire*, The New Cambridge History of India II (Cambridge University Press, 1988), chapter 1.
[138] Irfan Habib, "Introduction: An Essay on Haidar Ali and Tipu Sultan," in *Confronting Colonialism: Resistance and Modernization under Haidar Ali and Tipu Sultan*, ed. Irfan Habib (Anthem Press, 2002); Burton Stein, "State Formation and Economy Reconsidered: Part One," *Modern Asian Studies* 19, no. 3 (1985).
[139] Benjamin B. Cohen, *Kingship and Colonialism in India's Deccan, 1850–1948* (Palgrave Macmillan, 2007).

reduce the sovereignty of the subordinate polity, constituting informal empire.

Once these institutions had been established, the interests of both domestic and international actors converged around them. The European powers were then able to extend and maintain their position of dominance through a mix of coercion and appeals to the material interests of important actors within the Ottoman Empire and China. This was possible because the decentralized politics in both these cases shaped the interests of local actors so that they sought accommodation with the hierarchical institutions.

In Egypt the opposite occurred. Initially able to achieve their aims through informal empire, the British, because of the breakdown of the institutions established by the Ottoman Empire in Egypt, were forced to assert greater levels of control in the form of colonialism. The institutions the European powers had relied on to facilitate their economic activity had stopped functioning. Increased centralization and independence from the Ottomans meant that the institutional complex of which informal empire was a part no longer corresponded with the incentives of domestic political order in Egypt. Ultimately, despite attempts at reform, the imperialist institutions gave way, and Britain occupied Egypt through formal colonization.

The implication of these cases is that the various literatures that attempt to explain the emergence or failure of different forms of empire are inadequate. Accounts of imperial breakdown and hierarchy rely too readily on exogenously given factors such as the power differences between the core and the periphery. The cases here show that persistence, change, and breakdown of imperial institutions can only be explained through the endogenous interactions of empire and domestic political structures in the subordinate state.

The Egyptian case also highlights an important fact about the role of hierarchy and control in the international system. That is, great powers, such as Britain, often do not respond to increasing cost of governance and control by reducing their demand; instead, they are willing to pay more, increasing their level of control through force and demonstrating an increased demand for hierarchy and empire. In other words, great powers are often prepared to give up other goods in order to continue their domination.

The European powers began their expansion using informal techniques of control despite the possibility of formal empire in some cases. Where competition was present informal empire matched the first preferences of both the metropole and the periphery and the result was stable informal imperial regimes. Where competition over rents was absent, these incentives and preferences did not align; the result because of the permissive international system was colonialism and occupation.

6 Cross-National Variation in Sovereignty and Hierarchy

The end of World War II marked the conclusion of the imperial era. The European powers began their long, often painful and bloody, withdrawal from their colonies. The changed international environment, the diffusion of technology, and the growth of nationalism had reduced the power advantage that had permitted European domination of most of the globe. However, hierarchy has remained an important part of the international system. Throughout the postwar period great powers have made efforts, successful or not, to reduce the sovereignty of others in pursuit of their own security, economic, and ideological goals.

This chapter uses statistical analysis to explore variation in the level of hierarchy among states and whether some of this variation is explained by the combination of rent-seeking and contestation or political threat to rent-seeking in the subordinate state. I use two empirical strategies. The first focuses on the former Soviet Republics and their relationship with Russia. Narrow, focused tests of broad theories allow a more comprehensive understanding of the conditions under study, even if they limit generalizability to a certain extent.[1] The second strategy tests the theory in a larger, global sample. While this increases the difficulty of modeling the processes under study, it does provide some evidence of generalizability. Combined, these two aspects of the study will increase confidence in the findings if they support the arguments presented in this book.

The chapter uses quantitative analyses to demonstrate how domestic political institutions have influenced the development of hierarchy globally and in the post-Soviet space. In the post-Soviet space, the interaction between rent-seeking and contestation is first directly measured and then examined indirectly using regime type as a proxy, to test the relationship's robustness using slightly different assumptions. This analysis demonstrates how the theoretical relationship generalizes to other post-Soviet

---

[1] Paul R. Rosenbaum, "Choice as an Alternative to Control in Observational Studies," *Statistical Science* 14, no. 3 (1999); Kevin A. Clarke, "The Phantom Menace: Omitted Variable Bias in Econometric Research," *Conflict Management and Peace Science* 22, no. 4 (2005).

Republics not discussed in the qualitative chapters. This is further highlighted by a brief discussion of the findings in relation to recent political developments in Kyrgyzstan and Armenia. Finally, the larger, global sample is analyzed to test the generalizability of the theory beyond Russia's sphere of influence.

Cross-National Variation in Russian Hierarchy

The argument states that where high levels of rent-seeking raise the consequences of political power being lost and political institutions increase the probability that power will be lost or negatively affect future access to rents, hierarchy should be higher. In other words, those who are profiting from rent-seeking should seek Russian hierarchy if they also face a threat or potential threat from domestic sources.

To test this, a time-series cross-sectional data set was constructed using yearly observations from all non-Russian former Soviet states from 1992 to 2016. The sample includes all the post-Soviet states as they are plausible targets for Russian hierarchy. While some of the states might have become oriented toward the west and its institutions such as NATO, these alternative institutions are not hierarchical as such, as they are more symmetrical in terms of rights and responsibilities.[2] The data set includes indicators of Russian hierarchy, rent-seeking, political competition, and various control variables related to alternative accounts for hierarchy.

Measuring Russian Hierarchy

Hierarchy results when the roles that normally fall to an independent state exercising its authority are arrogated to another.[3] The capacity of the subordinate state to decide policy is diminished to benefit the interests of one or many superordinate states. Issue areas that can be arrogated to another party can concern politics, security, and economics. The subordinate state can further increase the level of hierarchy by surrendering control over more issues

A measure for the level of hierarchy, the authority of one state over another, must encompass a range of issue areas. In the post-Soviet space a variety of Russian dominated international organizations exist that some countries opt into. These organizations can be political, economic, or security oriented. Several countries also host Russian military

---

[2] For a more detailed discussion of this issue, see the definition of hierarchy in Chapter 1.
[3] D. A. Lake, "Escape from the State of Nature: Authority and Hierarchy in World Politics," *International Security* 32, no. 1 (2007).

installations, some including large numbers of military personnel. The number and type of such international organizations reflect the variety of issue areas affected by Russian hierarchy.

Membership in these organizations established by Russia was used as indicators of the underlying willingness to accept Russian hierarchy. These indicators were combined using an Item Response model to construct a continuous measure of Russian hierarchy. Membership of the following international organizations was counted for each state: the Commonwealth of Independent States (CIS) and several of its subagreements – the Council of Defense Ministers, the Economic Court, and the Council of Border Guards; the Collective Security Treaty, and later the Collective Security Treaty Organization (CSTO); Treaty of Deepening Integration; the Eurasian Economic Community; the Common Economic Space; and the Air Defense Integration. Hosting a Russian military installation in the country was an additional indicator.

As states can opt in or out of such organizations, these indicators capture hierarchy of a voluntary nature, not just an arrangement based on coercion. Various states have joined and then left the CSTO and CIS, demonstrating that membership is not a matter of force or coercion. For example, Uzbekistan left the CSTO, rejoined and then left again. Others such as Georgia and Azerbaijan have left without rejoining.[4] Georgia was also able to negotiate the removal of Russian military bases.[5] Hierarchy can be measured by the degree of control over an issue area, but also the number of areas the dominant state controls. Counting organizations across a variety of issue areas can determine if a state has authority over greater or lesser number of sovereign rights, and hence has a greater or lesser amount of hierarchical authority.

Even if the sovereignty surrendered is limited in the case of some of these organizations, it does indicate a willingness to accept Russian primacy in the region. If joining these organizations was just cheap talk or had no effects, then we would not expect the consistent patterns that we observe in the following analyses, as states might join organizations randomly. While sovereignty, in some instances, is not circumscribed to a large extent, joining an organization does seem to indicate a commitment to Russian involvement in the region. Most importantly, even if the absolute level of hierarchy measured is limited, it still allows the analysis of differences between states and over time within states.

---

[4] T. Kuzio, "Geopolitical Pluralism in the CIS: The Emergence of GUUAM," *European Security* 9, no. 2 (2000).

[5] R. L. Larsson, "The Enemy Within: Russia's Military Withdrawal from Georgia," *Journal of Slavic Military Studies* 17, no. 3 (2004).

Membership of these institutions is indicative of a willingness to join in Russian-led projects, but for some more so than others. The levels of hierarchy captured by these raw indicators therefore may vary substantially. The CIS, for example, requires relatively little of states in a formal sense. This is in part due to its focus on soft law and agreements, and due to opposition from CIS "minimalists" like Ukraine, Moldova, and Georgia. It is worth noting, however, that some states within the organization, such as Kazakhstan, wished to increase the degree of integration that organization demanded. Furthermore, nested within the CIS agreements are bilateral treaties that often provide Russia with substantial influence in a variety of areas.

Other organizations require substantially more sovereignty be surrendered. For example, the Joint Air Defense agreement was run through the Russian air force; it also resulted in a certain technological dependency, as radars and other equipment are sourced from Russia. For example, Kazakhstan, as part of their cooperation with Russia on Air Defense, allows Russia to run their Balkash Radar base; this provides Russia with control over a Kazakh military asset on Kazakh territory.[6] Such military arrangements and technological dependence are an expected outcome of hierarchy.[7]

The use of the item response theory (IRT) model to estimate the latent level of authority allowed me to account for this variation. Item response models estimate the level of a latent variable as a function of observed indicators and therefore do not assume that membership of all these institutions demands the surrender of an equivalent level of sovereignty. Some states have joined almost all these institutions while others have kept themselves separate, while others have joined some but not others. This variation suggests that these institutions provide a means to discriminate between states' latent willingness to accept integration with Russia

Item response models assume that some indicators are harder to achieve than others and this then provides a means to determine the latent value of the dependent variable. In other words, if states join all or most of these institutions it indicates a higher underlying willingness to accept Russian leadership in the region, as while some organizations might make few demands on states others will make more, and only states with a comparatively high willingness to accept hierarchy will join these latter type. An alternative dependent variable was created by simply

---

[6] "Kazakhstan Lawmakers OK Deal with Russia on Radar Complex for Missile Attack Warning," TASS, accessed January 22, 2016, http://tass.ru/en/defense/825174.

[7] Jonathan D. Caverley, "United States Hegemony and the New Economics of Defense," *Security Studies* 16, no. 4 (2007); David Lake, "Beyond Anarchy: The Importance of Security Institutions," *International Security* 26, no. 1 (2001): 129–60.

counting the number of organizations that each country was a member of, with an additional point for hosting a Russian military installation, and normalizing by the total possible score for that year. This raw index of Russian hierarchy was bounded at 0 and 1 and therefore did not fit the modeling assumptions of ordinary least squares regression as well as the continuous IRT measure of hierarchy. While the raw hierarchy index assumed that each organization contributed equally to Russian hierarchy, its more straightforward construction made it a useful robustness check.

Contestation, Rent-Seeking, and Political Institutions: Direct Measures

The independent variables measure contestation and threats to political survival. The prediction is that as the level of corruption and rent-seeking increase accompanied by political competition, this should result in reduced levels of autonomy and increased hierarchy. I first directly modeled the interaction between the level of political corruption and the existence of political forces outside of the ruling coalition. Combined competition and corruption should result in lower levels of autonomy and increased hierarchy.

To measure rent-seeking, I used a variable from the Varieties of Democracy (V-Dem) database measuring corruption within the states. The authors of the V-Dem database obtained this variable by first surveying country experts on the level of corruption, and then aggregating their responses using a latent variable model. The result was a continuous variable measuring corruption.

To measure competition or political threat I used two alternative variables. First, I used Defacto2, a variable from the Cheibub, Gandhi, and Vreeland (CGV) database. This database includes a variety of variables measuring regime characteristics. Defacto2 is a dummy variable measuring organized political forces outside of regime control. In addition, I used the Polity Polcomp variable. This variable measures both how regulated and controlled political competition is and how widespread participation is in political competition. Unlike the CGV Defacto2 variable, the Polcomp variable is continuous. As the Polcomp variable increases, so does the level of political competition. Using these variables it is possible to model the interaction between rent-seeking and political competition; the expectation is that where corruption is high, more competition should increase the level of Russian hierarchy.[8]

---

[8] A possible alternative to using these institutional variables would be to estimate regime time horizons as a proxy for political survival. However, there are problems with this

Controlling for Alternative Explanations Control variables were selected to account for alternative explanations described in Chapter 2 and aggressively deal with potential confounding variables. These control variables are designed to account for the various factors that may have pushed Russia to assert control in certain areas rather than others, and those that may have pulled them back. By providing a detailed specification it should be possible to determine not only if domestic politics plays a role in the establishment of Russian hierarchy but what other variables have an effect. This will provide a richer understanding of how Russia has pursued its interests in post-Soviet space.

The first factor to be controlled for was the presence of fixed or site-specific assets. Several authors have argued that particular types of economic structures are more likely to foster higher levels of hierarchy.[9] Fixed assets in this case are things such as mines or oil, that cannot be shipped or moved, and do not rely a great deal on technical expertise. Where site-specific assets exist that a dominant state wishes to take advantage of, they need to appropriate them by force because simple investments, not guaranteed by hierarchical institutions, could easily be appropriated by local governments. To control for this, the total resource revenue of the state was included in the models. The World Bank's measure of natural resource revenue was used to account for these factors.

There are further reasons to include oil and other natural resources in as a control. Part of Russia's newfound influence and power is often attributed

---

approach. The theory presented in the book argues that hierarchy should increase the probability of political survival. As the theoretical mechanism relies on Russia transferring resources to keep leaders in power, it is not possible to use outcomes or leaders losing power to measure contestation. The reason for this is, if the theory is correct, then any models that estimate the probability of losing power will underestimate the true probability as leaders will stay in power due to outside support even though domestic pressures might lead to their ouster. Finding a null result based on authoritarian leader time horizons is not suitable for falsifying the argument in this context. An additional problem is that it makes it difficult to assess the differences between authoritarian and democratic regimes, as democratic regimes have regularized and institutionalized means of removing leaders from power.

[9] For general theoretical statements, see Jeffrey Frieden, "The Economics of Intervention: American Overseas Investments and Relations with Underdeveloped Areas, 1890–1950," *Comparative Studies in Society and History* 31, no. 1 (1989); Jeffrey Frieden, "International Investment and Colonial Control: A New Interpretation," *International Organization* 48, no. 4 (1994); Charles Lipson, *Standing Guard: Protecting Foreign Capital in the Nineteenth and Twentieth Centuries* (University of California Press, 1985). For the application of these sorts of approaches to the former Soviet cases, see Alexander Cooley, "Imperial Wreckage: Property Rights, Sovereignty, and Security in the Post-Soviet Space," *International Security* 25, no. 3 (2001); Alexander Cooley and Hendrick Spruyt, Contracting States: Sovereign Transfers in International Relations (Princeton University Press, 2009); Kathleen Hancock, "The Semi-sovereign State: Belarus and the Russian Neo-empire," *Foreign Policy Analysis* 2, no. 2 (2005).

to its wealth in oil and gas and its ability to use other states' needs for these resources as a source of leverage. If this were the case, such power would be more useful in dealing with states without oil and gas, as those possessing their own would not be subject to Russia's manipulation of access to energy resources. Oil exportation may also affect the independent variables of interest. Oil and natural resources can strongly influence the nature of political institutions. In particular, resource rents can strongly reduce the degree of freedom within a state.[10] In addition, the multinational corporations that are conduits of this business can influence conflict or establish relationships between actors which can be used as a form of leverage or influence.[11] Because of its potential to affect both the independent variable and the dependent variable it is important to include oil as a control.

Power is another important factor that could affect the level of hierarchy. This is controlled for through a measure of military capability and population. The natural log of the SIPRI measure of military spending was used to measure military capabilities.[12] In addition, the natural log of population was included in the model. These data were taken from the World Bank's World Development Indicators.[13] Controlling for the level of GDP is of particular importance as the relationship between economic development and political and social rights is strong and robust.[14] Economic development could also increase the relative power and capacity of the state. Moreover, Hale suggests that the level of development affects the incentives of states to pursue integration.[15]

To further control for realist arguments based on threat I included two variables dealing with security threat. One variable indicates whether the state faces an external threat, while the other measures if the state faces a potential secessionist threat domestically. Both of these variables were coded according to Darden's scheme.[16] States are considered to face an

---

[10] Thad Dunning, *Crude Democracy: Natural Resource Wealth and Political Regimes*, Cambridge Studies in Comparative Politics (Cambridge University Press, 2008); M. L. Ross, "Does Oil Hinder Democracy?," *World Politics* 53, no. 3 (2001).

[11] Rawi Abdelal, "The Profits of Power: Commerce and Realpolitik in Eurasia," *Review of International Political Economy* 20, no. 3 (2013); Rawi Abdelal, "The Multinational Firm and Geopolitics: Europe, Russian Energy, and Power," *Business and Politics* 17, no. 3 (2015).

[12] Stockholm International Peace Research Institute, Military Expenditure Database, www.sipri.org/databases/milex.

[13] World Development Indicators, World Bank, http://data.worldbank.org/data-catalog/world-development-indicators.

[14] C. Boix and S. C. Stokes, "Endogenous Democratization," *World Politics* 55, no. 4 (2003).

[15] H. E. Hale, *The Foundations of Ethnic Politics: Separatism of States and Nations in Eurasia and the World*, Cambridge Studies in Comparative Politics (Cambridge University Press, 2008).

[16] Keith A. Darden, *Economic Liberalism and Its Rivals: The Formation of International Institutions among the Post-Soviet States* (Cambridge University Press, 2009).

internal threat if they have faced a separatist or insurrectionary movement. An external threat was coded if the states border another state that has made territorial claims over the target state.

Another possible source of Russian hierarchy could be the need to protect Russian minorities in the region. The existence of 25 million ethnic Russians outside of Russia has been a motivating factor for Russian foreign policy and assertiveness since the Soviet collapse.[17] A dummy variable measuring whether a Russian minority was present and politically active in the country as coded by Ethnic Power Relations data set.[18] Ethnic Fractionalization was used as a control as well.[19] Higher levels of ethnic fractionalization might allow Russia greater opportunities to engage in divide and rule. Furthermore, ethnic fractionalization is often related to competition over rent-seeking.[20]

Geographic region and membership in the EU may have important implications for Russian hierarchy. Arguments have been made concerning the existence of outside alternatives that might allow subordinate states to escape the influence of potential dominant states.[21] Where alternatives exist, weaker states are able to turn to these outsiders for protection, knowledge, and other resources, mitigating the need for hierarchy. The most relevant "White Knights" in this instance are NATO and EU membership. Norms may have diffusion effects; proximity to Europe might lead to more liberal institutions and policies at a domestic level in former Soviet countries.[22] In addition, the desire to join the EU creates incentives for elites to adopt liberal economic and social institutions in order fulfill the demands of EU countries.[23] Simultaneously, these factors might drive countries away from illiberal authoritarian Russia. To address this a variable measuring membership or an association agreement with the EU was included, as was a region variable, coding whether a state was in Europe, the Caucasus, or Central Asia.

Level of nationalism is important to control for if possible. It has been shown that nationalism correlates strongly with important political

---

[17] Andrei P. Tsygankov, *Russia and the West from Alexander to Putin: Honor in International Relations* (Cambridge University Press, 2012), 182–83.
[18] Manuel Vogt et al., "Integrating Data on Ethnicity, Geography, and Conflict: The Ethnic Power Relations Data Set Family," *Journal of Conflict Resolution* 59, no. 7 (2015).
[19] A. Alesina et al., *Fractionalization* (National Bureau of Economic Research, 2003).
[20] Jose G. Montalvo and Marta Reynal-Querol, "Ethnic Diversity and Economic Development," *Journal of Development Economics* 76, no. 2 (2005).
[21] Cooley and Spruyt, *Contracting States*; Hancock, "Semi-Sovereign State."
[22] J. Kopstein and D. A. Reilly, "Geographic Diffusion and the Transformation of the Postcommunist World," *World Politics* 53, no. 1 (2000).
[23] Frank Schimmelfennig, "The Community Trap: Liberal Norms, Rhetorical Action, and the Eastern Enlargement of the European Union," *International Organization* 55, no. 1 (2001).

outcomes in the postcommunist world. High levels of precommunist literacy led to a strong sense of national identity within certain countries because it allowed the transmission of nationalist education. These effects persisted through the communist and postcommunist era, leading to a rejection of Russian influence.[24] The control variable used measured the percentage of the population who were literate prior to the imposition of communism. This variable should positively correlate with nationalism and thus would predict reduced levels of hierarchy. To further control for the level of nationalism, I included the number of weeks it took these states to secede from the Soviet Union.[25]

Analysis and Results The theory argues that the combined effect of rent-seeking and contestation is to increase the willingness of actors to accept hierarchy. Pooled ordinary least squares (OLS) regression, including all the control variables, was used to estimate the effects of the interaction of rent-seeking and political competition on hierarchy. The variables measuring corruption and political competition were included in the model as were the interaction terms between these variables. The expectation is that as these variables increase together, the level of Russian hierarchy should be higher as well.

The models included a lagged dependent variable to account for autocorrelation. The lag was included for theoretical reasons; the causal theory presented above assumes that hierarchy in the present should be somewhat correlated with hierarchy in the future. This implies a dynamic process for which including the lagged dependent variable is the best modeling choice.[26]

There are situations in which the inclusion of a lagged dependent variable can be problematic for obtaining a correct estimate of the effect.[27] Specifically, doing so can suppress the effects of other independent variables and, even more troubling, cause the sign of coefficients to reverse in some circumstances.[28] However, there is controversy surrounding whether the prevalence and significance of these problems may be overstated, and including a lagged dependent variable is usually a conservative choice when dealing with time-series data.[29] The dynamic

---

[24] K. Darden and A. Grzymala-Busse, "The Great Divide: Literacy, Nationalism, and the Communist Collapse," *World Politics* 59, no. 1 (2006).

[25] Hale, *Foundations of Ethnic Politics*.

[26] Luke Keele and Nathan J. Kelly, "Dynamic Models for Dynamic Theories: The Ins and Outs of Lagged Dependent Variables," *Political Analysis* 14, no. 2 (2006).

[27] C. H. Achen, "Why Lagged Dependent Variables Can Suppress the Explanatory Power of Other Independent Variables," *Ann Arbor* 1001 (2000).

[28] Achen.

[29] Nonetheless, to be certain of the robustness of the results, it is worth considering alternative specifications, and the models were rerun without the lagged dependent

relationship implied by the theory strongly suggests that the lagged dependent variable specification is appropriate.[30]

Due to the use of the lagged dependent variable, fixed effects for country were not included in the model. The relatively short time dimension of the panel means including fixed effects would have raised concerns regarding Nickell bias.[31] Moreover, in the face of dynamic misspecification, fixed effects can introduce more bias than naïve OLS.[32] Fortunately, the focused nature of the sample allowed me to explicitly account for many of the factors that might contribute to hierarchy, obviating the need for country-level fixed effects.[33]

The truncation of the raw hierarchy index, by creating an artificial floor at 0 and ceiling at 1, raised a possible concern of predicting outcomes outside of this range using OLS. As the focus of these analyses was the marginal effects rather than prediction, this was not a major concern. OLS was used as it has many of the same advantages as a linear probability model when using binary dependent variables. It is easy to estimate and interpret marginal effects.[34] However, to assuage concerns about this issue, a fractional logit model was also run for the raw Hierarchy index.[35] This analysis was not performed using the CGV Defacto2 variable due to concerns about separation issues when using the fractional logit. In total four models were run. The first model examined the relationship between the IRT Hierarchy variable and the interaction of corruption and Polcomp (Model 1), while the second used the interaction of corruption and the CGV variable (Model 2), both using OLS. Next, the relationship between the raw hierarchy index and the interaction between corruption and Polcomp was examined using OLS (Model 3). Finally, this model was rerun using a fractional logit (Model 4).

variable. This was tested both with and without country-level fixed effects. As expected, the results were stronger and the predicted effects substantially larger than those presented here (see Appendix B for results of these alternative specifications).

[30] Keele and Kelly, "Dynamic Models for Dynamic Theories."
[31] Nathaniel Beck and Jonathan N. Katz, "Modeling Dynamics in Time-Series-Cross-Section Political Economy Data," *Annual Review of Political Science* 14 (2011).
[32] Thomas Plümper and Vera E. Troeger, "Not So Harmless After All: The Fixed-Effects Model," *Political Analysis* 27, no. 1 (2019).
[33] While results for the model described above are discussed below, the models were thus run in three different ways: with a lagged dependent variable excluding fixed effects; with fixed effects and no lagged dependent variable; and with no lagged dependent variable and no fixed effects. In the models without lagged dependent variables, Driscoll Kraay standard errors were used to address autocorrelation (these additional specifications are included in Appendix B).
[34] Jeffrey M. Wooldridge, *Econometric Analysis of Cross Section and Panel Data* (MIT Press, 2010).
[35] Leslie E. Papke and Jeffrey Wooldridge, *Econometric Methods for Fractional Response Variables with an Application to 401 (k) Plan Participation Rates* (National Bureau of Economic Research, 1993), www.nber.org/papers/t0147.

To aid interpretation of the results, the marginal effects of political corruption were calculated across the full range of the corruption variables. This is important as interaction terms do not have straightforward interpretations.[36] These marginal effects provide strong support for the theory. Where corruption is low, competition has a negative effect on Russian Hierarchy. As corruption increases this negative effect gets smaller and eventually becomes positive. This indicates that at high levels of corruption, competition increases Russian hierarchy. The relationship holds for both the Polcomp variable (Figure 6.1a) and the CGV measure of competition (Figure 6.1b).

Next, the marginal effects for corruption were explored along the range of the competition variables. Figure 6.2a shows that the marginal effect of increasing corruption on the IRT measure of hierarchy is negative when competition as measured by Polcomp is low, and positive and significantly different from zero, when competition is high. In other words, the graphs show that where competition is absent a one unit increase of

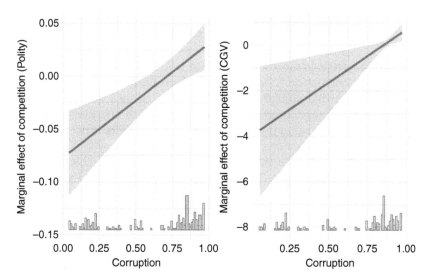

Figure 6.1 Marginal effect of competition when modified by corruption: (a) effect for the IRT hierarchy variable and Polcomp; (b) IRT and CGV. 90% CIs.

[36] T. Brambor, W. R. Clark, and M. Golder, "Understanding Interaction Models: Improving Empirical Analyses," *Political Analysis* 14, no. 1 (2006); William D. Berry, Matt Golder, and Daniel Milton, "Improving Tests of Theories Positing Interaction," *Journal of Politics* 74, no. 3 (2012); B. F. Braumoeller, "Hypothesis Testing and Multiplicative Interaction Terms," *International Organization* 58, no. 4 (2004).

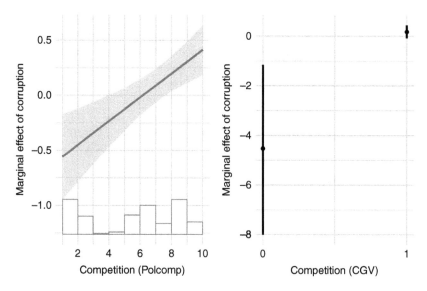

Figure 6.2 Marginal effect of corruption when modified by competition: (a) modified by Polcomp; (b) modified by CGV. 90% CIs.

corruption results in more autonomy and less hierarchy. Where competition is high, corruption is associated with increased hierarchy. Figure 6.2 shows a somewhat similar relationship when using CGV to measure competition. Increased corruption is associated with lower levels of hierarchy when competition is absent, but in this case there is no significant difference from zero when competition is present.

The results are a little anomalous but provide a reasonable degree of support for the argument. The interaction is significant and in the predicted direction. While on average, for this cross-national sample, corruption has a negative effect on hierarchy; this effect is reduced as competition increases. Hence, countries with high corruption and competition should have higher levels of hierarchy. The reduction of hierarchy associated with increased corruption when competition is absent is more difficult to explain. It may be that absent competition, highly corrupt regimes have incentives to avoid outside interference so as not to surrender rents (see Table 6.1).

Cross-National Variation in Russian Hierarchy and Regime Type

The following analysis captures issues related to competition and corruption using the proxy of regime type. The previous measurement strategy

Table 6.1 *Relationship results for Models 1–4*

	\multicolumn{4}{c}{Dependent variable}			
	IRT Hierarchy		Raw Hierarchy	
	OLS	OLS	OLS	GLM: quasi-binomial link = logit
	(1)	(2)	(3)	(4)
Corruption	−0.665**	−4.601**	−0.124*	−5.984***
	(0.266)	(2.117)	(0.063)	(1.225)
Polcomp	−0.077***		−0.011*	−0.580***
	(0.025)		(0.006)	(0.127)
CGV		−4.053**		
		(1.898)		
GDP Per Capita	−0.085	−0.154	0.017	0.098
	(0.091)	(0.131)	(0.022)	(0.214)
Precommunist Literacy	−0.009**	−0.012**	−0.001	−0.064***
	(0.004)	(0.006)	(0.001)	(0.019)
Referendum	−0.0004	−0.001	0.001	0.090**
	(0.003)	(0.005)	(0.001)	(0.039)
Caucasus	0.209**	0.248*	0.014	4.004***
	(0.094)	(0.143)	(0.022)	(0.890)
Central Asia	−0.264	−0.571	−0.003	0.487
	(0.261)	(0.363)	(0.061)	(2.683)
Russian Minority	0.109	0.218	0.044	−1.298**
	(0.124)	(0.203)	(0.029)	(0.608)
Population	−0.010	0.006	−0.037*	0.901***
	(0.091)	(0.154)	(0.022)	(0.340)
Military Spending	0.033	0.024	0.009	−0.030
	(0.029)	(0.042)	(0.007)	(0.074)
Resource Revenue	−0.018	−0.024	0.001	0.108**
	(0.019)	(0.030)	(0.005)	(0.051)
ELF	0.781	1.255	−0.052	7.984*
	(0.611)	(0.922)	(0.145)	(4.071)
Internal Threat	−0.319	−0.535*	0.033	−1.682*
	(0.201)	(0.298)	(0.049)	(0.885)
External Threat	−0.005	0.008	−0.025	−2.685
	(0.200)	(0.301)	(0.047)	(2.152)
EU	0.104	−0.010	0.030*	
	(0.075)	(0.085)	(0.018)	
IRT Hierarchy$_{t-1}$	0.810***	0.798***		
	(0.036)	(0.047)		
Raw Hierarchy$_{t-1}$			0.946***	5.188***
			(0.024)	(0.351)
Corruption × Polcomp	0.108***		0.020**	0.711***

Table 6.1 *(cont.)*

	Dependent variable			
	IRT Hierarchy		Raw Hierarchy	
	OLS	OLS	OLS	GLM: quasi-binomial link = logit
	(1)	(2)	(3)	(4)
	(0.035)		(0.008)	(0.161)
Corruption × CGV		4.775**		
		(2.168)		
Constant	1.430	5.247	0.488	−19.010***
	(1.381)	(3.570)	(0.325)	(4.991)
Observations	285	192	285	285
Adjusted R^2	0.972	0.963	0.989	
F statistic	251.688***	157.890***	618.200***	
	(df = 40; 244)	(df = 32; 159)	(df = 40; 244)	

*$p < 0.1$. **$p < 0.05$. ***$p < 0.01$.

for political competition mostly measured the presence of political threats outside of the regime, focusing on what Zimmerman calls "the ejectorate."[37] Using regime type can capture the effects of different elite or intraregime dynamics as well. This variable will mainly measure contestation over control of leadership or the regime itself, rather than more general forms of contestation.

Regimes are the institutionalized rules that govern the politics of a society or state.[38] Different types of regime, including subtypes of authoritarian regimes, have different political and economic logics.[39] This may be because institutions constrain and enable certain actions on the part of insiders and opposition elites.[40] Alternatively, institutions might be epiphenomenal, reflecting underlying cleavages and forms of competition.[41] Regardless of this distinction, regime characteristics can

---

[37] William Zimmerman, *Ruling Russia: Authoritarianism from the Revolution to Putin* (Princeton University Press, 2014).
[38] Gerardo L. Munck, "The Regime Question: Theory Building in Democracy Studies," *World Politics* 54, no. 1 (2001): 119–44.
[39] H. E. Hale, "Regime Cycles," *World Politics* 58, no. 1 (2005).
[40] Jason Brownlee, *Authoritarianism in an Age of Democratization* (Cambridge University Press, 2007), 10.
[41] Thomas Pepinsky, "The Institutional Turn in Comparative Authoritarianism," *British Journal of Political Science* 44, no. 3 (2014).

proxy for the concepts of rent-seeking and contestation. We may expect that elites in authoritarian regimes engage in more corruption and rent-seeking compared to more democratic systems, while others feature more competition, and others still combine elements of both competition and rent-seeking. By observing the type of political regime or institutions that govern a society, it is possible to measure the types of political contestation and relationships that occur within a state.

Measuring Rent-Seeking and Competition by Regime Type The causal theory presented in this book is about both the presence of competition and how that competition influences access to rents. Variables measuring different types of institutional environments can proxy for contestation and rent-seeking, what the consequences of competition are and how these consequences are managed. The independent variable was the type of authoritarian regime taken from Geddes, Wright, and Frantz. Different regime institutions affect how resources are distributed and the nature of political contestation. The variation is more fine-grained than the differences between democracy and autocracy. Regime types capture the nature of domestic political institutions and how elite groupings and factions interact with one another and society.

Open political institutions that are more common in nonauthoritarian regimes allow greater monitoring and policing of elites.[42] For this reason rent-seeking is more constrained in nonauthoritarian regimes. In contrast, rent-seeking will be higher in autocratic regimes.[43] The type of authoritarian regime also reflects the nature of political contestation.[44] The Autocratic Regimes data set from Geddes, Wright, and Frantz shows that two types of autocratic regime were prominent in Eurasia during the period under observation.[45] These regimes are classified as Personalist and Party regimes.[46] These regime types possess different institutional characteristics leading to differing levels of contestation and rent-seeking and also influence the effects of contestation on access to rents and future well-being.

---

[42] Alicia Adsera, Carles Boix, and Mark Payne, "Are You Being Served? Political Accountability and Quality of Government," *Journal of Law, Economics, and Organization* 19, no. 2 (2003).

[43] Douglass North, *Institutions, Institutional Change, and Economic Performance* (Cambridge University Press, 1990); North, *Violence and Social Orders: A Conceptual Framework for Interpreting Recorded Human History* (Cambridge University Press, 2009).

[44] Barbara Geddes, *Paradigms and Sand Castles: Theory Building and Research Design in Comparative Politics* (University of Michigan Press, 2003).

[45] Barbara Geddes, Joseph Wright, and Erica Frantz, "Autocratic Breakdown and Regime Transitions: A New Data Set," *Perspectives on Politics* 12, no. 2 (2014).

[46] There are also three country years where a party-based regime exists. This is discussed below in more detail.

The regimes Uzbekistan and Kyrgyzstan illustrate some of these differences. In Uzbekistan under Karimov, classified as a party regime by Geddes, Wright, and Frantz, there were no or few groupings of power outside of the state/regime.[47] Economic and political opportunities all flowed through the dominant state apparatus limiting the ability of outside groups to gain resources or benefit and threaten regime stability.[48] In contrast, while the personalist Kyrgyz regime was more liberal, particularly early on, it relied on narrower base of power. Akyaev directed resources to a small group and his family and was far less successful at coopting other actors in the country.[49] This made his regime unstable and unable to resist opposition.

Nonautocracies are a mixed bag of regimes. They are those that do not fit the definition of authoritarian regimes. In the post-Soviet sphere this ranges from the established and relatively consolidated democracies such as the Baltic States of Estonia, Latvia, and Lithuania, to regimes that verge on competitive authoritarian regimes such Georgia post Rose Revolution and Ukraine for the entire period of its independence. Power in these latter states has changed hands after elections, but these elections have been far from free and fair.

The threat to elites is higher in personalist regimes than party regimes. Personalist regimes are authoritarian regimes where political power is controlled by an individual or small group. Personalist regimes are less institutionalized and hence evince higher levels of threat from rival groups.[50] Personalist regimes are exclusionary; this increases their instability as other elite factions need to overthrow the regime for control of resources and rent-seeking opportunities. Personalist leaders also often attempt to eliminate all potential rivals.[51] While party regimes may have greater numbers of factions, these factions are usually better managed.

Personalist regimes are less stable for both the ruling coalition and the leader. Using Geddes, Wright, and Frantz's measure, Personalist regimes fail at almost twice the rate as party regimes.[52] Escriba-Folch shows that

---

[47] As an authoritarian subtype, Geddes Wright and Frantz code Uzbekistan as a Party-Personalist regime, it thus has some hybrid characteristics.

[48] Scott Radnitz, *Weapons of the Wealthy: Predatory Regimes and Elite-Led Protests in Central Asia* (Cornell University Press, 2010); Alisher Ilkhamov, "Neopatrimonialism, Interest Groups and Patronage Networks: The Impasses of the Governance System in Uzbekistan," *Central Asian Survey* 26, no. 1 (2007).

[49] Edward Schatz, "The Soft Authoritarian Tool Kit: Agenda-Setting Power in Kazakhstan and Kyrgyzstan," *Comparative Politics* 41, no. 2 (2009); Radnitz, *Weapons of the Wealthy*, 62–67.

[50] Geddes, *Paradigms and Sand Castles*.

[51] Abel Escribà-Folch, "Accountable for What? Regime Types, Performance, and the Fate of Outgoing Dictators, 1946–2004," *Democratization* 20, no. 1 (2013).

[52] Geddes et al., "Autocratic Breakdown and Regime Transitions."

personalist leaders are replaced through irregular means more than 60 percent of the time, while party leaders suffer the same fate less than 30 percent of the time.[53]

Leaders and elites in personalist regimes are more likely to face exile, imprisonment, or death as a result of losing political competition.[54] Party regimes usually have more institutionalized control of factions within the regime than personalist regimes, resulting in a lower probability of being overthrown by outside forces.[55] Party regimes are more stable and hence the probability of regimes losing power due to political contestation or overthrow is lower. In addition, because of the larger size of the winning coalition, elites who make up party regimes are more likely to be partial beneficiaries of a regime transition.[56]

These regimes also share rent-seeking opportunities differently. The nature of personalist regimes means that benefits tend to be distributed to smaller groups, ethnic or kin-based, forcing elite factions to compete over these resources if they want access. In contrast, party regimes often share and manage resources among different groups in the larger ruling coalition.

Many of the traits attributed to the different regime types are demonstrated in the former Soviet Republics. The two party-based regimes have seen no coerced leadership changes. Uzbekistan had been ruled continuously since independence by Karimov, and the regime has demonstrated a remarkable stability.[57] Following Karimov's natural death, the regime managed a relatively peaceful transition of power with the promise of reforms.[58] Turkmenistan was ruled by Niyazov until his death, when power transferred relatively peacefully to his successor Berdymukhamedov.[59] In contrast, the various personalist regimes have seen many violent or coerced transfers of power. In Georgia, Gamsakhurdia was forced from power and ended up dead, either through suicide or murder.[60] Later Shevardnadze was also forced

---

[53] Abel Escribà-Folch, "Accountable for What? Regime Types, Performance, and the Fate of Outgoing Dictators, 1946–2004," *Democratization* 20, no. 1 (2013): 165.
[54] Escribà-Folch, "Accountable for What?" [55] Geddes, *Paradigms and Sand Castles*.
[56] J. Wright, "How Foreign Aid Can Foster Democratization in Authoritarian Regimes," *American Journal of Political Science* 53, no. 3 (2009).
[57] Jennifer Murtazashvili, "Coloured by Revolution: The Political Economy of Autocratic Stability in Uzbekistan," *Democratization* 19, no. 1 (2012).
[58] Navbahor Imamova, "Uzbekistan's New Era Might Just Be Real," *Foreign Policy* (blog), accessed May 8, 2019, https://foreignpolicy.com/2018/06/21/uzbekistans-new-era-might-just-be-real/.
[59] Richard Pomfret, "Turkmenistan after Turkmenbashi," in *Institutional Reform in Central Asia: Politico-Economic Challenges*, ed. Joachim Ahrens and Herman Hoen (Routledge, 2013).
[60] Stephen Francis Jones, *Georgia: A Political History since Independence* (I. B. Tauris, 2013).

from power.[61] In Azerbaijan, Elchibey was overthrown.[62] In Armenia, Levon Ter-Petrosyan was forced to resign by Robert Kocharyan, resulting in a change of regime.[63] In Tajikistan, Nabiyev was forced from power in a civil war and replaced by Emomali Rahoman.[64] Kyrgystan has seen two forced changes in leadership.[65] Personalist leaders tend to be forced from power more often than party leaders globally, and the Eurasian cases are no exception.[66]

More open political systems should lower the stakes of contestation. A quick comparison of Kyrgyzstan and Ukraine demonstrates this point. Kyrgyzstan, which has been coded as a Personalist regime since its independence, has seen two dictators toppled. First, Akayev was overthrown during the Tulip Revolution. Akayev was forced to flee the country and now resides in Moscow.[67] Similarly, when his successor Bakiyev was removed from power, Bakiyev fled to Minsk in Belarus for safety.[68] In contrast, in Ukraine, when Kravchuk and later Kuchma lost or ceded power they were able to remain in the country, and they and their relatives continued to benefit economically.[69] Even in highly flawed democracies such as Ukraine, the costs of losing power have often been lower, and economic opportunities can still be pursued by elites.

In summary, the combination of rent-seeking and political threats to rent-seeking will be highest in Personalist regimes. Therefore, the theory predicts that support for Russian hierarchy should be greatest in these states. In contrast, where threats to political survival are lower such as in Party regimes, there will be less willingness to give up sovereignty. Alternatively, in regimes where contestation is high, but the more open political systems somewhat constrain rent-seeking or at least lower the costs of losing power, then support for hierarchy should also be lower. These predictions are outlined in Table 6.2.

---

[61] l. Mitchell, "Georgia's Rose Revolution," *Current History – New York Then Philadelphia* 103 (2004).

[62] Jones, *Georgia*.

[63] Charles H. Fairbanks, "Disillusionment in the Caucasus and Central Asia," *Journal of Democracy* 12, no. 4 (2001): 49.

[64] Martha Brill Olcott, "Central Asia on Its Own," *Journal of Democracy* 4, no. 1 (1993): 102.

[65] Kathleen Collins, "Kyrgyzstan's Latest Revolution," *Journal of Democracy* 22, no. 3 (2011).

[66] Geddes et al., "Autocratic Breakdown and Regime Transitions."

[67] Scott Radnitz, "What Really Happened in Kyrgyzstan?," *Journal of Democracy* 17, no. 2 (2006): 131.

[68] Collins, "Kyrgyzstan's Latest Revolution," 157.

[69] Kravchuk remained a prominent part of the political scene through the Social Democratic Party. Serhy Yekelchyk, *Ukraine: Birth of a Modern Nation* (Oxford University Press, 2007), 208.

Table 6.2 *Predicted relationship between regime type and hierarchy*

Regime type	Predicted outcome
Personalist (Belarus, 1995–2010; Kyrgyzstan, Kazakhastan; Tajikistan, Georgia, 1992–2003)	Support for hierarchy (rent-seeking high, greater potential for elites to lose power, and instability high)
Party (Belarus, 1992–94; Turkmenistan, Uzbekistan)	Moderate support for hierarchy (rent-seeking high, elite contestation better managed, higher levels of stability)
Nonauthoritarian regimes (Estonia, Georgia, 2004–10; Latvia, Lithuania, Moldova, Ukraine)	Lowest support for hierarchy (rent-seeking low, contestation high)

Bivariate Relationship between Hierarchy and Regime Type There was a strong bivariate relationship between regime type and the IRT Russian hierarchy measure. Among authoritarian regime types, there was a large observed difference between Party regimes and Personalist regimes. For nonauthoritarian regimes, the mean level of hierarchy was far lower than the level of hierarchy for Personalist regimes (see Figure 6.3). Personalist regimes are more inclined to support Russian hierarchy than either Party regimes or nonauthoritarian regimes.

One caveat concerns Belarus; for the first three years after independence Belarus was coded as Party-Based, by the GFW data set. During this period, Belarus had high levels of hierarchy. Qualitative analysis can explain this aberration. While Belarus was still a Party-Based regime at the time, this was due to inertia more than a reflection of the underlying political conditions. The communist regime, left in power following the Soviet collapse, was in fact riddled with rent-seeking and political rivalries.[70] Leaders were removed from power; Belarus had three leaders between 1991 and 1994. Ultimately, the system collapsed after a brief period when Lukashenko won an election and instituted a new regime.[71] Hence, despite the coding of the regime as Party-Based, there was a high level of political contestation and instability. This means that the difference between regime types presented in Figure 6.3 might underestimate the true effect.

The relationships between hierarchy and regime type were consistent across time as well (Figure 6.4). The level of hierarchy for Personalist

---

[70] Steven Levitsky and Lucan Way, *Competitive Authoritarianism: Hybrid Regimes after the Cold War* (Cambridge University Press, 2010), 201–3; R. Abdelal, *National Purpose in the World Economy: Post-Soviet States in Comparative Perspective* (Cornell University Press, 2001), 142–44.

[71] Andrew Wilson, *Belarus: The Last European Dictatorship* (Yale University Press, 2011).

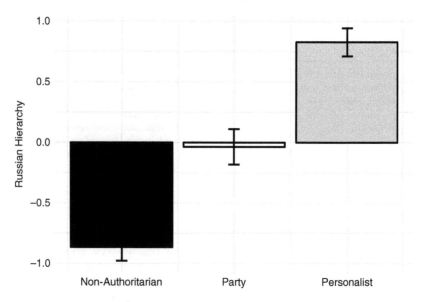

Figure 6.3 Mean level of hierarchy and standard errors conditional on regime type.

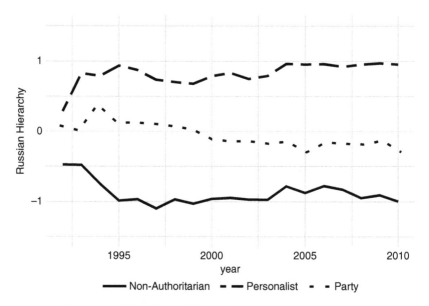

Figure 6.4 Mean level of hierarchy across time conditional on regime type.

regimes from 1992 to 2016 was consistently high. In contrast, nonauthoritarian regimes showed a sharp drop off from 1994 as the last Russian soldiers left the Baltic States, and then a consistent rate of hierarchy from that point onward. Finally, Party regimes showed a higher level of hierarchy than nonauthoritarian regimes, but still substantially lower than that of the Personalist regimes. One interesting difference is that while nonauthoritarian and party regimes saw declines in Russian hierarchy as politics settled after the collapse of the Soviet Union, the level of hierarchy jumped in Personalist regimes. This decline in some types of states helps rule out the idea of reverse causation. That is, hierarchy does not necessarily perpetuate itself and change the nature of regimes in political contexts that are unfavorable to its existence.

These patterns demonstrate a strong, observable difference among regimes in their willingness to give up some sovereignty to Russia. However, regime type is the culmination of many different factors which may be driving these states to align themselves with Russia. In the following section, multivariate regression analysis is used to determine the relationship between Regime Type and Russian Hierarchy while accounting for alternative explanations and other possible factors that might contribute to the outcome.

Multivariate Analysis As with the continuous independent variables measuring rent-seeking and contestation, the relationship between the regime type and hierarchy was modeled using multivariate regression. The IRT Hierarchy measure and the raw hierarchy were again used as dependent variables. Again, OLS was used to provide a simple interpretation, along with a fractional logit model for the raw hierarchy measure. Control variables were included as in the previous analysis. Models were run with and without lagged dependent variables, and time dummies were included.

As predicted, even with the control variables included, there was a significant association between Regime Type and Russian Hierarchy. In the various models, Personalist regimes were used as the reference category in the regressions. This means that the regression coefficients can be interpreted as the level of hierarchy relative to Personalist regimes. Figure 6.5 shows the difference between Personalist regimes and Democracies and Party regimes. A negative point on the graphs means that on average those regimes were associated with lower levels of hierarchy than Personalist regimes. Model 5, using the IRT measure, showed that hierarchy in both nonauthoritarian regimes was significantly lower than Personalist Regimes. For Party regimes the effect was negative, but not significant at traditional levels, $p = 0.15$ (see Figure 6.5).

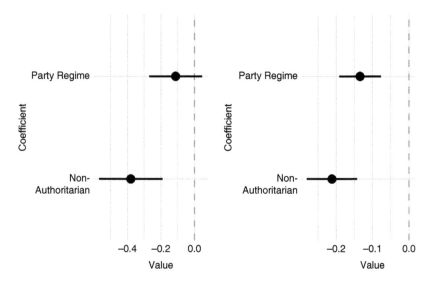

Figure 6.5 Relationship between hierarchy and independent variables (Model 15, year dummies and lagged dependent variable included in model, 95% CIs): (a) IRT hierarchy; (b) raw hierarchy.

The relationship between the raw Hierarchy index and Regime Type provides stronger support for the theory. Both party and nonauthoritarian regimes were significantly associated with lower levels of Hierarchy when compared to Personalist regimes (see Figure 6.5).

Discussion

The analyses so far in this chapter indicate that political competition has an important effect on whether a state will join Russian-led organizations or agree to host a Russian military base. The findings are consistent with political survival microfoundations. Domestic politics of a particular kind drive part of the decision of states to surrender their sovereignty. A state's interest in hierarchy cannot simply be read from a state's position in the international system, a state's capabilities or its assets, or its identity. Instead, domestic politics must be considered and the politics of these states must be disaggregated.

Lake has made the argument that regimes with smaller selectorates are more likely to display lower levels of hierarchy.[72] Personalist regimes

[72] David Lake, "Legitimating Power: The Domestic Politics of US International Hierarchy," *International Security* 38, no. 2 (2013).

often have smaller selectorates than Party regimes.[73] Consequently, the regime type variable used in this analysis may pick up contestation, rent-seeking, and a smaller selectorate. However, Lake's argument is less consistent with the finding that regimes with lower levels of competition display lower levels of hierarchy. Lake's arguments would predict that where contestation was higher and more open within authoritarian regimes, hierarchy would be lower as the selectorate is larger. For this reason, the political survival and rent-seeking argument provides a more complete explanation.

The interpretation of control variables is problematic.[74] However, of the other variables in included in the models, several show some relationship with Russian hierarchy (see Table 6.1 and Appendix B). There is some evidence that producing revenue through resources is associated with Russian hierarchy, though the direction of the effect is not consistent, nor is there a reliably significant association. This is inconsistent with arguments that Russia can use its energy resources to gain leverage over countries.[75] However, to the extent that oil has a causal effect on the independent variable, it may be that the natural resources works through its effects on politics rather than directly.

Internal secessionist threats are sometimes associated with lower levels of hierarchy. A possible reason for this may be that Russia has often supported secessionist movements in countries such as Azerbaijan, Georgia, and Moldova,[76] and by providing such support they have alienated the government, reducing the amount of influence they can wield through formal institutions. In contrast, the ethnic fractionalization variable is associated with higher levels of hierarchy, and is significant in some of the models. This association could be the result of divide and conquer tactics by Russia, but is also consistent with the rent-seeking argument. In post-Soviet countries, ethnic identity has often become a focal point and a source of competition over resources.[77] External threat is significantly associated with hierarchy in some of the models, but the direction of the effect changes depending on the model. This provides little support for

---

[73] Jessica L. P. Weeks, "Autocratic Audience Costs: Regime Type and Signaling Resolve," *International Organization* 62, no. 1 (2008).

[74] The reason for this is intuitive. The variables are confounders and hence suffer posttreatment bias. In addition, they suffer from potential problems because there are no controls for their own confounders that may be correlated with the controls, but not the independent variable of interest.

[75] Marshall I. Goldman, *Petrostate: Putin, Power, and the New Russia* (Oxford University Press, 2008).

[76] C. King, *Extreme Politics: Nationalism, Violence, and the End of Eastern Europe* (Oxford University Press, 2010), 116–19.

[77] Hale, *Foundations of Ethnic Politics*. These issues are explored in more detail in Chapter 3.

the argument that hierarchy and integration might be motivated by a need for security.

However, these macro measures of contestation and rent-seeking may not capture all contestation that occurs. An example of this can be found in Uzbekistan's relationship with Russia, which worsened in the late 1990s. They withdrew from many regional agreements and joined the anti-Russian bloc constituted by Georgia, Azerbaijan, Ukraine, and Moldova. However, in 2005, the regime faced domestic opposition and political competition in the form of protests in the town of Andijan concerning the arrest of an Uzbek businessman. This has been attributed to internal clan politics and competition.[78] In response, the government cracked down, and the conditions in terms of civil liberties worsened.[79] Following these events, Uzbekistan realigned slightly with Russia, and the hierarchy index rose from 2005 to 2006. The mechanism of external protection can be seen as the CSTO provided Uzbekistan diplomatic cover and help to crack down on "extremists."[80] While these changes are consistent with the argument of the book, increased threat to political survival led to increased hierarchy, these changes were not captured by the macro-variables used in this chapter.

An additional limitation of this analysis concerns reverse causation. It could be possible that Russia is affecting the type of regime that exists in neighboring countries.[81] To a degree, such a causal relationship is consistent with the theoretical arguments made here. Russia provides resources to elite actors engaging in political contestation over rents to keep them in power. The process thus implies a certain degree of endogeneity. A relationship between hierarchy and domestic political institutions must be an endogenously self-enforcing one. If Russia were to upset the environment of contestation too much, subordinate actors would lose incentives to support Russian hierarchy. Nonetheless, the theory requires that changes in levels of competition and rent-seeking should result in changed levels of hierarchy or willingness to give up sovereign rights.

In practical terms, how might these relationships help us understand political events that have occurred in the post-Soviet region, particularly those of recent interest? Previous chapters have highlighted these dynamics in detail for the cases of Georgia and Ukraine. I conclude this

---

[78] *New York Times*, May 19, 2005. [79] RFE/RL, August 31, 2006.
[80] See the response of Russian foreign minister Sergei Lavrov in an interview with *Izvestia* shortly after the events in Andijan, accessed March 31, 2012, www.mid.ru/brp_4.nsf/e 78a48070f128a7b43256999005bcbb3/6730c35e15d679b2c3257005002be494? OpenDocument.
[81] David R. Cameron and Mitchell A. Orenstein, "Post-Soviet Authoritarianism: The Influence of Russia in Its" Near Abroad," *Post-Soviet Affairs* 28, no. 1 (2012).

section with a discussion of the results in the context of two different illustrative cases: Kyrgyzstan and Armenia.

Kyrgyzstan One case that the results here shed light on is that of Kyrgyzstan over the last couple of decades. Kyrgyzstan has been considered almost a Russian client state. It has participated in numerous Russian-led integration efforts in the region such the CTSO and the Eurasian Economic Union and it also hosts a Russian military air base. In recent years it has arguably moved even closer toward the Russian sphere. The arguments of the book provide us particular insight into the events that have occurred since the fall of Bakiyev in 2010.

Bakiyev was the president of Kyrgyzstan between 2005 and 2010. Bakiyev during his tenure sought to play off the interests of Russia and the United States. In these hierarchical relationships with both Russia and the United States, the ruling elites were able to profit from rent-seeking. They profited directly through the rents they extracted from the United States paying for basing rights. In addition, other elites were able to profit through corruption that coagulated around the base, primarily in the form supplying gas to the base. However, Russia soon perceived that Bakiyev was no longer a pliable client. They began to provide resources to the opposition and other actors and they imposed duties on energy imports. Following the growth of opposition and riots in 2010, Bakiyev was forced to resign. In this period of unrest, there were numerous appeals from the Kyrgyz interim leaders for Russia to intervene through the CTSO. However, Russia did not intervene.

Following the fall of Bakiyev, Russia expanded its repertoire of control. Whereas in the past, they had focused their support of the leaders of regimes, Russia now extended the provision of support to both the regime and the opposition. The resources they provided were both symbolic and material. They provided financial support for officials seeking election, and many of these actors sought out connections with Russia, traveling to Moscow to elicit support. In addition to these resources, Russia also started providing more military assistance as well as more economic investment in strategic areas such as energy. Notably, the failure of the CTSO to provide direct protection led to the certain reworking of the institutions. This institutional reform was meant to facilitate action in the future if similar situations arose.

In this context, Russia was able to increase its influence to a certain extent. While Kyrgyzstan had not participated in the earlier treaty version of the Eurasian Economic Space and Customs Union, they did agree to join the Eurasian Economic Community as it was established in 2015. Kyrgyzstan gave up on their basing relationship with the United States in

2013.[82] They agreed to extend the lease on the Russian Kant airbase in return for Putin writing down almost US$500 million in debt.[83] In addition, Russia asserted more informal control, promoting policies through the Kyrgyz parliament that reflected Russian interests. These included socially conservative policies, but also policies aimed at reducing the role of western NGOs in the country.[84] This latter issue has long been a fixation of Russian domestic and international policy. In other words, we can see both in the formal and informal practices, an increase in Russian hierarchy post 2010.

The theory and quantitative results presented above shed some light on these processes and events, and much of what occurred fits well with the empirical implications of the theory. First and most obviously, the increase in political competition among elites in 2010 and afterward has been associated with an increase in Russian influence and hierarchy over Kyrgyzstan. This increase in contestation has occurred in the context of particularly high levels of corruption that has both domestic and international sources. Secondly, Russia has provisioned resources to elites to aid in the political competition and help them maintain access to resources. Another factor is that Bakiyev lost power after alienating his external patrons in Moscow. While this does not directly prove they kept him in power, it is consistent with the idea. Furthermore, Bakiyev arguably lost support in part because he alienated society and other elites by constructing a patronage network that was too narrowly focused on his own family.

Armenia The results also shed some light on developments in Armenia. During the post-Soviet era, the regime in Armenia has been highly corrupt, but featured a reasonable amount of political competition through formal and informal mechanisms. Despite the weakness of many of its political institutions, Armenia has had a relatively flourishing civil society. Armenia has also been one of Russia's closest allies in the regions in the security sphere, while for a long while avoiding economic integration with Russian-led institutions. However, the economic relationship was strengthened in the mid-2010s.

In many ways, Armenia's close relationship with Russia is overdetermined. Armenia's conflict with Azerbaijan over Nagorno-Karabakh has

---

[82] Alexander Cooley and Daniel H. Nexon, "'The Empire Will Compensate You': The Structural Dynamics of the US Overseas Basing Network," *Perspectives on Politics* 11, no. 4 (2013): 1043.

[83] Anna Matveeva, "Russia's Changing Security Role in Central Asia," *European Security* 22, no. 4 (2013): 485.

[84] David Lewis, "Reasserting Hegemony in Central Asia: Russian Policy in Post-2010 Kyrgyzstan," *Comillas Journal of International Relations* 1, no. 31 (2015): 65.

forced them to pursue an alliance. Similarly, concerns about other powers and historical enemies such as Turkey have also pushed Armenia closer to Russia. These factors, however, have been relatively constant, and thus cannot explain shifts in behavior. The economic shift toward Russia in the mid-2010s needs another explanation, as does the failure of an ostensibly reforming politician such as Pashinyan to explore new avenues for Armenia's foreign policy.

After over a decade or so of pursuing integration with the west rather than Russia in the economic sphere,[85] Armenia abruptly shifted its policy in 2013. In 2013, Serzh Sargaysan the then president of Armenia, announced that Armenia would join the Russian-led Customs Union. This would ultimately translate into them joining the Eurasian Economic Union.[86]

Political contestation has been a regular feature in Armenian politics and was notable at this period as well. In 2013, there were mass protests motivated by concerns of electoral fraud. In 2015, there were once again large protests, this time the cause was a hike in electricity prices. It is during these 2015 protests that we can most clearly see the role of Russia in providing support to governing elites. Russia provided a military loan valued at almost US$200 million.[87] The Russian owned utility responsible for electricity was also transferred to Armenian control, through the ownership of an Russian-Armenian oligarch with connections to the ruling Republican Party, Samvel Karapetyan.[88] This transfer of resources momentarily dampened opposition.

In 2018, opposition flared again. The protests were in response to Serzh Sargysan pursuing the nomination as PM after serving his allowed terms as president.[89] This time Russia provided little or no support to the incumbent regime initially, but has begun to increase pressure on the Pashinyan government.[90] In the end, Sargysan was forced to resign his post as PM.

Russia's failure to support their allies in Armenia is unexpected considering the theory of this book.[91] However, the dynamics at play

---

[85] Darden, *Economic Liberalism and Its Rivals*, 184–90.
[86] Sean Roberts and Ulrike Ziemer, "Explaining the Pattern of Russian Authoritarian Diffusion in Armenia," *East European Politics* 34, no. 2 (2018): 162.
[87] Syuzanna Vasilyan, "'Swinging on a Pendulum': Armenia in the Eurasian Economic Union and with the European Union," *Problems of Post-Communism* 64, no. 1 (2017): 34.
[88] Ursula Kazarian, "Energy Security in Armenia and the South Caucasus," *Fletcher Security Review* 5 (2018): 52.
[89] Georgi Derluguian and Ruben Hovhannisyan, "The Armenian Anomaly: Toward an Interdisciplinary Interpretation," *Demokratizatsiya* 26, no. 4 (2018): 461.
[90] Miriam Lanskoy and Elspeth Suthers, "Armenia's Velvet Revolution," *Journal of Democracy* 30, no. 2 (2019): 95.
[91] It has been speculated that this failure to support the Republican Party leaders was due to miscalculation on Russia's part. Distracted by global events and involvement in Syria, Russia took its eyes off the ball.

postleadership change are consistent with the book. Despite some speculation that Sargysan's replacement, Pashinyan, was more pro-western than the previous regime, there is little evidence that he is pursuing a more pro-western path. Indeed, during the protests that brought down Sargysan and the Republican Party, what is now called a Velvet Revolution, there were efforts to downplay links to the west.[92] In power, Pashinyian has adopted policies under Russian guidance, most notably sending a small military contingent to Syria.[93]

Global Sample, 1945–2011: Analysis and Results

It is important to consider whether rent-seeking and competition can also explain the level of hierarchy outside of the post-Soviet space. Russia itself has taken opportunities to extend its influence where high levels of rent-seeking and competition are present outside of its usual sphere of influence in recent years. In 2018 and 2019, Russia provided resources, including covert military support to a variety of different regimes in Africa and South America as well. Russia has played a role attempting to prop up leaders in Sudan, in the Central African Republic, and Venezuela. The final analysis tests for the external validity of the argument outside of Russian hierarchy and the post-Soviet region. To do this, data was gathered from the V-Dem data set. The constructed data set contains 155 countries from 1950 to 2011.

The V-Dem data set includes variables that measure the degree of autonomy, both domestic and international that a state possesses. These two variables were used as the dependent variables in separate models. These variables were constructed the same way as the measure of corruption taken from the V-Dem data set – by surveying experts and aggregating the results using item response theory models. Increasing values of these variables indicated that the country possessed more autonomy. While these variables captured perceptions of autonomy held by country experts, it is not clear that it necessarily measures the kinds of asymmetrical hierarchies that are the major focus of this work. That said, they are close enough approximations to provide a reasonable test of how well the argument generalizes.

In the original data, the variables measure the degree of autonomy. For the purposes of this analysis, the autonomy variables were reversed so as

[92] Alexander Iskandaryan, "The Velvet Revolution in Armenia: How to Lose Power in Two Weeks," *Demokratizatsiya* 26, no. 4 (2018): 480.
[93] "Armenia Sends Non-Combat Team to Syria at Russia's Request," accessed May 31, 2019, www.aljazeera.com/news/2019/02/armenia-sends-combat-team-syria-russia-request-190209144531602.html.

to measure the degree of hierarchy. That is, a positive association between the independent variables and the outcome variable measures an increase in hierarchy and a reduction of sovereignty.

The estimation strategy for these tests is slightly different from that of the earlier models. The large sample, and particularly the long time component, means that it is possible to combine a lagged dependent variable and country-level fixed effects in the same model without the same concern for Nickell bias.[94] The fixed effects are important in this context as well; while in the more narrow context of the post-Soviet space it is possible to control for slow-moving factors that might contribute to the level of nationalism and the interests of multiple great powers, globally this is a more daunting task. The country-level fixed effects account for these issues.

To test the causal argument, the interactions of the variables measuring political competition and the variable measuring corruption were included in the models and their marginal effects were calculated. These variables were the same as those in the previous section. Polcomp and CGV's Defacto2 variables were used to measure competition, while the Varieties of Democracy corruption variable was used to measure corruption. In addition, control variables measuring GDP per capita, population, oil resources, and military capabilities were included in the models.

The results demonstrate that the combination of rent-seeking and threat leads to lower levels of political autonomy both domestically and in international politics. The interaction term was significant in all the models. Figure 6.6 shows the marginal effects of increasing corruption as the level of contestation is held constant for the models with country-level fixed effects. Examining the effect of competition at different levels of corruption using the CGV Defacto variable shows that competition increases the overall level of hierarchy when combined with corruption. Where corruption is low, the existence of political forces outside of the regime results in reduced hierarchy. As corruption increases, the effect of competition is diminished and where corruption is very high sovereignty is reduced as competition is increased. This relationship holds for both international autonomy and domestic autonomy (see Figures 6.6a and 6.6b, respectively). Using the Polity data, increasing competition reduces hierarchy and increases autonomy when corruption is low. The effect is moderated and reduced as corruption increases, until it has a relatively small effect on autonomy, but it never positively associated with an increase of hierarchy (see Figure 6.7).

---

[94] Beck and Katz, "Modeling Dynamics in Time-Series-Cross-Section Political Economy Data."

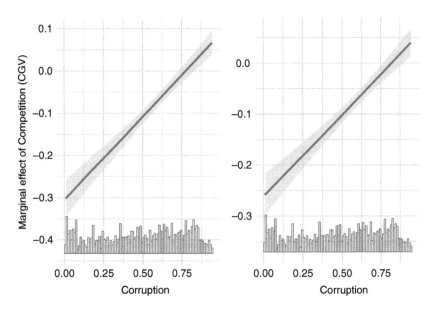

Figure 6.6 Marginal effects of competition (CGV) on (a) external control over international autonomy and (b) domestic autonomy as corruption varies. 90% CIs.

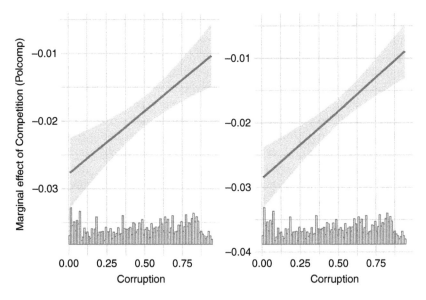

Figure 6.7 Marginal effects of competition (Polcomp) on (a) external control over international autonomy and (b) domestic autonomy as corruption varies. 90% CIs.

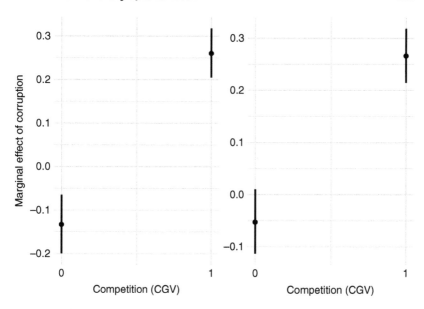

Figure 6.8 Marginal effects of corruption modified by competition (CGV) on (a) external control over international autonomy and (b) domestic autonomy as competition varies. 90% CIs.

The results provide further support for the hypothesis when the marginal effects of corruption are examined. When competition is measured by the binary CGV, we find rent-seeking reduces hierarchy when competition is absent, and hierarchy is significantly increased by rent-seeking in the presence of competition (see Figure 6.8). When exploring the effects of corruption modified by the Polcomp variable, we find that corruption has a slight, and not statistically significant, positive effect on sovereignty when competition as measured by Polcomp is low, and large positive effect when competition is higher (see Figure 6.9).

Discussion

Rent-seeking and political competition are correlated with lower levels of autonomy on a global scale. High levels of competition as measured by Polity are strongly correlated with consolidated democracy. In addition, there are lower levels of corruption and rent-seeking in the global sample, which may affect the results. Overall, the results show that the combination of rent-seeking and competition reduce the level of autonomy a state possesses. There seems to be some evidence, as Lake suggests,[95] that expanding the

---

[95] Lake, "Legitimating Power."

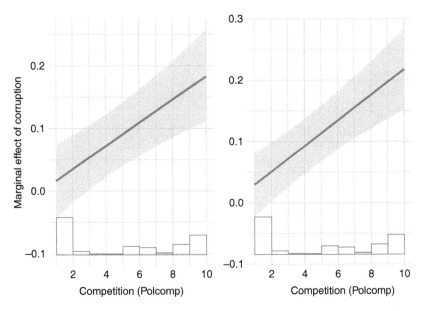

Figure 6.9 Marginal effects of corruption modified by competition (Polcomp) on (a) external control over international autonomy and (b) domestic autonomy as competition varies. 90% CIs.

selectorate leads to lower levels of hierarchy, but these effects are dramatically curtailed or even reversed when combined with high levels of corruption and rent-seeking.

The above results provide an opportunity to discuss hierarchical arrangements other than those of Russia. While the data presented here do not allow us to directly examine US hierarchy, we can make some indirect inferences by looking at specific cases where the United States has been known to wield outsized influence. Specifically, we can examine how the results here might shed light on some notable cases in Latin America and the Caribbean, a relationship that can be appropriately described as hierarchical.[96]

One obvious insight that can be gleaned from examining the data is that US hierarchy in the Americas has not been constant. Using the V-Dem measures of autonomy, both across countries and within cases, the level of political autonomy within the countries of the Americas has varied. This may be due to US preference. The United States' motivation for pursuing

---

[96] David A. Lake, *Hierarchy in International Relations* (Cornell University Press, 2009); Ahsan I. Butt, "Anarchy and Hierarchy in International Relations: Examining South America's War-Prone Decade, 1932–41," *International Organization* 67, no. 3 (2013).

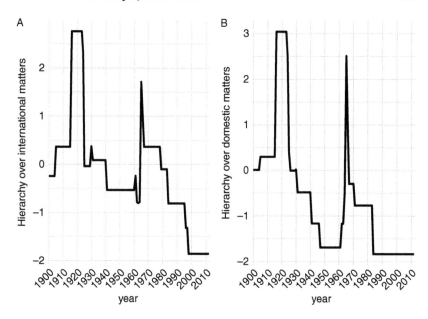

Figure 6.10 Level of hierarchy over Dominican Republic using V-Dem's measure of autonomy.

influence and control in Latin America and the Caribbean have not been constant, rather, the extent of their desire for control has varied over time.[97] Furthermore, the asymmetry in the power relationship has not been sufficient for the United States to consistently get is own way; the states of Latin America have been able to adopt different strategies to avoid dominance.[98]

That said, from early in the nineteenth century, the United States expressed a desire for influence in the region. The United States has sought for whatever reasons to limit the independence of countries in the region, at least informally, and from the late nineteenth through the twentieth century can be said to have wielded hierarchy.[99] As with the other cases discussed, there is no claim that domestic politics explain all the variation in US success at establishing hierarchy in the region; coercive power and other factors play a large role. However, the influence of domestic politics is clear qualitatively in some cases, as in the following example case of the Dominican Republic.

---

[97] Peter H. Smith, *Talons of the Eagle: Latin America, the United States, and the World* (Oxford University Press, 2008).
[98] Tom Long, *Latin America Confronts the United States: Asymmetry and Influence* (Cambridge University Press, 2015).
[99] Butt, "Anarchy and Hierarchy," 584–87; Lake, *Hierarchy in International Relations*, 10.

Figure 6.10 shows hierarchy or the lack of autonomy in the Dominican Republic using the V-Dem variables used above. What is immediately noticeable when examining the graphs are the two peaks in hierarchy, one in the 1920s and another in the 1960s. Both these increases in hierarchy can be attributed to increase US intervention into the country.

Both of these US interventions and assertions of hierarchy occurred at times of extreme instability when ruling elites were threatened by conflict among themselves. In both cases, US intervention helped one faction gain and hold on to power and continue to extract rents from the country. While both examples are consistent in many ways with the theory of the book, the following discussion focuses on the latter intervention, which occurred during the peak of the Cold War. The US government feared a second Castro rising in the region and consequently had strong incentives to control the politics of states that seemed to be veering in that direction.

The assassination of President Trujillo triggered a struggle for power that ultimately resulted in the United States invading and establishing an increased measure of control. Trujillo, who had been president from the 1930s, was assassinated in 1961. Initially the country was governed by a council of state. After various machinations between factions, elections were announced. The elections, held in December 1962, were won by Juan Bosch.[100] Bosch's performance as president eventually alienated some parts of the military and Wessin y Wessin launched a coup.

However, rather than restoring order the coup seemed to exacerbate divisions within the country. The result was a civil conflict between actors affiliated with the Trujillo regime and those that had rallied around the former president Bosch.[101] In this context, the United States under Johnson was initially hesitant to intervene, believing that those opposed to Bosch, the more conservative side of the conflict, would prevail. However, the pro-Bosch forces achieved some success and the result became more uncertain. Both sides requested US involvement. The rebels sought the United States to use its authority to negotiate a settlement and eventually the Junta in charge of the Republic, now led by Pedro Benoit, requested a US invasion.[102] The United States hesitated at first, but as the rebels achieved more success, the United States eventually intervened. The final result was the defeat of the Boschist rebels.

---

[100] Russell Crandall, *Gunboat Democracy: US Interventions in the Dominican Republic, Grenada, and Panama* (Rowman and Littlefield, 2006), 48–50.
[101] Crandall, 53–57; Lindsey A. O'Rourke, *Covert Regime Change: America's Secret Cold War* (Cornell University Press, 2018), 214–16.
[102] Lester D. Langley, *The United States and the Caribbean in the Twentieth Century* (University of Georgia Press, 1985), 239–40; Crandall, *Gunboat Democracy*, 57–60.

While obviously impossible to explain exactly, many aspects of these events are consistent with the theory if the book. The political killing of Trujillo occurred after the external patron, the United States, had withdrawn support for Trujillo. The reason for this withdrawal of support was fear that Trujillo's brutal rule was losing support and could not be sustained. As political contestation intensified there were invitations from those threatened by this political contestation for the United States to intervene and increase the level hierarchy. These events played out in a context where status and power was central to economic life.[103]

The events following US intervention also provide some indirect support for the theory. The United States continued to provide support in the form of economic and technical assistance to the Balageur regime that assumed control. The United States also provided support for Balageur in the election immediately following the civil war, when Balageur defeated Bosch.[104] As Balageur consolidated his hold on power the level of US support dropped and so did Balageur's focus on the United States, shifting to an emphasis on Spanish culture and connections rather than the Dominican Republic's connections to the United States.

The results presented here provide good evidence that the relationship between high levels of contestation and rent-seeking and hierarchy holds outside of the qualitative cases discussed in the previous chapters and outside of the more limited sphere of the former Soviet Union. They also help demonstrate, as does the case of the Dominican Republic, that countries other than Russia take advantage of the same sorts of opportunities to extend hierarchy over countries that they desire to control.

Conclusion

Building off the qualitative insights of the previous chapters, the analysis in this chapter has shown that domestic political institutions are associated with different degrees of willingness to give up sovereignty. Where political institutions increased threats to political survival and raised the level of rent-seeking, states or domestic elites surrendered more sovereignty to Russia. Where the effects of rent-seeking and contestation were reduced, states have been less prepared to give up sovereignty.

---

[103] Wasiq N. Khan, "Economic Growth and Decline in Comparative Perspective: Haiti and the Dominican Republic, 1930–1986," *Journal of Haitian Studies* 16, no. 1 (2010): 123–24; Mats Lundahl and Claudio Vedovato, "The State and Economic Development in Haiti and the Dominican Republic," *Scandinavian Economic History Review* 37, no. 3 (1989): 49–50.
[104] Crandall, *Gunboat Democracy*, 91.

Moreover, these relationships hold outside of the post Soviet Space. Contestation and rent-seeking combine to reduce the autonomy of states in the global sample as well. This implies that it is not only Russia that takes advantage of pliable elites, other great powers are possibly doing the same either globally or in their respective spheres of influence.

In addition, the illustrative cases studies presented in this chapter demonstrate that the models and theory of this book can be used to explain certain aspects of contemporary events. In both Kyrgyzstan and Armenia, contestation and rent-seeking played a role in actors willingness to accommodate Russian demands and provided Russia with opportunities to extend or maintain its influence in situations where we might expect it to decline. If we want to understand how great powers extend their influence and interfere in others' sovereign affairs, we need to pay attention to these variables.

7 Hierarchy, Political Order, and Great Power Politics

Hierarchy is a means for great powers to pursue their interests in international politics. For example, in terms of security, hierarchy can involve gaining the right to station military forces on another state's territory. Hierarchy can also be used to achieve economic goals. Great powers can establish authority relationships to secure access to markets or guarantee the property of transnational economic actors. To do this, states prefer informal forms of hierarchy rather than taking direct control, as it allows them to achieve their aims without paying the greater costs generated by direct forms of rule.

Great powers are more successful establishing informal hierarchy when elites in the subordinate states support the imposition of hierarchy. The incentives of these elites in subordinate states to submit to the demands of the great power are influenced by the political and economic institutions of their own states. Stable international orders in the form of hierarchy can often depend on disorder at a domestic level, while the reverse is also true: stable functioning domestic politics can lead to greater incentives to resist the establishment of hierarchical international orders. Strong domestic order can lead to the breakdown of international hierarchy when they create incentives to resist hierarchy.

This book has highlighted important constraints and limitations placed on great powers by the systems and structures with which they interact. The cases have demonstrated that the relationship between domestic and international order is complex and often paradoxical. Specifically, elites who are engaging in contestation with other elites in high-rent-seeking environments are more likely to give up sovereignty. Rent-seeking increases the value of political power, as political power is essential for economic gain. Contestation increases the probability that elites will lose access to power. In this environment, elites trade sovereignty for political support, hoping to hold on to power and preserve access to rent-seeking opportunities. Somewhat counterintuitively, elite actors who place a high value on political power are more likely to give up sovereignty than those who do not.

The theoretical argument presented in the book contributes to the existing literature on hierarchy by extending explanations for hierarchy beyond the central government, incorporating nonstate and regional actors into the explanation. Russia, for example, has attempted to exert its control over neighboring countries by fostering relationships and garnering support from local actors. In Georgia, Russia established relationships with ethnic and political powerbrokers in Abkhazia, South Ossetia, and Adjara. In Ukraine, Russia tried to maintain a foothold using local actors in Crimea, Donetsk, and Lugansk. By incorporating local powerbrokers along with the central state, it is possible to provide a more complete and general account of how authority relations and hierarchy develop in the international system.

The following sections draw out the implications of these findings for international relations theory and policy. From a policy perspective, semi-sovereign relationships can be somewhat effective at promoting domestic political development, but within severe constraints. Elites who agree to give up sovereignty also have a strong incentive to limit dramatic reforms of domestic political institutions that might threaten their rent-seeking behavior. From a theoretical perspective, the institutions within smaller states constrain the type and form of hierarchical order that can develop in the international system. The degree of hierarchy and anarchy will depend on how willing subordinate actors are to accept such arrangements.

State-Building, Nationalism, and Sovereignty

In 2009, noted economist Paul Romer proposed his notion of "Charter Cities."[1] Using the examples of Hong Kong and Mauritius, Romer argued that some countries had developed stronger institutions and economies when their sovereignty was abrogated.[2] He suggested that surrendering sovereignty was a means of promoting development, as it placed some aspects of political and legal sovereignty beyond the control of corrupt local elites.

In 2011, Honduras took up some of Romer's ideas, proposing a series of Special Development Zones.[3] Romer was meant to sit on a supervision board, which was to take control of some aspects of Honduran

---

[1] Maya Kroth, "Under New Management," *Foreign Policy*, September 1, 2014, www.foreignpolicy.com/articles/2014/09/01/under_new_management_amapala_honduras_charter_cities.

[2] Brandon Fuller and Paul Romer, *Success and the City: How Charter Cities Could Transform the Developing World* (Macdonald-Laurier Institute for Public Policy, 2012).

[3] Kroth, "Under New Management."

sovereignty. However, soon issues of governance arose. The Honduran government signed agreements with private interests without referring them to the supervision board.[4] This meant that there was no external monitoring of the agreements. Honduran elites proposed they would surrender sovereignty, but in the pursuit of rent-seeking as much as promoting economic development.

Why did Romer's proposal run into trouble so quickly? As Lake and Fariss have pointed out, trusteeships and semi-sovereign arrangements potentially result in principal-agent problems.[5] The preferences and goals of the external actor and local actor will not always align, limiting the effectiveness of indirect rule as a tool for promoting development. Building off Lake's and Fariss's insights, the analysis presented in this book shows that this problem is fundamental – the actors most prepared to support semi-sovereign authority and hierarchies are the ones who benefit most from a corrupt and dysfunctional institutional environment. The principal-agent problems are immense.

If the external actors aim to promote development, then it may be difficult to find agents with similar preferences who also have the requisite political power and authority to influence outcomes substantially. Alternatively, actors who do agree to surrender sovereignty also have a strong incentive to shirk and limit the effectiveness of development policies. These principal-agent problems place strict limitations on hierarchy as a tool for promoting development.

However, Romer is not alone in arguing that semi-sovereign relationships or trusteeships are a means to promote development.[6] And there is some evidence that hierarchies and semi-sovereign arrangements can be successful.[7] The argument here demonstrates why in some cases trusteeship might be successful despite these principal-agent problems. Where threats to political survival are extreme, subordinate actors have an

---

[4] Jonathan Watts and Latin America correspondent, "Plans for Honduras Start-up City Hit by Transparency Concerns," *Guardian*, September 8, 2012, sec. World news, www.theguardian.com/world/2012/sep/08/honduras-city-project-paul-romer.

[5] David A. Lake and Christopher J. Fariss, "Why International Trusteeship Fails: The Politics of External Authority in Areas of Limited Statehood," *Governance*, 2014, http://onlinelibrary.wiley.com/doi/10.1111/gove.12066/full.

[6] Stephen Krasner, "Sharing Sovereignty: New Institutions for Collapsed and Failing States," *International Security* 29, no. 2 (2004); James D. Fearon and David D. Laitin, "Neotrusteeship and the Problem of Weak States," *International Security* 28, no. 4 (2004); Aila M. Matanock, "Governance Delegation Agreements: Shared Sovereignty as a Substitute for Limited Statehood," *Governance*, 2014, http://onlinelibrary.wiley.com/doi/10.1111/gove.12067/full; Stephen D. Krasner and Thomas Risse, "External Actors, State-Building, and Service Provision in Areas of Limited Statehood: Introduction," *Governance*, 2014, http://onlinelibrary.wiley.com/doi/10.1111/gove.12065/full.

[7] Matanock, "Governance Delegation Agreements."

incentive to support the establishment of hierarchy, and the order will be relatively stable. Hierarchy can secure elites' position and political survival in the short run. This creates incentives to support it. Elites are unlikely to undermine their rent-seeking position to too great an extent, however. Furthermore, as elites become more certain of their political survival, they may develop incentives to resist.

The empirical evidence presented in the book shows how in extreme circumstances state and nation-building enterprises can create short-term incentives for elites to surrender sovereignty to outside forces. This finding perhaps suggests that an external role in state-building is possible. However, the effects may be short-lived or self-defeating. Examples of these dynamics can be found in the three cases from the nineteenth century. In all three cases – China, the Ottoman Empire, and Egypt – elites surrendered sovereignty in return for resources from outside powers to carry out modernization and reform efforts, with varying success. There was also evidence of similar processes in a case from the current era, where Shevardnadze gave up sovereign rights to build the Georgian state in the early 1990s.

In Egypt, interactions between state-building imperatives and the establishment of informal control persisted for several decades. During the period of Muhammed Ali's rule in Egypt, Ali gave up rights such as extraterritoriality to the European powers in return for aid asserting his autonomy against the Ottoman Empire, but also to carry out reforms at the domestic level. It was during this period that the hierarchy was at its most stable. In the subsequent decades the dynamic persisted. Ali's grandson Ismail also required access to European financing to carry out educational, military, and governmental reforms. In this period these domestic problems forced the Egyptian rulers to accept European hierarchy.

However, Ismail managed to gain independence from the Ottoman Empire, and his political survival was no longer immediately threatened by the Ottoman Empire. The changed institutions altered the incentives of Egyptian political elites. The institutions of hierarchy were no longer as stable and eventually failed. Egyptian resistance forced the British to intervene and assume direct control. Egypt's eventual resistance demonstrates the self-defeating nature of hierarchy if it successfully promotes development.

The mid-nineteenth century when the Chinese state was wracked by rebellion was the point that hierarchy in the country was at its most stable. European officers such as Colonel Gordon were even in charge of armies within China; in this way the Chinese were giving up one of the most fundamental attributes of statehood to outsiders. Despite helping with the provision of order, hierarchy only lost legitimacy over the next decades.

In China we also saw incentives to surrender sovereignty for the benefit of state-building efforts. The Chinese government during the nineteenth century saw European interference, even if undesirable ex ante, as a means of carrying out reforms and strengthening the state. European funds and expertise played a role in suppressing regional, provincial and ethnic or religious uprisings. Moreover, European control of government institutions such as the Chinese Maritime Customs increased the bureaucratic efficiency of the Chinese state and increased their capacity to raise revenue domestically. Europeans were involved in the modernization of the Chinese government and military.

The European powers played a similar role providing resources but limiting sovereignty in the Ottoman Empire. In this case, the need to carry out political reforms drove the Ottoman government to borrow heavily from European sources.[8] When the Ottoman government could no longer service the debt, it was required to give up control of some revenue-raising activities.[9] This led directly to the establishment of the Ottoman Administration of Public Debt, a body that controlled 27 percent of Ottoman revenue.[10] Despite aiding development in some ways, European involvement also placed strict limitations on Ottoman sovereignty and growth.[11]

European efforts did not increase the legitimacy of hierarchy. If anything, the great powers were seen for the imperialists that they were and resented by local leaders and the population. There is an inherent trade-off for those who hope to use hierarchical relationships as a tool for state-building; providing resources to local elites may undermine hierarchy more than legitimate it, as these leaders suffer the humiliations of empire, while increasing their incentive and capacity to resist.

These processes are still active in the contemporary era. In the early 1990s Georgia was beset with political disorder and was on the verge of becoming a failed state. In order to gain aid in building and saving the Georgian state, Shevardnadze agreed to join the CIS and allowed Russia a role in appointing ministers in the Georgian government, such as the

---

[8] Edhem Eldem, "Ottoman Financial Integration with Europe: Foreign Loans, the Ottoman Bank and the Ottoman Public Debt," *European Review* 13, no. 3 (2005); Murat Birdal, *The Political Economy of Ottoman Public Debt: Insolvency and European Financial Control in the Late Nineteenth Century* (I. B. Tauris, 2010).

[9] Eldem, "Ottoman Financial Integration with Europe."

[10] M. S. Hanioglu, *A Brief History of the Late Ottoman Empire* (Princeton University Press, 2008), 135–37.

[11] See Sunar Ilkay Sunar, "State and Economy in the Ottoman Empire," in *Ottoman Empire and the World Economy*, ed. Huri Islamoglu-Inan (Cambridge University Press, 1987).

defense minister. This provided Shevardnadze the space and resources to carry out his reform of the government and military and build a somewhat stable state in Georgia. Russia's influence over the country was most stable when the country was wracked by the civil war and still controlled by militias. It was at this point in time that hierarchy was most stable. As Georgian politics became more stable, and as the government increased its capacity, reduced competition, and limited rent-seeking, hierarchy faced more and broader resistance.

One key finding of the book is that international and domestic orders are often substitutes, not complements. Hierarchy was most stable and most supported by subordinate elites when disorder was prevalent in the subordinate state. When political competition and political instability were high, when corruption and rent-seeking were rife, this was when subordinate elites supported hierarchy. The provision of resources from the dominant to the subordinate state did not lead to greater levels of legitimacy or stability of imperial order. When the politics of the subordinate state had either lower levels of rent-seeking or lower levels of political competition, resistance to the order arose.

Nationalism, Resistance, and the Loss of Sovereignty

Resistance to hierarchy can often result in reduced sovereignty rather than increased autonomy. Those working on hierarchy in the international system have often adopted an institutionalist approach, which has hypothesized that increases in the cost of governance lead to reduced authority and hierarchy in the international system.[12] This result is also a puzzle if one adopts a cultural or constructivist understanding of hierarchy.[13] Resistance implies, at least to an extent, illegitimate rule. If legitimacy and beliefs were to explain the level of hierarchy, then resistance should be associated with reduced levels of hierarchy.

In Egypt, hierarchy functioned when the local elites saw hierarchy as to their benefit. Once this ceased to be the case, however, the local elites began to resent the impositions of empire more. When Egypt achieved independence from the Ottoman state, the institutions of the regime became centralized and noncompetitive. The mechanisms that had led

---

[12] David A. Lake, "Anarchy, Hierarchy, and the Variety of International Relations," *International Organization* 50, no. 1 (1996).

[13] Alexander Wendt and Daniel Friedheim, "Hierarchy under Anarchy: Informal Empire and the East Germany State," in *State Sovereignty as Social Construct*, ed. Thomas Biersteker and Cynthia Weber (Cambridge University Press, 1996); John M. Hobson and J. C. Sharman, "The Enduring Place of Hierarchy in World Politics: Tracing the Social Logics of Hierarchy and Political Change," *European Journal of International Relations* 11, no. 1 (2005).

to stability of hierarchy vanished. Resistance emerged, leading to the failure of hierarchy and the British occupation of Egypt. Egyptian sovereignty, as a result of their resistance, was curtailed far more than it had been under informal hierarchy.

Perversely, increased nationalism can increase the level of hierarchy. Nationalism can do this in two ways. First, it increases the incentives of some actors to resist. This then results in increased coercion and the imposition of greater levels of hierarchy as described above. Second, nationalism can exacerbate tensions domestically, increasing the level of contestation and threat to political survival for some elites.[14] This then drives those threatened elites to support external actors.

These patterns can be seen repeatedly in Georgia. During the period of Soviet breakdown, Gamsakhurdia, the Georgian president, defined competition in terms of culture, not competition over rents. During this period, Gamsakhurdia tried to resist Russian presence, and the result was increased violence. Because this intensified competition between groups within Georgia, it also increased the support for Russia from groups that were threatened by Gamsakhurdia's nationalist policies. In later periods, when Saakashvili resisted Russian influence in the region, Russia intensified its control over South Ossetia and Abkhazia. Georgia fought a war with Russia to remove their agents in South Ossetia. Following the defeat of Georgia, Russia recognized the independence of these two regions and increased their presence and funding in these regions.

Resistance from subordinate elites increased the costs of governance for the dominant state. The dominant state, however, was prepared to pay the higher costs and assert greater levels of control. This indicates something important about the nature of authority in the international system. Hierarchy is not a normal good. There are few substitutes for authority in certain situations; states are simply forced to pay the higher cost and forgo other goods as a result. What the cases show is that hierarchy and empire, within certain bounds, can be described as Giffen goods. That is, as the price of these goods increases, more of the good is consumed not less.[15] This occurs when consumers have few substitutes for a good and the good is a staple. In other words, as resistance causes hierarchy to become more costly, the demand for control can often become higher; the dominant state will establish more extensive forms of hierarchy rather than withdrawing and consequently pay more for governance.

---

[14] For a similar argument regarding competing nationalisms, see Stephen Shulman, "Nationalist Sources of International Economic Integration," *International Studies Quarterly* 44, no. 3 (2000).

[15] R. T. Jensen and N. H. Miller, "Giffen Behavior and Subsistence Consumption," *American Economic Review* 98, no. 4 (2008).

Hierarchy and the Future of International Order

The influence of domestic politics in the subordinate state on the development of hierarchy has important implications for international outcomes as well as domestic state-building. These factors influence how great powers behave in the international system, whether they can establish authority relations or are forced to rely on coercion. For these reason, the findings also speak to debates regarding rising powers, their strategies and options as their power grows.[16] Formal imperial relationships are more or less obsolete. Norms against territorial expansion and strong respect for sovereignty mean that direct, territorial control requires states pay an excessive normative cost.[17] However, informal hierarchy is still a viable option.

The success of Russia's attempts at recreating its sphere of influence and control will continue to be mixed. Where there are institutional complementarities between the orders that Russia seeks to create and the domestic politics of those countries it seeks to control, Russian hierarchy should be stable. Where these incentives do not exist, Russia should face resistance. Expansion, control, and stability of the regional order will rely on the willingness of smaller states to facilitate this order.

The same incentives and constraints will influence the choices of other rising powers. Scholars cannot explain these dynamics by focusing solely on the nature of these rising states. It is not enough to understand the history and culture of these new powers. The fact that China was a "civilizational-state" will only tell part of the story about China's rise.[18] To understand how rising powers will construct or influence international orders, it is necessary to understand how the institutions and character of the subordinate states create incentives to accommodate themselves to a new order or not.

The findings of this book tell us that the control and informal domination by these rising powers will be strongest when there is disorder within those state that are targeted for control. Rising powers will have the most success promulgating their new order when there is political competition and rent-seeking in the domestic sphere of the subordinate states. This

---

[16] Edward D. Mansfield, "Rising Powers in the Global Economy: Issues and Questions," *International Studies Review* 16, no. 3 (2014); Stephan Haggard, "Liberal Pessimism: International Relations Theory and the Emerging Powers," *Asia and the Pacific Policy Studies* 1, no. 1 (2014); Randall Schweller, "Emerging Powers in an Age of Disorder," *Global Governance* 17, no. 3 (2011).

[17] Tanisha M. Fazal, *State Death: The Politics and Geography of Conquest, Occupation, and Annexation* (Princeton University Press, 2007).

[18] See, e.g., M. Jacques, *When China Rules the World: The Rise of the Middle Kingdom and the End of the Western World* (Allen Lane, 2009).

domestic disorder will be an enabling feature of hierarchy and control, not a product of it.

China's growing role in African politics has been characterized as a form of neo-imperialism or neo-colonialism.[19] The findings provide a likely explanation for China's success in spreading its influence in Africa. The fragmented, patrimonial politics that characterizes many sub-Saharan states provide fertile ground for the establishment of informal forms of hierarchy.[20] While some this may be characterized as the spread the influence, China has been ratcheting up its direct control, assuming rights to run ports in places like Djibouti and establishing military installations.[21] It is in this environment that China has spread its authority.

The findings also speak to the debates regarding China's role in Asia. Some scholars have foreseen a return to hierarchical arrangements.[22] Others have been more skeptical of this possibility.[23] Where historical trends have resulted in stronger, more cohesive states, Chinese efforts to extend hierarchy and control may run into more resistance. Where states are fragmented and beset with corruption, China may succeed. Different types of states exist throughout Asia, some stronger, some weaker, some more fragmented.[24] Any international order China establishes in Asia is likely to be a mixture of hierarchy and anarchical elements as they receive support from some states and are resisted by others.

Hierarchy will have a continuing and ambiguous place in the international system. Great powers are still prepared to pay a relatively high cost to preserve their control. For example, Russia was willing to attack Georgia and Ukraine even if it earned the opprobrium of the world. The theory and findings presented here show that we need to understand the pull as well as the push, the supply side and the demand side, of

---

[19] Alison J. Ayers, "Beyond Myths, Lies and Stereotypes: The Political Economy of a 'New Scramble for Africa,'" *New Political Economy* 18, no. 2 (2012).

[20] Nicolas Van de Walle, *African Economies and the Politics of Permanent Crisis, 1979–1999* (Cambridge University Press, 2001).

[21] Andrew Jacobs and Jane Perlez, "US Wary of Its New Neighbor in Djibouti: A Chinese Naval Base," *New York Times*, August 7, 2018, sec. World, www.nytimes.com/2017/02/25/world/africa/us-djibouti-chinese-naval-base.html.

[22] David C. Kang, "Hierarchy and Legitimacy in International Systems: The Tribute System in Early Modern East Asia," *Security Studies* 19, no. 4 (2010).

[23] Amitav Acharya, "Will Asia's Past Be Its Future?," 2006, www.mitpressjournals.org/doi/pdf/10.1162/016228803773100101; Amitav Acharya, "Power Shift or Paradigm Shift? China's Rise and Asia's Emerging Security Order," *International Studies Quarterly* 58, no. 1 (2014).

[24] Dan Slater, *Ordering Power: Contentious Politics and Authoritarian Leviathans in Southeast Asia* (Cambridge University Press, 2010).

hierarchy in international relations. Simply condemning Russia for its expansionism in Georgia and Ukraine or China for its move into Africa, without studying the subordinate state in depth, fails to appreciate the dynamics that have led them there and the interests some local actors might have in giving up sovereignty to these powers.

Appendix A

Additional Tests (Georgia)

Alternative measures of the main variables of interest were used to test the robustness of the findings. *Accountability* was used as a second measure of attitudes toward rent-seeking. Accountability asked whether "high officials are punished for their unlawful actions." The responses ranged between strongly disagree, disagree, agree, and strongly agree. This also measured the extent to which officials can take advantage of their position for gain and arbitrarily use their power to benefit themselves and their clients. These results were similar to those in the main text.

Connections, another measure of rent-seeking, asked respondents what was the most important factor in finding a job. If the respondent selected "connections," this indicated that they believed that nonmarket factors were crucial aspects of the economy. The type of connections was not specified, and hence could mean nonpolitical connections such as friends or family, but it is likely that it measured some aspect of rent-seeking. The interaction was significant and in the predicted direction for the Trust Local category (Model 6).

Other measures of support for hierarchy were used in additional models. *CIS* asked respondents if "Georgia should focus on closer cooperation with the Commonwealth of Independent States (CIS), because that is where we belong" or if "Georgia should pursue closer cooperation with the European Union (EU), because this will help us develop in the right direction." Russia has reduced Georgian sovereignty and control over its territory in the post-Soviet era; support for the CIS was an indication of support for a higher level of hierarchy than support for the EU. The effect for the interaction between Rule of Law and Trust Local category was significant at the 5 percent level in a logistic regression (Model 7),[1] supporting the hypothesis. The Accountability variable (Model 8) was

---

[1] Only the three major ethnic groups were used for the Ethnic Identity variable because of separation.

not significant, possibly because Cooperate with CIS was a less direct measure of support for hierarchy than Protect from Russia. The EU could play a role similar to that of Russia for improving an individual's prospects for political survival, representing a milder alternate form of hierarchy.

Territorial Integrity asked respondents to name the most important issue facing Georgia. The territorial integrity of the country was one option. Territorial integrity is connected to issues of sovereignty and Russia's role in the country. The government at the time viewed the breakaway regions as Russian proxies.[2] Unencumbered control over a given territory forms part of the definition of the state going back to Weber.[3] Believing territorial integrity is the most important issue in Georgia demonstrates a rejection of Russia's role in reducing Georgia's sovereignty. Logistic regressions showed the probability of claiming territorial integrity was the most important issue facing Georgia was higher for those who believe that the rule of law was widespread, and that high officials were punished for their crimes (Models 9 and 10).

There are other powerful international actors, notably the United States and the EU, that are potential sources of external resources with different normative agendas and identities than Russia. The political survival argument for hierarchy would be strongly supported if the same variables explained resistance to all three. Ordered logistic regressions were run using *Protect from USA* and *Protect from EU* as dependent variables. The question was similar to Protect from Russia.[4] This analysis largely supported the hypothesis. In the case of the United States, Elite–Societal Relations interacted with Rule of Law did not produce a significant effect but did when interacted with Accountability (Models 11 and 12). Both variables interacted with Elite–Societal Relations were significantly correlated with a lower probability that those that trust local officials believe that EU influence should be resisted.[5]

Additional Tests (Ukraine)

Again, several additional models were run to check the robustness of the results. First, the independent variable measuring rent-seeking was dichotomized, to check the parallel odds assumptions. In contrast to the

---

[2] Yakobashvili, author interview, July 29, 2010.
[3] Max Weber, *Max Weber: Essays in Sociology* (Oxford University Press, 1958).
[4] *Friends with American* and *Friends with German* replaced Friends with Russian.
[5] For the Trust Executive category, the interaction predicted a lower probability of wanting to resist Russia, contrary to theoretical predictions. This might be explained by the demands concerning governance that the EU could make on the central government.

Appendix A

results from Georgia, while the results were in the predicted direction, the coefficient was no longer significant at 0.75 ($p = 0.35$).

Models were also run using two additional dependent variables.[6] *Russian Threat* is a variable that asked the respondent to rank the threat Russia posed to Ukraine, from very threatening to not threatening at all. This variable may not get directly at the issue of sovereignty. It does, nonetheless, reflect some of the respondents' attitudes to Russian attempts to influence the region. Russia being viewed as nonthreatening would indicate a lack of concern with Russia's attempts to spread its authority. The variable ranged from 1 (a large threat) to 4 (not threatening at all).

Using Russian Threat as the dependent variable, there was a positive coefficient of 0.63 for the trust parliament variable, which was significant at the $p < 0.1$ level. This indicates that as corruption increased, people in this category became more inclined to surrender sovereignty to Russia. In this model the trust neither category was also significant with a coefficient of 0.52 ($p < 0.01$). This test provides some evidence that competition over rent-seeking influenced attitudes toward sovereignty.

The second variable, *NATO*, asks whether Ukraine should join a security alliance with the Commonwealth of Independent States or NATO, with the intermediate responses being do not join NATO but cooperate with them and do not join NATO and not cooperate with them. As was the case with the question regarding the EU and the CIS in Georgia, this variable was best construed as a question concerning different levels of hierarchy. Being more closely aligned with Russia and joining the CIS indicated a higher level of hierarchy because of Russia's stronger interests in the region. Russia's security interests were already reducing Ukrainian sovereignty, for example in their control over the Black Sea Fleet in Crimea.

Using NATO, the only competition variable that had a significant interaction with corruption was the trust parliament category (coefficient = 0.72, $p = 0.05$). The trust neither category was not significant at either the 0.05 or 0.1 level. Moreover, this coefficient, −0.03, was small and negative. Consequently, the only variable that was consistently robust across most of these checks was the coefficient for the interaction between corruption and the trust parliament category.

---

[6] Calculating the predicted probabilities shows substantive effects in these two models as well.

Table A.1 *Main results and Accountability variable*

Dependent variable	1 Protect from Russia	2 Protect from Russia	3 Protect from Russia	4 Protect from Russia	5 Protect from Russia	6 Protect from Russia
Rule of Law	0.110 (0.07)	0.444*** (0.193)				
Accountability			0.203*** (0.070)	0.551** (0.197)		
Connections					−0.242** (0.107)	−0.631** (0.310)
Trust Executive	0.088 (0.289)	−0.454 (0.999)	−0.064 (0.282)	0.012 (1.061)	0.069 (0.246)	−0.069 (0.317)
Trust Both	−0.060 (0.212)	0.841 (0.765)	−0.114 (0.209)	0.826 (0.781)	0.105 (0.183)	0.007 (0.233)
Trust Neither	−0.290 (0.192)	0.758 (0.564)	−0.282 (0.191)	0.906 (0.611)	−0.225 (0.167)	0.450** (0.217)
Rule of Law × Trust Executive		0.186 (0.361)				
Rule of Law × Trust Both		−0.344 (0.261)				
Rule of Law × Trust Neither		−0.431** (0.215)				
Accountability × Trust Executive				−0.047 (0.351)		

Accountability × Trust Both				−0.339	
				(0.257)	
Accountability × Trust Neither				−0.447**	
				(0.216)	
Connections × Trust Executive					0.349
					(0.507)
Connections × Trust Both					0.222
					(0.378)
Connections × Trust Neither					0.541
					(0.340)
Armenian	−0.826***	−0.806***	−1.010***	−1.005***	−1.020***	−1.000***
	(0.227)	(0.228)	(0.222)	(0.223)	(0.198)	(0.199)
Azerbaijani	0.316	0.288	0.287	0.261	0.199	0.178
	(0.365)	(0.371)	(0.364)	(0.368)	(0.334)	(0.337)
Age	0.003	0.003	0.003	0.003	0.005	0.005
	(0.004)	(0.004)	(0.004)	(0.004)	(0.003)	(0.003)
Income	0.027	0.031	0.027	0.030	0.008	0.010
	(0.044)	(0.045)	(0.044)	(0.044)	(0.040)	(0.040)
Education	0.008	0.004	−0.005	−0.007	−0.013	−0.014
	(0.021)	(0.021)	(0.020)	(0.020)	(0.018)	(0.018)
Sex	−0.165	−0.170	−0.201*	−0.209*	0.097	−0.119
	(0.122)	(0.122)	(0.120)	(0.120)	(0.108)	(0.109)
Friends with Russian	0.479**	0.448***	0.580***	0.545***	0.605***	0.598***
	(0.157)	(0.158)	(0.156)	(0.157)	(0.140)	(0.140)
Family in Local Government	−0.033	−0.028	0.058	−0.066	−0.118	0.122
	(0.222)	(0.224)	(0.216)	(0.217)	(0.188)	(0.189)
Family in National Government	−0.328	−0.349	−0.244	−0.259	−0.369	−0.355
	(0.350)	(0.351)	(0.324)	(0.326)	(0.293)	(0.294)
Cut 2	−1.753***	1.02*	−1.761***	−0.826	−2.443***	−2.613***

Table A.1 (cont.)

Dependent variable	1 Protect from Russia	2 Protect from Russia	3 Protect from Russia	4 Protect from Russia	5 Protect from Russia	6 Protect from Russia
	(0.434)	(0.63)	(0.429)	(0.677)	(0.383)	(0.400)
Cut 3	−0.184	−.56	−0.207	0.730	−0.905**	−1.075***
	(0.427)	(0.62)	(0.422)	(0.673)	(0.375)	(0.392)
Cut 4	1.277***	−2.01***	1.301***	2.245***	0.647	0.480
	(0.428)	(0.63)	(0.424)	(0.677)	(0.374)	(0.390)
N	968	968	1,006	1,006	1,264	1,264
AIC	2,539	2,538	2,625	2,625	3,274	3,277

Note. Rule of Law or Accountability shows effect for Trust Local category in models with interactions.
*$p < 0.1$. **$p < 0.05$. ***$p < 0.01$, from two-tailed significance.

Table A.2 *Additional tests, Georgia*

Variables	7 CIS	8 CIS	9 Territorial Integrity	10 Territorial Integrity	11 Protect from USA	12 Protect from USA	13 Protect from EU	14 Protect from EU
Rule of Law	−0.449** (0.227)		−0.069 (0.294)		0.169 (0.191)		0.391** (0.188)	
Accountability		0.008 (0.218)		−0.031 (0.275)		0.524** (0.18)		0.541** (0.186)
Trust Executive	−1.094 (1.218)	−1.508 (1.382)	2.117 (1.541)	−3.866** (1.901)	0.359 (1.008)	0.645 (1.060)	3.120*** (1.040)	1.607 (1.099)
Trust Both	−1.680* (0.960)	−2.141** (1.035)	−0.058 (1.185)	−0.617 (1.220)	0.100 (0.777)	1.241* (0.759)	0.729 (0.771)	1.683** (0.764)
Trust Neither	−1.429** (0.661)	−0.626 (0.711)	−0.266 (0.850)	0.405 (0.854)	0.507 (0.574)	1.257** (0.577)	1.225 (0.565)	1.216** (0.585)
Rule of Law × Trust Executive	0.439 (0.439)	0.317	0.988* (0.520)		−0.264 (0.360)		−1.247*** (0.372)	
Rule of Law × Trust Both	(0.527)	(0.105)	0.044 (0.401)		−0.202 (0.262)		−0.354 (0.261)	
Rule of Law × Trust Neither	0.428 (0.261)		0.226 (0.324)		−0.334 (0.215)		−0.608** (0.214)	
Accountability × Trust Executive		0.593 (0.439)		1.368** (0.579)		−0.343 (0.354)		−0.658* (0.367)
Accountability × Trust Both		0.542* (0.323)		0.135 (0.389)		−0.629** (0.249)		−0.651** (0.249)
		0.117	...	−0.183		−0.597***		−0.508*

Table A.2 (cont.)

Variables	7 CIS	8 CIS	9 Territorial Integrity	10 Territorial Integrity	11 Protect from USA	12 Protect from USA	13 Protect from EU	14 Protect from EU
Accountability × Trust Neither		(0.249)		(0.306)		(0.205)		(0.206)
N	891	910	1,071	1,110	946	964	952	991
AIC	1,022	1,037	874	880	2,397	2,480	2,395	2,517

Note. Rule of Law or Accountability shows effect for Trust Local category in models with interactions (all control variables included).
*$p < 0.1$. **$p < 0.05$. ***$p < 0.01$, from two-tailed significance.

Appendix A

Table A.3 *Main results, Ukraine*

Dependent variable	1 Relationship with Russia	2 Relationship with Russia	3[+] Relationship with Russia	4[+] Relationship with Russia
Corruption	0.22**	0.11	0.23	−0.009
	(0.08)	(0.14)	(0.17)	(0.27)
Trust President	−0.02	−0.11	−0.04	−0.15
	(0.17)	(0.72)	(0.17)	(0.37)
Trust Parliament	0.90***	−1.97	0.92***	0.27
	(0.25)	(1.21)	(0.25)	(0.76)
Trust Neither	0.62***	0.15	0.68***	0.12
	(0.14)	(0.66)	(0.14)	(0.41)
Corruption × Trust Executive	...	0.02	...	0.12
		(0.23)		(0.42)
Corruption × Trust Parliament	...	0.85**	...	0.75
		(0.35)		(0.81)
Corruption × Trust Neither	...	−0.14**	...	0.63
		(0.19)		(0.43)
Language	.56***	.55***	0.58***	0.59***
	(0.16)	(0.16)	(0.015)	(0.15)
Russian	0.31**	.33**	0.32***	0.31**
	(0.15)	(0.26)	(0.15)	(0.16)
Income	0.0003	0.0004	−0.0004	−0.0004
	(0.0005)	(0.0005)	(0.0005)	(0.0005)
Education	−0.15***	−0.15***	−0.15***	0.004
	(0.03)	(0.03)	(0.03)	(0.03)
Sex	0.23*	0.23*	0.22*	0.22*
	(0.12)	(0.12)	(0.13)	(0.12)
Age	0.003	0.003	0.003	0.003
	(0.004)	(0.004)	(0.003)	(0.003)
Family in Government	−0.31	−0.23	−0.23	−0.24
	(0.27)	(0.36)	(0.36)	(0.36)
Region	−1.09***	−1.11***	−1.08***	−1.09
	(0.14)	(0.14)	(0.15)	(0.14)
Cut 2	1.37***	1.75***	1.87***	2.84***
	(0.43)	(0.56)	(0.37)	(0.69)
Cut 3	−1.88***	−1.52***	−1.38***	1.26*
	(0.43)	(0.56)	(0.37)	(0.67)
N	1,278	1,278	1,278	1,278
AIC	2,203	2,203	2,208	2,212

+ Dichotomized dependent variable.
*$p < 0.1$. **$p < 0.05$. ***$p < 0.01$, from two-tailed significance.

Table A.4 *Additional tests, Ukraine*

Dependent variable	5 Russian Threat	6 Russian Threat	7 NATO	8 NATO
Corruption	0.09	−0.14	0.17**	0.12
	(0.08)	(0.15)	(0.08)	(0.13)
Trust President	−0.06	0.06	−0.01	−0.44
	(0.18)	(0.72)	(0.17)	(0.70)
Trust Parliament	0.30	−1.80	1.22***	−1.25
	(0.27)	(1.21)	(0.26)	(1.29)
Trust Neither	0.13	−1.64**	0.80***	0.92
	(0.14)	(0.68)	(0.14)	(0.66)
Corruption × Trust President	...	0.02	...	0.14
		(0.23)		(0.22)
Corruption × Trust Parliament	...	0.63*	...	0.72**
		(0.37)		(0.37)
Corruption × Trust Neither	...	0.52**	...	−0.03
		(0.20)		(0.19)
Language	.53***	.56***	0.35**	0.32**
	(0.16)	(0.16)	(0.15)	(0.15)
Russian	0.18	.17**	0.41**	0.43***
	(0.17)	(0.18)	(0.16)	(0.16)
Income	0.0003	0.0004	−0.001**	−0.001**
	(0.0005)	(0.0005)	(0.004)	(0.004)
Education	−0.07***	−0.08***	−0.09***	−0.09***
	(0.02)	(0.03)	(0.03)	(0.03)
Sex	0.03	0.04	0.21*	0.21*
	(0.11)	(0.12)	(0.11)	(0.11)
Age	0.01**	0.01**	0.03***	0.01***
	(0.004)	(0.004)	(0.003)	(0.003)
Family in Government	−0.11	−0.08	−0.05	−0.08
	(0.36)	(0.37)	(0.36)	(0.36)
Region	−1.05***	−1.05***	−0.63***	−0.65***
	(0.13)	(0.14)	(0.14)	(0.14)
N	1,192	1,192	1,089	1,089
AIC	2,526	2,522	2,749	2,750

*$p < 0.1$. **$p < 0.05$. ***$p < 0.01$, from two-tailed significance.

Appendix B

Table B.1 *Columns (1–2) fixed effects no lagged dependent variable, Columns (3–6) pooled autocorrelation adjusted for using Driscoll Kraay standard errors*

	Dependent variable			
	IRT Hierarchy			
	(1)	(2)	(3)	(4)
Corruption	−0.400	−10.425**	−2.944***	−21.431***
	(0.398)	(4.801)	(0.284)	(3.398)
Polcomp	−0.149***		−0.380***	
	(0.037)		(0.021)	
CGV		−9.030**		−18.605***
		(4.088)		(3.262)
GDP Per Capita	−0.287**	−0.068	−0.637***	−0.434
	(0.113)	(0.167)	(0.144)	(0.332)
Precommunist Literacy			−0.034***	−0.041***
			(0.007)	(0.010)
Referendum			−0.006	0.008
			(0.004)	(0.007)
Caucasus			0.890***	1.453***
			(0.177)	(0.150)
Central Asia			−0.454	−1.370***
			(0.431)	(0.492)
Minority			0.186	1.146***
			(0.130)	(0.179)
Population	0.361	0.134	0.099	−0.164
	(0.239)	(0.502)	(0.226)	(0.237)
Military Spending	−0.010	−0.059	0.156***	0.056
	(0.046)	(0.059)	(0.059)	(0.098)
Resource Revenue	−0.037	−0.040	−0.133***	−0.101
	(0.026)	(0.040)	(0.046)	(0.066)
ELF			3.192***	3.535***
			(1.004)	(1.324)
EU	0.357***	0.189	0.202	−0.413
	(0.102)	(0.116)	(0.130)	(0.266)
Internal Threatt			−1.707***	−1.477***
			(0.245)	(0.405)

Table B.1 *(cont.)*

	\(1\)	\(2\)	\(3\)	\(4\)
	\multicolumn{4}{c}{Dependent variable}
	\multicolumn{4}{c}{IRT Hierarchy}
External Threat			−0.257	−0.478
			(0.344)	(0.604)
Corruption × Polcomp	0.155***		0.462***	
	(0.049)		(0.043)	
Corruption × CGV		10.762**		21.587***
		(4.792)		(3.644)
Constant			6.182*	23.739***
			(3.571)	(8.315)
Observations	290	197		
R^2	0.356	0.259		
Adjusted R^2	0.237	0.086		
F statistic	4.210***	2.312***		
	(df = 32; 244)	(df = 24; 159)		

*$p < 0.1$. **$p < 0.05$. ***$p < 0.01$.

Table B.2 *Results for different time periods*

	(1)	(2)	(3)	(4)
	\multicolumn{4}{c}{Dependent variable}
	\multicolumn{4}{c}{IRT Hierarchy}
Corruption	−2.118**	0.694*	−19.043***	4.423
	(0.890)	(0.413)	(4.651)	(8.263)
Polcomp	−0.154***	0.026		
	(0.047)	(0.048)		
CGV			−16.598***	2.499
			(4.505)	(6.984)
GDP Per Capita	−0.158	0.082	0.169	0.153
	(0.247)	(0.112)	(0.389)	(0.181)
Precommunist Literacy	−0.013	−0.004	−0.039*	−0.001
	(0.012)	(0.005)	(0.021)	(0.006)
Referendum	0.007	0.008**	0.022	0.024***
	(0.011)	(0.004)	(0.017)	(0.006)
Caucasus	0.857***	0.195**	1.935***	0.663***
	(0.308)	(0.096)	(0.432)	(0.145)

Appendix B

Table B.2 *(cont.)*

	\multicolumn{4}{c}{Dependent variable}
	\multicolumn{4}{c}{IRT Hierarchy}
	(1)	(2)	(3)	(4)
Central Asia	0.028	−0.031	−1.034	0.522
	(0.825)	(0.359)	(1.355)	(0.398)
Russian Minority	0.145	1.116***	1.351**	2.355***
	(0.296)	(0.176)	(0.528)	(0.329)
Population	0.062	−0.576***	−0.267	−1.362***
	(0.254)	(0.124)	(0.450)	(0.253)
Military Spending	0.026	0.015	−0.047	0.078
	(0.066)	(0.036)	(0.110)	(0.064)
Resource Revenue	−0.055	0.016	−0.191	0.035
	(0.070)	(0.021)	(0.121)	(0.037)
ELF	1.146	−0.503	1.971	−2.247**
	(1.686)	(0.744)	(2.916)	(1.087)
EU	0.118	−1.395***	0.034	−2.347***
	(0.141)	(0.248)	(0.244)	(0.279)
Internal Threat	−0.302	0.0001	−0.506	0.584
	(0.577)	(0.258)	(0.900)	(0.368)
External Threat	−0.454	−0.434*	−0.752	−1.499***
	(0.622)	(0.248)	(0.988)	(0.422)
IRT Hierarchy$_{t-1}$	0.546***	0.530***		0.184**
	(0.106)	(0.054)		(0.089)
Corruption × Polcomp	0.159**	−0.047		
	(0.068)	(0.059)		
Corruption × CGV			18.973***	−3.782
			(5.250)	(8.252)
Constant	1.400	7.427***	18.157**	14.976*
	(3.836)	(1.953)	(8.588)	(7.965)
Observations	83	202	88	109
R^2	0.966	0.987	0.886	0.988
Adjusted R^2	0.952	0.985	0.845	0.985
Residual std. error	0.210	0.134	0.369	0.132
	(df = 59)	(df = 168)	(df = 64)	(df = 83)
F statistic	71.879***	399.968***	21.649***	280.703***
	(df = 23; 59)	(df = 33; 168)	(df = 23; 64)	(df = 25; 83)

Note. Models 1–2 show results from 1992–2000, models 3–4 results from 2000–2016.
*$p < 0.1$. **$p < 0.05$. ***$p < 0.01$.

Table B.3 *Regime type models 1–3 pooled with lagged dependent variable, models 4–5 fixed effects*

	Dependent variable					
	IRT Hierarchy	Raw Hierarchy	Raw Hierarchy	IRT Hierarchy	Raw Hierarchy	Raw Hierarchy
	(1)	(2)	(3)	(4)	(5)	(6)
Non–Authoritarian	−0.380***	−0.212***	−0.311	−0.262***	−0.172***	−3.459***
	(0.094)	(0.035)	(0.195)	(0.094)	(0.031)	(0.239)
Party	−0.113	−0.134***	−1.014**	−0.460***	−0.274***	−1.581***
	(0.079)	(0.029)	(0.408)	(0.176)	(0.045)	(0.341)
GDP Per Capita	−0.242**	−0.232***	−0.353	−0.167	−0.185***	−0.144
	(0.110)	(0.040)	(0.250)	(0.113)	(0.039)	(0.163)
Precommunist Literacy	−0.006	−0.001	−0.017			
	(0.005)	(0.002)	(0.018)			
Referendum	−0.002	−0.003**	0.071**			
	(0.004)	(0.001)	(0.028)			
Caucasus	−0.179	−0.200***	1.776**			
	(0.157)	(0.057)	(0.725)			
Central Asia	−0.329	−0.020	5.183**			
	(0.314)	(0.115)	(2.255)			
Russian Minority	−0.161	−0.204***	−3.312***			
	(0.163)	(0.060)	(0.901)			
Population	0.065	0.087**	1.225***	0.296	0.170*	1.200***
	(0.109)	(0.040)	(0.415)	(0.270)	(0.092)	(0.160)
Military Spending	0.067*	0.056***	0.170*	−0.003	0.018	−0.346***
	(0.036)	(0.013)	(0.090)	(0.041)	(0.015)	(0.126)
Resource Revenue	−0.019	−0.030***	0.049	−0.004	−0.011	−0.455***

ELF	(0.026)	(0.009)	(0.060)	(0.025)	(0.009)	(0.082)
	1.026	0.431	3.371			
	(0.772)	(0.282)	(3.527)			
EU	0.008	0.017		0.156**	0.093***	
	(0.075)	(0.028)		(0.078)	(0.028)	
Internal Threat	−0.469*	−0.383***	−2.904***			
	(0.257)	(0.094)	(1.018)			
External Threat	−0.044	0.015	−4.762***			
	(0.230)	(0.084)	(1.601)			
IRT Hierarchy$_{t-1}$	0.757***	0.237***		0.487***		
	(0.043)	(0.016)		(0.060)		
Raw Hierarchy$_{t-1}$			6.364***			
			(0.328)			
Constant	1.290	1.390**	−22.951***			
	(1.566)	(0.572)	(5.384)			
Observations	216	216	216	216	221	221
R^2	0.973	0.973		0.565	0.497	
Adjusted R^2	0.968	0.968		0.472	0.392	
Residual std. error (df = 182)	0.184	0.067				
F statistic	199.805*** (df = 33; 182)	200.349*** (df = 33; 182)		9.215*** (df = 25; 177)	7.205*** (df = 25; 182)	

*$p < 0.1$. **$p < 0.05$. ***$p < 0.01$.

Table B.4 *V–Dem global data*

	\multicolumn{4}{c}{Dependent variable}
	International	Domestic	International	Domestic
	(1)	(2)	(3)	(4)
CGV	−0.305***	−0.261***		
	(0.027)	(0.025)		
Polity			−0.028***	−0.029***
			(0.003)	(0.003)
Corruption	−0.133***	−0.052	−0.003	0.009
	(0.041)	(0.038)	(0.039)	(0.035)
Population	−0.027**	−0.021**	−0.013	−0.023**
	(0.011)	(0.010)	(0.011)	(0.010)
GDP Per Capita	−0.027***	−0.039***	−0.029***	−0.034***
	(0.008)	(0.007)	(0.008)	(0.007)
Resource Revenue	0.00000	−0.00000	0.00000	−0.00000
	(0.00000)	(0.00000)	(0.00000)	(0.00000)
Military Capabilities	1.430***	1.665***	−0.131	0.063
	(0.400)	(0.372)	(0.487)	(0.440)
CGV × Corruption	0.393***	0.318***		
	(0.043)	(0.040)		
Polity × Corruption			0.019***	0.021***
			(0.006)	(0.005)
Observations	6,977	6,977	6,560	6,560
R^2	0.728	0.717	0.733	0.724
Adjusted R^2	0.711	0.700	0.715	0.706
F statistic	2,281.660***	2,159.430***	2,192.644***	2,093.960***
	(df = 8; 6814)	(df = 8; 6814)	(df = 8; 6399)	(df = 8; 6399)

Note. Includes lagged dependent variables, standard errors in parentheses.
*$p < 0.1$. **$p < 0.05$. ***$p < 0.01$.

Bibliography

Abdelal, Rawi. *National Purpose in the World Economy: Post-Soviet States in Comparative Perspective.* Ithaca, NY: Cornell University Press, 2001.
"The Profits of Power: Commerce and Realpolitik in Eurasia." *Review of International Political Economy* 20, no. 3 (2013): 421–56.
"The Multinational Firm and Geopolitics: Europe, Russian Energy, and Power." *Business and Politics* 17, no. 3 (2015): 553–76.
Abernathy, David. *The Dynamics of Global Dominance: European Overseas Empires 1415–1980.* New Haven, CT: Yale University Press, 2000.
Abu-Lughod, Ibrahim. "The Transformation of the Egyptian Élite: Prelude to the 'Urābī Revolt." *Middle East Journal* 21, no. 3 (1967): 325–44.
Acharya, Amitav. "Will Asia's Past Be Its Future?" (2006). www.mitpressjournals.org/doi/pdf/10.1162/016228803773100101.
"Power Shift or Paradigm Shift? China's Rise and Asia's Emerging Security Order." *International Studies Quarterly* 58, no. 1 (2014): 158–73.
Achen, C. H. "Why Lagged Dependent Variables Can Suppress the Explanatory Power of Other Independent Variables." *Ann Arbor* 1001 (2000): 48106–1248.
Adsera, Alicia, Carles Boix, and Mark Payne. "Are You Being Served? Political Accountability and Quality of Government." *Journal of Law, Economics, and Organization* 19, no. 2 (2003): 445–90.
Ahmed, Faisal Z. "The Perils of Unearned Foreign Income: Aid, Remittances, and Government Survival." *American Political Science Review* 106, no. 1 (2012): 146–65.
Ai, Chunrong, and Edward C. Norton. "Interaction Terms in Logit and Probit Models." *Economics Letters* 80, no. 1 (2003): 123–29.
Albertus, Michael, Sofia Fenner, and Dan Slater. *Coercive Distribution.* Cambridge: Cambridge University Press, 2018.
Aleksandar Vasovic, Adrian Croft. "US, EU Set Sanctions as Putin Recognises Crimea Sovereignty." March 17, 2014. http://in.reuters.com/article/2014/03/17/ukraine-crisis-crimea-referendum-idINDEEA2G00620140317.
Al-Jazeera. "Armenia Sends Non-Combat Team to Syria at Russia's Request." February 2019. www.aljazeera.com/news/2019/02/armenia-sends-combat-team-syria-russia-request-190209144531602.html.
Al-Sayyid-Marsot, Afaf Lufti. *Egypt in the Reign of Muhammad Ali.* Cambridge: Cambridge University Press, 1984.

"The British Occupation of Egypt from 1882." In *The Oxford History of the British Empire: The Nineteenth Century*, edited by Andrew Porter, 3:651–64. Oxford: Oxford University Press, 1999.

Alt, James E., and David D. Lassen. "The Political Economy of Institutions and Corruption in American States." *Journal of Theoretical Politics* 15, no. 3 (2003): 341–65.

Ambrosio, Thomas. "The Fall of Yanukovych: Structural and Political Constraints to Implementing Authoritarian Learning." *East European Politics* 33, no. 2 (April 3, 2017): 184–209.

Amos, Howard. "Ukraine Crisis Fuels Secession Calls in Pro-Russian South." *Guardian*, February 24, 2014, sec. World news. www.theguardian.com/world/2014/feb/23/ukraine-crisis-secession-russian-crimea.

Aphrasidze, David, and David Siroky. "Frozen Transitions and Unfrozen Conflicts, or What Went Wrong in Georgia?" *Yale Journal of International Affairs* 121 (2010).

Åslund, Anders. "Oligarchs, Corruption, and European Integration." *Journal of Democracy* 25, no. 3 (2014): 64–73.

Åslund, Anders, and Michael McFaul. *Revolution in Orange: The Origins of Ukraine's Democratic Breakthrough*. Washington, DC: Carnegie Endowment for International Peace, 2006.

Auyero, Javier. "'From the Client's Point (s) of View': How Poor People Perceive and Evaluate Political Clientelism." *Theory and Society* 28, no. 2 (1999): 297–334.

Aves, Jonathan. *Georgia, from Chaos to Stability?* London: Royal Institute of International Affairs Russia and Eurasia Programme, 1996.

Aydingün, Ayşegül, Pinar Köksal, and Alter Kahraman. "Conversion of Ajarians to Orthodox Christianity: Different Narratives and Perceptions." *Europe-Asia Studies* 71, no. 2 (February 7, 2019): 290–314.

Ayers, Alison J. "Beyond Myths, Lies and Stereotypes: The Political Economy of a 'New Scramble for Africa.'" *New Political Economy* 18, no. 2 (May 21, 2012): 227–57.

Baev, Pavel. "Civil Wars in Georgia." In *Potentials of Disorder*, edited by Jan Koehler and Christoph Zurcher, 127–44. Manchester: Manchester University Press, 2003.

Bakke, Kristin M., Andrew M. Linke, John O'Loughlin, and Gerard Toal. "Dynamics of State-Building after War: External-Internal Relations in Eurasian de Facto States." *Political Geography* 63 (March 1, 2018): 159–73.

Balmaceda, Margarita Mercedes. *The Politics of Energy Dependency: Ukraine, Belarus, and Lithuania between Domestic Oligarchs and Russian Pressure*. Vol. 40. Toronto: University of Toronto Press, 2013.

Barkey, Karen. *Empire of Difference: The Ottomans in Comparative Perspective*. Cambridge: Cambridge University Press, 2008.

BBC News. "Pro-Russians Storm Ukraine Buildings." April 7, 2014. www.bbc.com/news/world-europe-26910210.

Beck, Nathaniel, and Jonathan N. Katz. "Modeling Dynamics in Time-Series-Cross-Section Political Economy Data." *Annual Review of Political Science* 14 (2011): 331–52.

Bedwell, Helena, and Henry Meyer. "Georgia Pushes for Fast-Track NATO Entry to Ward Off Russia (3)." *BusinessWeek*, April 29, 2014. www.businessweek.com/news/2014-04-29/georgia-pushes-for-fast-track-nato-membership-to-ward-off-russia.

Beissinger, Mark R. *Nationalist Mobilization and the Collapse of the Soviet State*. Cambridge: Cambridge University Press, 2002.

Berman, Illan. "How Russia Is Paying for the Crimean Annexation." *Foreign Affairs*, September 9, 2015. www.foreignaffairs.com/articles/ukraine/2015-09-08/paradise-lost-crimea.

Berry, William D., Matt Golder, and Daniel Milton. "Improving Tests of Theories Positing Interaction." *Journal of Politics* 74, no. 3 (2012): 653–71.

Birch, Sarah. "The Parliamentary Elections in Ukraine, March 2002." *Electoral Studies* 22, no. 3 (September 2003): 524–31.

Birdal, Murat. *The Political Economy of Ottoman Public Debt: Insolvency and European Financial Control in the Late Nineteenth Century*. London: I. B. Tauris, 2010.

Blagov, Sergei. "Military Issues Block Russia-Georgia Detente." *EurasiaNet*, January 5, 2003. www.eurasianet.org/departments/insight/articles/eav010603.shtml.

Blaisdell, Donald C. *European Financial Control in the Ottoman Empire: A Study of the Establishment, Activities, and Significance of the Administration of the Ottoman Public Debt*. New York: Columbia University Press, 1929.

Blauvelt, Timothy. "Abkhazia: Patronage and Power in the Stalin Era." *Nationalities Papers* 35, no. 2 (May 2007): 203–32.

———. "Status Shift and Ethnic Mobilisation in the March 1956 Events in Georgia." *Europe-Asia Studies* 61, no. 4 (June 1, 2009): 651–68.

Brambor, Thomas, William R. Clark, and Matt Golder. "Understanding Interaction Models: Improving Empirical Analyses." *Political Analysis* 14, no. 1 (2006): 63–82.

Bratton, Michael. "Formal versus Informal Institutions in Africa." *Journal of Democracy* 18, no. 3 (2007): 96–110.

Braumoeller, Bear F. "Hypothesis Testing and Multiplicative Interaction Terms." *International Organization* 58, no. 4 (2004): 807–20.

Brooks, Risa. *Shaping Strategy: The Civil-Military Politics of Strategic Assessment*. Princeton, NJ: Princeton University Press, 2008.

Brown, Ian. "British Financial Advisers in Siam in the Reign of King Chulalongkorn." *Modern Asian Studies* 12, no. 2 (1978): 193–215.

Brownlee, Jason. *Authoritarianism in an Age of Democratization*. Cambridge: Cambridge University Press, 2007.

———. *Authoritarianism in an Age of Democratization*. Cambridge: Cambridge University Press, 2007.

Brzezinski, Zbigniew, and Paige Sullivan. *Russia and the Commonwealth of Independent States: Documents, Data, and Analysis*. New York: M. E. Sharpe, 1997.

Bukkvoll, Tor. "Private Interests, Public Policy: Ukraine and the Common Economic Space Agreement." *Problems of Post-Communism* 51, no. 5 (2004): 11–22.

Bunce, Valerie. *Subversive Institutions: The Design and the Destruction of Socialism and the State*. Cambridge Studies in Comparative Politics. Cambridge: Cambridge University Press, 1999.

Subversive Institutions: The Design and the Destruction of Socialism and the State. Cambridge Studies in Comparative Politics. Cambridge: Cambridge University Press, 1999.

Burbank, Jane. *Empires in World History: Power and the Politics of Difference*. Princeton, NJ: Princeton University Press, 2010.

Burke-White, William W. "Crimea and the International Legal Order." *Survival* 56, no. 4 (July 4, 2014): 65–80.

Bussell, Jennifer. "Typologies of Corruption: A Pragmatic Approach." In *Greed, Corruption, and the Modern State Essays in Political Economy*, 21–46. Cheltenam, UK: Edward Elgar, 2015.

Butt, Ahsan I. "Anarchy and Hierarchy in International Relations: Examining South America's War-Prone Decade, 1932–41." *International Organization* 67, no. 3 (2013): 575–607.

Cain, P. J., and A. G. Hopkins. *British Imperialism 1688–2000*. London: Longman, 2002.

Cameron, David R., and Mitchell A. Orenstein. "Post-Soviet Authoritarianism: The Influence of Russia in Its 'Near Abroad.'" *Post-Soviet Affairs* 28, no. 1 (2012): 1–44.

Cassel, Kristoffer. *Grounds of Judgment: Extraterritoriality and Imperial Power in Nineteenth-Century China and Japan*. Oxford: Oxford University Press, 2012.

Caverley, Jonathan D. "United States Hegemony and the New Economics of Defense." *Security Studies* 16, no. 4 (2007): 598–614.

Centeno, Miguel Angel. *Blood and Debt: War and the Nation-State in Latin America*. University Park: Penn State University Press, 2002.

Charap, Samuel, and Timothy J. Colton. *Everyone Loses: The Ukraine Crisis and the Ruinous Contest for Post-Soviet Eurasia*. New York: Routledge, 2018.

Cheterian, Vicken. *War and Peace in the Caucasus: Ethnic Conflict and the New Geopolitics*. New York: Columbia University Press, 2008.

"The August 2008 War in Georgia: From Ethnic Conflict to Border Wars." *Central Asian Survey* 28, no. 2 (June 1, 2009): 155–70.

"The August 2008 War in Georgia: From Ethnic Conflict to Border Wars." In *War and Revolution in the Caucasus*, edited by Stephen F. Jones, 63–78. London: Routledge, 2010.

Chiaberashvili, Zurab, and Gigi Tevzadze. "Power Elites in Georgia: Old and New." In *From Revolution to Reform: Georgia's Struggle with Democratic Institution Building and Security Sector Reform*, 187–207. Vienna: National Defense Academy, 2005.

Citrin, Jack. "Comment: The Political Relevance of Trust in Government." *The American Political Science Review* 68, no. 3 (1974): 973–88.

Clarke, Kevin A. "The Phantom Menace: Omitted Variable Bias in Econometric Research." *Conflict Management and Peace Science* 22, no. 4 (2005): 341–52.

Clogg, Rachel. "The Politics of Identity in Post-Soviet Abkhazia: Managing Diversity and Unresolved Conflict." *Nationalities Papers* 36, no. 2 (2008): 305–29.

Coenders, Marcel, and Peer Scheepers. "The Effect of Education on Nationalism and Ethnic Exclusionism: An International Comparison." *Political Psychology* 24, no. 2 (2003): 313–43.
Cohen, Warren I. *Empire without Tears: America's Foreign Relations, 1921–1933*. Philadelphia: Temple University Press, 1987.
Cole, Juan. *Colonialism and Revolution in the Middle East*. Princeton, NJ: Princeton University Press, 1993.
Collier, David. "Understanding Process Tracing." *PS Political Science and Politics* 44, no. 4 (2011): 823.
Collins, Kathleen A. "Economic and Security Regionalism among Patrimonial Authoritarian Regimes: The Case of Central Asia." *Europe-Asia Studies* 61, no. 2 (2009): 249–81.
 "Kyrgyzstan's Latest Revolution." *Journal of Democracy* 22, no. 3 (2011): 150–64.
Commission on Security and Cooperation in Europe. "Georgia's Parliamentary Election." October 31, 1999.
Cooley, Alexander. *Great Games, Local Rules: The New Power Contest in Central Asia*. Oxford: Oxford University Press, 2012.
Cooley, Alexander, and Lincoln A. Mitchell. "No Way to Treat Our Friends: Recasting Recent U.S.–Georgian Relations." *The Washington Quarterly* 32, no. 1 (January 2009): 27–41.
 "Abkhazia on Three Wheels." *World Policy Journal* 27, no. 2 (2010): 73–81.
Cooley, Alexander, and Daniel H. Nexon. "'The Empire Will Compensate You': The Structural Dynamics of the U.S. Overseas Basing Network." *Perspectives on Politics* 11, no. 4 (2013): 1034–50.
Cooley, Alexander, and Hendrik Spruyt. *Contracting States: Sovereign Transfers in International Relations*. Princeton, NJ: Princeton University Press, 2009.
Cornell, S. E. "Autonomy as a Source of Conflict: Caucasian Conflicts in Theoretical Perspective." *World Politics* 54, no. 2 (2002): 245–76.
Crandall, Russell. *Gunboat Democracy: US Interventions in the Dominican Republic, Grenada, and Panama*. New York: Rowman and Littlefield, 2006.
Cuffe, John, and David S. Siroky. "Paradise Lost." In *Secessionism and Separatism in Europe and Asia: To Have a State of One's Own*, 37–52. Abingdon, UK: Routledge, 2012.
Dadalauri, Nina. "Political Corruption in Georgia." In *Corruption and Development*, edited by Sarah Hacking, 155–66. London: Palgrave Macmillan, 2007.
D'Anieri, Paul. "The Last Hurrah: The 2004 Ukrainian Presidential Elections and the Limits of Machine Politics." *Communist and Post-Communist Studies* 38, no. 2 (2005): 231–49.
 Understanding Ukrainian Politics: Power, Politics, and Institutional Design. Armonk, NY: M. E. Sharpe, 2007.
Darchiashvili, David. "Georgia: A Hostage to Arms." In *The Caucasus: Armed and Divided*, 76–78. London: SaferWorld, 2003.
 "Georgian Defense Policy and Military Reform." In *Statehood and Security: Georgia after the Rose Revolution*, edited by Bruno Coppieters and Robert Legvold, 117–52. Cambridge, MA: MIT Press, 2005.

Darden, Keith A. *Economic Liberalism and Its Rivals: The Formation of International Institutions Among the Post-Soviet States*. Cambridge: Cambridge University Press, 2009.

Resisting Occupation: Mass Literacy and the Creation of Durable National Loyalties. New York: Cambridge University Press, forthcoming.

Darden, Keith, and Anna Maria Grzymala-Busse. "The Great Divide: Literacy, Nationalism, and the Communist Collapse." *World Politics* 59, no. 1 (2006): 83–115.

Darwin, John. *After Tamerlane: The Global History of Empire Since 1405*. New York: Bloomsbury Press, 2008.

De Mesquita, Bruce B., Alastair Smith, Randolph M. Siverson, and James D. Morrow. *The Logic of Political Survival*. Cambridge, MA: MIT Press, 2005.

Department of State, Office of Website Management, Bureau of Public Affairs. "Evidence of Russian Support for Destabilization of Ukraine." Press release, April 13, 2014. www.state.gov/r/pa/prs/ps/2014/04/224762.htm.

Derluguian, Georgi. "The Tale of Two Resorts: Abkhazia and Ajaria before and since the Soviet Collapse." In *The Myth of "Ethnic Conflict": Politics, Economics, and "Cultural" Violence*, edited by Beverly Crawford and Ronnie Lipschutz, 261–92. Berkeley: University of California Press, 1998.

Bourdieu's Secret Admirer in the Caucasus: A World-System Biography. Chicago: University of Chicago Press, 2005.

Derluguian, Georgi, and Ruben Hovhannisyan. "The Armenian Anomaly: Toward an Interdisciplinary Interpretation." *Demokratizatsiya* 26, no. 4 (Fall 2018): 441–64.

De Waal, Thomas. *The Caucasus: An Introduction*. Oxford: Oxford University Press, 2010.

Deyermond, Ruth. "Assessing the Reset: Successes and Failures in the Obama Administration's Russia Policy, 2009–2012." *European Security* 22, no. 4 (December 1, 2013): 500–523.

Dillon Savage, Jesse. "The Stability and Breakdown of Empire: European Informal Empire in China, the Ottoman Empire and Egypt." *European Journal of International Relations* 17, no. 2 (2011): 161.

Doyle, Michael. *Empires*. Ithaca, NY: Cornell University Press, 1986.

Dreyfus, Emmanuel. "Expectations for Kyiv-Moscow Relations after Ukraine's Presidential Election." *PonarsEuarasia – Policy Memos*, May 13, 2019. www.ponarseurasia.org/memo/expectations-kyiv-moscow-relations-after-ukraines-presidential-election.

Driscoll, Jesse. *Warlords and Coalition Politics in Post-Soviet States*. Cambridge: Cambridge University Press, 2015.

Economist. "Ukraine's Unhappy Ceasefire." September 7, 2014. www.economist.com/blogs/easternapproaches/2014/09/war-ukraine.

Edelstein, David M. *Occupational Hazards: Success and Failure in Military Occupation*. Cornell Studies in Security Affairs. Ithaca, NY: Cornell University Press, 2008.

Eisenstadt, Shmuel Noah, and Luis Roniger. *Patrons, Clients and Friends: Interpersonal Relations and the Structure of Trust in Society*. Cambridge: Cambridge University Press, 1984.

Ekedahl, Carolyn, and Melvin A. Goodman. *Wars of Eduard Shevardnadze*. University Park: Penn State University Press, 2010.

Eldem, Edhem. "Ottoman Financial Integration with Europe: Foreign Loans, the Ottoman Bank and the Ottoman Public Debt." *European Review* 13, no. 3 (2005): 431–45.

Elliot, John. *Empires of the Atlantic World: Spain and Britain in the Americas 1492–1830*. New Haven, CT: Yale University Press, 2006.

Elman, Benjamin A. "Naval Warfare and the Refraction of China's Self-Strengthening Reforms into Scientific and Technological Failure, 1865–1895." *Modern Asian Studies* 38, no. 2 (2004): 283–326.

Elster, Jon. "Rational Choice History: A Case of Excessive Ambition." *The American Political Science Review* 94, no. 3 (2000): 685–95.

Engvall, Johan. "From Monopoly to Competition." *Problems of Post-Communism* 65, no. 4 (2018): 271–83.

Escribà-Folch, Abel. "Accountable for What? Regime Types, Performance, and the Fate of Outgoing Dictators, 1946–2004." *Democratization* 20, no. 1 (2013): 160–85.

Etkind, Alexander, and Andrei Shcherbak. "The Double Monopoly and Its Technologists: The Russian Preemptive Counterrevolution." *Demokratizatsiya* 16, no. 3 (Summer 2008): 229–39.

Fahmy, Khaled. *All the Pasha's Men: Mehmed Ali, His Army and the Making of Modern Egypt*. Cambridge: Cambridge University Press, 1997.

Mehmed Ali: From Ottoman Governor to Ruler of Egypt. Makers of the Muslim World. Oxford: Oneworld, 2009.

Fairbanks, Charles H. "II. The Postcommunist Wars." *Journal of Democracy* 6, no. 4 (1995): 18–34.

"Disillusionment in the Caucasus and Central Asia." *Journal of Democracy* 12, no. 4 (2001): 49–56.

Fairbanks, Charles H., Jr., and Alexi Gugushvili. "A New Chance for Georgian Democracy." *Journal of Democracy* 24, no. 1 (2013): 116–27.

Fazal, Tanisha M. *State Death: The Politics and Geography of Conquest, Occupation, and Annexation*. Princeton, NJ: Princeton University Press, 2007.

Fearon, James. "Rationalist Explanations for War." *International Organization* 49, no. 3 (1995): 379–414.

Fearon, James D., and David D. Laitin. "Neotrusteeship and the Problem of Weak States." *International Security* 28, no. 4 (2004): 5–43.

Fearon, J. D., D. D. Laitin, and J. M. Box-Steffensmeier. "Integrating Qualitative and Quantitative Methods." In *The Oxford Handbook of Political Methodology*, 756–76. XXXX: XXXX, 2008.

Feuerwerker, Albert. *The Foreign Establishment in China in the Early Twentieth Century*. Ann Arbor: Center for Chinese Studies, University of Michigan, 1976.

Financial Times. "Ukraine: An Oligarch Brought to Heel." March 25, 2015. www.ft.com/cms/s/0/b0b04474-d232-11e4-a225-00144feab7de.html.

Findlay, Ronald, and Kevin H. O'Rourke. *Power and Plenty: Trade, War, and the World Economy in the Second Millennium*. Princeton Economic History of the Western World. Princeton, NJ: Princeton University Press, 2007.

Fisman, Raymond, and Roberta Gatti. "Decentralization and Corruption: Evidence across Countries." *Journal of Public Economics* 83, no. 3 (2002): 325–45.
Foreign Policy Research Institute. "Russia in Venezuela: Geopolitical Boon or Economic Misadventure?" January 2019. www.fpri.org/article/2019/01/russia-in-venezuela-geopolitical-boon-or-economic-misadventure/.
Freese, Theresa. "Russia's Troop Withdrawal from Georgia: The Start of a New Friendship?" *EurasiaNet*, August 9, 2005. www.eurasianet.org/departments/insight/articles/eav081005.shtml.
Frye, Timothy. "What Do Voters in Ukraine Want? A Survey Experiment on Candidate Ethnicity, Language, and Policy Orientation." *Problems of Post-Communism* 62, no. 5 (2015): 247–57.
Frye, Timothy, and Ekaterina Zhuravskaya. "Rackets, Regulation, and the Rule of Law." *Journal of Law, Economics, and Organization* 16, no. 2 (2000): 478–502.
Fuller, Brandon, and Paul Romer. *Success and the City: How Charter Cities Could Transform the Developing World*. Ottawa, ON: Macdonald-Laurier Institute for Public Policy, 2012.
Fuller, Elizabeth. "Aslan Abashidze: Georgia's Next Leader?" *RFE/RL Research Report* 2, no. 44 (1993): 23–26.
Gallagher, John, and Ronald Robinson. "The Imperialism of Free Trade." *The Economic History Review* 6, no. 1 (1953): 1–15.
Gallagher, Mary E., and Jonathan K. Hanson. "Power Tool or Dull Blade? Selectorate Theory for Autocracies." *Political Science* 18 (2015). www.annualreviews.org/eprint/5N4i9qp8RfQTmPzxZtke/full/10.1146/annurev-polisci-071213-041224.
Gallup. "World-Low 9% of Ukrainians Confident in Government." March 21, 2019. https://news.gallup.com/poll/247976/world-low-ukrainians-confident-government.aspx.
Gambetta, Diego. "Fragments of an Economic Theory of the Mafia." *European Journal of Sociology/Archives Européennes de Sociologie* 29, no. 1 (May 1988): 127–45.
———. *Codes of the Underworld: How Criminals Communicate*. Princeton, NJ: Princeton University Press, 2009.
Geddes, Barbara. *Paradigms and Sand Castles: Theory Building and Research Design in Comparative Politics*. Ann Arbor: University of Michigan Press, 2003.
Geddes, Barbara, Joseph Wright, and Erica Frantz. "Autocratic Breakdown and Regime Transitions: A New Data Set." *Perspectives on Politics* 12, no. 2 (2014): 313–31.
Gehlbach, Scott, and Philip Keefer. "Investment without Democracy: Ruling-Party Institutionalization and Credible Commitment in Autocracies." *Journal of Comparative Economics* 39, no. 2 (2011): 123–39.
George, Julie A. "Minority Political Inclusion in Mikheil Saakashvili's Georgia." *Europe-Asia Studies* 60, no. 7 (2008): 1151–75.
———. "The Dangers of Reform: State Building and National Minorities in Georgia." *Central Asian Survey* 28, no. 2 (2009): 135–54.
———. "Can Hybrid Regimes Foster Constituencies? Ethnic Minorities in Georgian Elections, 1992–2012." *Electoral Studies* 35 (2014): 328–45. www.sciencedirect.com/science/article/pii/S0261379414000304.

Georgian Times. "Ivanishvili on Foreign Policy, Territorial Integrity." October 21, 2011. www.geotimes.ge/index.php?m=home&newsid=26072.

Gerring, John, Daniel Ziblatt, Johan Van Gorp, and Julian Arévalo. "An Institutional Theory of Direct and Indirect Rule." *World Politics* 63, no. 03 (2011): 377–433.

Gervasoni, Carlos. "A Rentier Theory of Subnational Regimes: Fiscal Federalism, Democracy, and Authoritarianism in the Argentine Provinces." *World Politics* 62, no. 2 (2010): 302–40.

Geyer, Georgie Anne. "Conversations with Eduard Shevardnadze." *The Washington Quarterly* 23, no. 2 (2000): 55–66.

Goddard, Stacie E., and Daniel H. Nexon. "The Dynamics of Global Power Politics: A Framework for Analysis." *Journal of Global Security Studies* 1, no. 1 (February 1, 2016): 4–18.

Goldman, Marshall, I. *Petrostate: Putin, Power, and the New Russia*. Oxford: Oxford University Press, 2008.

Gordadze, Thornike. "Georgia-Russia Conflict in August 2008: War as a Continuation of Politics." In *Reassessing Security in the South Caucasus: Regional Conflicts and Transformation*, 11–31. Farnham, UK: Ashgate, 2011.

Granovetter, Mark. "Economic Action and Social Structure: The Problem of Embeddedness." *The American Journal of Sociology* 91, no. 3 (1985): 481–510.

Grzymala-Busse, Anna. "Beyond Clientelism: Incumbent State Capture and State Formation." *Comparative Political Studies* 41, no. 4–5 (2008): 638.

Grzymala-Busse, Anna, and Pauline Jones Luong. "Reconceptualizing the State: Lessons from Post-Communism." *Politics and Society* 30, no. 4 (2002): 529–54.

Gunitsky, Seva, and Andrei P. Tsygankov. "The Wilsonian Bias in the Study of Russian Foreign Policy." *Problems of Post-Communism* 65, no. 6 (2018): 385-93.

Guretski, Voitsekh. "The Question of Javakheti." *Caucasian Regional Studies* 3, no. 1 (1998): 301–5.

Haggard, Stephan. "Liberal Pessimism: International Relations Theory and the Emerging Powers." *Asia and the Pacific Policy Studies* 1, no. 1 (2014): 1–17.

Haggard, Stephan, Andrew MacIntyre, and Lydia Tiede. "The Rule of Law and Economic Development." *Annual Review of Political Science* 11 (2008): 205–34.

Hale, Henry E. "Regime Cycles." *World Politics* 58, no. 1 (2005): 133–65.

"Democracy or Autocracy on the March? The Colored Revolutions as Normal Dynamics of Patronal Presidentialism." *Communist and Post-Communist Studies* 39, no. 3 (2006): 305–29.

The Foundations of Ethnic Politics: Separatism of States and Nations in Eurasia and the World. Cambridge Studies in Comparative Politics. Cambridge: Cambridge University Press, 2008.

"Formal Constitutions in Informal Politics: Institutions and Democratization in Post-Soviet Eurasia." *World Politics* 63, no. 4 (2011): 581–617.

"Regime Change Cascades: What We Have Learned from the 1848 Revolutions to the 2011 Arab Uprisings." *Annual Review of Political Science* 16 (2013): 331–53.

Patronal Politics: Eurasian Regime Dynamics in Comparative Perspective. Cambridge: Cambridge University Press, 2014.

"The Uses of Divided Power." *Journal of Democracy* 21, no. 3 (2010): 84–98.

Hall, Peter, and Rosemary Taylor. "Political Science and the Three Institutionalisms." *Political Studies* 44, no. 4 (1996): 936–57.

Hanioglu, M. Sukru. *A Brief History of the Late Ottoman Empire.* Princeton, NJ: Princeton University Press, 2008.

Hao, Yen-P'ing, and Erh-min Wang. "Changing Chinese Views of Western Relations, 1840–95." In *The Cambridge History of China,* edited by John K. Fairbank and Kwang-Ching Liu, 142–201. Cambridge: Cambridge University Press, 1980.

Hardin, Russell. *Trust.* Cambridge: Polity, 2006.

Hart, Robert, and James Duncan Campbell. *The I. G. in Peking: Letters of Robert Hart, Chinese Maritime Customs, 1868–1907.* Cambridge, MA: Harvard University Press, 1975.

Headrick, D. R. *The Tools of Empire: Technology and European Imperialism in the Nineteenth Century.* Oxford: Oxford University Press, 1981.

Helmke, Gretchen, and Steven Levitsky. "Informal Institutions and Comparative Politics: A Research Agenda." *Perspectives on Politics* 2, no. 4 (2004): 725–40.

Herron, Erik S. "Electoral Influences on Legislative Behavior in Mixed-Member Systems: Evidence from Ukraine's Verkhovna Rada." *Legislative Studies Quarterly* 27, no. 3 (2002): 361–82.

Herszenhorn, David M. "Facing Russian Threat, Ukraine Halts Plans for Deals with EU." *New York Times,* November 21, 2013, sec. World/Europe. www.nytimes.com/2013/11/22/world/europe/ukraine-refuses-to-free-ex-leader-raising-concerns-over-eu-talks.html.

Hicken, A. "Clientelism." *Annual Review of Political Science* 14 (2011): 289–310.

Hierman, Brent. "What Use Was the Election to Us? Clientelism and Political Trust amongst Ethnic Uzbeks in Kyrgyzstan and Tajikistan." *Nationalities Papers* 38, no. 2 (2010): 245–63.

Higgins, Andrew. "In Eastern Ukraine, a One-Building, Pro-Russia Realm Persists Despite Criticism." *New York Times,* April 9, 2014. www.nytimes.com/2014/04/10/world/europe/ukraine-russia.html.

Higgins, Andrew, and Steven Erlanger. "Gunmen Seize Government Buildings in Crimea." *New York Times,* February 27, 2014. www.nytimes.com/2014/02/28/world/europe/crimea-ukraine.html.

Higley, John, and Michael G. Burton. "The Elite Variable in Democratic Transitions and Breakdowns." *American Sociological Review* 54, no. 1 (1989): 17–32.

Hobson, John M., and J. C. Sharman. "The Enduring Place of Hierarchy in World Politics: Tracing the Social Logics of Hierarchy and Political Change." *European Journal of International Relations* 11, no. 1 (March 1, 2005): 63–98.

Hopkins, A. G. "The Victorians and Africa: A Reconsideration of the Occupation of Egypt, 1882." *The Journal of African History* 27, no. 2 (1986): 363–91.
Horowitz, Richard. "Politics, Power and the Chinese Maritime Customs: The Qing Restoration and the Ascent of Robert Hart." *Modern Asian Studies* 40, no. 3 (2006): 549–81.
Hoyle, Mark. *Mixed Courts of Egypt*. London: Graham and Trotman, 1991.
Hsu, Immanuel. "Late Ch'ing Foreign Relations, 1866–1905." In *The Cambridge History of China: Volume 2 Late Ch'ing 1800–1911*, edited by John Fairbank and Kwang-Ching Liu, 2:70–141. Cambridge: Cambridge University Press, 1980.
Ilkhamov, Alisher. "Neopatrimonialism, Interest Groups and Patronage Networks: The Impasses of the Governance System in Uzbekistan." *Central Asian Survey* 26, no. 1 (March 1, 2007): 65–84.
Imamova, Navbahor. "Uzbekistan's New Era Might Just Be Real." *Foreign Policy* (blog), June 21, 2018. https://foreignpolicy.com/2018/06/21/uzbekistans-new-era-might-just-be-real/.
Independent International Fact-Finding Mission on the Conflict in Georgia. "Report." Brussels: European Union, September 2009.
International Crisis Group. "Georgia: Avoiding War in South Ossetia." 2004.
——— "Saakashvili's Ajara Success: Repeatable Elsewhere in Georgia?" August 18, 2004.
——— "Abkhazia Today." *Europe Report* 176 (2006).
——— "Georgia's Armenia and Azeri Minorities." November 2006.
——— "Abkhazia: Deepening Dependence." February 26, 2010.
Iskandaryan, Alexander. "The Velvet Revolution in Armenia: How to Lose Power in Two Weeks." *Demokratizatsiya* 26, no. 4 (Fall 2018): 465–82.
Jackson, Robert. *Quasi-States: Sovereignty, International Relations and the Third World*. Cambridge: Cambridge University Press, 1990.
——— "The Weight of Ideas in Decolonization." In *Ideas and Foreign Policy*, edited by Judith Goldstein and Robert Keohane, 111–38. Ithaca, NY: Cornell Univesity Press, 1993.
Jacobs, Andrew, and Jane Perlez. "U.S. Wary of Its New Neighbor in Djibouti: A Chinese Naval Base." *New York Times*, August 7, 2018, sec. World. www.nytimes.com/2017/02/25/world/africa/us-djibouti-chinese-naval-base.html.
Jacques, Martin. *When China Rules the World: The Rise of the Middle Kingdom and the End of the Western World*. London: Allen Lane, 2009.
Jensen, Robert T., and Nolan H. Miller. "Giffen Behavior and Subsistence Consumption." *American Economic Review* 98, no. 4 (2008): 1553–77.
Jones, Stephen Francis. *Georgia: A Political History since Independence*. New York: I. B. Tauris, 2013.
——— *The Making of Modern Georgia, 1918–2012: The First Georgian Republic and Its Successors*. New York: Routledge, 2014.
Kandelaki, Giorgi. "Shevardnadze's Chisinau Concessions Shatter Georgia's Political Unity." *EurasiaNet*, October 8, 2002. www.eurasianet.org/departments/insight/articles/eav100902.shtml.

Kang, David C. "Hierarchy and Legitimacy in International Systems: The Tribute System in Early Modern East Asia." *Security Studies* 19, no. 4 (2010): 591–622.

Kasaba, Reşat. "Treaties and Friendships: British Imperialism, the Ottoman Empire, and China in the Nineteenth Century." *Journal of World History* 4, no. 2 (1993): 215–41.

Kaufman, Stuart J. "Spiraling to Ethnic War: Elites, Masses, and Moscow in Moldova's Civil War." *International Security* 21, no. 2 (1996): 108–38.

― *Modern Hatreds: The Symbolic Politics of Ethnic War*. Ithaca, NY: Cornell University Press, 2001.

Kayaoglu, Turan. "The Extension of Westphalian Sovereignty: State Building and the Abolition of Extraterritoriality." *International Studies Quarterly* 51, no. 3 (2007): 649–75.

― *Legal Imperialism: Sovereignty and Extraterritoriality in Japan, the Ottoman Empire, and China*. Cambridge: Cambridge University Press, 2010.

Kazarian, Ursula. "Energy Security in Armenia and the South Caucasus." *Fletcher Security Review* 5 (2018): 50–57.

Keefer, Philip. "Clientelism, Credibility, and the Policy Choices of Young Democracies." *American Journal of Political Science* 51, no. 4 (2007): 804–21.

Keele, Luke. "The Authorities Really Do Matter: Party Control and Trust in Government." *Journal of Politics* 67, no. 3 (2005): 873–86.

Keele, Luke, and Nathan J. Kelly. "Dynamic Models for Dynamic Theories: The Ins and Outs of Lagged Dependent Variables." *Political Analysis* 14, no. 2 (2006): 186–205.

Khan, Mushtaq H. "Rent-Seeking as Process." In *Rents, Rent-Seeking and Economic Development: Theory and Evidence in Asia*, edited by Mushtaq H. Khan and K. S. Jomo, 70–144. Cambridge: Cambridge University Press, 2000.

Khan, Wasiq N. "Economic Growth and Decline in Comparative Perspective: Haiti and the Dominican Republic, 1930–1986." *Journal of Haitian Studies* 16, no. 1 (2010): 112–25.

KIIS. "Corruption in Ukraine 2015." 2015. https://kiis.com.ua/materials/pr/20161602_corruption/Corruption%20in%20Ukraine%202015%20ENG.pdf.

King, Charles. "The Benefits of Ethnic War: Understanding Eurasia's Unrecognized States." *World Politics* 53, no. 4 (2001): 524–52.

― *Extreme Politics: Nationalism, Violence, and the End of Eastern Europe*. New York: Oxford University Press, 2010.

Kitschelt, Herbert, and Steven I. Wilkinson. "Citizen-Politician Linkages: An Introduction." In *Patrons, Clients, and Policies: Patterns of Democratic Accountability and Political Competition*, 1–49. Cambridge: Cambridge University Press, 2007.

Kivelson, Valerie A., and Ronald Suny. *Russia's Empires*. Oxford: Oxford University Press, 2017.

Kohut, Zenon E. *Russian Centralism and Ukrainian Autonomy: Imperial Absorption of the Hetmanate, 1760s–1830s*. Vol. 66. Cambridge, MA: Harvard Ukrainian, 1988.

Kollmann, Nancy Shields. *The Russian Empire 1450–1801*. Oxford: Oxford University Press, 2016.
Kolstø, Pal, and Helge Blakkisrud. "Living with Non-recognition: State- and Nation-Building in South Caucasian Quasi-States." *Europe-Asia Studies* 60, no. 3 (2008): 483–509.
Kou, Ting-Yee, and Kwang-Ching Liu. "Self Strengthening: The Pursuit of Western Technology." In *The Cambridge History of China: Vol. 2. Late Ch'ing 1800–1911*, edited by John Fairbank, 491–452. Cambridge: Cambridge University Press, 1978.
Krasner, Stephen. *Organized Hypocrisy*. Princeton, NJ: Princeton University Press, 1999.
—— "Sharing Sovereignty: New Institutions for Collapsed and Failing States." *International Security* 29, no. 2 (2004): 85–120.
Krasner, Stephen D., and Thomas Risse. "External Actors, State-Building, and Service Provision in Areas of Limited Statehood: Introduction." *Governance* 27, no. 4 (2014): 545–67.
Kravchenko, Stepan, and Henry Meyer. "Ukraine's Top Oligarch Walks a Fine Line." *BusinessWeek*, July 10, 2014. www.businessweek.com/articles/2014-07-10/in-ukraine-separatist-war-rinat-akhmetov-walks-fine-line.
Kroth, Maya. "Under New Management." *Foreign Policy*, September 1, 2014. www.foreignpolicy.com/articles/2014/09/01/under_new_management_amapala_honduras_charter_cities.
Kucera, Joshua. "Batumi: Making a Break for the West." *Eurasia Insight*, May 17, 2007.
Kudelia, Serhiy. "The Sources of Continuity and Change of Ukraine's Incomplete State." *Communist and Post-Communist Studies* 45, no. 3 (2012): 417–28.
—— "When External Leverage Fails." *Problems of Post-Communism* 60, no. 1 (2013): 29–42.
—— "The House That Yanukovych Built." *Journal of Democracy* 25, no. 3 (2014): 19–34.
Kuhn, Philip. "The Taiping Rebellion." In *The Cambridge History of China: Vol. 2. Late Ch'ing 1800–1911*, 264–317. Cambridge: Cambridge University Press, 1978.
Kukhianidze, Alexandre. "Organized Crime and Smuggling through Abkhazia and South Ossetia." *Abkhazia*, July 3, 2007. https://abkhazia.com/research-blogs/history/66-Ethnic-Conflicts-in-the-Caucasus/401-organized-crime-and-smuggling-through-abkhazia-and-south-ossetia.
—— "Corruption and Organized Crime in Georgia before and after the 'Rose Revolution.'" *Central Asian Survey* 28, no. 2 (2009): 215–34.
Kulyk, Volodymyr. "Language Identity, Linguistic Diversity and Political Cleavages: Evidence from Ukraine." *Nations and Nationalism* 17, no. 3 (2011): 627–48.
—— "Shedding Russianness, Recasting Ukrainianness: The Post-Euromaidan Dynamics of Ethnonational Identifications in Ukraine." *Post-Soviet Affairs* 34, no. 2–3 (2018): 119–38.

"Identity in Transformation: Russian-Speakers in Post-Soviet Ukraine." *Europe-Asia Studies* 71, no. 1 (2019): 156–78.

Kuran, Timur. "The Economic Assent of the Middle East's Religious Minorities: The Role of Islamic Legal Pluralism." *Journal of Legal Studies* 33 (2004): 475–515.

"Why the Middle East Is Economically Underdeveloped: Historical Mechanisms of Institutional Stagnation." *Journal of Economic Perspectives* 18, no. 3 (2004): 71–90.

Kuzio, Taras. "Geopolitical Pluralism in the CIS: The Emergence of GUUAM." *European Security* 9, no. 2 (2000): 81–114.

"From Kuchma to Yushchenko Ukraine's 2004 Presidential Elections and the Orange Revolution." *Problems of Post-Communism* 52, no. 2 (2005): 29–44.

"Regime Type and Politics in Ukraine under Kuchma." *Communist and Post-Communist Studies* 38, no. 2 (2005): 167–90.

"Strident, Ambiguous and Duplicitous." *Demokratizatsiya: The Journal of Post-Soviet Democratization* 17, no. 4 (2009): 350–72.

Kyiv International Institute of Sociology. "Geopolitical Orientations of the Residents of Ukraine: February 2019." Press release, n.d. www.kiis.com.ua/?lang=eng&cat=reports&id=827&page=4&t=3.

Kyiv Post. "Factbox: Russia's Black Sea Fleet in Ukraine." April 26, 2010. www.kyivpost.com/content/ukraine/factbox-russias-black-sea-fleet-in-ukraine-65036.html.

Lachowski, Zdzislaw. *Foreign Military Bases in Eurasia*. Stockholm: International Peace Research Institute, 2007. http://kms1.isn.ethz.ch/serviceengine/Files/ISN/31819/ipublicationdocument_singledocument/b72b4442-d2b3-4684-af9f-b0b136a4c622/en/Policypaper18.pdf.

Lake, David. "Anarchy, Hierarchy, and the Variety of International Relations." *International Organization* 50, no. 1 (1996): 1–33.

"Beyond Anarchy: The Importance of Security Institutions." *International Security* 26, no. 1 (2001): 129–60.

Hierarchy in International Relations. Ithaca, NY: Cornell University Press, 2009.

"Legitimating Power: The Domestic Politics of US International Hierarchy." *International Security* 38, no. 2 (2013): 74–111.

Lake, David A., and Christopher J. Fariss. "Why International Trusteeship Fails: The Politics of External Authority in Areas of Limited Statehood." *Governance* 27, no. 4 (2014): 569–87.

Lakoba, Stanislav. "History: 18th Century-1917." In *The Abkhazians: A Handbook*, edited by Brian Hewitt, 67–88. Richmond: Curzon, 1999.

Landes, David. *Bankers and Pashas: International Finance and Economic Imperialism in Egypt*. Cambridge, MA: Harvard University Press, 1958.

Langley, Lester D. *The United States and the Caribbean in the Twentieth Century*. Athens: University of Georgia Press, 1985.

Lanoszka, Alexander. "Beyond Consent and Coercion: Using Republican Political Theory to Understand International Hierarchies." *International Theory* 5, no. 03 (2013): 382–413.

Lanskoy, Miriam, and Giorgi Areshidze. "Georgia's Year of Turmoil." *Journal of Democracy* 19, no. 4 (2008): 154–68.
Lanskoy, Miriam, and Elspeth Suthers. "Armenia's Velvet Revolution." *Journal of Democracy* 30, no. 2 (April 13, 2019): 85–99.
Larsson, Robert L. "The Enemy Within: Russia's Military Withdrawal from Georgia." *The Journal of Slavic Military Studies* 17, no. 3 (2004): 405–24.
Lawrence, Adria. *Imperial Rule and the Politics of Nationalism: Anti-colonial Protest in the French Empire*. Cambridge: Cambridge University Press, 2013.
Lee, Eric. *The Experiment: Georgia's Forgotten Revolution 1918–1921*. London: Zed Books, 2017.
Levitsky, Steven, and Lucan Way. *Competitive Authoritarianism: Hybrid Regimes after the Cold War*. New York: Cambridge University Press, 2010.
Lewis, David. "Reasserting Hegemony in Central Asia: Russian Policy in Post-2010 Kyrgyzstan." *Comillas Journal of International Relations* 1, no. 31 (2015): 58–80.
Libman, Alexander, and Anastassia V. Obydenkova. "Understanding Authoritarian Regionalism." *Journal of Democracy* 29, no. 4 (October 17, 2018): 151–65.
Lieven, Anatol. "Imperial Outpost and Social Provider: The Russians and Akhalkalaki." *EurasiaNet*, February 19, 2001. www.eurasianet.org/departments/insight/articles/eav022001.shtml.
Listhaug, Ola. "The Dynamics of Trust in Politicians." In *Citizens and the State*, edited by Hans-Dieter Klingmann and Dieter Fuchs, 261–97. New York: Oxford University Press, 1995.
Lohm, H. "Javakheti after the Rose Revolution: Progress and Regress in the Pursuit of National Unity in Georgia." ECMI Working Paper, 2007.
Lomnitz, Larissa Adler. "Informal Exchange Networks in Formal Systems: A Theoretical Model." *American Anthropologist* 90, no. 1 (1988): 42–55.
Long, Tom. *Latin America Confronts the United States: Asymmetry and Influence*. Cambridge: Cambridge University Press, 2015.
Losaberidze, David, Konstantine Kandelaki, and Niko Orvelashvili. "Local Government in Georgia." In *Developing New Rules in the Old Environment*, 165–322. Budapest: OSI/LGI, 2001.
Lowrey, Mark, Annie Landler, and Steven Lee Myers. "Obama Steps Up Russia Sanctions in Ukraine Crisis." *New York Times*, March 20, 2014. www.nytimes.com/2014/03/21/us/politics/us-expanding-sanctions-against-russia-over-ukraine.html.
Lühiste, Kadri. "Explaining Trust in Political Institutions: Some Illustrations from the Baltic States." *Communist and Post-Communist Studies* 39, no. 4 (2006): 475–496.
Luhmann, Niklas. *Trust and Power*. Hoboken, NJ: John Wiley, 1979.
Lundahl, Mats, and Claudio Vedovato. "The State and Economic Development in Haiti and the Dominican Republic." *Scandinavian Economic History Review* 37, no. 3 (September 1989): 39–59.
Lynch, Dov. "Separatist States and Post–Soviet Conflicts." *International Affairs* 78, no. 4 (2002): 831–48.

Lynch, Dov, and Royal Institute of International Affairs. *Russian Peacekeeping Strategies in the CIS: The Cases of Moldova, Georgia and Tajikistan*. Basingstoke, UK: Macmillan, 2000.

MacDonald, Paul. *Networks of Domination: The Social Foundations of Peripheral Conquest in International Politics*. Oxford: Oxford University Press, 2014.

———. "Embedded Authority: A Relational Network Approach to Hierarchy in World Politics." *Review of International Studies* 44, no. 1 (2017): 128–50.

MacFarlane, S. Neil. "Colliding State-Building Projects and Regional Insecurity in Post-Soviet Space: Georgia versus Russia in South Ossetia." In *Troubled Regions and Failing States: The Clustering and Contagion of Armed Conflicts*, 103–26. New York: Emerald, 2010.

———. "Georgia: National Security Concept versus National Security." *CAUCASUS SOCIAL SCIENCE REVIEW* 1 (2013).

MacKinnon, Stephen R. *Power and Politics in Late Imperial China: Yuan Shi-Kai in Beijing and Tianjin, 1901–1908*. Berkeley: University of California Press, 1980. www.ucpress.edu/op.php?isbn=9780520040250.

Magaloni, Beatriz. *Voting for Autocracy: Hegemonic Party Survival and Its Demise in Mexico*. New York: Cambridge University Press, 2006.

———. "Credible Power-Sharing and the Longevity of Authoritarian Rule." *Comparative Political Studies* 41, no. 4–5 (2008): 715–41.

Magaloni, Beatriz, and Ruth Kricheli. "Political Order and One-Party Rule." *Annual Review of Political Science* 13 (2010): 123–43.

Magocsi, Paul R. *A History of Ukraine: The Land and Its Peoples*. Toronto: University of Toronto Press, 2010.

Mahoney, James. "After KKV: The New Methodology of Qualitative Research." *World Politics* 62, no. 1 (2009): 120–47.

Malyarenko, Tetyana, and Stefan Wolff. *The Dynamics of Emerging De-Facto States: Eastern Ukraine in the Post-Soviet Space*. New York: Routledge, 2019.

Mansfield, Edward D. "Rising Powers in the Global Economy: Issues and Questions." *International Studies Review* 16, no. 3 (2014): 437–42.

Marten, Kimberly. *Warlords: Strong-Arm Brokers in Weak States*. Ithaca, NY: Cornell University Press, 2012.

Matanock, Aila M. "Governance Delegation Agreements: Shared Sovereignty as a Substitute for Limited Statehood." *Governance* 27, no. 4 (2014): 589–612.

Matsuzato, Kimitaka. "All Kuchma's Men: The Reshuffling of Ukrainian Governors and the Presidential Election of 1999." *Post-Soviet Geography and Economics* 42, no. 6 (2001): 416–39.

Mattern, Janice Bially, and Ayşe Zarakol. "Hierarchies in World Politics." *International Organization* 70, no. 3 (2016): 623–54.

Mattes, Michaela, and Mariana Rodríguez. "Autocracies and International Cooperation." *International Studies Quarterly* 58, no. 3 (2014): 527–38.

Matveeva, Anna. "Russia's Changing Security Role in Central Asia." *European Security* 22, no. 4 (December 2013): 478–99.

Maurer, Noel. *The Empire Trap: The Rise and Fall of US Intervention to Protect American Property Overseas, 1893–2013*. Princeton, NJ: Princeton University Press, 2013.

McConaughey, Meghan, Paul Musgrave, and Daniel H. Nexon. "Beyond Anarchy: Logics of Political Organization, Hierarchy, and International Structure." *International Theory* 10, no. 2 (2018): 181–218.

Mclean, David. "Finance and 'Informal Empire' before the First World War." *The Economic History Review* 29, no. 2 (1976): 291–305.

Migdal, Joel S. *Strong Societies and Weak States: State-Society Relations and State Capabilities in the Third World*. Princeton, NJ: Princeton University Press, 1988.

Miller, Eric A. "Smelling the Roses: Eduard Shevardnadze's End and Georgia's Future." *Problems of Post-Communism* 51, no. 2 (2004): 12–21.

Milner, Helen V. *Interests, Institutions, and Information: Domestic Politics and International Relations*. Princeton, NJ: Princeton University Press, 1997.

Mitchell, Lincoln A. "Georgia's Rose Revolution." *Current History* 103 (2004): 342–48.

"What's Next for Georgia?" *World Affairs* 175, no. 5 (2013): 75–82.

Mitchell, Lincoln A. *Uncertain Democracy: US Foreign Policy and Georgia's Rose Revolution*. Philadelphia: University of Pennsylvania Press, 2009.

Mitchell, Lincoln A., and Alexander A. Cooley. "After the August War: A New Strategy for US Engagement with Georgia." 2010.

Montalvo, Jose G., and Marta Reynal-Querol. "Ethnic Diversity and Economic Development." *Journal of Development Economics* 76, no. 2 (2005): 293–323.

Morris, Chris. "Crimea 'Votes for Russia Union.'" BBC News, March 16, 2014. www.bbc.com/news/world-europe-26606097.

Moscow Times. "Internal Rifts in Ukraine Play in Russia's Favor – Analysts." March 24, 2015. https://themoscowtimes.com/articles/internal-rifts-in-ukraine-play-in-russias-favor-analysts-45110.

Munck, Gerardo L. "The Regime Question: Theory Building in Democracy Studies." *World Politics* 54, no. 01 (2001): 119–44.

Murtazashvili, Jennifer. "Coloured by Revolution: The Political Economy of Autocratic Stability in Uzbekistan." *Democratization* 19, no. 1 (2012): 78–97.

Nexon, Daniel. "What's This Then? 'Romanes Eunt Domus'?" *International Studies Perspectives* 9, no. 3 (2008): 300–308.

Nilson, Douglas C., and Linda Burzotta Nilson. "Trust in Elites and Protest Orientation: An Integrative Approach." *Political Behavior* 2, no. 4 (1980): 385–404.

Nodia, Ghia. "Georgia: Dimensions of Insecurity." In *Statehood and Security: Georgia after the Rose Revolution*, edited by Robert Legvold and Bruno Coppieters, 39–82. Cambridge, MA: MIT Press, 2005.

North, Douglass. *Institutions, Institutional Change, and Economic Performance*. Cambridge: Cambridge University Press, 1990.

Violence and Social Orders: A Conceptual Framework for Interpreting Recorded Human History. Cambridge: Cambridge University Press, 2009.

O'Brien, Patrick K., and Geoffrey Allen Pigman. "Free Trade, British Hegemony and the International Economic Order in the Nineteenth Century." *Review of International Studies* 18, no. 2 (April 1992): 89–113.

O'Brien, Patrick Karl, and Leandro Prados de la Escosura. "Balance Sheets for the Acquisition, Retention and Loss of European Empires Overseas." *Itinerario* 23, no. 3–4 (1999): 25–52.

Olcott, Martha Brill. "Central Asia on Its Own." *Journal of Democracy* 4, no. 1 (1993): 92–103.

O'Loughlin, John, Vladimir Kolossov, and Gerard Toal. "Inside Abkhazia." *Post-Soviet Affairs* 27, no. 1 (2011): 1–36.

O'Rourke, Lindsey A. *Covert Regime Change: America's Secret Cold War.* Ithaca, NY: Cornell University Press, 2018.

Papava, Vladimir. "The Political Economy of Georgia's Rose Revolution." *Orbis* 50, no. 4 (2006): 657–67.

Papke, Leslie E., and Jeffrey Wooldridge. *Econometric Methods for Fractional Response Variables with an Application to 401 (k) Plan Participation Rates.* Boston: National Bureau of Economic Research Cambridge, 1993. www.nber.org/papers/t0147.

Peimani, Hooman. *Conflict and Security in Central Asia and the Caucasus.* San Diego, CA: ABC-CLIO, 2009.

Pelkmans, Mathijs. *Defending the Border: Identity, Religion, and Modernity in the Republic of Georgia.* Ithaca, NY: Cornell University Press, 2006.

Pepinsky, Thomas. "The Institutional Turn in Comparative Authoritarianism." *British Journal of Political Science* 44, no. 3 (2014): 631–53.

Phillips, David L. "Shevardnadze under Fire: Pulling Georgia from the Brink." *New York Times*, November 12, 2003, sec. Opinion. www.nytimes.com/2003/11/12/opinion/12iht-edphillips_ed3_.html.

Plümper, Thomas, and Vera E. Troeger. "Not so Harmless After All: The Fixed-Effects Model." *Political Analysis* 27, no. 1 (2019): 21–45.

Pomfret, Richard. "Turkmenistan after Turkmenbashi." In *Institutional Reform in Central Asia: Politico-Economic Challenges*, edited by Joachim Ahrens and Herman Hoen, 63–88. Abingdon, UK: Routledge, 2013.

Pop-Eleches, Grigore, and Graeme B. Robertson. "Identity and Political Preferences in Ukraine – before and after the Euromaidan." *Post-Soviet Affairs* 34, no. 2–3 (May 4, 2018): 107–18.

Pouliot, Vincent. *International Pecking Orders: The Politics and Practice of Multilateral Diplomacy.* Cambridge: Cambridge University Press, 2016.

Powell, Robert. *In the Shadow of Power: States and Strategies in International Politics.* Princeton, NJ: Princeton University Press, 1999.

"The Inefficient Use of Power: Costly Conflict with Complete Information." *American Political Science Review* 98, no. 2 (2004): 231–41.

RadioFreeEurope/RadioLiberty. "Georgia Finalizes Withdrawal from CIS." August 18, 2009, sec. News. www.rferl.org/content/Georgia_Finalizes_Withdrawal_From_CIS/1802284.html.

Radnitz, Scott. "What Really Happened in Kyrgyzstan?" *Journal of Democracy* 17, no. 2 (2006): 132–46.

Weapons of the Wealthy: Predatory Regimes and Elite-Led Protests in Central Asia. Ithaca, NY: Cornell University Press, 2010.

Rayfield, Donald. *Edge of Empires: A History of Georgia.* New York: Reaktion Books, 2013.

Reiter, Dan. "Exploring the Bargaining Model of War." *Perspectives on Politics* 1, no. 1 (2003): 27–43.

Reuters. "Ukraine Leader Fires Powerful Oligarch Kolomoisky as Regional Chief." March 25, 2015. www.reuters.com/article/us-ukraine-crisis-oligarch-idUSKBN0ML0CG20150325.

Roberts, Sean, and Ulrike Ziemer. "Explaining the Pattern of Russian Authoritarian Diffusion in Armenia." *East European Politics* 34, no. 2 (April 3, 2018): 152–72.

Robinson, Ronald. "Non-European Foundations of European Imperialism: Sketch for a Theory of Collaboration." In *Studies in the Theory of Imperialism*, 117–42. London: Longman, 1972.

"The Conference in Berlin and the Future in Africa, 1884–1885." In *Bismark, Europe, and Africa: The Berlin Africa Conference 1884–1885 and the Onset of Partion*, edited by Stig Forster, Wolfgang J. Mommsen, and Ronald Robinson. Oxford: Oxford University Press, 1988.

Robinson, Ronald, and John Gallagher. *Africa and the Victorians: The Official Mind of Imperialism.* London: Macmillan, 1961.

Roeder, Philip G. *Where Nation-States Come From: Institutional Change in the Age of Nationalism.* Princeton, NJ: Princeton University Press, 2007.

Rose, Richard, and William Mishler. "Negative and Positive Party Identification in Post-Communist Countries." *Electoral Studies* 17, no. 2 (1998): 217–34.

Rosenbaum, Paul R. "Choice as an Alternative to Control in Observational Studies." *Statistical Science* 14, no. 3 (1999): 259–78.

Reuters. "RPT-INSIGHT – How the Separatists Delivered Crimea to Moscow." March 13, 2014. http://in.reuters.com/article/2014/03/13/ukraine-crisis-russia-aksyonov-idINL6N0M93AH20140313.

RFE/RL's Ukrainian Service. "Crimean Parliament Fires Government, Sets Autonomy Referendum." *RadioFreeEurope/RadioLiberty*, February 27, 2014, sec. Ukraine. www.rferl.org/content/ukraine-turchynov-appeal-calm-crimea-buildings-seized/25278931.html.

RT. "Interview with Tengiz Kitovani." *Question More* (blog), September 28, 2007. http://rt.com/politics/interview-with-tengiz-kitovani/.

Sakwa, Richard, and Mark Webber. "The Commonwealth of Independent States, 1991–1998: Stagnation and Survival." *Europe-Asia Studies* 51, no. 3 (1999): 379–415.

Sanborn, Joshua A. *Imperial Apocalypse: The Great War and the Destruction of the Russian Empire.* New York: Oxford University Press, 2014.

Schatz, Edward. "The Soft Authoritarian Tool Kit: Agenda-Setting Power in Kazakhstan and Kyrgyzstan." *Comparative Politics* 41, no. 2 (2009): 203–22.

Schölch, Alexander. "The 'Men on the Spot' and the English Occupation of Egypt in 1882." *The Historical Journal* 19, no. 03 (1976): 773–85.

Schultz, Kenneth A. *Democracy and Coercive Diplomacy.* Vol. 76. Cambridge: Cambridge University Press, 2001.

Schweller, Randall. "Emerging Powers in an Age of Disorder." *Global Governance* 17, no. 3 (2011): 285–97.
Scott, James C. "Patron-Client Politics and Political Change in Southeast Asia." *The American Political Science Review* 66, no. 1 (1972): 91–113.
Seawright, Jason. "Better Multimethod Design: The Promise of Integrative Multimethod Research." *Security Studies* 25, no. 1 (2016): 42–49.
Multi Method Social Science. Cambridge: Cambridge University Press, 2016.
Sharman, Jason C. "International Hierarchies and Contemporary Imperial Governance: A Tale of Three Kingdoms." *European Journal of International Relations* 19, no. 2 (2013): 189–207.
Empires of the Weak: The Real Story of European Expansion and the Creation of the New World Order. Princeton, NJ: Princeton University Press, 2019.
Shulman, Stephen. "Nationalist Sources of International Economic Integration." *International Studies Quarterly* 44, no. 3 (2000): 365–90.
Simpson, Gerry. *Great Powers and Outlaw States: Unequal Sovereigns in the International Order*. Cambridge: Cambridge University Press, 2004.
Siroky, David S., and John Cuffe. "Lost Autonomy, Nationalism and Separatism." *Comparative Political Studies* 48, no. 1 (2014).
Slater, Dan. *Ordering Power: Contentious Politics and Authoritarian Leviathans in Southeast Asia*. Cambridge: Cambridge University Press, 2010.
Slater, Dan, and Daniel Ziblatt. "The Enduring Indispensability of the Controlled Comparison." *Comparative Political Studies* 46, no. 10 (2013): 1301–27.
Slider, Darrell. "Crisis and Response in Soviet Nationality Policy: The Case of Abkhazia." *Central Asian Survey* 4, no. 4 (1985): 51–68.
"Recent Elections in Georgia: At Long Last, Stability?" *Demokratizatsiya* 8, no. 4 (2000): 517–32.
Slinko, Irina, Evgeny Yakovlev, and Ekaterina Zhuravskaya. "Laws for Sale: Evidence from Russia." *American Law and Economics Review* 7, no. 1 (2005): 284–318.
Smith, Peter H. *Talons of the Eagle: Latin America, the United States, and the World*. New York: Oxford University Press, 2008.
Smith, Richard J. "Foreign-Training and China's Self-Strengthening: The Case of Feng-Huang-Shan, 1864–1873." *Modern Asian Studies* 10, no. 02 (1976): 195–223.
Solnick, Steven Lee. *Stealing the State: Control and Collapse in Soviet Institutions*. Russian Research Center Studies 89. Cambridge, MA: Harvard University Press, 1998.
Sonyel, Salahi R. "The Protégé System in the Ottoman Empire." *Journal of Islamic Studies* 2, no. 1 (1991): 56–66.
Spruyt, Hendrik. *The Sovereign State and Its Competitors: An Analysis of Systems Change*. Princeton Studies in International History and Politics. Princeton, NJ: Princeton University Press, 1994.
Ending Empire: Contested Sovereignty and Territorial Partition. Cornell Studies in Political Economy. Ithaca, NY: Cornell University Press, 2005.

Steele, David. "Three British Prime Ministers and the Survival of the Ottoman Empire, 1855–1902." *Middle Eastern Studies* 50, no. 1 (2014): 43–60.
Strom, Kaare. "A Behavioral Theory of Competitive Political Parties." *American Journal of Political Science* 34, no. 2 (1990): 565–98.
Sullivan, Tim, and Yaras Karmanau. "Crimea's New Leader, a Man with a Murky Past." Associated Press, March 8, 2014.
Sunar, Ilkay. "State and Economy in the Ottoman Empire." In *Ottoman Empire and the World Economy*, edited by Huri Islamoglu-Inan, 63–87. Cambridge: Cambridge University Press, 1987.
Suny, Ronald Grigor. *The Making of the Georgian Nation*. Bloomington: Indiana University Press, 1994.
 "Provisional Stabilities: The Politics of Identities in Post-Soviet Eurasia." *International Security* 24, no. 3 (1999): 139–78.
TASS. "Putin Signs Laws on Reunification of Republic of Crimea and Sevastopol with Russia." March 21, 2014. http://en.itar-tass.com/russia/724785.
 "Kazakhstan Lawmakers OK Deal with Russia on Radar Complex for Missile Attack Warning." October 1, 2015. http://tass.ru/en/defense/825174.
Têng, Ssū-yü. *The Taiping Rebellion and the Western Powers: A Comprehensive Survey*. London: Clarendon Press, 1971.
Thelen, Kathleen. "Historical Institutionalism in Comparative Politics." *Annual Review of Political Science* 2, no. 1 (1999): 369–404.
Tilly, Charles. *Coercion, Capital and European States A.D. 990–1992*. Cambridge, MA: Blackwell, 1992.
 "Trust and Rule." *Theory and Society* 33, no. 1 (2004): 1–30.
 Trust and Rule. Cambridge: Cambridge University Press, 2005.
Toal, Gerard. *Near Abroad: Putin, the West, and the Contest over Ukraine and the Caucasus*. Oxford: Oxford University Press, 2017.
Toft, Monica D. "Multinationality, Regions and State-Building: The Failed Transition in Georgia." *Regional and Federal Studies* 11, no. 3 (2001): 123–42.
Tomz, Michael. *Reputation and International Cooperation: Sovereign Debt across Three Centuries*. Princeton, NJ: Princeton University Press, 2007.
Trier, Tom, Hedvig Lohm, and David Szakonyi. *Under Siege: Inter-ethnic Relations in Abkhazia*. New York: Columbia University Press, 2009.
Tsygankov, Andrei P. *Russia's Foreign Policy: Change and Continuity in National Identity*. New York: Rowman and Littlefield, 2010.
 Russia and the West from Alexander to Putin: Honor in International Relations. Cambridge: Cambridge University Press, 2012.
Tsygankov, Andrei P., and Matthew Tarver-Wahlquist. "Duelling Honors: Power, Identity and the Russia–Georgia Divide." *Foreign Policy Analysis* 5, no. 4 (2009): 307–26.
Tuchynska, Svitlana. "All In The Family." *Kyiv Post*, March 2, 2012. www.kyivpost.com/content/ukraine/all-in-the-family-123517.html.
Turadze, Eter. "Ajaria: Concern over Missing Funds." *Caucasus Reporting Service* 263 (2004).

Ufford, Letitia W. *The Pasha: How Mehemet Ali Defied the West, 1839–1841.* New York: McFarland, 2007.
Ukrainska Pravda. "Azarov Otkazalsya Ot Coglasheniya Ob Assotsiatsii s ES." November 23, 2013. www.pravda.com.ua/rus/news/2013/11/21/7002657/.
Umland, Andreas. "Starting Post-Soviet Ukrainian Right-Wing Extremism Studies from Scratch." *Russian Politics and Law* 51, no. 5 (2013): 3–10.
Van Den Boogert, Maurits. *The Capitulations and the Ottoman Legal System: Qadis, Consuls and Beraths in the 18th Century.* Leiden, Netherlands: Brill, 2005.
Van de Walle, Nicolas. *African Economies and the Politics of Permanent Crisis, 1979–1999.* Cambridge: Cambridge University Press, 2001.
Vasilyan, Syuzanna. "'Swinging on a Pendulum': Armenia in the Eurasian Economic Union and with the European Union." *Problems of Post-Communism* 64, no. 1 (2017): 32–46.
Vogt, Manuel, Nils-Christian Bormann, Seraina Rüegger, Lars-Erik Cederman, Philipp Hunziker, and Luc Girardin. "Integrating Data on Ethnicity, Geography, and Conflict: The Ethnic Power Relations Data Set Family." *Journal of Conflict Resolution* 59, no. 7 (2015): 1327–42.
Wakeman, Fredric. "The Canton Trade and the Opium Wars." In *The Cambridge History of China: Vol. 2. Late Ch'ing 1800–1911*, 163–212. Cambridge: Cambridge University Press, 1978.
Walker, Shaun. "Petro Poroshenko Wins Ukraine Presidency, According to Exit Polls." *Guardian*, May 26, 2014, sec. World news. www.theguardian.com/world/2014/may/25/petro-poroshenko-ukraine-president-wins-election.
Walter, Barbara F. *Committing to Peace: The Successful Settlement of Civil Wars.* Princeton, NJ: Princeton University Press, 2002.
———. "The Critical Barrier to Civil War Settlement." *International Organization* 51, no. 3 (2003): 335–64.
Waltz, Kenneth. *Theory of International Politics.* Boston: McGraw-Hill, 1979.
Warren, Mark. "Trust and Democracy." In *The Oxford Handbook of Social and Political Trust*, edited by Eric M. Uslaner. Oxford: Oxford University Press, 2018.
Watts, Jonathan. "Plans for Honduras Start-up City Hit by Transparency Concerns." *Guardian*, September 8, 2012, sec. World news. www.theguardian.com/world/2012/sep/08/honduras-city-project-paul-romer.
Way, Lucan. "Kuchma's Failed Authoritarianism." *Journal of Democracy* 16, no. 2 (2005): 131–45.
Weber, Max. *Max Weber: Essays in Sociology.* Oxford: Oxford University Press, 1958.
Weeks, Jessica L. P. "Autocratic Audience Costs: Regime Type and Signaling Resolve." *International Organization* 62, no. 1 (2008): 35–64.
———. *Dictators at War and Peace.* Ithaca, NY: Cornell University Press, 2014.
Wendt, Alexander, and Daniel Friedheim. "Hierarchy under Anarchy: Informal Empire and the East Germany State." In *State Sovereignty as Social Construct*, edited by Thomas Biersteker and Cynthia Weber, 240–77. Cambridge: Cambridge University Press, 1996.

Wheatley, Jonathan. *Georgia from National Awakening to Rose Revolution: Delayed Transition in the Former Soviet Union*. Post-Soviet Politics. Aldershot, UK: Ashgate, 2005.
"The Integration of National Minorities in the Samtskhe-Javakheti and Kvemo Kartli Provinces of Georgia." European Center for Minority Issues, 2009.
Wilson, Andrew. *Ukraine's Orange Revolution*. New Haven, CT: Yale University Press, 2005.
The Ukrainians: Unexpected Nation. New Haven, CT: Yale University Press, 2009.
Belarus: The Last European Dictatorship. New Haven, CT: Yale University Press, 2011.
Ukraine Crisis: What It Means for the West. New Haven, CT: Yale University Press, 2014.
Windler, Christian. "Diplomatic History as a Field for Cultural Analysis: Muslim-Christian Relations in Tunis, 1700–1840." *The Historical Journal* 44, no. 1 (2001): 79–106.
"Representing the State in a Segmentary Society: French Consuls in Tunis from the Ancien Regime to the Restoration." *The Journal of Modern History* 73 (2001): 233–74.
Wooldridge, Jeffrey M. *Econometric Analysis of Cross Section and Panel Data*. Cambridge, MA: MIT Press, 2010.
Wright, Joseph. "How Foreign Aid Can Foster Democratization in Authoritarian Regimes." *American Journal of Political Science* 53, no. 3 (2009): 552–71.
Yekelchyk, Serhy. *Ukraine: Birth of a Modern Nation*. Oxford: Oxford University Press, 2007.
The Conflict in Ukraine: What Everyone Needs to Know. Oxford: Oxford University Press, 2015.
Zarakol, Ayşe. *Hierarchies in World Politics*. Vol. 144. Cambridge: Cambridge University Press, 2017.
Zhang, Yongjin. "China's Entry into International Society: Beyond the Standard of 'Civilization.'" *Review of International Studies* 17, no. 1 (1991): 3–16.
Zhukov, Yuri M. "Trading Hard Hats for Combat Helmets: The Economics of Rebellion in Eastern Ukraine." *Journal of Comparative Economics* 44, no. 1 (2015): 1–15. www.sciencedirect.com/science/article/pii/S01475967 1500092X.
Zimmerman, William. *Ruling Russia: Authoritarianism from the Revolution to Putin*. Princeton, NJ: Princeton University Press, 2014.
Zollinger, Daniel, and Daniel Bochsler. "Minority Representation in a Semi-democratic Regime: The Georgian Case." *Democratization* 19, no. 4 (2012): 611–41.
Zurcher, Christoph. *Post-Soviet Wars: Rebellion, Ethnic Conflict, and Nationhood in the Caucasus*. New York: New York University Press, 2007.

Index

Abashidze, Aslan, 67, 68, 74, 103
  and Zviad Gamsakhurdia, 104
  loss of support, 125
  militia, 104
  relationship with Shevardnadze, 103, 104
  Support for Russia, 103
  Support from Russia, 107
Abkhaz
  Support from Russia, 113
Abkhazia, 1, 7, 10, 13, 19, 40, 49, 100, 102
  autonomy, 99
  civil war with Georgia, 112
  de facto state, 1
  demographics, 111, 113
  economy, 102
  Georginization, 109
  privileges, 109
  priviliged position of Abkhazians, 60
  protests, 111
  refugees, 113
  rent-seeking, 113
  Russian military, 110
  Russian military bases, 110
  separatism, 1
  Soviet Economy, 111
  Soviet Union, 109
Abkhazian parliament, 112
Accommodation, 12
Adjara, 11, 19, 40, 68, 70, 100, 102
  autonomy, 99
  conflict with Georgian government, 103
  corruption and rent-seeking, 106, 107, 108
  economy, 102, 108
  ethnic makeup, 102
  lack of titular minority, 102
  media, 106
  post Rose Revolution, 34, 71, 108–109
  religion, 103
  Rose Revolution, 107
  Russian Empire, 103
  Russian military base, 102, 103, 109
  Soviet Union, 103
  support for Russia, 102
  taxation, 105
Adjarans
  culture, 103
Afghanistan, 2
aggregate social actors, 39
Air Defense Integration, 183
Akhalkalaki, 13, 116
  pro-Russian protest, 97
Akhalkalaki. *See also* Javakheti
  Russian Military Base, 97
Akhmetov, Rinat, 93
Aksyonov, Sergey, 91
Akyaev, Askar, 196
Alexandria, 168
Algiers, 176
Ali, Muhammed, 166
  relationship with Ottoman Empire, 169
  service with Ottomans, 168
  state-building, 169
anarchy, 5
Andijan, 204
annexation, 21
Armenia, 107, 117, 182
  conflict with Azerbaijan, 206
  protests, 207
  Turkey, 206
Armenians, 14, *See* Georgia, Armenians
Austro-Hungarian Empire, 79
authoritarian regimes
  mass politics, 35
authority, 4, 6
autonomous institutions, 102
  effects on politics, 102
autonomous regions, 59
autonomous republics, 59
Azerbaijan, 51
Aztecs, 9

Bakiyev, Kurmanbek, 198
Balageur, Joaquin, 215

Index

balance of power, 15
Balkash Radar base, 184
Baltic regions, 78
Baltic States, 16, 196
  NATO, 8
bargaining, 2, 27, 106, 159
  information, 42
Batkivshchyna, 84, 94
Belarus, 46, 78
Berdymukhamedov, Gurbanguly, 197
Berlin Conference, 26
Beyical states. *See* Ottoman Empire, North Africa
Black Sea Fleet, 78, 92
Blunt, Wilfred, 172
Bolsheviks, 79
Bosch, Juan, 214
Boxer Rebellion, 160, 177
Britain
  China, 158
  Persia, 153
  Thailand, 153
  threats to India as motivation, 175
British colonialism, 4
British occupation of Egypt, 167, *See* Egypt, British Occupation
Bull, Hedley, 176
Burjanadze, Nino, 68, 70
Bush administration, 75

Canton, 161
Canton trade system, 157
capitulations, 162
Caucasus, the, 46
Central African Republic, 208
Central Asia, 5, 36, 46, 54
Chakhalyan, Vahagn, 116
Chanturia, Gia, 59
Charter Cities, 218
Chechen terrorists, 69
Chechnya, 2
China, 4, 224
  Africa, 225
  army and western support, 158
  Boxer Rebellion, 2
  Canton, 159
  contrast with Ottoman Empire, 152
  corruption and rent-seeking, 160
  culture, 152
  duration of extraterritoriality, 177
  empire, 155
  gentry, 156, 159
  informal empire, 154
  Japanese invasion, 161
  local actors and trade, 33
  minining concessions, 159
  Mongols, 157
  Muslim rebels, 159
  navy and western support, 158
  origins of extraterritoriality, 157
  Qing, 18
  Qing and decentralization, 155
  rebellions, 156, 158
  Revolution, 161
  Russian Empire, 156
  state-building, 220
  treaties, 158
  Unequal treaties, 23
  warlords, 177
  Western coastal traders, 157
  Western loans, 154
  World War II, 161
Chinese Maritime Customs, 154, 158, 160
Chinese nationalism, 157
Citizen Union of Georgia, 105
civil war
  post Soviet, 51
civilization, 53
civilizational-state, 224
client states, 8
clinetelism and patronage, 37
club goods, 130
coercion, 6
  costs, 24
  out of equilibrium outcome, 42
cold war, 27
Cole, Juan, 168
Collective Security Treaty Organization, 183
Collier, David, 18
Colored Revolutions, 36
commitment problems, 27, 177
  domestic politics, 34
Common Economic Space, 183
Commonwealth of Independent States, 33, 183
  Council of Border Guards, 183
  Council of Defense Ministers, 183
  Economic Court, 183
  Georgia, 1
Communist Party of the Soviet Union, 79
competitive authoritarian regimes, 196
concessions, 154
Constantinople, 175
constructivism, 17, 45
contracting, 7
  subnational actors, 7
cooperation between empires, 175
Correlates of War, 153
corruption, 13, 29

Index

Cossacks, 79
  autonomy, 79
coups, 13
credible commitments, 54
Cretan revolt, 166
Crimea. *See* Russia, annexation of Crimea
  Annexation, 49
  annexation of Crimea, 90–92
  referendum, 90
critical geopolitics, 54
culture, 10, 53
Customs Union
  Armenia, 207
  Kyrgyzstan, 205

D'anieri, Paul, 80
Daoguang Emperor, 43
Darden, Keith, 53
Darwin, John, 23
de facto states, 7, 13
defection, 9
Dehli, 179
democracy, 34
Disraeli, Benjamin, 175
divide and rule, 45
Djibouti, 225
Dnieper river, 79
Dnipropetrovsk, 83, 93
Dominican Republic, 213
Donbas, 7, 92, 94
  de facto state, 94
Donetsk, 83, 89, 93, 218

East India Company, 179
Eastern Ukraine, 11, 81, 84, 92
economic development, 15, 16, 17, 47, 99, 100, 121, 156, 187, 219
Egypt, 4, 10, 24–25
  capitulations, 167
  consequences of autonomy, 170
  debt, 171
  European advisers, 25
  extraterritoriality, 167
  importance of cotton trade, 169
  mixed courts, 170
  occupation, 43
  Ottoman authority, 167
  Ottoman Empire, 43
  Ottoman identity, 171
  rent-seeking and patronage, 170
  state-building, 168, 220
  Suez Canal, 168, 174, 175
  trade, 169
  Turko-Circassian, 170

Egyptian military, 12
  uprising, 172
ejectorate, 31, 194
Elchibey, Abulfaz, 198
elites
  definition, 31
  political survival, 29
Elliott, Henry, 164
Elster, Jon, 39
empire, 3, 46
  formal, 52
energy producers, 16
English School, 176
Ergneti Market, 73
Escriba-Folch, Abel, 196
Estonia, 196
ethnic fractionalization, 188
ethnicity
  politics, 99
Eurasia, 153
Eurasian Economic Community, 183
  Kyrgyzstan, 205
Eurasian Economic Space
  Kyrgyzstan, 205
Eurasian Economic Union
  Armenia, 207
Euromaidan. *See* Ukraine, Euromaidan
Euromaidan protests
  effects, 146
European empires
  relative military power, 25, 26
European Union, 188
  empire, 3
exogenous shocks, 12, 40, 44, 153
exploration, 25
external validity, 152
extraterritoriality, 7, 12, 26, 154
  definition, 154

feedback loop, 40
Feuerwerker, Albert, 154
fixed assets, 186
Fokin, Vitold, 81
formal empire, 5
  obsolescence, 21
formal institutions, 13
France
  China, 158
  Egypt, 168, 172
  occupation of Egypt, 168
Frieden, Jeffrey, 174
frozen conflict, 49. *See also* de facto states

Index

Gallagher, John, 10
Gamsakhurdia, Zviad, 1, 38, 56, 59, 64, 67, 104, 111, 112, 197
  coup, 62
  ethnic minorities, 60
  nationalism, 59, 60, 61
  relationship with warlords, 60, 61
Georgia, 1, 9, 97
  1990 elections, 60
  2000 presidential elections, 105
  2003 parliamentary election, 69
  2004 presidential elections, 70
  2008 parliamentary elections, 70
  2008 war with Russia, 2
  2012 parliamentary elections, 76
  Armenians, 14, 31, 99, 146
  autonomous republics, 99
  Azerbaijanis, 99
  civil wars, 60
  Collective Security Treaty Organization, 64, 66
  comaprison with Ukraine, 55–56
  Commonwealth of Independent States, 57, 64, 72, 104
  Communist Party, 59
  constitution, 112
  constitutional reform, 76
  corruption and rent-seeking, 63, 71
  Democratic Republic of Georgia, 58
  early modern period, 58
  electoral fraud, 69
  ethnic conflict, 60
  ethnic identity, 131
  ethnic minorities, 1, 98
  ethnic minorities and territorial concentration, 100
  frozen conflicts, 67
  internally displaced people, 113, 114
  Josef Stalin, 58
  language politics, 111
  membership of Collective Security Treaty Organization, 57
  Military Council, 62
  militias and warlords, 31, 61, 63, 68, 100
  Mkhedrioni, 61
  nationalist protests, 111
  political institutions, 68
  reforms, 70
  regional governors, 68
  rent-seeking and corruption, 61, 68
  Rose Revolution, 57
  Russian Empire, 57
  Russian language, 59
  Russian military bases, 57, 72
  Russian military support, 1, 64
  secessionist movements, 63
  sovereignty, 1
  Soviet military, 60
  Soviet Union, 58, 99
  state weakness, 61
  state-building, 1, 72
  status in Russian Empire, 58
  the Supreme Council, 60
  United States, 74–75
  War with Russia, 44, 49, 72–75
  weakening of regions, 71
Georgia 1999 parliamentary election, 105
Georgian Dream, 70, 76, 77
Georgian military, 64, 66, 117
  rent-seeking and corruption, 64
Georgian nationalism, 10
Georgian nationalist movement, 59
Georgian nobility, 58
Germany, 79
Geyrat, 121
Giorgadze, Igor, 64, 67–68
Gladstone, William, 44, 172
Glasnost, 79
global order, 2
Gorbachev, Mikhail, 50, 80
governance, 5
Grachev, Pavel, 62
Grand Duchy of Lithuania, 78
Granovetter, Mark, 137
Group for Economic Development, 90
Gryszlov, Boris, 57
GUAM, 57, 66
Guentsadze, Roman, 112

Hale, Henry, 30, 34, 35, 36, 54, 85, 100, 126, 187, 189, 194, 203
Hart, Robert, 160
hierarchy, 224–226
  as Giffen good, 223
  Coercion and Resistance, 15, 42
  costs for subordinate elites, 34
  costs to subordinate, 33
  definitions, 4–8
  Governance Costs, 24–25
  governance hierarchies, 8
  great power competition, 5
  greed versus political survival, 35
  institutions, 7
  military occupations, 5
  ramifications, 5–6
  social hierarchy, 8
  types of support for subordinate elites, 32–33
holodomor, 79
Honduras, 218

Hong Kong, 218
hoop tests, 126
Hopkins, Anthony, 174
Hyderabad, 179

ideas, 53
identity, 11
Imereti, 68
Incas, 9
incomplete contracts, 41
India, 176, 179
informal empire, 6, 12, 25, 46, 156, 159, 178, 179
informal hierarchy, 22, 28
informal institutions, 13
institutions, 31, 47
  legal, 47
insurgencies, 52
international organizations, 8
International society. *See* English School
international system, 18, 26
  constraints, 27–28
Ioseliani, Jaba, 61, 112
Iran, 153
Ismail, Khedive, 12
  greater autonomy from Ottoman Empire, 170
Ivanishvili, Bidzina, 76–77
Ivano-Frankivsk, 82
Ivanov, Sergei, 107

Japan, 153
Javakheti, 1, 19, 31, 98, 100
  contestation with Georgian government, 116
  corruption and rent-seeking, 117
  demographics, 114
  economy, 115
  language politics, 118
  Ottoman Empire, 116
  post Rose Revolution, 117
  protests, 118
  rent-seeking and corruption, 14
  Russian Empire, 116
  Russian military, 115
  Russian military base, 116
Jiangnan, 159
Jianxi, 159
joint-stock companies, 163

Kadyrov, Ramzan, 2
Kant airbase. *See* Kyrgyzstan, Russian military base
Karapetyan, Samvel, 207
Karimov, Islam, 196, 197

Kaufmann, Stuart, 35
Kavsadze, Alexander, 112
Kayoglu, Turan, 26
Kazakhstan, 16
  preference for increased integration, 184
  Russian military cooperation, 184
Kitovani, Tengiz, 61, 62, 67, 107, 112
  relationship with Russia, 62
Kocharyan, Robert, 198
Kokoity, Eduard, 73
Kolomoyskiy, Ihor, 92–93, 148
Krasner, Stephen, 9
Kravchuk, Leonid, 80–81, 198
Kuchma, Leonid, 81–83, 145, 198
Kvemo Kartli, 19, 68, 98, 100, 118
  economy, 120
Kvemo Kartli,
  demographics, 114
Kyiv, 79, 89, 91
Kyrgyzstan, 16, 33, 182
  Parliament, 206
  personalist regime, 196
  rent-seeking, 29
  Russia, 41
  Russian military base, 206
  United States, 41

Lake, David, 11, 202
Latin America, 153
Latvia, 196
legal pluralism, 157
legitimacy, 6, 9, 10
Lithuania, 196
Lugansk, 218
Lukashenko, Alexander, 199
Lutsenko, Yuri, 88, 92
Lviv, 82

MacDonald, Paul, 11
Maduro, Nicolas, 33
Magalioni, Beatrice, 35
Maghrebi states, 179
Maghreb, 26
Mahrattas, 179
Mamaladze, Levan, 71, 106, 120
Manas Airbase, 42
Manchus, 157
Mariupol, 94
mass politics, 35
  patronage, 35–37
Mauritius, 218
Medvedchuk, Viktor, 82
merchants, 23, 58
method of agreement, 152
Mexico, 9

Index 271

Midlothian campaign, 173
migration, 33
military assistance, 205, 207
Mingrelia, 1, 64, 112
Minsk, 198
missionaries, 23
Mkhedrioni, 61, 64
Mohyliov, Anatolii, 91
Moldova, 46, 51
    Commonwealth of Independent States, 184
Molotov-Ribbentrop pact, 79
Mongols, 78, 157
Moscow, 198
Mughal Empire, 26, 179
    informal empire, 179
Muhammed Ali
    conflict with Ottoman Empire, 169
    desire to westernize Egypt, 169
multiethnic nations, 56
multipolarity, 27, 152, 177
Muscovy, 58, 78

Nabiyev, Rahmon, 198
Nadibaidze, Vardiko, 64, 66
Nagorno-Karabakh, 115, 206
Nanking, 161
Napoleonic Wars, 168, 178
National Guard, 112
national identity, 53
nationalism, 10, 21, 27, 188
NATO, 8, 54, 77, 188
neo-colonialism, 225
New Zealand
    South Pacific, 3
Ninotsminda, 117
Niyazov, Sapamurat, 197
Nodia, Ghia, 66, 116
Noghaideli, Zurab, 57, 68
nonauthoritarian regimes
    hierarchy, 198
nonstate factors, 11, 13
norms, 10, 27
    against territorial annexation, 51
    territoral expansion, 21
North Africa
    French imperialism, 26
    French imperialism, Algiers, 27
North Ossetia, 73
Northern Alliance, 2

Obama administration, 75
oligarchs, 83
Opium Wars, 27, 43

Orange Revolution, 126, *See* Ukraine, Orange Revolution
Ottoman Administration of Public Debt, 7
Ottoman bureaucracy, 164
Ottoman Empire, 4
    Armenians, 164
    capitulations, 162
    collapse, 167
    contrast with China. *See* China, contrast with Ottoman Empire
    culture, 152
    decentralizatoin, 164
    Georgia, 58
    Greeks, 164
    importance of trade, 162
    inheritance laws, 163
    local actors and trade, 33
    minorities, 163
    North Africa, 178
    protégé system, 163
    protégés, 166
    state-building, 221
    tax farming, 165
    Taxation, 165
    taxation of foreigners, 163
Ottoman state, 164, 165
Ottomanization, 165

Palmerston, John, 169
Pankisi Gorge, 69
Party of Regions, 87, 90, 94
Party regime, 195, 197
    hierarchy, 198
    rent-seeking, 197
    stability of, 197
Pashinyan, Nikol, 207
patrimonialism, 152
patronage
    negative consequences, 37
patronage and clientelism, 14
patronal regimes, 34
patron–client relationships, 2
Pavlovsky, Gleb, 85
People's Republic in Donetsk, 92
Perestroika, 79
Persian Empire
    Georgia, 58
Personalist regimes, 195, 196
    hierarchy, 198
    instability, 196
    political threats, 196
    rent-seeking, 197
Poland, 79
political authority. *See* authority

Political contestation
  definition, 30
Polity, 185
Poroshenko, Petro, 94
  decline in popularity, 148
post-Soviet region, 16–17
power, 4, 8, 9, 10, 47, 54
precommunist literacy, 189
preferences, 40
preferences and beliefs, 39
principal-agent problem, 219
protection pacts, 41
protests, 13
Putin, Vladimir, 86

Qinghai, 157

Radnitz, Scott, 36
Rahoman, Emomali, 198
Rational Choice
  critiques, 39
  information, 15
regime type, 45, 194
regional organizations, 51
relational contracting, 9
remittances, 33
rent-seeking, 29–30
  and trust, 37
  definition, 13
  mass politics, 36
  private good, 130
  regulation, 14
  subnational variation, 32
  subsidies, 14
Republican Party (Armenia), 207
resolve, 43
Revival, 104
Rice, Condoleezza, 75
Robinson, Ronald, 10
Roki Tunnel
Romer, Paul, 218
Rose Revolution, 69–70, *See* Georgia, Rose Revolution
Round Table-Free Georgia bloc, 60
rule of law, 32, 128, 130
Russia
  annexation of Crimea, 6, 12
  China, 152, 157
  Civil war in Ukraine, 30
  costs of Crimean annexation, 92
  hierarchy, 51
  hierarchy and Central Asia, 5
  integration, 50
  interests in Georgia, 57, 98
  military bases, 8, 23, 51, 183

Ottoman Empire, 152
  Persia, 153
  preference for hierarchy, 50
  preferences for hierarchy, 46, 52
  regional integration, 51
  sanctions, 92
  war with Georgia. *See* Georgia War with Russia
Russia
  Civil War in Ukraine, 11
  Russian air force, 184
  Russian media, 85
  Russian minorities, 188
  Russification, 79

Saakashvili, Mikhail, 34, 57, 62, 70, 107, 116
  anticorruption efforts, 71
  political strength, 71
Salt administration, 7, 154, 158
sanctions. *See* Russia, sanctions
Sargaysan, Serzh, 207
scramble for Africa, 26
Second Polish Republic, 79
selectorate, 31, 212
self-determination, 92
self-strengthening movement, 158
Sevastopol, 77, 91
Shamba, Sergei, 114
Shevardnadze, Eduard, 1, 13, 32, 56, 59, 63, 74, 103
  assasination attempts, 66
  Georgian Soviet Socialist Republic, 59
  personalism, 68
  political outlook, 63
  relationship with warlords, 63
  return to power, 62
  Russian support, 32
Shikai, Yuan, 160
Siam. *See* Thailand
Sigua, Tengiz, 112
site-specific assets, 186
Slater, Dan, 16, 41, 151, 225
Svoboda Ukraine, 79
Social Democratic Party, 82
social status, 4
social trust, 37
South Ossetia, 1, 7, 10, 40, 49, 72–74
  de facto state, 1
  Russian support, 1
  separatism, 1
  smuggling, 145
sovereign rights, 2, 5, 13

Index

sovereignty, 8
  de jure, 6
  economic, 8
Soviet military, 62
Soviet nationality policy, 58
Soviet Republics, 50
Soviet Union
  federal structure, 50, 101
  nationalism, 50
Stalin, Josef, 59
state, 46
  modern, 46
state-building, 51, 53
  post-Soviet, 51
status, 8
stratification, 4
Sublime Porte, 169, 170
subnational actors, 2, 98
subnational analysis, 99
subordinate actor preferences, 37–38
subregional hegemon, 54
Sudan, 208
Sukhumi, 112
Supreme Council, 60
Svoboda, 38
systematic crises of empire, 177

Taiping Rebellion, 158
Tajikistan, 16, 51
Taliban, 2
Taruta, Serhiy, 92–94
Tawfiq Pasha, 171
Tbilisi, 62, 105
technology, 15, 52
Ter-Petrosyan, Levon, 198
territorial expansion, 21, 23, 27, 28, 43, 51, 52, 92, 150, 176, 178, 224
territorial partition, 157
Tevzadze, Davit, 66
Thailand, 7
Tilly, Charles, 137
Tippu Sultan, 179
titular minorities, 50
Toal, Gerard, 54
trade, 47
Transcaucasian Republic, 58
transnational actors, 23–24
Transnistria, 7
treaties, 8
Treaty of Deepening Integration, 183
Tripoli, 178
Trujillo, Rafael, 214
trust, 136–138
  general, 127

particularized, 37, 127
trust differential, 136
trusteeships, 219
Tulip Revolution, 198
Tunis, 153
Turkmenistan, 51, 52, 54
  regime type, 34
  Russia, 34
Tymoshenko, Yulia, 84, 85, 88, 126
  nationalism, 86
  prime minister, 86

Ukraine, 16, 46
  2002 Rada elections, 84
  2004 election fraud, 85
  2004 presidential election, 32, 84
  2010 presidential election, 87
  2014 parliamentary election, 94
  2019 presidential elections, 148
  Austro-Hungarian Empire, 133
  Belarusians, 133
  Black Sea fleet, 77, 88
  blackmail, 83
  CIS minimalist, 184
  civil war, 94
  Common Economic Space, 84
  Commonwealth of Independent States, 80
  comparison with Georgia, 55–56
  constitution, 83, 86, 87
  Eastern Ukraine, 97, 133
  ethnicity, 133, 146
  EU association agreement, 89
  Euromaidan, 88–89
  gas industry and rent-seeking, 30, 83
  Hetmanate, 79
  language, 134
  militias, 93
  Moldovans, 133
  multivector foreign policy, 84
  nationalism, 147
  oligarchs, 92
  Orange Revolution, 77, 85–87
  presidential election, 81
  presidential election, 82
  privatization, 83
  public perceptions of corruption, 147
  regionalism, 133
  rent-seeking and corruption, 83
  response to 2008 Russo-Georgian War, 86
  Russian Empire, 78, 133
  Russian language, 79
  Separatists Eastern Ukraine, 92–94
  Soviet Union, 79–80, 133

Ukraine (cont.)
  subnational actors, 92
  Western Ukraine, 133
Ukrainian civil war, 94
Ukrainian nationalism
  gender, 134
UN Security Council, 90
uncertainty, 48
United National Movement, 69, 70, 74–75
  Adjara, 108
United States
  Caribbean, 212
  empire, 3
  hierarchy and Central Asia, 5
  South America, 3, 6, 23
Urabi, Ahmed, 2, 172, 173, 175, 177
Uzbekistan, 54
  Collective Security Treaty Organization, 183
  party regime, 196

Varieties of Democracy (V-Dem), 185
Velvet Revolution, 208
Venezuela, 33, 208
Viceroy of Chihli, 159

Watson, Adam, 176
Western Ukraine, 81, 135
Wheatley, Jonathan, 66
White Knights, 188
World War I, 12, 167
World War II, 12
world wars, 153
Wuchang, 161

Yakobashvili, Temuri, 113
Yanukovych, Victor, 32, 49, 94, 126
  election campaign, 32
  Russia, 88
Yanukovych, Viktor, 85, 87, 90
Yatsenyuk, Arseniy, 90
Yeltsin, Boris, 80
Yushchenko, Victor, 77, 83–84
  prime minister, 83

Zelenskiy, Volodomyr, 148
Zhili, 160
Zhukov, Yuri, 30
Zhvania, Zurab, 70
Ziblatt, Daniel, 16
Zimmerman, William, 31, 194
Zviadist rebels, 1, 32, 40, 63, 65, 112, 113

Lightning Source UK Ltd.
Milton Keynes UK
UKHW020018120320
360210UK00006B/46